LEADERS

'*Leaders* rexamines old notions of leadership – especially
the outdated view that history is shaped by great men going
it alone. General McChrystal shows us that leadership can take
many forms, leaders often have different strengths, and
great leaders can come from anywhere'
Sheryl Sandberg, COO of Facebook and
founder of LeanIn.Org

'*Leaders* is a superb, thought-provoking challenge to conventional
understanding of the nature of leadership. An enlightening,
entertaining must-read about why we revere so many leaders
who are often deeply flawed and even unsuccessful, and the
lessons for thinking about and teaching leadership in the future'
Robert M. Gates, former US Secretary of Defense

'Leadership, we learn, is complex. At a time when Americans
yearn for leaders we can admire and respect, this book . . . will
help you think differently about both leadership and our history'
Walter Isaacson, author of *Steve Jobs* and *Leonardo da Vinci*

'No living American has more convincingly combined the
practice and teaching of leadership than General Stanley
McChrystal: that's why Yale students flock to his classes.
Now, in *Leaders*, he invites us to join them, with Plutarch
as his teaching assistant. No current or aspiring leader can
afford to miss this shrewd and surprising book'
John Lewis Gaddis, Yale University

'*Leaders* is a must-read for all leaders – whether they're
just beginning their careers or whether they're already
leading an entire organization'
Ken Langone, author of *I Love Capitalism!*

'Whenever Stanley McChrystal talks, I take notes. I am so drawn to his ability to cut through pop-culture theories about leadership to get to the core of what actually makes a leader. *Leaders* takes us deeper than most other leadership books into the true and often messy mechanics of leadership. Anyone who considers themselves a student of leadership must read this book'
Simon Sinek, optimist and author of *Start With Why* and *Leaders Eat Last*

ABOUT THE AUTHORS

Stanley McChrystal retired from the US Army as a four-star general after thirty-four years of service. His previous books, *My Share of the Task* and *Team of Teams* were both *New York Times* bestsellers. He is a senior fellow at Yale University's Jackson Institute for Global Affairs and a partner at the McChrystal Group, a leadership consulting firm based in Virginia.

Jeff Eggers served for twenty years as a US Navy SEAL and also in government as a special assistant to the president for National Security Affairs. He is now executive director of the McChrystal Group Leadership Institute.

Jason Mangone served for four years in the US Marine Corps, followed by positions at the Aspen Institute, the Service Year Alliance and the New York City Department of Veterans' Services.

LEADERS

MYTH AND REALITY

Stanley McChrystal,
Jeff Eggers *and* Jason Mangone

PORTFOLIO
PENGUIN

PORTFOLIO PENGUIN

UK | USA | Canada | Ireland | Australia
India | New Zealand | South Africa

Portfolio Penguin is part of the Penguin Random House group of companies
whose addresses can be found at global.penguinrandomhouse.com.

First published in the United States of America by
Portfolio/Penguin, an imprint of Penguin Random House LLC 2018
First published in Great Britain by Portfolio Penguin 2018
001

Copyright © McChrystal Group LLC 2018

The moral right of the authors has been asserted

Printed and bound in Great Britain by Clays Ltd, Elcograf S.p.A.

A CIP catalogue record for this book is available from the British Library

ISBN: 978–0–241–33632–8

To John Lewis and John McCain, who remind us that it's possible to keep our humanity while leading with courage and commitment.

CONTENTS

PROLOGUE

And when our work is done,
Our course on earth is run,
May it be said, "Well done"
Be thou at peace.

—WEST POINT'S ALMA MATER

The book is just eight inches tall and fourteen wide, with a fraying orange cloth cover. Some of the pages are torn but after two lifetimes of rough service, it is in remarkably good shape. I should be so lucky.

The tattered children's book *Greek Tales for Tiny Tots* was originally purchased in Chattanooga, Tennessee, in 1929 for a young girl named Mary, who treasured it. In the late 1950s Mary, by then my mother, read from it to me. In the 1980s I read it to my son and recently gave my oldest granddaughter, Emmylou, her first look at the worn pages.

The work is special to me. With simply drawn pictures and brief text, it tells stories of Greek and Roman heroes: Theseus, Hercules, Ulysses, Ariadne, and others who struggled against nature, fate, and sometimes each other. It is mythology, but the narratives of individuals whose heroism, vision, or genius, often combined with dogged perseverance, were the dominant force in shaping events resonated deeply with me.

When I could read larger volumes my mother shared Roland, Julius Caesar, William Wallace, and Robin Hood. In my grade school library I found biographies crafted for young readers and remember being caught during arithmetic by my second grade teacher reading a book on John Paul Jones, too intently focused on the story to pretend I was paying attention in class. Later in life, I was given a chess set inscribed with the truism that "pawns are the soul of the game." But as a boy, to me history seemed a game in which leaders were kings, queens, bishops, rooks, and knights who stood in sharp contrast in stature, power, and importance to the lowly pawns.

My early lessons in leadership didn't come only from ancient history. My father was a soldier, and I was ten when he deployed on his first tour in Vietnam. Although young, I read to understand the geopolitical labyrinth my father, and my nation, had entered. I came to view the unfolding events primarily as the actions of leaders, political and military—those who would be successful heroes if the story would cooperate. It did not, but I still believed.

West Point, the familiar name for the United States Military Academy, was founded in 1802 at a scenic bend in the Hudson River. During the Revolutionary War it had been the Continental Army's most strategic post, as it denied British access to the vital waterway north from New York City. In July 1942, my father, himself the son of a career soldier, traveled to West Point to join the Corps of Cadets. Thirty years later, I followed him.

The Academy likes to remind visitors that "much of the history we teach was made by leaders we taught," and today it celebrates the role of leadership in America's past while forging military leaders for her future. West Point's mission is, in part, "to educate, train, and inspire the Corps of Cadets so that each graduate is a commissioned leader of character."

But it is not the mission statement that dominates the future soldier's experience. From the first day, cadets' expectations of leaders, and of themselves, are shaped by the visceral experience of being physically surrounded by reminders of past leaders. Cadets clad in traditional gray move among icons of those who once wore the same uniform. I lived in Pershing Barracks, named for the officer who led America's Expeditionary Force to France in World War I. When I walked to attend class in Thayer Hall, named for the officer who set the course of West Point in its early years, I passed a bronze George Patton, the aggressive World War II commander. Portraits of famous officers gazed down on every meal, never letting us forget that West Point's raison d'être was to mold us into leaders.

At the same time, we were reminded, it was not about us. We were being developed to serve the larger purpose of the nation by extending West

Point's Long Gray Line, the term used to describe West Point's alumni who kept unbroken commitments to the Academy and the nation's ideals.

We were taught the beliefs and behaviors of great leaders, not by academics, but largely by young officers recently off the battlefields of Southeast Asia. We inhaled their stories of combat and envied their accomplishments. We admired their integrity, courage, and sense of duty, and we learned to look, walk, and talk in the way they taught us. If we did so, we were told, and believed, we might not be famous leaders, but we would serve well. And we suspected, but never openly speculated, that some of us would make the history future cadets would study.

Soon after graduation it was my turn to lead, first as a Platoon Leader—an infantry lieutenant responsible for twenty 1970s American paratroopers. Although the post-Vietnam Army was a troubled institution, the majority of soldiers, like generations before them, did their jobs with stoic patience. And like leaders of generations before me, I progressed through the ranks to Captain (commanding 150 men), Battalion (commanding 600), and Regiment (about 2,200), before becoming a General Officer.

At that point, my experience took me into territory I'd not studied at West Point. In the post–9/11 environments of Iraq and Afghanistan I spent almost five years commanding the Joint Special Operations Command, a one-of-a-kind Task Force composed of the nation's most elite forces. As an over-fifty-year-old product of earlier-era leadership models, I was challenged by this new environment. I found command on a twenty-first-century, technology-enabled battlefield required not just traditional skills, but also intuitive adaptations.

Throughout my years in military leadership, my reading continued. I had a strong preference for history, frequently reading biographies, like those of George Washington and George Marshall, and the memoirs of Ulysses S. Grant. Novels periodically crept onto my nightstand, although typically they were historically and often militarily grounded. I remember being fascinated by *The Killer Angels*, in which author Michael Shaara made me feel like a confidant of the well-known leaders at the battle of Gettysburg.

While I enjoyed the study of history and leaders, as I matured, the concepts of leadership that I had willingly accepted increasingly contrasted with some of what I read, and much of what I experienced. The patrician warrior Robert E. Lee lost to nondescript "Sam" Grant. The inspiring ideas of Thomas Jefferson stood in contrast to his position as a slaveholder. And emerging insights about Allied successes in breaking Axis codes revealed that victories once attributed to superior generalship were actually the result of a combination of other factors.

I found that leaders who exhibited all the right traits often fell short, while others who possessed none of the characteristics of traditional leadership succeeded. The things we sought and celebrated in leaders had confusingly little linkage to outcomes. The study of leadership increasingly seemed to be a study of myth, with a significant gap between how we speak of it and how it is experienced.

In the fall of 2010 this mythology of leadership became more personal. Partnered with Sam Ayres, a recent Yale graduate who would later enlist in the Army and serve as a Sergeant in the 75th Ranger Regiment, I undertook the task of writing my memoir. Having not kept records or a journal (to avoid retaining classified information), I had to begin by creating a decades-long timeline of my life.

The process was invaluable but humbling. As we deconstructed events, we discovered that even where my recollections were accurate, they were stunningly incomplete accounts of history. I was often unaware of the actions, decisions, and drama that had actually driven outcomes. Successes I credited to a decision I'd made felt less impressive once I recognized the myriad factors and players who often had far more to do with the result than I had. The idea that my memoir would convey a story of which I was the central figure shifted. I mattered, just not to the extent I thought I had.

This was the final push toward accepting the reality that over a lifetime, my leader-centric view of the world had increasingly come into conflict with uncomfortable questions.

IN 2013, author and journalist David Brooks gave a talk at Yale titled "Who Would Plutarch Write About Today?" The first-to-second-century Greek-turned-Roman historian's *Lives*—in which he profiled forty-eight ancient personalities—was not long ago a staple of nearly all educated readers. References to Plutarch may sound pretentious to an audience less familiar with him today, but Brooks's inquiry into which leaders a modern Plutarch would choose was a fascinating one and, for me, a compelling and consuming one.

Brooks's question might be reformulated: "What is leadership today?" Leaders are the subject of constant scrutiny and study, but too many of us, seduced by the mythology of what good leadership looks like, miss the reality. As a result, our models for identifying, educating, and evaluating leaders falter, or feel incomplete. We intuitively know that leadership is critical to success in the modern world, but we don't really understand what that leadership consists of.

In 1905, Albert Einstein redefined how we consider time, space, and motion. He overturned Newtonian physics, but his special theory of relativity wasn't complete, since it didn't account for acceleration. For the next ten years, Einstein struggled before producing his general theory of relativity that more completely described the reality of our universe.

We lack the leadership equivalent to a general theory of relativity, a theory that accurately and comprehensively predicts which leadership qualities and strategies result in success. Such a model is still out of reach, far beyond the scope of this book, but a step in its direction is possible. That first step is learning where the mythology and reality diverge.

As authors, we come at this endeavor with the experience and curiosity of practitioners who know there is a deeper understanding to be had. We each began in uniform. Jason Mangone graduated from Boston College to serve as a United States Marine Corps Infantry Officer in Iraq before graduate school at Yale and then two years as director of the Service Year Alliance, a nonprofit effort to make a year of national service a reality for every young American. Jeff Eggers is a United States Naval Academy graduate and former SEAL officer with a graduate degree from Oxford University, combat service in Iraq and Afghanistan, and six years in the White House on the National Security staff. I spent more than thirty-eight years in uniform from West Point to command of all US and NATO forces in Afghanistan before leaving the Army in 2010. Since retiring, I've focused on leadership, teaching at Yale's Jackson Institute and authoring two books.

Each of us carries successes, failures, lessons, and scar tissue from years of leading, but more than anything else we bring unanswered questions. We all share a fascination with, and passion for, leadership, along with a sense that despite all the scholarship, more understanding of leadership is needed.

This book is our attempt to take that first step toward a general theory of leadership. Inspired by Brooks's question, we have mimicked Plutarch's structure by profiling thirteen famous leaders in six pairs and one stand-alone: Robert E. Lee. Like Plutarch, each of our paired chapters opens with a brief introduction and ends with a comparison of the two profiled leaders, in hopes that the juxtaposition of the profiles will reveal the complexity of leadership and shed light on the way most of us end up seeing the myth instead of the reality. Readers will notice that the authors occasionally use personal pronouns. Where "I" is used, most often in the introductions of every profile, it refers to me, Stan. Where "we" is used, this refers to all three authors, myself included.

The profiles are selected and crafted to be educational and entertaining. Not all of our figures were good leaders, or even good people. Some succeeded because they were talented, some because they were extraordinarily committed, some through luck, and some never truly tasted success at all. Right or wrong, success or failure, each was a significant factor in the outcome we see as history today. Their relevance is indisputable. But they are not the entire story.

We've consciously chosen the experiences of thirteen leaders as a lens through which to view leadership. But they are not laboratory animals best viewed with clinical detachment. Their stories are human and are better *experienced* rather than read with analytical dispassion. No life is lived, no crisis navigated, in anticipation of being an interesting case study. Let yourself into the character's world, and into the experience of the leaders themselves.

Don't scan the text for new leadership checklists. We will use stories to challenge traditional leadership models, but we stop short of prescribing how to lead. It is our hope that by helping to dismantle some common myths we will create space for you and other leaders to interact with reality and respond to your challenges with clear thinking and humility.

Finally, by itself, *Leaders* will not make you into a great leader. It won't overcome weak values, a lack of self-discipline, or personal stupidity.

Instead of simplifying the challenge of leading, *Leaders* will outline and underscore the complexities. Leadership has always been difficult, and in the face of a rapidly changing environment, it will only get harder.

But it won't be impossible, and it will be essential.

—GENERAL STAN MCCHRYSTAL (US ARMY, RETIRED)

LEADERS

One

THE MYTHOLOGY

*Things are not always as they seem;
the first appearance deceives many.*

—PHAEDRUS, ROMAN POET, CA. 15 BCE–50 CE

I n 49 BCE, with the dramatic proclamation "The die is cast," Julius Caesar made the fateful decision to cross the Rubicon River at the head of his
13th Legion. The crossing of the Rubicon was momentous because the
river demarcated the boundary between Italy and the province of Gaul to
the north, where Caesar was serving as governor. Suspicious of his growing
power, the Senate had ordered him to disband his army and return to
Rome. But Caesar, defying the Senate, decided to return not in submission
but in rebellion, marching on Rome with his legion. By crossing into Italian territory with an army, Caesar had irrevocably made himself a traitor.

For all its notoriety, Caesar's river crossing was a relatively modest affair in which the future ruler and his legionnaires merely waded across a
shin-deep stream. Nonetheless, this act put him in irreconcilable opposition to Rome's Senate, making the expression "crossing the Rubicon" forever synonymous with passing a point of no return.

The story about how Caesar and his legion marched on Rome survived on
the parchment of the *Lives*, a series of profiles of famous men recorded by the
Greek biographer Plutarch. Plutarch also recorded that the Senate—five years
later—"in the hope that the government of a single person would give them
time to breathe after so many civil wars and calamities," made Caesar

The original and iconic Washington Crossing the Delaware.
(PHOTOGRAPH BY VCG WILSON/CORBIS VIA GETTY IMAGES)

"dictator for life." And yet within two months he was assassinated, the knives wielded by many of those same senators. As Plutarch explains, Caesar's "pretension" and the "extravagance" of his new title had motivated the group, including Caesar's close friend Marcus Junius Brutus, to conspire against him.

Today, those of us who know Julius Caesar's story most likely learned it not from reading Plutarch, but from Shakespeare's *Julius Caesar.* In the bard's telling of the assassination, Caesar struggles until he sees Brutus among the attackers and realizes the depth of his betrayal. Famously, his dying utterance is the poignant "Et tu, Brute? Then fall, Caesar!"

ALMOST TWO MILLENNIA LATER, another General would become famous by crossing a river. Unlike the modest Rubicon, the Delaware could not be crossed by wading, so George Washington had no choice but to cross by boat, a scene memorialized in *Washington Crossing the Delaware,* one of America's most recognizable paintings. On a canvas measuring over twenty-one feet wide, Emanuel Leutze captured the daring of America's founding father and first president.

The parallels between Caesar and Washington go beyond the rivers they crossed as generals. Just as Caesar's final phase of leadership was reenacted by Shakespeare through the rhythm of iambic pentameter, the final act of Washington's leadership was depicted by the playwright Lin-Manuel Miranda, who four centuries later chose hip-hop as the rhythm to dramatize Washington's retirement in his theatrical story of Alexander Hamilton. And where Shakespeare had turned to Plutarch's *Lives*, Miranda found his inspiration within the pages of Ron Chernow's biography *Alexander Hamilton*.

The musical closes with the rap song "One Last Time," in which George Washington's 1796 decision to step down after his second term is met by a disbelieving Hamilton:

> **Hamilton:** Why do you have to say goodbye?
> **Washington:** If I say goodbye, the nation learns to move on.
>   It outlives me when I'm gone.

Miranda said later that he sought to celebrate Washington's "humanity" and "frailty," lifting up the rare example of a leader who voluntarily relinquishes power. In the playwright's drama, Washington selflessly prioritizes the fledgling nation's democracy over the pursuit of power, consistent with the founding father's legacy of leadership.

For would-be leaders, the oft-told stories of audacious river crossings and of the dramatic finales of Julius Caesar and George Washington are both inspiring and intimidating. The stories would be more helpful, though, if leadership actually worked the way the legends imply. In fact, for both Caesar and Washington, leadership was hardly so simple.

History codified Caesar's "The die is cast" as a declaration of courage and decisiveness, but the proclamation also marked a moment of profound doubt. Plutarch tells us, but popular history forgets, that Caesar "ordered a halt" when he approached the river, and that he "wavered much in his mind . . . and often changed his opinion one way and the other." Before pressing on, he sought counsel when "his purposes fluctuated most." And yet "halting," "wavering," and "fluctuating" are not how we tend to view leaders, nor how leaders seek to be remembered. Truly effective leaders, we like to believe, are not susceptible to the fog of doubt—they act decisively and face the consequences. But few real leaders have actually operated this way.

So, too, Caesar's dying words, "Et tu, Brute?" were likely dramatic license taken by Shakespeare and other Elizabethan playwrights. Plutarch's version of the assassination itself was the stuff of a very different drama.

When he is first attacked, rather than make an exclamation that might endear him to history, Caesar, more naturally, grabbed the offending dagger and tried to stop himself from being stabbed. Instead of calling to Brutus, he exclaims, "Vile Casca, what does this mean?" The rest of the struggle is an awkward affair, the great Caesar writhing to avoid the blows of his attackers, who in their own bungling efforts end up stabbing one another: "Some say that he fought and resisted all the rest, shifting his body to avoid the blows, and calling out for help, but that when he saw Brutus's sword drawn, he covered his face with his robe and submitted. . . . And the conspirators themselves were many of them wounded by each other, whilst they all levelled their blows at the same person."

Where Shakespeare's play focuses on the tension and conflict between two of his play's main characters, Plutarch's account zeroes in on Caesar's behavior in the course of dying a violent death.

In truth, neither Plutarch nor Shakespeare knew exactly what happened, and neither do we. We have no choice but to interpret events through the words they've given us. Both the biographer and the playwright do their best to capture the complexity in their own way. Alas, what we remember selectively is that Caesar crossed the Rubicon boldly and then died while uttering the three famous words that he probably never said.

LOOKING AT THE BIOGRAPHER'S and playwright's versions of history side by side, we see that Caesar's leadership was not as heroic as it's often remembered. So too was the case with Washington.

Inside the West Wing lobby of the White House hangs a reproduction of Leutze's *Washington Crossing the Delaware*. The painting is a favorite stop for White House staffers giving tours to guests, who are entertained with a catalog of the painting's historical flaws: the Delaware River never froze in this way, the river is far too wide, the boat is heading the wrong way, the flag is wrong for the period, and so on. But the most interesting factual flaw is the boat itself. Rather than the rickety whaling rowboat

Mort Künstler's modern and more realistic depiction of Washington's crossing.
(FROM THE ORIGINAL PAINTING BY MORT KÜNSTLER, *WASHINGTON'S CROSSING* © 2011 MORT KÜNSTLER, INC.)

depicted by Leutze, Washington is believed to have used a sixty-foot flat-bottom barge complete with artillery, a far better option for an army conducting a winter's night river crossing.

In 2011, a radically different depiction of the crossing was unveiled at the New-York Historical Society, complete with the flat-bottom barge. Artist Mort Künstler had been commissioned by a Mr. Thomas R. Suozzi, who told him, "I want to go up against the existing painting. The other painting is great, but it doesn't tell the realistic story." Aside from the boat, the most striking difference between the Leutze and Künstler versions is Washington himself. In the original, the General is fully upright in the tiny boat, seemingly lunging forward, his center of gravity elevated and perched over a miniature iceberg. In the remake, he's still standing, but he's carefully balanced, his right hand holding a firm grip on a nearby cannon to steady himself.

Künstler's work corrected inaccuracies of history, while also fixing a critical flaw in how we often depict the practice of leadership. It is, of course, human nature to steady oneself in a boat at night, for human balance is imperfect. Few real leaders, even military generals, present themselves riskily in a rowboat, refusing support, as if posing for posterity.

And yet observers rarely see the depiction of Washington towering above a small boat in a freezing body of water—at night—as peculiar. Instead, we often accept such absurdly displayed feats of heroic leadership as normal.

Miranda's depiction of Washington as the American founder too selfless to accept a crown was similarly skewed, and there was more to the idealized story. As Chernow explains, by the time of his resignation, Washington "was suffering from an aching back, bad dentures, and rheumatism; visitors noted his haggard, careworn look." America's founding father was, after all, still human. Washington was certainly motivated by the principle of civic rule—but he was also physically and mentally tired.

A quick scan of these various accounts of two leaders tells us as much about methods of storytelling as about the leaders themselves. Biographers typically tell the stories of individual leaders, emphasizing the significance of their decision making. Unsurprisingly, leaders who draw most of their leadership ideas from biographies learn to adjust their own narrative frames to keep themselves at the center. The stories they tell themselves and others are misleading in a way that we humans crave in a complex world; biography simplifies the complexity of collective human systems down to more manageable individual elements.

The playwright often has a different perspective, focusing on the relationships *among* individuals, particularly when those relationships contain conflict or comedy. While the biographer helps the reader to *know* the attributes of the leader, the playwright gets the theatergoer to *experience* the drama of relationships enveloping that leader.

In truth, we crave both the biographer *and* the playwright. As individuals we appreciate the biographer's focus on the actors, and as social animals we enjoy the playwright's dramatic depiction of their relationships. Yet both storytellers have contributed to the mythology of leadership. Where the biographer fuels our leader-centrism, the playwright (or the painter) enables leader romanticism. Between the two effects, we devise narratives that obscure the role of followers and wrongly attribute complex outcomes to mere individuals: Caesar's strength both defined and ended his empire, and Washington won the Revolutionary War and founded the United States.

In reality, the lessons of leadership are not the ones we most naturally derive from the legends. The Rubicon reminds us that real leaders experience doubt and consult with others. Similarly, the lesson of the Delaware is not that good leaders are blasé in taking on unnecessary risk. A real leader might not utter a pithy line upon being stabbed; he might just quietly die of internal bleeding. When a real leader relinquishes power, he might be upholding the principles of democracy, or he might also simply be fatigued.

"LEADERSHIP" IS A FAMOUSLY difficult term to define. As *The Bass Handbook of Leadership* observes, "often, a two-day meeting to discuss leadership has started with a day of argument over the definition." Bass also notes that leadership expert Joseph Rost found 221 definitions of leadership in 587 examined publications.

Of course, few leaders are so concerned with quibbling over definitions. In our experience, most people think of leadership as the *process* of influencing a *group* toward some defined *outcome*. This definition suggests that leadership is the process of one person herding the group toward goals, and that leaders at the top craft and direct those endpoints. Perhaps worse, our quest to understand leadership has followed a consistent but always insufficient pattern: we've studied individual leaders and come to think of leadership as simply what leaders do.

Here lies the root cause of the mythology of leadership—its relentless focus on the leader. For years, human beings have searched for the secret of leadership by studying why certain leaders achieve enviable results where others do not. To the detriment of the study of leadership, rarely do we look to the individuals around the senior leader. We assume the leader controls the process, undervaluing the role of followers and situational context. Moreover, we pretend that leadership is goals-driven, and that good *outcomes* can be gained through the correct formula of effective leadership. We wrongly believe that what happened in one leadership instance can be replicated in another.

This common understanding of leadership, when held up against the reality of how leadership actually works, reveals three myths, which we'll discuss in more detail in the book's final two chapters:

The Formulaic Myth: In our attempt to understand process, we strive to tame leadership into a static checklist, ignoring the reality that leadership is intensely contextual, and always dependent upon particular circumstances.

The Attribution Myth: We attribute too much to leaders, having a biased form of tunnel vision focused on leaders themselves, and neglecting the agency of the group that surrounds them. We're led to believe that leadership is what the leader does, but in reality, outcomes are attributable to far more than the individual leader.

The Results Myth: We say that leadership is the process of driving groups of people toward outcomes. That's true, to a point, but it's much broader than that. In reality, leadership describes what leaders symbolize more than what they achieve. Productive leadership requires that followers find a sense of purpose and meaning in what their leaders represent, such as social identity or some future opportunity.

The power and prevalence of this mythology of leadership rival those of religion or romance—these myths seem universal and inseparable from our existence as humans. They reflect a disconnect between how things should be and how we find them in practice and yet we knowingly live with this disconnect. For instance, corporate executives often speak of the importance of leadership, but when they're asked to list the threats to their business, they generally list exogenous factors, rarely listing their own leadership as a risk factor.

In part, we live with this mythology because it serves a useful function. As with religion, leadership offers value by crafting a narrative that helps make sense of the world around us, even when it eludes our comprehension. Leadership provides a framework for assigning causality when things go well, and equally a way to assign blame when things go otherwise. And as with romance, leadership holds our attention and captures our imagination, stirring feelings that we don't always understand.

Despite this utility, the mythology often leads us astray with adverse consequences and risks to society. When we buy into the mythology, our leadership models are made less effective, and we construct elaborate processes to select, assess, and train leaders who perpetuate existing weaknesses.

And dangerously, we create and sustain false expectations about leaders. In some cases, savvy leaders exploit the mythology, enriching themselves while corroding the prosperity of the organizations they lead. In others, the mythology becomes exposed, leading to disappointment and cynicism about leadership.

So we might ask, Why do we live with this mythology and how might leadership be redefined? Is it really a process, or more a property? What is the role of leadership in human systems, and why does it seem so necessary in the first instance?

In reality, and across the profiles in this book, we see that leadership is about much more than outcomes; it is equally concerned with how complex human groups optimize their cooperation and how individuals find symbols of meaning and purpose in life. This optimization and sense of meaning emerge from the interaction of a wide range of constantly shifting variables that include far more than the individual leader. Leadership is coproduced by leaders and followers, emerging between the influential and charismatic who crave it and the hopeful and fearful who demand it.

The mythology of leadership is caught up in the duality that makes us human, whereby we find value as part of a social collective and also as autonomous individuals. Being human, we're also wired to experience some separation between how things should be and how things are within the human experience, with the cognitive gift of being able to imagine the future and the unreal. The flip side is that things are never precisely as we wish them to be. And perhaps leadership is no different, bound up in our tendency to always want more from it than it is capable of delivering.

IN LATE 1777, a year following his famous crossing of the Delaware, then-General Washington dispatched Captain Alexander Hamilton to travel to upstate New York and assess the situation. Returning in early 1778, the trusted aide rejoined Washington at winter quarters in Valley Forge, Pennsylvania.

It had been a busy winter for Hamilton. In addition to his survey north, he had been helping his commander in chief draft a letter to the Continental Congress on the almost desperate state of the Army. And so, fatigued from travel and the cold, and in the midst of a war his side was losing, he focused his mind on the future—by looking back.

At day's end, in a room shared with several others, Hamilton sat down at a small desk and removed a worn little notebook from his bag. On its cover was stamped "Pay Book of the State Company of Artillery"—a reference to the New York artillery company he'd commanded when he'd first written in it in August 1776. But the notebook, and its owner, had moved on to bigger things. He set the repurposed book on the desk, opened it to where his last set of notes had ended, prepared his quill, and turned his attention to a 1,700-year-old text: Plutarch's *Lives*.

In the winter of 1777–78, while holed up at Valley Forge, Hamilton took copious notes on the *Lives* in the margins of his notebook, analyzing the stories of Theseus and Romulus, the mythical founders of Athens and Rome, as well as Lycurgus and Numa, lawgivers of Sparta and Rome. Reading the *Lives* was then a common practice, and would continue to be for another 150 years. Teddy Roosevelt kept a copy in his breastpocket: "'I've read this little volume close to a thousand times,' he said, 'but it is ever new.'" Plutarch's works were found in Machiavelli's Florentine court; in President John Adams's letters; and in the libraries and writings of Montaigne, Montesquieu, Rousseau, and Emerson. Well through the early twentieth century, Plutarch's biographical profiles of famous Greeks and Romans were a standard companion for leaders.

Plutarch was a Greek writer who lived from about 46 to about 120 CE. In his *Lives,* he profiled forty-eight leaders, creating pairs of Greek and Roman leaders who shared a common experience or trait—such as Theseus and Romulus. Each of Plutarch's paired—or "parallel"—lives generally begins with an informal introduction that speaks to his motives, followed by one Greek and one Roman "life," and then concludes with a comparison of the two lives. Four of the lives are unpaired. This book mimics Plutarch's structure with thirteen famous leaders profiled in six pairs and one standalone profile. Like Plutarch, each of our paired chapters opens with a brief introduction and ends with a comparison of the two profiled leaders.

Plutarch wrote ancient biography, not history. He was more interested in the question "What sort of man was he?" rather than "What did he do?"

*The cover of Hamilton's notebook
and his first page of notes on
Plutarch's* Lives.

(LIBRARY OF CONGRESS, MANUSCRIPT DIVISION, ALEXANDER HAMILTON PAPERS)

He was focused on matters of personal character. Plutarch's aim was to study virtue so that it could be imitated. In his introduction to the "Life of Pericles," he writes:

> . . . Virtue, by the bare statement of its actions, can so affect men's minds as to create at once an admiration of the things done and desire to imitate the doers of them. . . . Moral good is a practical stimulus; it is no sooner seen, than it inspires an impulse to practice, and influences the

mind and character not by a mere imitation which we look at, but by the statement of fact creates a moral purpose which we form. And so, we have thought fit to spend our time and pains in writing of the lives of famous persons.

While the structure of our book is similar, our intent is different. We offer accounts of those who have led and, importantly, also their context and surroundings, with the hope that these stories will help frame a deeper understanding of what it means to lead and what we mean by leadership. Where Plutarch asked, "What sort of man was he?" we started by asking, "What sort of leader was she?"

Why Plutarch chose his comparisons, or even his precise reason for pairing Greeks and Romans, remains the subject of debate. We are more transparent about our intent and method. In that spirit, we offer some preliminary notes to the reader.

First, unlike Plutarch, we did not select our pairings with any formal structure, such as one Greek and one Roman. Nor did we select them with an end in mind, cherry-picking those who would stand up to a thesis that we sought to prove. Rather, our selection process was incremental, mostly organic, and we applied only a few simple criteria. We began with the idea that we sought a group of leaders that would be interesting to read about, and from whose stories we might learn something about the realities of leadership.

Second, and unlike the relatively limited set of Plutarch's orators and military generals, we were far less constrained in our selection process. Not by design, our six genres of leaders—zealots, founders, power brokers, geniuses, reformers, and heroes—encompass several different leadership types. This is not to say that we thought leadership is the same as political leadership, or that to lead a cause is comparable to leading a start-up. Rather, we take such an expansive approach because we hope to learn more about leadership as a broad concept, rather than further segmenting an already fragmented field of inquiry.

In doing so, we made our task more difficult, for this breadth reflects the challenge that leadership is often an ill-defined, loose mosaic of disciplines. Ultimately, this breadth reflects the slipperiness of leadership and how and where it is practiced; it is something that is everywhere, and yet difficult to pin down. There are of course alternative ways of dividing leadership into different types and genres, but this book is interested in the prevalence of mythologies that emanate through them all.

Third, in considering notable leaders in human history, it was not easy to settle on thirteen. Reviewing the hundreds of candidates who might qualify, we sought a cohort who would be representative across a number of dimensions: profession, region, gender, race, and so on. Unsurprisingly, we found women and minorities to be poorly represented in the canon on leaders. In the end, we settled on leaders who would offer the most diversity in terms of how they led, while remaining clear-eyed to the fact that leadership's history has been a largely patriarchal one.

Fourth, Plutarch hoped that his leaders would offer an example to emulate, or, where he chose immoral examples, to teach us to "avoid the wildness of extremes. . . ." Readers will notice, through our inclusion of leaders most would abhor, that we believe there is much to learn from immoral leaders. Such people have always led and will continue to do so, and so our study must consider this reality carefully. Good leaders, we want to believe, are virtuous, but immoral leaders have been just as effective as the most admirable.

Finally, a major historical criticism of Plutarch is that he judged leaders across a millennium of history by a single moral standard, rather than in the context of their own times. Plutarch thought about context mostly as it related to how much credit a hero deserved for his success, or, in his words, "whether they owe their greatest achievements to good fortune, or their own prudence and conduct." Our view is that effective leadership is intensely behavioral, and not necessarily virtuous, so we see context as a central determinant of whether leaders are remembered or celebrated, much more than moral integrity. Using an individual's actions to tell a story of change comes at the cost of understanding networks, group agency, and contextual restraints. Accordingly, our reliance on the individual leader is contingent.

But there is an obvious irony in this method. If leadership is more than the aggregate of leader behavior, how could a useful landscape be generated by aggregating the portraits of thirteen leaders? Where possible, we looked at our leaders from the point of view of their followers and were particularly sensitive to their environment and the role of context. But it is admittedly difficult to step out of the trap of leader-centrism, even for authors looking to reframe leadership as less leader-centric. Ultimately, this book became an exploration of why this is so.

We say "ultimately" because the fundamental questions that drove our research changed as we wrote the book. Plutarch wrote of a shift in his own motivations as he went about writing his forty-eight *Lives*, telling readers that "it was for the sake of others that I first commenced writing biographies; but I find myself proceeding and attaching myself to it for my own. . . ." Each of the authors of this book began with self-centered motivations—we wanted to be able to explain leadership as we'd experienced it. We began the writing of our profiles with the simple question "How did they lead?" Over time, we came to explore more illuminating questions such as "Why did they emerge as a leader?" and "What was it about the situation that made this style of leadership effective?"

We do draw some conclusions, and even suggest a new definition for leadership in the book's final chapter—one that addresses some of the embedded assumptions of the one described earlier. The three myths, we suggest, are sticky for a reason, and so we return to them in the penultimate and final chapters to reiterate the gap between the myths and the realities of leadership.

Reading Plutarch's *Lives* inspired us to profile leadership as it was experienced. But it also opened our eyes to the fact that individual leaders are never sufficient to understanding cause and effect. As such, our lens of leadership shifts the focus toward the ecosystem of which the leader is a part. We strive to contextualize these leaders' actions into the messy realities they faced, insistent that a less mythological model cannot be prescriptive and should instead describe leadership in the context of the variability and duality of the human condition.

Accordingly, we make contingent our reliance on the individual leader, for using an individual's actions to serve a story of change comes at the cost of understanding networks, group agency, and contextual restraints. Leading is more about being part of a feedback loop within a system than it is about being at the top of a command chain. Indeed, the age-old mythology of leadership may yet come to be understood best through the more modern lens of complex adaptive systems, where outcomes are irreducibly driven by the interplay of followers and context as much as they are by the visionary privilege of the leader.

While an improved understanding of leadership would necessarily be less dependent on—and expect less of—our leaders, they remain indispensable. Indeed, leaders matter tremendously, just not in the way we typically think they do.

Two

THE MARBLE MAN: ROBERT E. LEE

In all of us, however common-place we may be, there lurks an enigma, something which neither we nor others understand. We call it personality, a vague word meaning many things—courage, common sense, quick wit, frankness, determination, self-command, and many other qualities, none of which can openly express themselves unless occasion is propitious and circumstances are favourable. Most of us live and die in a dungeon, and the enigma dies with us; a few of us escape, mostly by chance, and then, if our personality is strong, we accomplish something worth accomplishing, and by doing so the enigma is more often than not transformed into a myth. We cease to be what we really were, and become something we never could be—something which flatters the common mind.

—MAJOR-GENERAL J. F. C. FULLER

The Picture

On a Sunday morning in 2017 I took down his picture, and by afternoon it was in the alley with the other rubbish awaiting transport to the local landfill for final burial. Hardly a hero's end.

The painting had no monetary value; it was really just a print of an original overlaid with brush strokes to appear authentic. But forty years earlier it had been a gift from a young Army wife to her Lieutenant husband when the $25 price (framed) required juggling other needs in our budget.

The dignified likeness of General Robert E. Lee in his Confederate Army uniform had been a prized possession of mine. I'd grown up not far from the Custis-Lee Mansion and been an impressionable seven-year-old boy when the nation's Civil War centennial began. At West Point, Lee, the near-perfect cadet, Mexican War hero, Academy Superintendent, and finally the commander of the Confederacy's Army of Northern Virginia, cast a long, ever-present shadow. Later, in Army quarters from Fort Benning, Georgia, to Fort Lewis, Washington, the painting reflected my fascination with leadership, and spoke of duty and selfless service.

Although a portrait of a man, to many it evoked wider ideas and emotions. For like an object bathed in the light of the setting sun, Robert E. Lee's shadow took on exaggerated size and grew steadily as America's Civil War retreated ever further into the softer glow of history.

A mythology grew around Lee and the cause he served. For many, Lee's qualities and accomplishments, already impressive, took on godlike proportions. This was the Lee I first came to know: a leader whose flaws and failures were sanded off, the very human figure recast as a two-dimensional hero whose shadow had eclipsed the man from whom it came.

But as time passed, the myth was reexamined. The darker side of Lee's legacy, and the picture in my office, now communicated ideas about race and equality with which I sought no association. Down it came.

It was not a simple decision. For almost 150 years, Lee had been a subject of study, and of admiration, not only for his skill, but also as a symbol of stoic commitment to duty, a term he once supposedly described as "the sublimest word in the English language." And while I could appreciate the visceral association with slavery and injustice that images of the Confederacy's most famous commander evoke, for a lifetime, that's not the association I'd drawn. I'd read and largely believed Winston Churchill's statements that "Lee was one of the noblest Americans who ever lived and one of the greatest captains known to the annals of war." And President Franklin Roosevelt's tribute when unveiling a statue of Lee in 1936:

> All over the United States we recognize him as a great leader of men, as a great general. But, also, all over the United States I believe that we recognize him as something much more important than that. We

*The picture of Robert E. Lee, the
soldier, that hung in many of the
Army quarters Annie and I occupied
for more than thirty years.*
(PHOTOGRAPH BY BUYEN LARGE/GETTY IMAGES)

recognize Robert E. Lee as one of our greatest American Christians and
one of our greatest American gentlemen.

Ironically, at age sixty-three, the same age at which Lee died, I concluded I was wrong. To some extent, wrong about Lee as a leader, but certainly about the message that Lee as a symbol conveyed. And although I
was slow to appreciate it, a significant part of American society, many still
impacted by the legacy of slavery, had felt it all along.

Still, as I pondered Plutarch, and began a personal journey to consider
leadership through a lens of notable leaders, I knew that without Lee, whatever list I chose would be incomplete. Not because Lee was the most intelligent, most powerful, or most successful leader, but because his story was
personal to my own. I'd lived a soldier's life. I'd traveled a similar road,
often walking the very same pathways, attempting to master the art and
science of leading. Like Lee, I'd savored success and known bitter failure.
And often the role model against which I'd measured my conduct, sometimes deliberately, and sometimes not, was the soldier Robert E. Lee.

Including Lee in a study of leadership carries risk of misinterpretation, controversy, and even outrage. When Plutarch profiled the Roman general Coriolanus, who vanquished the Volscians only to later lead his former foe against Rome, it allowed him to deepen his study of virtue. Similarly, examining Lee offers us an opportunity to deepen our understanding of leadership. It is a conscious choice to begin with the leader I thought I knew best, and to take a new, clear-eyed look, leavened with a lifetime of personal experiences that have shaped and matured my thoughts on leadership.

Most accounts of Lee as a man, and a leader—his physical presence, demeanor, valor, and apparent serenity—reflect almost quintessentially desirable leadership traits. But staring into a bright light makes it difficult to see clearly. More than most, Lee is portrayed either in a glare of adulation or, more recently, under a dark shadow of disdain.

It is often difficult to separate the leader from the mythology that has grown around him or her, and Lee is no exception. As we look more closely, the reality of Lee's story pushes back the myth. We fixate on him as a major player in the drama of the Civil War, but many of the outcomes of that war were the result of a combination of other factors, not the results of his actions. As for his character? In some ways, he was a good man, and in other ways a bad one. Yet this shouldn't frame our reading of his leadership. Leadership is itself neither good nor evil. Malevolent leaders emerge with surprising frequency, as often as those we judge to be good. Leadership is better judged as either effective or not. Was Lee effective? In large ways yes, and in many ways no.

The Intersection

"With my whole command," the younger general said firmly, and the die was cast.

The two men, fifty-six-year-old General Robert E. Lee and thirty-nine-year-old Thomas Jonathan Jackson, the latter nicknamed "Stonewall" since the opening days of the Civil War, had arrived on horseback, discussed the day's fighting, and laid plans for the morrow.

I remember the scene well. Their meeting was romantically depicted in an 1869 oil painting by an immigrant from St. Helena named Everett B. D. Julio, a black-and-white print of which had hung prominently in my

A print of Everett B. D. Julio's 1869 romantic, and largely inaccurate, depiction of Generals Lee and Jackson's final meeting on the battlefield in Chancellorsville. A copy hung in Stonewall Jackson Elementary School in Arlington, Virginia, where I attended first through fourth grades.

Virginia elementary school. In the picture, the generals, on horseback, in immaculate uniforms, seemed poised for battle. A distinctive ridge-line, nonexistent on Chancellorsville's actual terrain, dramatizes the depiction.

War is rarely like that, and neither was it then. The two generals met at night, after dismounting where Plank and Furnace roads met, an obscure intersection of dirt tracks in thickly wooded terrain, appropriately called "The Wilderness." They were just south of another intersection—ambitiously named Chancellorsville for the lone home there, a brick dwelling owned by the Chancellor family.

It was Friday, May 1, 1863, and the temperature in nearby Washington, DC, that afternoon had reached 74 degrees. But as darkness fell, the chill infiltrating the forest caught up with soldiers who had been too active earlier to notice. The ground was damp after recent rains and greatcoats were hastily pulled over uniform tunics. Joints, veterans of countless campaigns, stiffened in the cool night air, and hats covered hair matted with sweat. Moist wool uniforms retain some warmth, but also the stains and smells of uninterrupted wear. As it is in combat, the men looked, and felt, old beyond their years.

The discussion was in earnest. The previous days' fighting had been bloody but inconclusive, and like boxers cautiously testing their opponent, they sought an advantage against their foe. As they conversed, a familiar cavalry commander, thirty-year-old General J. E. B. Stuart, in knee-high boots, arrived in the darkness. At about that time the three generals learned that the enemy's flank was vulnerable and additional scouting soon found a route through the thick forest to reach it.

For Robert E. Lee, the murkiness of the entire situation mirrored the darkened woods around him. The North's Army of the Potomac, after months of relative inactivity following their defeat at Fredericksburg in December 1862, had reorganized under a new commanding general, Major General "Fighting Joe" Hooker, and was on the move headed south. It was Lee's job to stop them, and in response to Union movement on his flank, he had already split his outnumbered army once, detaching roughly 12,000 soldiers (or 20 percent of his force) to enable him to maneuver the remaining forces to confront Hooker's 70,000-man main body.

Now, at the night-shrouded trail junction, he needed to decide whether to split his small force again. Jackson and Lee discussed the risky option and Lee asked Jackson how much of his unit he would place on the flanking wager. Jackson's answer was simple—all of it.

As was his nature, Lee accepted his trusted subordinate's decision. He decided to retain just two divisions, about 14,000 Confederate soldiers, to face Hooker's entire command—gambling he could hold long enough for Jackson's now-separate force to conduct a fourteen-mile forced march on poorly mapped forest roads, and that Jackson's attack would then succeed. If Hooker attacked aggressively at midday and cracked Lee's line, disaster was likely. Defeat could end the South's existence as a fledgling nation.

In violation of conventional military doctrine, in the face of an enemy army of superior strength led by a seasoned, aggressive commander, they would split their poorly equipped and inadequately supplied force—again. It was a decision for which generals are labeled audacious—if they win.

The next day, the 750th of a war that would grind on for 711 more, was difficult. As they do in war, things went awry from the start. Union pressure on Lee's army's weakened front threatened ruin while Jackson's corps moved.

Jackson's columns were late in beginning their march and were spotted by Federal forces early in the movement. But fate smiled, and by late afternoon Confederate regiments, preceded by a rush of frightened wildlife, burst upon Union General Oliver O. Howard's XI Corps and the deed was done. Jackson's infantry caved in the Union right wing at Chancellorsville in a victory capping a string of battlefield successes that seemed to confirm stories of Lee's extraordinary military genius. As Richmond's *Daily Dispatch* explained at the conclusion of the Battle of Chancellorsville,

> By a prompt and rapid movement by Gen. Lee, [the Yankees] were routed. . . . Saturday and Sunday are amongst the most brilliant in the annals of the Southern Confederacy, already illumined with triumphs which, for number and magnitude, are not surpassed in history.

The scene, and the actors in it, fit comfortably into a narrative of heroism and sacrifice. Lee, the noble patrician with snow-white hair and beard and a fatherly countenance, provided a calming foil to the disheveled appearance and boiling intensity of Jackson and the youthful, dashing Stuart. Two years earlier Lee had forsworn command of Union forces to reluctantly take up arms in the defense of his beloved Virginia, and was the inspiration and architect of victory, with his passionate lieutenant, Jackson, the decisive thrust that humbled their foe. Defending their native state and newly formed nation against foreign invaders, they had triumphed. And as if in a tragedy, the meeting of brothers-in-arms would be their last. In the evening, after victory was complete, Jackson was wounded and with his devoted wife beside his bed, died a hero's death eight days later. Lee noted the magnitude of the loss, saying that he had lost his "right arm."

The generals who had met that evening were seasoned soldiers. All were graduates of West Point, had served with distinction in the pre–Civil War United States Army and, as time passed, were fated to achieve almost mythological status. In the years ahead, statues and paintings proliferated. Lee and Jackson appeared on a 1925 US half dollar, a World War II tank was named after J. E. B. Stuart, and the United States Army would name a military installation after Lee. I began my own education in 1960 at Stonewall Jackson Elementary School and later played sports for the Washington-Lee High

School Generals. Although long dead as soldiers (only Lee survived the war and died five years later), as heroes often do, they lived on.

From 1942 to 1944, Lee biographer and devoted admirer Douglas Southall Freeman published his magisterial work, *Lee's Lieutenants*. The three-volume study of Lee's army commanders became a consistent part of the professional reading of twentieth-century American military leaders, and I remember thumbing through my father's copies while still a boy.

Freeman began the trilogy with a question: "Were ever men more consistently themselves?" When applied to Robert E. Lee and his celebrated subordinates, the question is illuminating. In many ways, Lee was remarkably reliable in reflecting the standards he set for himself, although some of his choices are confounding. In his continual search for rules to govern his conduct, Lee dependably adhered to values and responsibilities he felt appropriate for himself as a soldier, a husband, a father, a Christian, an American, a Southern slaveholder, and a Virginian.

One hundred and nine years after Chancellorsville, in the shadow of monuments to heroes that stand on West Point's Trophy Point, I'd taken the same oath Lee, Jackson, Stuart, and others had. From my first day wearing the cadet gray uniform, one that had changed little in the intervening years, I was determined to become a leader. At the time it felt straightforward enough, but I found there was much of life and leadership to learn.

New soldiers expect, and in some ways seek, hardship and periodic danger; it is the inevitable complexity of life that is always the harshest reality. In the end, the West Point–trained heroes of Chancellorsville became icons of Southern heritage. But they also betrayed the oath we shared, took up arms against their nation, and fought to kill former comrades—all in the defense of a cause ultimately committed to the morally indefensible maintenance of slavery.

The Perfect Cadet

Thirty-eight years before General Robert E. Lee led his army to victory at Chancellorsville, the eighteen-year-old son of Revolutionary War hero Henry "Light Horse Harry" Lee had entered the United States Military Academy at West Point to begin a soldier's life. And as I found when I followed in 1972, he'd never really left. A portrait of Academy Superintendent Colonel Lee in the blue uniform of the United States Army reminded me and my classmates of his thirty-one years of service before secession, and massive granite barracks named in his honor spoke volumes about the unique place where my chosen profession positioned his memory.

In many ways, this reverence was a curious outcome. In 1780, General Benedict Arnold had conspired to betray his army and his country by surrendering the same West Point, then a strategic fort dominating the vital Hudson River, to the British, and has suffered unrelenting condemnation since. Other generals like Eisenhower, MacArthur, and Patton were depicted in statues and held up for study, but for Lee was reserved the special honor of emulation. I, along with many other young leaders, venerated him for his unwavering dignity, stoic commitment, and courageous leadership, allowing these qualities to eclipse the reality of his service against the nation he'd sworn to defend. The naturally studious, self-disciplined Cadet Lee had grown up in Alexandria, Virginia, ten miles from George Washington's Mount Vernon estate, with the first president's legacy of duty omnipresent. Young Robert was acutely aware of the Lee family's respected position in Virginia society, which implied a noblesse oblige for those who carried the famous name.

The perceptive youth admired his own father's Continental Army service but from an early age eschewed the older Lee's financial and familial irresponsibility. Bright, handsome, and willing to accept West Point's rigorous, yet often petty discipline, during his four years at the Academy, Lee set a rarely achieved record of zero demerits and enviable academic marks. More fundamentally, he seemed to internalize the Academy's values captured in her motto of "Duty, Honor, Country." At some point, fellow cadets, who included a number of future comrades and battlefield opponents, gave their charismatic yet serious comrade the moniker of "Marble Man," as though anticipating the role he would play for the last decade of his life, and the first 150 years following his death.

The Engineer Officer

In 1829, recently graduated Robert E. Lee entered the 6,332-strong United States Army as a Lieutenant of Engineers, joining what was then the most respected branch of the service. But it was peacetime, and there was little glory. He spent the first seventeen years of his career working on projects fortifying America's extensive coastline against foreign invasion and improving navigation on the vital Mississippi River. Although keenly aware that the glory of his task paled in comparison to that of his father's combat exploits, or Napoleon Bonaparte's battlefield mastery, Lee had studied at West Point, his work was a duty to be performed with skill and diligence.

Lee's marriage in 1831 to Mary Anna Custis, the great-granddaughter of George Washington's wife, Martha Custis Washington, reinforced his already strong psychological and emotional ties to Virginia and her patrician class. Stately Arlington House, overlooking Washington City, became his home. When not deployed on military service, Lee focused on his growing family.

The young officer matured as a leader. Dignified and reflexively courteous, to others Lee exuded quiet professionalism and a self-control that eluded many of his peers, who often turned to alcohol to deal with the loneliness of remote postings in a peacetime force. Instinctively self-disciplined, Lee acted out a part he'd written for himself. The examples of those he admired, like Washington, the values he had inherited from the society he came from, the history he read, and his incubation at West Point shaped the image of the leader he wanted to be, and the leader he molded himself into.

The Mexican War Hero

By most measures, the Mexican War that began in 1846 was an unfortunate, unnecessary, and unfair conflict between two mismatched opponents, and like many, Lee was distressed by these realities. But it's doubtful that the thirty-nine-year-old Captain was entirely unhappy when it began. It is axiomatic that soldiers abhor war, but that is primarily true of those who

A young Robert E. Lee. Highborn, disciplined, and bright, his pre–Civil War career centered on his oversight of engineering projects around the United States, valor on the battlefield in Mexico, and leadership of West Point.
(BETTMANN / CONTRIBUTOR)

have already experienced one. In reality, most members of the profession quietly yearn for an opportunity to test themselves in battle. For some, it is in hope of promotion or glory; in most it is a subtler need to prove to themselves and justify to others their legitimacy as soldiers. My military peers and I had few strong views on Grenada in 1983, Panama in 1989, or even Saddam Hussein's occupation of Kuwait in 1990, but the vast majority sought battlefield service. It would have been natural for Lee to feel the same.

Still, like those of his future opponent, Ulysses S. Grant, Lee's feelings about the war were conflicted. In Mexico, Lee was not fighting in a war he wanted his country to fight and would write that "we bullied [Mexico] . . . for that I am ashamed, for she was the weaker party." Still, by instinct, upbringing, and education he, as soldiers still do, mentally compartmentalized the broader politics to pursue what he considered his duty.

On the ground, the war with Mexico was a complex endeavor, and Lee's previous experiences building coastal fortifications bore little resemblance to his new role. Instead of supervising workers laboriously sinking piles into muddy American coastal soil, Lee found himself on foreign soil in what was, for its time, a fast-moving and risky military operation. For all soldiers, until tested, performance in combat is a great unknown, and Lee was no different. He knew his father's reputation for courage would not automatically pass to him, and peacetime proficiency is an incomplete predictor of wartime competence. But assigned to a prestigious position on Winfield Scott's staff, Lee found that war suited him well. Whether siting artillery while under enemy fire or conducting nighttime reconnaissance to locate and determine the best route on which to attack the foe, Lee performed brilliantly.

Ahead of the Battle of Cerro Gordo in April 1847, Lee was sent to reconnoiter a path through the mountains, in doing so bringing himself within several feet of gossiping Mexican soldiers. Lee spent hours lying silently and motionlessly under a log until darkness allowed him to escape and return to his own army.

He'd nearly been captured, but he'd found a route by which the American army might be able to outflank their enemy. After relaying his discovery back to General Scott, plans were changed, and it was decided that a group of "pioneers" would hack out a path through the inhospitable terrain. A force of soldiers under the aggressive General David Twiggs would then be guided by Lee along the route, surprising the Mexican defenders.

It was a clever plan, but all hell broke loose when Twiggs's poorly disciplined troopers made so much noise they lost the element of surprise. Mexicans began assembling in formation on the mountaintop, and the impetuous Twiggs suddenly gave an order to "charge them to hell." The Americans initially overran the Mexican positions but, while attempting to gain the next summit of Cerro Gordo, found themselves pinned down by cannon fire. Lee responded and rapidly deployed three light artillery pieces to ease the pressure on Twiggs's men—saving them from certain slaughter. Praise came in reports from the grateful Twiggs and other high-ranking witnesses to his "intrepid coolness and gallantry" in the midst of this ordeal. For soldiers, from such exploits legends begin.

Lee's performance in Mexico established his reputation in the eyes of the Army as a gifted professional and, in the view of some, as the most impressive officer to emerge from the conflict. His credibility grew from his noted competence as an engineer, from his courage under fire, and for the kind of noteworthy leadership that periodically appears in the crucible of combat. Even the formidable, if somewhat pompous, Major General Winfield Scott, nicknamed "Old Fuss and Feathers," who commanded an outnumbered force in a brilliant campaign to capture Mexico's capital city, frequently mentioned Lee in his dispatches, judging him to be "the very best soldier I ever saw in the field." The achievement was significant, and improbable, because Lee had served as a staff officer, advising, interpreting, and executing the orders of others, and not as a commander. Still, it identified him within the Army as a man to watch.

The Southerner

Lee returned from Mexico in 1848 to an Army quickly reverting to its peacetime culture and size, which meant that Brevet Colonel Lee returned to his regular Army rank of Captain and his prewar role constructing fortifications along the American coastline. He also returned to his family, now including four sons, three daughters, and a wife, and to the Virginia society from which he had come and to which he still felt a gravitational pull—to his family legacy, his earliest loyalties, and the things that were deeply familiar and deeply rooted in how he defined himself.

But he remained in uniform, taking the high-profile post as the Superintendent of West Point in 1852 and, in 1855, a promotion to Lieutenant Colonel and transfer to the cavalry. His posting to Texas as second in command of the 2nd Cavalry Regiment meant another separation from his family, who remained in Arlington, but offered active service against Comanches—and greater possibility for promotion.

The death in 1857 of his wife's father, George Washington Parke Custis, the owner of Arlington House and several other income-producing properties in Virginia, caused Lee to take extended leave from his unit in order to settle family affairs. That process involved more than executing Custis's last will and testament. The slave-worked estates were poorly run and heavily in debt, and the professional soldier found himself in an active role within the landed, slave-owning gentry for which the South was known.

For that culture in the first half of the nineteenth century, slavery was always an issue. It was the subject of often-contentious discussion, political wrangling, and periodic violence, as in 1859, when Lieutenant Colonel

Robert E. Lee was directed to lead United States military operations to end John Brown's aborted abolitionist uprising at Harpers Ferry, Virginia. From birth, Lee was intimately familiar with slavery. His father's old commander, George Washington, whom Lee idolized, had owned slaves for fifty-six years of his life, only directing the 123 he owned fully (of the 317 on his estate) to be freed following his wife, Martha's, death. And although Lee's family lacked the wealth for large holdings, from childhood, Lee was part of a culture built on the ownership of slaves.

Lee's own statements on slavery are conflicting, but his overall record is clear. Lee repeatedly expressed his theoretical opposition to slavery, but he in fact reflected the conventional thinking of the society from which he came and actively supported the "peculiar institution" of slavery. Well before joining the Confederacy, Lee loathed abolitionists and his feelings hardened as the Civil War dragged on. Following President Lincoln's Emancipation Proclamation, Lee wrote:

> In view of the vast increase of the forces of the enemy, of the savage and brutal policy he has proclaimed, which leaves us no alternative but success or degradation worse than death, if we would save the honor of our families from pollution, our social system from destruction, let every effort be made, every means be employed, to fill and maintain the ranks of our armies, until God, in his mercy, shall bless us with the establishment of our independence.

From as far back as 1859, Lee's personal treatment of slaves has been a public issue. Although accusations that he beat his slaves are impossible to prove after 150 years, their veracity is arguably beside the point.* Lee was

---

* In 1859, the *New York Tribune* printed accusations that Lee had beaten some of his runaway slaves, and an account of the beatings, provided by Wesley Norris, one of the slaves, was published in an antislavery newspaper in 1866. For a full discussion of Lee's treatment of his slaves, see Elizabeth Brown Pryor, *Reading the Man: A Portrait of Robert E. Lee Through His Private Letters* (New York: Viking, 2007), chapter 16. With respect to the question of whether or not Lee beat his slaves, Pryor concludes that "Wesley Norris's testament was given to an antislavery newspaper in 1866 and is one of several accounts of this incident. . . . Its veracity has been questioned by generations of Lee aficionados, and we might be tempted to dismiss it as the exaggerated ranting of a bitter ex-slave. Except for one thing: all of its facts are verifiable."

a willing and active participant in a society and economy that rested on slavery, and he fought ferociously to defend it. Lee was a Southerner, and efforts to depict him in opposition to slavery run contrary to his actions.

"The Greatest Mistake"

*While I wish to do what is right, I am unwilling to do
what is wrong at the bidding of the South or of the North.*

—ROBERT E. LEE, IN A LETTER, DECEMBER 1860

On April 20, 1861, newly promoted Colonel Robert E. Lee tendered his resignation from the United States Army, the institution he had served since entering West Point three and a half decades before. "You have made the greatest mistake of your life, and I feared it would be so," General Scott, his mentor since the Mexican War, told him.

The drama surrounding Lee's choice to abandon both the Army and the nation to which he had sworn allegiance and dedicated his life has been the subject of extensive analysis and debate. In one sense, it helps us define Lee the man, but only partially. In both Iraq and Afghanistan our enemies represented movements I opposed, but I came to appreciate how a rational, moral person could see things from a perspective diametrically opposed to mine, and in their position, I would likely have shared that view. As uncomfortable as it might be, most soldiers understand that our cause might be no more right than our enemy's.

For leaders, it can be exquisitely complex. Whether out of strong belief, a sense of duty, or another purpose, a leader may work, politic, or fight for a cause some judge reprehensible. But the moral validity of the cause doesn't determine the success or effectiveness of the leadership. Great leaders can serve bad causes as often as lousy leaders represent the most noble of efforts.

With Robert E. Lee, it is particularly difficult to judge—in some measure because of the hagiography that arose following his death, but also because, intentionally or not, Lee painted a somewhat contradictory picture of his underlying motives.

Lee was offered command of soldiers on opposing sides of the Civil

War—a Plutarchian moment in American history if there ever was one. The soldier for whom the concept of loyalty and the obligation of duty were sacred could not well have taken the choice lightly. Lee, who instinctively sought refuge in the simplicity of the values he tried to embody, found himself in a complex collision of competing ethics and responsibilities. The decision to join Virginia, and ultimately the Confederacy, resulted in contradictions Lee spent the remainder of his life trying to rationalize, and admirers have attempted to ignore or justify.

The road to Lee's fateful decision and the chaos and carnage of America's Civil War was a long one. Rather than erupting suddenly, the building pressure between the North and South grew over decades. Issues of economic development and states' rights were trumpeted, but ultimately the dispute was about slavery, which following the rise of labor-intensive cotton as a source of tremendous wealth underpinned the South's economic model. Independent of the moral contradictions of slavery in a nation conceived in liberty and the rights of man, abolition would fundamentally upend Southern society. Everyone in the South knew it, and few whites relished the prospect.

The final straw for most in the Deep Southern states was the November 1860 election of Republican candidate Abraham Lincoln of Illinois, and on December 20, 1860, South Carolina voted to secede (the eight slaveholding states of the Upper South and border did not see Lincoln's election as reason to leave the Union). While views of secession ranged across the nation from long-awaited liberation to existential tragedy, for soldiers like Lieutenant Colonel Robert E. Lee, then commanding the 2nd United States Cavalry Regiment at Fort Mason, Texas, the immediate challenge was to lead, and carefully manage, a mass of officers and soldiers who were individually challenged to choose between loyalty to their state, their nation, or the new Confederacy that might arise.

Secession was not a single event completed with raucous celebrations in Charleston, but a process that played out over months. In this uncharted territory, no one knew whether it was to be the first scene in a years-long tragedy or a mere season of discontent from contemptuous South Carolinians. At remote Fort Mason, Lee sought to maintain as much order and normalcy as possible, but pressures from outside events threatened to contort or rupture long-held loyalties and bonds between soldiers, producing an assault on the very premise upon which the United States had been created some eight decades earlier.

As pressures mounted, Lee read Edward Everett's *Life of George Washington* as if for guidance from the nation's first president, spending these months meditating on where his own obligations lay. Was his duty, as he had sworn, to the United States, or more basically, to her Army? Or did he owe allegiance to older ties like those to his beloved Virginia and, if she should secede, to the South? For Lee the choice could not have been entirely the product of political analysis; that's not how he functioned. Family, friendships, and visceral ties to the land and society from which he came all entered the calculus.

Everett's tome made it no easier. Washington's legacy seems to have reaffirmed to Lee the magnitude of his impending decision: "How his great spirit would be grieved if he could see the wreck of his mighty labors," he wrote on January 23. These times of solitary reflection likely brought more questions than answers, however, while his men outside asked questions of their leader to which his answers necessarily had to remain both equivocal and professionally exacting.

Increasingly, events forced the hand of Lee and other similarly conflicted soldiers. On January 9, 1861, just three weeks after seceding, cadets of South Carolina's military college, The Citadel, fired upon a Union steamer, *Star of the West*, which was attempting to resupply and reinforce the Federal-held Fort Sumter in Charleston Harbor. The march to war quickened. On February 1, the crisis grew nearer as Texas voted to secede, and after removing Unionist governor Sam Houston, joined six other states of the slaveholding Deep South to form the Confederate States of America.

Although war had not begun, the United States Army garrison at Fort Mason was now in potentially hostile territory—a delicate position for any commander. But Lee was spared the task of navigating this uncertainty alongside his troops when he was ordered to "report in person" to Washington, DC. Ironically, en route, the blue-uniformed Lee was briefly detained in San Antonio by armed secessionists who declared him to be a "prisoner of war," forcing him to abandon his luggage in order to progress on to the capital.

Events would soon force a personal decision. Although Lee saw secession as tragic, he had confessed to his friend and outspoken Unionist and
abolitionist Charles Anderson that he felt his "loyalty to Virginia ought to
take precedence over that which is due to the Federal government." Reaching Arlington on March 1, 1861, the dutiful Lee looked to Virginia to guide
his choice.

Virginia, however, had not yet decided to join the Confederacy, and her
choice, along with that of three other states of the Upper South—Arkansas,
Tennessee, and North Carolina—appeared to depend upon the turn of fast-
moving events surrounding besieged Fort Sumter and the willingness and
ability of President Lincoln's United States government to assuage Southern fears over the future of slavery under a Republican administration.

Apparently firm in his conviction to attach his loyalty to Virginia but
awaiting the South's most populous and powerful state's decision, Lee sent
a somewhat mixed signal on March 28 by accepting a promotion to Colonel
in the United States Army.

Opinion in Virginia, which had rejected a proposal for secession on
April 4, shifted after President Lincoln's call on April 15 for 75,000 soldiers
to be raised to put down the growing rebellion in the South. Virginia's departure from the United States was put into motion, with the state's legislature conditionally approving secession.

Against this backdrop, on the morning of April 18 President Lincoln
requested the highly regarded Lee to remain loyal to the Union. Pressed in
person by Francis Preston Blair Sr. at the request of Secretary of War Simon
Cameron, Lee was offered command of the army of Federal volunteers being raised to put down the rebellion. Lincoln's overture to secure Lee as a
leader of Union military forces was a shrewd move. The new president had
been told of Lee's capability as a soldier, but he was also acutely aware of
the cultural significance of having Lee the Virginian lead Union soldiers, a
premonition that would hold true as the dual weight of the Lee name and
Virginia's swing to the Confederacy became a tipping point for the secession of a further three states. Lincoln's cautious use of an intermediary in
extending this invitation to avoid embarrassment to his administration
should Lee reject the Union's overtures was warranted. Lee refused "the
offer he made me to take command of the army . . . though opposed to

secession and deprecating war, I could take no part in an invasion of the Southern States."

Lee's position clear, Winfield Scott told him that he must now formally resign. On Sunday, April 20, Lee expressed alarm at the pro-war sentiments he noticed in fellow churchgoers at Christ Church, Alexandria, when he attended worship, but later that day submitted his resignation from the United States Army.

Virginia's decision followed a month later when, in a referendum on May 23, 1861, 128,884 Virginians voted for secession against the 32,134 who voted to remain in the Union. Lee the Virginian now became a Confederate.

Although many historians view Lee's loyalty to Virginia, and therefore his decision to fight for the Confederacy, as preordained, evidence and human nature suggest how excruciatingly difficult it actually was. Lee's loyalties remained conflicted. He'd written extensively on his patriotism and faith in his nation: "there is no sacrifice I am not ready to make for the preservation of the Union, save that of honour," but more fundamentally, Lee defined himself by duty. From his earliest days, Lee's conduct, his diligence, and willing sacrifices were rooted in fulfilling responsibilities he set for himself, and in meeting the expectations of others. It was a persona he crafted carefully and projected intentionally. It was not a false depiction, but instead was remarkably accurate in reflecting the very essence of the man. For Lee, the torture came when the institutions and values to which he felt obligations came into conflict. For the first time in his life, he could not simultaneously meet all the commitments he'd made. In simply tying his decision to the course chosen by his native Virginia, he essentially passed the most important moral decision of his life to the popular vote of others. Soon he would find himself supporting the greatest evil in American history, slavery, and not only opposing, but ultimately trying to destroy, some of the very institutions and ideas he'd held dear.

On April 22, 1861, when Lee accepted command of Virginia's forces, with the strong likelihood of opposing the United States, he did it inside the state capitol at Richmond. That same building housed Jean-Antoine Houdon's iconic statue of George Washington. As a boy in northern Virginia, Lee had walked the same streets as Washington; Lee's wife was Washington's step-great-granddaughter; Lee's father-in-law collected Washington relics around his estate at Arlington House; and Lee had referenced the definitive biography of Washington when considering his loyalties at Fort Mason. In the Virginia statehouse in 1861, Lee was quite literally standing in his hero's shadow. When he was named commander of Virginia's forces, the president of the state convention even handed Lee one of Washington's swords. In accepting, Lee would eventually commit himself to tearing asunder the nation that his role model had spent a life creating.

The Confederate

For three months in 1863, a British Army officer took a personal leave of absence from his regiment, the Coldstream Guards, to tour the Confederacy. Entering through Texas, Lieutenant Colonel Arthur James Lyon Fremantle traveled east, eventually joining the Army of Northern Virginia as it moved north into Pennsylvania, ultimately to the Battle of Gettysburg. Fremantle's journal, published following his return to London, reflects the observations of a professional soldier, but his unabashedly glowing description of the Army commanding general stands out:

> General Lee is, almost without exception the handsomest man of his age I ever saw. He is fifty-six years old, tall, broad-shouldered, and well made, well set up—a thorough soldier in appearance; and his manners are most courteous and full of dignity. He is a perfect gentleman in every respect. I imagine no man has so few enemies, or is so universally esteemed. Throughout the South, all agree in pronouncing him to be as near perfection as a man can be.

When Virginia decided to join the Confederacy, Lee's military affiliation followed. But he did not ascend to his most famous role, Commander of the Army of Northern Virginia, until after General Joseph E. Johnston, a former US Army colleague, was wounded at the Battle of Seven Pines on May 31, 1862. Lee's most recent role had been as military adviser to another West Point graduate, Confederate president Jefferson Davis. But the highly

Lee in the uniform of a Confederate officer. After agonizing over which side to fight for in the Civil War, he eventually elected to fight for Virginia, the Confederacy, and, by connection, the institution of slavery.
(PHOTOGRAPH © CORBIS/CORBIS VIA GETTY IMAGES)

touted Lee had little to show for the first year of the war. He'd lost a minor battle in western Virginia and had been labeled the "King of Spades" for supervising extensive field fortifications along the South's Atlantic coast. In an Army and society that prized a swaggering cavalier culture, deliberate professionals were not automatically respected.

Three weeks into command, however, in late June 1862, Lee launched a series of hammerlike attacks known as the Seven Days' Battles, causing a superior Union Army under the command of Major General George Mc-Clellan to withdraw from a position threatening the Confederate capital of Richmond. The fast-moving campaign was imperfectly executed and costly in Southern casualties, but it ended a near-term threat to the city, undermined confidence in McClellan, and instantaneously brought the fifty-five-year-old Lee to the forefront of Confederate generals. It began a record of accomplishment that gave him a special place among American military leaders, where he has remained for 155 years.

Lee, who had attained only the rank of Colonel in the United States Army after more than thirty-one years, commanded the Army of Northern Virginia in the field for almost three years. In the end, he lost. But

before surrendering his poorly provisioned Army in April 1865 at Appomattox Court House, Virginia, he led his forces through a series of campaigns and battles that included such familiar names as the Second Bull
Run, Antietam, Fredericksburg, Chancellorsville, Gettysburg, the Wilderness, and Petersburg. Together with his key lieutenants, Lee earned an impressive record of tactical successes against a stronger foe led by five
successive commanding generals.

The General once derisively called "Granny Lee" became famous for his
aggressiveness and willingness to take battlefield risks. In an era when even
senior commanders had to put themselves in extreme physical danger in
order to observe and direct combat operations, personal courage was admired, but expected. Less common was the courage of commanders to risk
defeat through bold action in uncertain circumstances. As I found in Iraq
and Afghanistan, leaders most often fear responsibility for failure more
than enemy fire. For some, reputation is zealously protected and, overall,
caution and timidity are more common than physical cowardice. Lee
had no such reputation. One of his former artillery commanders, Edward
Porter Alexander, once described Lee, writing "his very name might be
Audacity."

Lee's battlefield successes had an unnerving effect on his foes in blue. Just
as opponents often felt little confidence in their ability to defeat Napoleon,
Lee's reputation and those of his key lieutenants were practical combat
multipliers for the Confederacy. General Grant, frustrated by his troops'
excessive regard for their legendary foe, once said:

> Oh, I am heartily tired of hearing about what Lee is going to do. Some
> of you always seem to think he is suddenly going to turn a double som-
> ersault, and land in our rear and on both of our flanks at the same time.
> Go back to your command, and try to think what we are going to do
> ourselves, instead of what Lee is going to do.

Even at the time, separating Lee the leader from the myth was difficult,
and until today assessing his record and effectiveness as a military commander is the subject of endless scholarship and argument rivaling the passions produced during the war itself. On an objective level, despite his

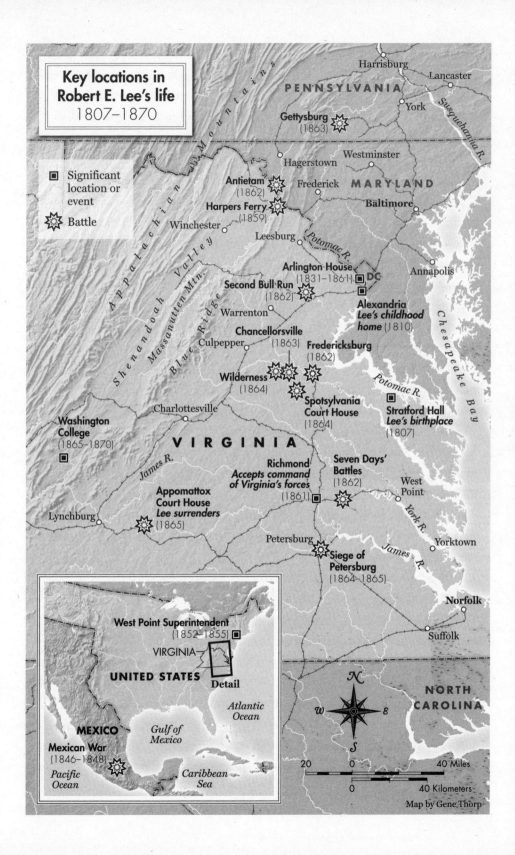

Key locations in Robert E. Lee's life
1807–1870

- ▣ Significant location or event
- ✸ Battle

PENNSYLVANIA

Harrisburg
Lancaster
York
Susquehanna R.

Gettysburg (1863) ✸

Hagerstown
Westminster
Frederick
MARYLAND
Baltimore

Antietam (1862) ✸
Harpers Ferry (1859) ✸

Winchester
Leesburg
Potomac R.
Annapolis

Arlington House (1831–1861) ▣ DC

Second Bull Run (1862) ✸
Alexandria
Lee's childhood home (1810)

Warrenton
Chesapeake Bay

Chancellorsville (1863) ✸
Fredericksburg (1862) ✸
Culpepper
Potomac R.

Wilderness (1864) ✸✸✸
Spotsylvania Court House (1864) ✸
Stratford Hall *Lee's birthplace* (1807) ▣

Charlottesville

Washington College (1865–1870) ▣

VIRGINIA

James R.

Richmond *Accepts command of Virginia's forces* (1861) ▣
Seven Days' Battles (1862) ✸
West Point

Appomattox Court House *Lee surrenders* (1865) ✸

Lynchburg

Petersburg
York R.
Yorktown

Siege of Petersburg (1864–1865) ✸
James R.

Norfolk

Suffolk

NORTH CAROLINA

N
W · E
S

Inset map

West Point Superintendent (1852–1855) ▣

VIRGINIA
Detail

UNITED STATES

Atlantic Ocean

MEXICO
Gulf of Mexico

Mexican War (1846–1848) ✸

Pacific Ocean
Caribbean Sea

20 0 40 Miles
0 40 Kilometers

Map by Gene Thorp

repeated tactical victories, the Confederacy's overall strategy and Lee's two major thrusts into the North failed. An 1862 push into Maryland was blunted at the Battle of Antietam, and the following year's invasion of the North that climaxed in Pennsylvania at Gettysburg foreshadowed the Confederacy's ultimate military defeat.

Lee's competence as a professional soldier is well grounded. But the reality is that while many of the Confederacy's shortcomings were the result of material limitations and the Confederacy's awkward relationship with the individual state governments, accounts that the Army of Northern Virginia was also a less disciplined and efficient force than circumstances demanded are convincing. In an age of mass armies, how well an army executed the mundane functions of logistics, field sanitation, and medical operations, or managed personnel, furlough, and legal requirements, was (and remains) as critical as battlefield brilliance.

One of Lee's most noted critics, the retired British Major General J. F. C. Fuller, lays responsibility directly at the feet of the Commanding General: "this lack of appreciation that administration is the foundation of strategy; this lack of interest in routine, and abhorrence to exert his authority, maintained his army in a state of semi-starvation and were the causes of much of its straggling and ill-discipline." Historians differ on the validity of Fuller's critique, but throughout the war, Lee's forces, hamstrung by sources of supply dependent upon individual states, fragile transportation networks, and his personal inattention, remained less effective than they needed to be.

Ironically, where the much-maligned George McClellan, twice Lee's opponent as commander of the Union's Army of the Potomac, was known for his overly cautious, slow maneuvers, he was also a gifted trainer, organizer, and manager—qualities much appreciated by his soldiers—and established the foundation upon which the Army of the Potomac's later success was built.

At the center of Lee's legacy of exceptional leadership are his relationships with key subordinates. Figures as famous as James Longstreet, George Pickett, and John Bell Hood, not to mention Jackson and Stuart, create the image of a constellation of heroes led by the brightest of stars engaged in an intrepid struggle for the defense of Southern rights. In reality, the competence and interaction of the Confederacy's military leadership, like that in most armies, was more problematic. Although many of the commanders touted Mexican War experience, most had served as staff officers—none, save President Jefferson Davis, had senior command of troops in the field.

Strong-willed, even headstrong, personalities melded imperfectly in an environment of inflated expectations and political pressures. In these challenging circumstances, Lee's ability to leverage the talents of so many officers was undeniably impressive. Where commanders like Stonewall Jackson thrived on operational freedom of action, Lee's command approach of broad "mission style" instructions—where subordinates are told what they need to accomplish rather than how to accomplish it—was hugely successful. But with less confident commanders, these general, sometimes vague, orders intended to provide flexibility led to problems. Where both the commander and situation aligned, as with Jackson at Chancellorsville, the result was sublime. On other occasions, as with the failure of Lieutenant General Richard Ewell to capture the decisive terrain of Cemetery Hill on the first day at Gettysburg, Lee's reluctance to be clear and direct carried painful consequences.

As time passed and attrition bled talent and experience from his force, Lee was forced to adjust the level of autonomy he granted subordinates. But he found leading less-gifted commanders frustrating. After Gettysburg Lee is reported to have exclaimed: "Had I Stonewall Jackson at Gettysburg, I would have won a great victory."

PERHAPS MORE IMPORTANT and certainly more interesting than Lee's competence as a commander is the phenomenon represented by the aura that arose around the West Point–educated son of Virginia that persists to this day.

Seemingly without effort, Lee developed a stature while living that has few parallels. His decisive audacity, buttressed by his impressive physical appearance, obvious piety, and a fatherly, reassuring mien completed a persona that resonated with perfect pitch in the hero-seeking cavalier culture of the South. It was not an accident. While never self-promotional, the self-disciplined Lee had willed himself into reflecting the combined attributes of selfless service and a controlled, dignified demeanor that fit well into Southern concepts of nobility and leadership. Importantly, for both Lee and the South, it was an image that also reflected the memory of George Washington.

Within the Army of Northern Virginia, Lee was held in particularly reverent repute, a fact that is worthy of further contemplation. Although his veteran campaigners savored some of the highest-profile victories of the war highlighted by physical privation—soldiers often marching staggering distances barefoot—serving under General Lee was also a frighteningly lethal prospect. Even while routing their Union foes, Lee's ranks bled profusely. Over the course of his years in command, an infantryman in the Army of Northern Virginia had a 67.7 percent chance of becoming a combat casualty or being killed by disease. For those who joined Lee's Army in 1861, 74.4 percent of infantrymen would die of disease or become casualties, and for those who joined in 1862, the chances were 83.1 percent.

Typically, nothing erodes the support of soldiers as much as a sense of unnecessary losses, yet Lee's popularity both within his Army and with the population whose husbands, brothers, and sons fell remained strong during and long after the conflict. In assessing Lee as a leader, it is fascinating to note the loyalty he retained among those who bore the highest costs.

The Marble Man

In April 1865, General Robert E. Lee put on his finest remaining dress uniform and rode his horse, Traveller, to meet fellow West Pointer and Mexican War veteran General Ulysses S. Grant at Appomattox Court House, a small Virginia village, to discuss terms for the surrender of Lee's Army.

They met in the parlor of a house constructed in 1848 and owned by Wilmer McLean. After a short conversation about times long past, the dignified but deeply uncomfortable Lee pressed Grant, who was characteristically clad in a mud-spattered Union Private's uniform, to address the purpose of the meeting—terms of surrender. Grant sat at a small table and drafted generous provisions for Lee's now-defeated Confederates to go home and begin the long process of rebuilding home and lives. When this was completed, Grant walked Lee to his horse and, sitting erect, the vanquished Lee trotted stoically back to his loyal veterans.

Grant later summarized his feelings:

What General Lee's feelings were I do not know. But my own, which had been quite jubilant on the receipt of his letter, were sad and depressed. I felt like anything rather than rejoicing at the downfall of a foe who had fought so long and valiantly, and who had suffered so much for a cause.

The meeting, more than just ending the Civil War, was beginning the next chapter of the Lee legend.

Although Lee was not present, soon after, at a formal surrender ceremony in which the vanquished traditionally laid arms and treasured colors at the feet of the victors, Major General Joshua Chamberlain, a hero of Gettysburg, and future governor of Maine, brought his soldiers to attention and saluted their former foe.

For Lee, there was little left but to go home. The South was shattered, Arlington House was gone from the family forever, the lands appropriated for a US Army fort and, most important, for Arlington National Cemetery, the final resting place for American veterans of countless conflicts. Lee would have to choose a new home, and a new life. Lee accepted an offer to become the president of Washington College in Lexington, Virginia (later Washington and Lee University, from which my brother graduated), where he stayed until his death in 1870, and, along with Traveller, remains buried today.

The assassination of President Lincoln soon after, and the cessation of all hostilities, began a difficult period in the South called Reconstruction. The emancipation of slaves and expansion of voting rights, combined with the devastation of the prewar economy, brought the South into a period of turmoil that gradually settled over time into a white-dominated society that delayed for another century former slaves' true freedom or opportunity. While the war had been lost, in the view of many former secessionists, they had secured their position in the peace. In the five years following Appomattox until his death, Lee held strong opinions about the war, but declined to write his memoirs and carefully controlled his public statements—disciplined until the end.

What Lee did following the war was less important than the emergence of the mythology of the Lost Cause. The Southern war to defend the right to hold other human beings in slavery was recast as a struggle to defend their freedom to maintain a way of life and to safeguard the work of the founding generation—as they defined it. As the objectives were redefined, the war itself was also given a new narrative—that of an outnumbered, poorly supplied band of heroes who courageously and stoically fought until overwhelmed by the industrial North. As the historian and civil rights activist W. E. B. Du Bois captured powerfully:

> We fell under the leadership of those who would compromise with the truth in the past in order to make peace in the present and guide policy in the future.

Although he never sought the role, and while living played no part in its development, scrupulously avoiding political statements or controversy, no leader better fit the Lost Cause narrative than Robert E. Lee. Jefferson Davis's personality was too acerbic, Jackson's a bit too eccentric, and James Longstreet had joined the Northern-imposed postwar government. More than anyone, it was Lee the patrician hero, Lee the principled Southern patriot, and Lee the stoic warrior who fit the model in character and persona. Long after his death, he became the icon of the movement. As decades passed, Lee's name and likeness spread, and took on whatever messages and meanings were desired by the observer.

Considering the Man and the Myth

With the distance of time, amid the emotion and among the shadows, how do we judge Robert E. Lee—a leader I'd been raised to admire? The contradiction between the soldier whose qualities were held up for veneration and his effort to maintain slavery and divide the nation is clear. But apart from that, as a leader, what difference did he really make? How do we judge any leader? And what does our selection of leaders and heroes say about us?

For me, as for many others, assessing Lee is particularly difficult. From one angle, his stature is simply too big, his memory too venerated. Four years after his death, a Southern congressman, Benjamin Harvey Hill of Georgia, eulogized the soldier from Virginia:

> He was a foe without hate; a friend without treachery; a soldier without cruelty; a victor without oppression, and a victim without murmuring. He was a public officer without vices; a private citizen without wrong; a neighbour without reproach; a Christian without hypocrisy, and a man without guile. He was a Caesar, without his ambition; Frederick, without his tyranny; Napoleon, without his selfishness, and Washington, without his reward.

But from another angle, a bronze Lee on horseback as depicted in one of the many statues of the man, seemingly leading the South's successful resistance to equality and change, blurs our ability to assess. We know the reality that neither image is an accurate reflection of the man or the leader, but mythology overpowers reason.

With Robert E. Lee, the mythology is particularly strong. The persona he crafted of a disciplined, dutiful soldier, devoid of intrigue and strictly loyal to a hierarchy of entities that began with God and his own sense of honor, combined with an extraordinary aptitude for war, projects the most traditional of leadership models. It is when we reveal his shortcomings, or identify his failures, that the image becomes more lifelike, more believable— closer to leaders we've known. And when we admit that even the most

Known to peers and followers as the "Marble Man," Lee exuded a calm and genteel persona that resonated with a national audience, especially after the Civil War ended. Marble, metal, oil paint—many materials have been employed over time to re-create his visage.
(PHOTOGRAPH BY HANK WALKER/THE LIFE PICTURE COLLECTION/GETTY IMAGES)

exceptional of leaders is not the dominant factor in driving events, the mythology becomes fully porous.

As we look at leaders, sometimes staring into the glare of greatness, and other times toward a darkened soul, we will see that image is rarely the reality, and that the myth is not the leader. They will often impress, and sometimes disappoint, but we hope they will always help illuminate.

Three

THE FOUNDERS

*Most of the significant advances in the world have
been made by people with at least a touch of
irrational confidence in themselves.*

—JOHN GARDNER

The tiny princess is beguiling, with long blond hair. As she slips her
hand into mine, her stunning, wide-set brown eyes look up at me.
When frightened, she clings closer; when excited, her words come too
fast to fully understand. I love her and, just as important, I love the idea of
her, and how she makes me feel about myself.

Granddaughters will do that to you. And as we walked through the
herds of people migrating through Disney World, I realized I was one of a
common breed, parents and grandparents who had brought children to a
theme park, in large measure for the satisfaction of seeing their offspring
smile in joy or gaze in wonderment.

Amusement parks are not a recent invention. Bakken, north of Copenhagen, opened in 1583. But today one man's name has become synonymous
not only with immersive park experiences, but also with books, movies,
toys, clothing, and, most important, nostalgia for adventures we never actually experienced, and a life we never lived—but wish we could have. With

pen and ink, bricks and mortar, celluloid and imagination, Walt Disney founded an empire.

Founders are those who create. They don't tweak on the margins or incrementally improve what already exists. Instead, from whole cloth they conceive and build—simultaneously serving as both architect and engineer. Typically, it falls to them to visualize, design, and build, tasks demanding foresight, political skills, and the will to drive dream to reality. Statistically, most fail, and those who succeed sometimes admit luck or serendipity as two of the biggest factors. But there is a common bond that connects them, and it is made of more than an idea and good fortune. It is an unwavering commitment to a vision.

Former Red Cross ambulance driver Walt Disney began his creative journey young, and at twenty-six he cocreated the iconic Mickey Mouse. And the firm that would come to bear his first and last names was built, step by step, on his hard-driving ambition combined with expansive ideas. Nothing was guaranteed or preordained, and although Disney benefited from the post–World War II boom in America's fortunes, his success was anything but blind luck, and Disney's enterprise grew.

In seeking a founder to pair with the prototypical child, we selected the prototypical grown-up. Coco Chanel's provocative history, her iconic perfume, and the ubiquitous "little black dress" all beckon us from the innocence of Disney's perpetual childhood into an adulthood as much fantasy for most of us as princesses and toads.

And while empires can begin with dreams, they are forged in hard work, emerging from a Darwinian process of refinement or elimination. And in an intensely competitive environment, Coco Chanel and Walt Disney prevailed—so successful that the companies that bear their names are still thriving a century after their creations, with each founder an indelible part of their brands.

It wasn't always—or usually—pleasant to work for either of these leaders, and yet it was never hard for them to attract talent. In choosing Chanel and Disney, we wanted to explore founding business leaders with interesting stories. And as we explored, we confronted a question that was more about leadership in general than about the particulars of founding a successful company: If leadership is so dependent on people, why are we so energized by leaders who prioritize their mission over their people?

Key Books

- Neal Gabler, *Walt Disney: The Triumph of the American Imagination* (New York: Random House, 2006)
- Rhonda K. Garelick, *Mademoiselle: Coco Chanel and the Pulse of History* (New York: Random House, 2015)

WALT DISNEY

You can design and create, and build the most wonderful place in the world. But it takes people to make the dream a reality.

—WALT DISNEY

On Tuesday, December 21, 1937, after nearly three years of indebting production, Walt Disney's most ambitious project to date was about to be unveiled to the Tinseltown elite at Los Angeles's palatial Carthay Circle Theatre. He had led production of the world's first feature-length animated film, *Snow White and the Seven Dwarfs*, an effort that had become ridiculed as "Disney's Folly" by much of Hollywood. In doing so, Walt cemented himself as an iconoclast, but along the way nearly destroyed his already considerable reputation as an innovator.

A white scarf was draped over Walt's suited shoulders as he worked his way through the press gauntlet. At thirty-six years old he remained trim, sporting a trademark waxy-thin mustache and neatly parted dark hair. A pair of heavy eyebrows anchored his already wrinkling forehead. They were among his favorite weapons of management; their skeptical hitch toward his hairline had already broken the will of many a rebellious animator.

Among Hollywood's upper crust of actors, directors, and critics that night, and a far cry from his roots in working-class Missouri, Walt cut the dapper figure of a young American aristocrat. Despite the evening's festive

A young Walt Disney in his lifelong natural element—addressing the
American public, in this case informing them of his pioneering
upcoming film, Snow White and the Seven Dwarfs.

tone, he strode solemnly up the red carpet, stooped with worry about
how his endeavor would be received. One of the reviewers in the crowd
would later write that Walt looked like he could be the movie's eighth
dwarf, Nervous.

He was in one of his doubting moods: *Snow White*'s success depended
on the audience making an emotional connection with animated characters
the same way they did with live humans. No one in the theater that evening, Walt included, knew if it was possible. Costly delays and revisions in
the film's production process weighed on Walt physically and emotionally—
if the premiere went poorly, bankruptcy beckoned.

Then an announcement from a TV reporter on the scene rang out: "And
now, here's the gentleman I'm sure you'd all want to meet, it's Walt Disney,
the creator of *Snow White and the Seven Dwarfs.* . . ."

Walt heard himself being described and looked up impassively in the
direction of the sound, instinctively cocking his sharp eyebrows upward.
Finding himself staring into a live NBC camera, he overpowered his

anxieties with a broad, toothy smile. After all, his nation of followers was watching, and he wanted them to see him as more confident, happy, and pleasant than he was around those who knew him better.

"The Place I Wanted to Work"

There is a natural gap between the persona every leader exudes and his or her private character. For Walt, the gap was a chasm, and one he was very conscious of. As he once told a friend: "I'm not 'Walt Disney.' I do a lot of things that Walt Disney wouldn't do. Walt Disney doesn't smoke; I smoke. Walt Disney doesn't drink; I drink."

Walt Disney was a man, but he's more popularly understood as a brand. Many of us were raised on the children of his prodigious imagination— Mickey Mouse, the Seven Dwarfs, Bambi, and Pinocchio, to name a few. We have visited his parks and watched his movies, all the products of the sprawling company that bears his name. The man who built that company was compulsively driven to entertain generations he would never meet.

By the time of *Snow White*'s premiere, Walt was already among the greatest creative minds of the twentieth century. He was objectively ingenious, having personally jump-started the field of animation in the decade leading up to *Snow White*'s 1937 debut. While Walt was hardly the only cog spinning in what was branded the Disney creative machine, he was ever a defining one. Whenever technical, technological, or creative obstacles stood in the way of Walt's vision for entertaining audiences, he would innovate solutions around them—stunning his animators and "storymen," making them, and those who watched the cartoons as prefeature film shorts, instant acolytes.

In 1928, as a twenty-six-year-old animator, Walt became the first person to ever successfully sync sound to cartoons. The product of his efforts was *Steamboat Willie*, the seven-minute debut of the iconic character Mickey Mouse (whom he cocreated with fellow Missourian Ubbe Iwerks, and would personally voice until the mid-1940s). During its production, the orchestra he hired for the music was having great difficulty timing its notes to on-screen action, so Walt printed a bouncing ball in the film to act as a makeshift metronome. American audiences were awestruck by *hearing* the

animated Mickey's drumsticks plink out "Turkey in the Straw" on a cartoon cow's teeth.

This first runaway success of Walt's attracted a growing chorus of admirers in the expanding universe of animation. The nationally distributed
series *Silly Symphonies* was released after *Steamboat Willie*, the first epi-
sode of which was an eerie short called *The Skeleton Dance*. The cartoon
was financially successful and grabbed the attention of animators across
the country. Joseph Barbera (eventual creator of *The Jetsons*, *Scooby-Doo*,
and *The Flintstones*) later recalled watching *The Skeleton Dance* in a New
York theater and asking himself: "How do you *do* that? How do you make
that happen?" One of Disney Studio's eventual senior animators, Art Babbitt, also saw the short in New York and immediately quit his job to apply
for work in California with Walt. As soon as he saw the cartoon skeletons
dance and frolic in sync to sound effects, he "knew that was the place I
wanted to work." In the days immediately after the first *Silly Symphony*
Walt added several established artists to his roster. By August 1929, Disney
had eight animators on its payroll. With these new talents on board, in July
1930, Walt's studio released the first full Technicolor cartoon—the success
of which reportedly prompted Sam Goldwyn to begin planning production of the first Technicolor regular film, *The Wizard of Oz*.

Disney had assembled a small chorus of the world's best animators, and
they didn't come flocking to Walt because he was offering big paychecks, or
even because he knew how to draw—by industry standards, he was an average illustrator. His animators came because they had witnessed what his
studio could produce, and they wanted to be a part of the cutting edge of
their field.

Prior to Disney, cartoons were only several minutes long and mere
"filler," strictly shown as preview entertainment for movie audiences. Walt
had a vision of what cartoons were capable of that was far greater.

One evening in 1934, Walt gave out fifty cents to each of his key employees
for dinner money, then told them all to assemble soon in an auditorium on his
studio's lot. He knew what he was planning would be a hard sell for them, and
an even harder sell for his growing legion of fans. To enlist his closest employees to his side, he planned a demonstration of vision and passion.

In that auditorium, and in front of his senior employees, Walt acted out an old German folk tale involving singing dwarfs, a magical mirror, and a poisoned apple. He acted out the characters, jumping between different body postures and costumes, singing along to songs, and explaining the storyline he would demand they help him tell.

This is how Disney's *Snow White* ballad began.

For the artists in the room, it was a confirming event. Walt's concept had the markings of something new and genre-defining. Remarking on the atmosphere during Walt's vigorous performance, one animator recalled that "we were all so steamed up, so enthused for this project that it really didn't cross our minds to doubt that it could be done . . . if Walt thought there was a way to do it, we better find a way to do it." Never mind that no one had ever made a cartoon movie, or that it would take more than two million drawings to produce it, or that new technologies would need to be invented to make Walt's vision possible. Their leader was excited and wondrous, and his followers in the room felt it too.

"Jesus Christ Communism"

Across the span of his career, and as Disney's company grew in size, Walt's passionate playfulness could be both inspirational and maddening. At its best, it was a source of creative excitement; at its worst, it was an impediment to planning. Whenever more level-headed peers—like his strait-laced brother and business partner, Roy—or lenders raised reasonable questions about fresh decisions that popped into Walt's head, he rarely paid them any mind. When Walt got stuck on a particular idea, he was frustratingly impossible to shut up about it. On a multiday excursion with him to Santa Barbara, employee David Hand regularly fled from Walt on horseback to escape ramblings on the status of Hand's work.

Yet the adoration Walt commanded among his first workers has been described by Disney biographer Neal Gabler in cultlike terms—similar to "a messianic figure inspiring a group of devoted, sometimes frenzied acolytes." The term "messianic" is especially fitting. Whenever one of his projects faced external doubt and incredible risk, he fought through with a crusading spirit, and what repeatedly followed was a deluge of financial success and critical recognition. As a leader, he had all the appearances of a miracle worker.

Moreover, like a cult leader, Walt earned the fervent trust of his congregation early on through charisma and demonstrations of care. In the hallways he asked about his employees' kids, and invited his animators to barbecues at his home. Those who interacted with him before *Snow White*—many of whom would eventually come to resent his later leadership—also testified to his ability to excite others into reaching new levels of creativity. Disney acted as their communal catalyst, with employees noting he could make "you come up with things you didn't know were in you and that you'd have sworn you couldn't possibly do," and that Disney would "disarm people by using the word 'we' instead of 'I.'"

Beyond merely using inclusive language, he demonstrated a devotion to his employees' fulfillment at work. When he was excited about a project—like *Snow White*—Walt would regularly forgo material concerns in the interest of his studio's creative process. As he recalled during a later interview: "The first thing I did when I got a little money to experiment, I put all my artists back in school . . . now we were dealing with motion, and the flow of movement, the flow of things, you know . . . so we had to set up our own school."

Walt also reinvested his free capital in buying new furniture and creative space for his artists, as well as hiring outside experts like architects and instructors to teach them new techniques. Later in life, during the construction of Disneyland, Walt spoke about his fiscal philosophy to a particularly skeptical employee: "You and I do not worry whether anything is cheap or expensive. We only worry whether it's good. I have a theory that if it's good enough, the public will pay you back for it." He prioritized creative excellence over cost control and profit generation, to the great satisfaction of his early animators.

While competing studios offered only seasonal work to artists, hiring and cutting them on a project-by-project basis, Walt signed his artists to lengthy contracts—practically giving them tenurelike employment, firing them only rarely, and making them feel as though they were "family." Ken Anderson, who began his nearly half-century career at Disney around the time of *Snow White*, later explained that Walt had "the whole say on how long you were going to work for him and what it was going to be for and all that stuff." Once an artist was in his fold, Walt worked hard to provide for them—a gesture that they rewarded with ardent dedication. Many of those who took part in creating *Snow White* or attended Walt's seminars embraced the culture enthusiastically: "We worked Saturdays and Sundays, and we loved it—everything was new!" The studio's early rank and file shared his passion for extending the frontiers of animation, and so were well vested in Walt's leadership.

This allowed for a kind of productive anarchy to reign at the Disney Studio. Workers were allowed to set their own schedules and there was no overtime pay. Yet, per Anderson, they were "always there" late into the night.

Walt once pridefully described this organizational culture as "a kind of Jesus Christ communism." This did not represent an affinity for left-wing beliefs, but rather Walt's deprioritization of moneymaking as an objective in favor of a grander artistic goal. Walt did not want to simply do well by audiences. He had a bold vision of crafting wholly new kinds of entertainment that the public didn't even realize were possible. As he wrote in a memo to a colleague:

> The first duty of the cartoon is not to picture or duplicate real action or things as they actually happen—but to give a caricature of life and action—to picture on the screen things that have run thru the imagination of the audience—to bring to life dream fantasies and imaginative fancies that we have all thought of during our lives or have pictured to us in various forms during our lives. Also to caricature things of life as it is today—or make fantasies of things we think of today.

Walt's motivating goal was to realize his own imagination. He believed that the possible could always triumph over the actual. He knew it was a group effort, but the organizational "communism" he relied on to achieve this goal reaped profit that Walt protectively kept for himself: public acclaim and credit. While Walt may have made reference to the collective "we" rather than "I" when discussing the studio's creative output, he acted far more selfishly when it came to the singular identity written into and on his products. In a deviation from industry norms, very few of Disney's artists were included in the credits of the products they worked on, while Walt's name was prominently displayed. And whenever Walt got the impression that his animators were becoming a little too self-indulgent in their work, he cracked down hard.

One such instance was in 1934 when Walt called Ken Anderson into his office. Walt laid into him: "I have something that I want you to learn here. This is the *Walt Disney* Studio. If you're thinking of making a name for yourself, then you'd better get the hell out of here now, because the one thing we are selling here is 'Walt Disney.' Not because it's me. But because that's the name for the Studio."

Disney's insistence that he be the only individual to receive public acclaim for the studio's output was deeply frustrating to the highly accomplished animators who worked alongside him. But during these egotistical outbursts, Walt also sought to invoke the collective good. His obsessive purpose was to pioneer new forms of entertainment, at the expense of everything else. His early staff shared that vision and, to them, his obsessiveness was a catalyst.

Innovation

A recurring scene played out in Walt's studio between 1934 and 1937:

Sitting down in the dank closet, magnifying glass to his face and animation celluloids ("cels") spread in front of him, Walt meticulously reviewed *Snow White*'s progress. Several animators—often his "Old Men" like Les Clark, Marc Davis, and Milt Kahl—stood behind him in anticipation. The team called this examination room, which was free from air conditioning and the site of many brow beatings, "the sweatbox." Their boss was exacting in his attention to detail, and unrelenting in calling out what he perceived as subpar work. At the same time, he never complimented his artists for what others might have called "good work." Walt would not be remembered by his workers for ever offering direct praise.

Now overseeing the world's greatest collection of animators, Walt was finding new ways to contribute to and ensure the groundbreaking success of *Snow White*. He had many responsibilities, but the most important were

Ever raising his artistic and narrative standards from project to project, Walt was unrelenting in trying to improve the output of his studio's talented artists. Subpar animation was often met by Walt's raising an eyebrow and providing an emotionless sentence of critique. Acceptable work was received with silence. Here we see an older Walt overseeing the story development of Sleeping Beauty.
(PHOTOGRAPH BY GENE LESTER/GETTY IMAGES)

story generation, animation management, and thinking through new ways to improve the film's impact on the audience. Walt's view was that these talents were of far greater importance to the outcome of his projects than what even his best animators would produce.

When the studio had created the *Silly Symphony* and Mickey Mouse series, they exceeded and then raised audience expectations, and *Snow White* would need to do the same. What had previously passed for good no longer met Walt's standards, and so he discarded much of his animators' work.

After experimenting with personalizing individual characters in the *Silly Symphony* short *The Three Little Pigs,* for example, Walt exacted meticulous control over *Snow White*'s story. One key change he insisted upon was that the titular dwarfs (identity-free in the original German folktale) have seven distinct personalities centered on different human traits. Disney's bet was that the audience would connect emotionally to each of the animated characters—it depended on each dwarf having a distinct yet relatable personality. Mickey Mouse might have been able to make audiences laugh—but Walt now wanted protagonists who could make real people cry.

Toward this end, trait-laden names were assigned to each dwarf, with songs written that conveyed the corresponding emotions to the audience. Among the many unused names considered were "Awful," "Hungry," "Lazy," "Soulful," and "Shifty" with associated dwarfs sketched according to these characteristics, which together reflected the diverse spectrum of human traits Walt wanted audiences to recognize. Similarly, twenty-five songs were written for *Snow White*, but only eight made it in to the final picture.

Walt was always listening for fresh concepts from his artists and prioritized the inclusion of good new ideas over production timelines. For instance, when one animator made Dopey take a clumsy hitch-step to stay in line with his fellow dwarfs in one scene, Walt decided that this motion needed to be characteristic of Dopey and woven into every scene that he walked in. Similarly, Walt decided that the dwarf Happy would always need to be among the first and most frequent to speak, and Sleepy the last to react in conversation. Walt regularly interrupted existing work processes to address ad hoc priorities he'd identified. In the words of art director David Hand, "Walt didn't care anything about the details of organization. And he caused a great deal of trouble by ordering a certain man, or his group of men, to do something else *right now*."

These decisions infuriated many of the artists working for him, who often had to work backward to reanimate old scenes or stop progress on one project to cater to the unpredictable whims of their boss. Even with the studio's manpower steadily growing through this period, it would take several employees six months to complete the Dopey hitch-step reanimation alone. Yet despite the frustrations of those subjected to his erratic work process, Disney's instincts for creating a compelling narrative and empathetic character arc were undeniable—making his perfectionism a key part of why his early employees found him so compelling. Per Disney artist Ward Kimball, "He was the best storyman in the Studio. . . . Nobody even approached him [in terms of talent]."

Walt also used the *Silly Symphony* series as a testing ground for new animation technologies. In particular, he conceived of an invention that would be named the multiplane camera, a fourteen-foot-tall metal contraption on which different painted panes of glass could be stacked and photographed together to create a layered image. Walt was interested in giving *Snow White*'s forest scenes realistic depth, and so he asked his machinists to create this apparatus as a means of providing dimensionality to the film. The multiplane camera's first use was in the *Silly Symphony* short *The Old Mill*, in which immersive scenes of nature were generated through image layering. The effect of this new technology is obvious in the short's opening shot of a shimmering cobweb on a tree, with the titular mill in the background.

But these high standards did not come free of charge. The studio, and its founder, were mired in financial difficulty. To continue financing *Snow White*, Walt even mortgaged Mickey Mouse; Bank of America—his primary lender—required that Walt put up all of his short cartoon intellectual property (including the legendary Mouse) as collateral for further loans to his studio. Despite his mounting financial conundrums, or the lack of faith his lenders had in him, Walt didn't appear too bothered during film production. As he would later remark in an interview: "We had the family fortune, everything we had, all wrapped up in *Snow White*. In fact, the banker, I think, was losing more sleep than I was."

One person close to Walt, however, was likely losing more sleep: his older brother, Roy. Roy's professional life became defined by confronting Walt about the studio's chronically perilous financial state, reining in the fallout of his brother's impulsive style, and providing a buttress of corporate structure for the growing company. Following Walt's death from lung cancer in 1966, Roy assumed control of the Disney empire and brought its identity closer to that of the megalithic corporation we recognize today. He was characterized by early insiders as a naysayer, a "typical, tightfisted, Machiavellian businessman" who could be counted on to shoot down many of the studio's creative concepts. He and Walt had a tendency to play an amusing cat-and-mouse game inside the studio. Roy would creep into the office of Walt's animators when the boss was gone and beseech them to hold down costs, followed by Walt trying to catch his brother in the act and kick him out.

But by December 1937, these organizational concerns about the management and direction of the studio were inconsequential in employees' minds relative to the looming debut of *Snow White*. Would it be a failure, truly "Disney's Folly," as most of Hollywood anticipated? Or would it be something entirely new, a revelatory artistic work that would create an entirely new genre of film?

Walt, as "the Eighth Dwarf" standing in the theater, was initially wrapped in a knot of anxiety. But by the emotional climax of the movie, when *Snow White* lies catatonic surrounded by the somber dwarfs, his concerns were assuaged by the real-life scene around him. He could hear the audience crying in their seats.

Critical reaction to the movie was beyond laudatory. The *New Republic* declared it to be one of "the genuine artistic achievements of this country," and the *New York Times* saw it as a welcome escape from the militarizing world of the late 1930s, reflecting that as ". . . crimes are being committed; hatreds are being whetted; riots are being brewed . . . the world fades away when Mr. Disney begins weaving his spell and enchantment takes hold." Of greater satisfaction to Walt, regular audiences around the world were deeply impressed by the range of emotions the film stirred in them, which ranged from terror in the ominous forest scenes to glee at the dwarfs' singing of "Heigh-Ho" to grief at Snow White's apparent death. The film held sales records until the 1939 release of *Gone with the Wind*. Walt was presented with an honorary Academy Award for *Snow White*, plus seven miniature versions to signify the eponymous dwarfs, for having created "a significant screen innovation which has charmed millions and pioneered a great new entertainment field for the motion picture cartoon."

Walt had again transformed the world of entertainment through his ambitious vision.

Expansion, Inequality, and Apathy

The financial windfall from *Snow White*'s release was more than enough to pay back Walt's debts and free Mickey Mouse from the looming specter of Bank of America's ownership. The movie brought in more than $8 million worldwide, earning a huge profit that Walt could now invest in his studio.

Snow White had been produced in Hyperion, a modest one-story stucco building named after the street on which it was built. For an established studio now making a permanent move into the movie business, and with a staggering target output of two to three feature films a year, a more fitting complex had to be constructed from scratch. Accordingly, construction began on a new fifty-one-acre campus in Burbank in late 1938.

The new compound's Animation Building was designed to be as pristine and efficient as possible: a custom humidity-control system prevented the artists' paints from smearing or cracking, while sealed windows were installed to keep out dust particles. Carpets and drapes were banned for the same reason; every artist's office had a north-facing window for the glare-free light it afforded. The temperature was to be kept between 74 and 78 degrees to maintain optimum paint viscosity. A gym, massage parlor, barbershop, and steam room were also built, although some artists initially lacked access to some of these. Despite the success of *Snow White*, Bank of America was nonetheless still suspect about the Disney Studio's financial future. It eventually increased Walt's credit limit, but insisted that the new Animation Building be easily convertible into a hospital should the studio fold.

Aspects of Walt's managerial "communism" remained intact—for example, he installed a uniformed staff to deliver catered meals to artists around the clock. And during the construction in Burbank, an employee walked into Walt's office to find the boss disassembling his chair, trying to design one that would be more comfortable for his animators.

Yet as new movies like *Pinocchio* were born from Burbank and lauded by an adoring public, the studio's growth would forever change its culture. The new Burbank facilities now housed more than a thousand people and lacked the "ramshackle homeliness" of the Hyperion address. Predictably, Walt struggled to maintain the same relationship with his staff as he had in the past.

While Walt had always been difficult to work with—his obsessive control over all the studio's creative processes had been important to its earlier successes—the low-level artists and technicians at Burbank didn't get to see as clearly the operational returns on his erratic behavior, or develop an affection for his charisma in the same way the Hyperion veterans had. Instead, they saw a leader who was at once micromanaging yet distant, smiling yet tyrannical, ultimately a force to keep their distance from.

The setup of the new Burbank Animation Building didn't help the degraded perceptions of Walt's leadership style. His private office was now located on an entirely different floor from the production wing of the studio. He also stopped socializing with his employees—according to Disney biographer Neal Gabler, his public reputation had reached heights where he wasn't sure what others truly "wanted from him." In any case, his behavior and relationships in a company of a thousand people could never be what they were with thirty. Oddly enough, it was now the businesslike Roy who was more likely to pal around with studio workers in Burbank's ordered corridors.

In the changed environment of post–*Snow White* Disney, there was no better reflection of this standoffish dynamic than the role of Burbank's doorman. This uniformed employee not only served as an office guard, but also became a sentry who warned the staff about Walt's mood. On days when the boss seemed ornery on arrival—perhaps frowning or offering no reply to a cheery "Good morning"—the doorman would pass along the message that Walt was wearing his "bear suit," alerting workers to avoid interactions with their legendary boss that day.

Walt's veteran animators, his Old Men, were compensated well by industry standards at this point—enough to afford multiple cars as well as mansions with live-in servants—but the same could not be said for the majority of the staff that supported their efforts. Some of the so-called ink girls (female assistant artists), equipment technicians, and entry-level animators earned less than they could have on unemployment benefits. Unlike the Old Men in the days of *Snow White*, these workers were not ready to work through the night with no overtime pay, and desperately wanted standard compensation structures like those of other large studios.

But Walt established his own sort of bonus system. Though he rarely complimented his artists on their work, he did give rewards for perceived creative contributions. For example, for every "gag" a storyman put into a narrative, Walt would assign a one-time bump in pay of a few dollars. It was a haphazard meritocracy. Walt's handouts were inconsistent, dependent as they were on his occasionally warped perception of merit, and so many workers found the arrangement flatly unjust. Sometimes he'd hand out bonuses to certain employees for improving a production process, only to find out months later that they had actually *opposed* the change made.

The same arbitrariness was on display at the Burbank studio—only now with stock distribution rather than small bonuses. In 1940, Walt and Roy took the company public to raise capital and designated a portion of equity for studio employees. But stock ownership was left up to Walt's judgment, resulting in interrank jealousy and anger when some employees were granted stock while others were left with none.

And Walt was still hesitant to give film credits to employees—remaining outside the industry norm of recognizing contributions by rank-and-file workers. The majority of Disney employees were distant from the intoxicating, creative mania that had propelled *Snow White*'s production. To them, Walt's style, and particularly his refusal to credit low-level employees (thus hurting potential job prospects), was unacceptable.

Yet by 1941, and beyond these institutional sources of friction, something more profound had changed *within* Walt. His trajectory up to that point had followed a consistent pattern: rapid shifts from one groundbreaking success to another—from adding sound to cartoons to introducing full Technicolor in animation to developing the world's first animated feature film. For someone who was constantly pioneering new realms of entertainment, and whose patience for dispassionate organization was nonexistent, a corporate atmosphere geared toward churning out more of the same was desperately boring. This was obvious to his Old Men, one of whom remembered that Walt's previous level of enthusiasm—once so infectious—was largely gone.

The Burbank doorman voiced his warning more and more often: "The boss is in his bear suit."

Betrayal

Walt's office diary for May 28, 1941, contained a simple entry: "Strike—6:00AM—today."

The metal entrance gate to the Burbank campus was ringed that morning by a thick crowd of rebelling employees. The strikers carried protest signs that drew upon their considerable skills—angry incarnations of Mickey, Donald Duck, and Jiminy Cricket glared down at their creator as he drove past them into work. One sign bore a man-sized drawing of Mickey, pointing angrily in the studio's direction and carrying a placard of his own reading "Daddy Disney is unfair to his artists."

Once inside, Walt went about his day as usual—apparently a little happier than most had seen him in a while. But by the afternoon, he was pacing around his office in front of photographs of individual strikers he'd ordered taken that morning, smoking Marlboros and muttering things like "I didn't think he'd go against me! That sonofabitch." And "We can get along without him." All told, up to seven hundred employees, mostly junior artists and technicians, surrounded his studio demanding recognition of their union, and endangering Disney's sterling reputation and warm public persona.

He was initially enraged by hallway whispers of pro-union sentiment, so he fired the employees who seemed to be spreading the rumors. In a last-ditch attempt to avert the strikes, he offered up a pair of almost three-hour-long, soul-baring addresses to the entire company in February 1941, where he tried to talk the studio's staff off the ledge of unionization. For many Disney employees, it was the most they had ever seen of Walt firsthand.

He assembled the staff in a Burbank auditorium and, after making a joke about what his lawyers had told him to say, he began on a note of self-awareness: "I have had a stubborn, blind confidence in the cartoon medium . . . a determination to show the skeptics that the animated cartoon was deserving of a better place; that it was more than a mere 'filler' on a program; that it was more than a novelty; that it could be one of the greatest mediums of fantasy and entertainment yet developed."

From there, Walt's speeches jumped from qualm to qualm, offering rebuttals to different grievances. He rationalized his aloofness, saying that he didn't like getting "too close to anybody" in the studio because he thought it would be "dangerous and unfair" to the morale of his workers, and he wouldn't allow sycophantic "apple-polishers" among them to gain an advantage. Though he acknowledged wages were very low for most employees, Walt claimed that this was mainly due to ongoing financial difficulties, noting he'd personally taken a 75 percent pay cut. He also denied the existence of a class divide in the studio, adding that all of the recreational facilities in Burbank were now open for every employee.

These speeches were likely among the most challenging moments of Walt's post–*Snow White* career. For someone who had such a unique grasp of how to access the emotional core of his audience, Walt was remarkably lacking in empathy for the many hundreds of employees now critical to his studio's success. The effacing aspects of his February speeches were therefore difficult for him to speak aloud, and his attempt to ingratiate himself and explain his motivations to the Burbank staff reflects his desperation to keep them on board.

He wouldn't allow himself to seem apologetic, because he wasn't. As a self-made man who had grown up in poverty and had regularly put himself into financial peril for the sake of the art form, Walt attributed the dissatisfaction of his employees to their underlying personal weakness. He was willing to concede that he'd been aloof and chaotic as their boss, but he wouldn't tolerate disloyalty, not from those he'd provided—nay, *invented*—careers for. In his view, working for him was not a job, but a privilege, and threats of mobilization against him were a betrayal too far. So the tones of humble paternalism in his speeches came mixed in proportion with those of patronization. "My first recommendation to a lot of you is this," he chided, "put your own house in order. . . . If you're not progressing as you should, instead of grumbling and growling, do something about it. . . . Too many people are inclined to self-pity. . . . Don't forget this—it's the law of the universe that the strong shall survive and the weak must fall by the way, and I don't give a damn what idealistic plan is cooked up, nothing can change that."

As he realized he was losing his audience, Walt began to make punitive threats—including banning pro-union workers from dips in his swimming pool. Overall, his audacious attempt to retroactively heal the internal divides of his studio failed, with the negative reaction of employees making one newspaper claim that Walt's oratory had inadvertently rallied his workers to unionize. Walt's eventual firing of senior animator Art Babbitt for union sympathies was the final catalyst for the devastating walkout that followed.

The strike lasted just under two months, and its settlement inflicted permanent change on the studio culture. A structured, professional culture, more in line with Roy's organizational philosophy, was born at Burbank. In a telling sign of this new norm, time punch card machines were finally installed to track the comings and goings of Burbank's workforce. The settlement brought standard corporate regimentation to Disney, something Walt himself had resisted.

This was a profoundly painful time for Walt. He later wrote to a friend about his frustrated confusion at having (in his view) provided for his employees, only for them to demonize and abandon him: "I was willing to sacrifice everything I had. . . . The lies, the twisted half-truths that were placed in public prints cannot be easily forgotten. I was called a rat, a yellow-dog employer and an exploiter of labor . . . above all, I was accused of rolling in wealth. That hurt the most . . . every damned thing I have is tied up in this business. . . . I am thoroughly disgusted."

Six years later, Walt would testify to the House Un-American Activities Committee that the strikes had been part of a grand Communist plot against him. He had kept these cameramen, ink girls, and writers employed in industry-leading work conditions, through thick and thin. So Walt was left deeply puzzled: How could they walk out on him after all he had done for them, and the risks he had endured for their profession over the years? The only explanation that made sense to him was outside political manipulation.* While Walt mourned his studio's changed identity, he

---

*His reputation would never truly recover after the strike. Even today, there remains a popular perception that Walt was virulently anti-Semitic. Gabler questions whether this is deserved, noting his donations to Jewish charities, how Walt's Jewish employees (many of them Disney's critics) have

successfully managed its production of propaganda and training films for the American effort in World War II—one of which was the Academy Award–winning *Der Fuehrer's Face*.

The Happiest Place on Earth

Ironically, the spiritual falling-out between Walt and his studio staff would bring greater joy to the world. The ugly and public divorce forced a reckoning that eventually brought Walt to create what became known as "the Happiest Place on Earth."

Walt had inferred much from the ordeal of managing an unwieldy, bloated studio, and so in December 1952 he incorporated a business entity that he could exert full control over. He named it "WED Enterprises"— after his initials—with its business certification reading that it would be involved in "the designing of amusement parks . . . and other products of an entertainment, amusement and educational nature." WED also served as an exclusive corporate vehicle to license out Walt's name. Walt personally selected employees from the studio to work for him at WED.

John Hench, who was one of those poached, remembered Walt stopping by his desk at Burbank and telling him, "I want you to work on Disney-land, and you're going to like it." Hench complied. Some at the old studio thought Walt's new venture foolhardy (though Roy wasn't entirely against the concept), and yet again Walt had to scrounge up money to meet his ballooning costs. He was re-creating his early recipe for success—a small team with an abundance of technical skill and creative passion, combined with an ambitious, unprecedented, and possibly unrealistic creative vision. On top of this basic organizational framework, Walt could scale his eccentric obsessiveness.

He toured forty sites before settling on a 160-acre lot in Anaheim. He ordered WED's designers to make Disneyland's buildings slightly undersized, so that guests could subconsciously feel larger than life. He personally helped

---

defended him from this charge, and that he received a Los Angeles Jewish citizenship award. Some, including Gabler, have concluded that these rumors were partially disseminated by those organizing against Walt. Gabler, *Walt Disney: The Triumph of the American Imagination*, pp. 455–58.

*Walt obsessed over every aspect of Disneyland's design and construction,
with virtually no details or decisions considered beneath his purview—though
this image shows him presenting sketches of the park's buildings, he wasn't
above helping to paint rides when deadlines were close. Whenever Walt was
occupied with "passion projects," this was his natural state.*
(PHOTOGRAPH BY HULTON ARCHIVE/GETTY IMAGES)

to spray-paint attractions alongside his workers to meet deadlines and ate hot
dogs with them in their catering tent. When one laborer suggested using
"cut" glass rather than more elaborate stained glass on a feature called Sto-
rybook Land, Walt protested: "Look, the thing that's going to make Disneyland unique . . . is the detail. If we lose the detail, we lose it all." He soon
made a habit of living in the park—sleeping in a furnished apartment built
above Disneyland's Main Street firehouse, even after its opening to the
public.

There are many such moments that played out during the construction
of Disneyland—and they deserve their own book. Their common feature
was that Walt had again become possessed by a grand idea that he had conceived, and he was determined to control the minutiae and achieve perfec-
tion. WED's employees, his select corps on this project, would later be
dubbed "Imagineers."

But there was only one group of people whom Walt could trust to tell him whether his obsession had been worth a damn.

So, on July 17, 1955, Walt appealed to them—the American public—once more. Televised by ABC to millions of Americans watching the opening from home, Walt now cut a much different figure from the one some of them might have remembered from scenes of the 1937 Carthay Circle Theatre premiere of *Snow White*.

On camera, the previews of jowls were beginning to play on his face, while his shoulders were dropping into a permanent slouch. The mustache was there—as were those brows, and that megawatt smile—but the charisma of his public persona was no longer that of a dashing entertainment upstart, rather that of a kindly aged neighbor. He was now the neighborly "Uncle Walt" who would become embedded in the popular American psyche. He filled this archetype well, and in this early Cold War era, the Old Americana that Uncle Walt embodied was magnetic. And as his frontierish, wavering voice betrayed during his speech at Disneyland's televised opening, Walt yearned for the American public as well:

> To all who come to this happy place: welcome. Disneyland is your land. Here age relives fond memories of the past, and here youth may savor the challenge and promise of the future. Disneyland is dedicated to the ideals, the dreams, and the hard facts that have created America . . . with hope that it will be a source of joy and inspiration to all the world.

Those immortal words remain struck into a bronze plaque at Disneyland, implicitly asking the park's guests—his largest flock of followers—to be the ultimate arbiters of Walt's success. After all, they are the ones whose opinions always mattered most.

COCO CHANEL

Nature is commonplace. Imitation is more interesting.
—GERTRUDE STEIN, QUOTED IN *MY AUTOBIOGRAPHY* BY CHARLIE CHAPLIN

"A Woman's Perfume with a Woman's Scent"

One winter evening in 1921, in a restaurant in Cannes, Coco Chanel sat across from Ernest Beaux, a handsome man with dark, coiffed hair. Chanel was wearing a dress she'd designed, elegantly tailored to flow around her svelte frame. The scene was a familiar one—Chanel frequented the South of France, and usually kept attractive company. For her, such dinners were both work and play: Chanel was always modeling and marketing a lifestyle, one that was accessible by wearing her clothes. But tonight, she was also launching a new product.

It was the busiest time of year in one of France's most elite resorts. Around the pair, high society trendsetters bustled as Chanel discreetly applied pressure to a nozzle in her hand.

Eighty different scents left the perfume bottle and mingled as one with the Mediterranean air. Those who passed by might pause and wonder, What is that fragrance?

It was Chanel No. 5, the perfume that would go on to become one of the world's most popular scents. On that night in 1921, it was not yet for sale. Chanel concocted the plot to spritz fashionable women inconspicuously to generate buzz about the new fragrance, and invited Beaux—one of the world's foremost perfumers, and the inventor of Chanel No. 5—to join her. They were successful: Beaux recalled that the "effect was amazing. Whenever a woman passed by our table, she stopped and sniffed. We pretended we didn't notice." It was neither the first nor the last time Chanel the woman used a social outing to advance Chanel the brand—and the two would eventually merge as one.

At the time, the thirty-seven-year-old Chanel was a famous fashion designer, or couturier. Women from across France sought to imitate her style in loose dresses, bare legs, and boater hats. Today, Chanel No. 5 is iconic, but Chanel's decision in 1920 to merge her world of fashion with that of perfumes was nearly unprecedented.

Moreover, she wanted that unprecedented step to feature an unprecedented perfume, one that would be more modern than the ornately decorated bottles and overly romanticized scents like Mediterranean Peach or Waltz Dream that were then common. Instead, she desired "a woman's perfume with a woman's scent," not some flowery concoction reminiscent of the outdated Victorian era that she had just stripped of its excessive layers of fabric and tight corsets. And she'd been thinking about such a perfume for at least two years, since a friend had given her the recipe for a scent apparently worn by Catherine de Medici.

In search of this elusive scent, Chanel hired Ernest Beaux, their introduction the result of Coco's cosmopolitan social life. In the early 1920s, the Russian Grand Duke Dmitri Pavlovich Romanov was Chanel's lover. The Grand Duke was living on an allowance from Coco—one of a few exiled Russian elites living in Paris after the Bolshevik Revolution of 1917 and on the Chanel payroll. When Chanel started to think about making perfumes, Grand Duke Dmitri introduced her to Beaux, whose family had made fragrances for the Romanovs prior to World War I.

Beaux was exactly the person Chanel needed to realize her vision for a new perfume. He was on the cutting edge of the fragrance industry, and among the first in the world to incorporate compounds known as aldehydes, synthetic components that enhance natural scents, into perfumes. It was Beaux's task to translate Chanel's enigmatic but pathbreaking vision into an actual product. "I want a woman's perfume with a woman's scent," she'd said. "An artificial perfume. I insist on artificiality, just as a dress is artificial, fabricated. I am a fashion artisan. I don't want rose or lily of the valley; I want a perfume that is a compound."

While creating something that smelled at the same time "like a woman" and "artificial" might have been a seemingly difficult task, Chanel was the sort of person Beaux wanted to work with. She was not only beautiful and smart, but also rich and famous. As a boss, she may have been eccentric and demanding, but she had just revolutionized women's fashion. For Beaux, joining her orbit meant that he might have a hand in revolutionizing the field of perfumes, and perhaps become rich in the process. Chanel had this sort of magnetism, and she knew it, saying later in life that she had a reputation for being "Queen Midas." Chanel had become the sort of person to whom it was difficult to say no.

After a few weeks of working together, Beaux presented Chanel with ten small vials of perfume, with labels numbered one to five, and twenty to twenty-four. She chose vial number five, her lucky number, and the reason the perfume is named what it is today. The perfume she chose was actually a new version of a scent that Beaux had made for the Russian royal family before World War I had upended his business, and combines natural elements like flowers with the artificial aldehydes.

The perfume sold so well from the beginning that Beaux could barely keep up with production. Looking for help, in 1923 Chanel contacted Théophile Bader, a friend of hers who ran one of Paris's largest department stores. He, in turn, introduced Chanel to Pierre and Paul Wertheimer, who owned one of the world's largest perfume manufacturers. Insistent that she maintain complete control of her fashion business, she let the Wertheimers set up a new entity, Parfums Chanel, which would go on to sell dozens of other Chanel fragrances. The Wertheimers put up all the capital for Parfums Chanel in exchange for a 70 percent stake in the venture. Théophile Bader received a 20 percent stake as a finder's fee and to act as the distribution partner. Chanel herself retained a 10 percent stake in the company and had control over which scents were sold under the Chanel name.

Whatever the state of her business—and much would change over the remaining half century of her life—Coco Chanel always prioritized creative control over everything else. She was not always the majority owner of the House of Chanel or its various subsidiaries, but she was unbreakably the brand's indelible spirit. And that arrangement suited everyone just fine. The Wertheimers, for example, chose her name for their new company and all of its products in an era when perfumes weren't made by, let alone named after, fashion designers.

Others were also insistent about putting Chanel at the center of things.

In one of the first ads for Chanel No. 5 in 1921, the entire scene is drawn in neutral shades with the exception of a woman in a powder-blue flapper dress in the middle of the page. Her skin is peachy, her cheeks tinted, and her lips the only flecks of red in the ad. Her head is tilted upward toward the left corner, where a rectangular bottle of Chanel No. 5 perfume is drawn. The iridescent woman in the middle is undeniably Coco Chanel.

It's a typically stunning ad. Whatever she was making, Chanel used smart, sound, and occasionally groundbreaking business practices. Chanel No. 5 was no different: she created an innovative product, executed a brilliant marketing campaign, and assembled a great team, including one of the world's best perfume makers, best distributors, and best manufacturers. Her decision to sell Chanel No. 5 was good business, too—it opened up her perfumes, and her brand, to a much wider audience.

Notably, the ad promoting Chanel No. 5 advertised Coco Chanel more than the actual product it was selling. From any perspective, Coco Chanel the person became inseparable from Coco Chanel the brand. Many leaders model behavior so that their followers behave similarly, because the leader is convinced those behaviors are the best way to achieve some goal. For Chanel, emulation wasn't simply a means, it was the end. She modeled a lifestyle, inviting others to be just like her. She became the person everyone else wanted to be, and that's what everyone—her investors, her customers, her employees, and Coco herself—expected. People weren't just buying a product—they were buying the idea of a particular woman, with a particular lifestyle, and a particular fashion that went with that lifestyle, and so on. So her perfume ads naturally made her the main focus. Women didn't want to smell like Chanel No. 5, they wanted to smell like Coco Chanel.

To do this well required a paradoxical combination of ego and empathy. If Coco wanted everyone to be like her, she first needed to understand what everyone else wanted. The story of Chanel's leadership is a story of the history, the relationships, the creative processes, and the eccentricities that allowed one woman to transform her personal style into something women across the world wanted for themselves.

"Qui qu'a vu Coco?": *Chanel's Rise*

In a book released five years after she died, Paul Morand—a French writer, diplomat, and friend of Chanel's—released notes he had taken over a series of conversations with Coco. In them, she recalled parts of her childhood: "There we are arriving at my aunts' house. . . . My mother has just died. My two sisters have been sent to a convent. I, being the most sensible one, am entrusted to these aunts who are distant relations. . . ." Later in the same book, Morand writes that Chanel said her father "left for America" and "didn't come back . . . we never heard another word from him."

Chanel's recollections here—and in most other places—are fabrications. She never talked publicly about her childhood, and even her closest confidants heard only a version of the childhood that she wanted them to hear, and such versions were usually fiction. Later in life, she even went so far as to pay off her brothers to remain quiet about her upbringing.

In her book *Mademoiselle: Coco Chanel and the Pulse of History*, biographer Rhonda Garelick pieces together a true account of Chanel's upbringing. The woman history knows as Coco was born Gabrielle Chanel in 1883, not in Auvergne—as she usually claimed—but in Saumur, about two hundred miles northwest. She was impoverished: her father was an itinerant peddler, and when able, her twenty-year-old mother tried to follow him around the countryside, often seeking work as a kitchen maid or laundress. Gabrielle was the second of six children—three girls and three boys (though her youngest brother died at only six months).

Gabrielle's mother did indeed die young—when Gabrielle was only eleven—but after their mother's death, the Chanel girls were left not with aunts, as Coco frequently claimed, but at a convent in the town of Aubazine. And while Gabrielle never saw her father again after getting dropped off at the convent, he never went to America.

After leaving the Aubazine convent, and spending a couple of years as a seamstress, she and her aunt Adrienne (who, only one year older than Gabrielle, was more of a sister) moved in together in a small apartment in the town of Moulins. In the evenings, Gabrielle was a backup singer at local clubs, entertaining army officers garrisoned nearby. In between sets, she would also sing on her own, which is how she became Coco—a nickname earned from the club's regulars who heard her sing popular tunes, like "Ko-Ko-Ri-Ko" or *"Qui qu'a vu Coco?"*

One such regular was Étienne Balsan, a wealthy former cavalry officer. By the age of twenty-three, Coco was one of Balsan's *cocottes*, a courtesan—a sort of high-end prostitute, or a mistress on a stipend. It was common for French elites at the time to have such women on their payroll; and for a young, poor, unmarried woman like Coco, it was a pathway to stability. Coco found herself in a part of society that she would one day come to lead: a courtesan class, quite famous in Paris, that set standards for the day's fashion. Chanel lived at Balsan's estate, Royallieu, for about six years surrounded by French aristocrats and their lovers. The days were leisurely and the nights were filled with parties. Balsan spent much of his time with horses, traveling around the country to attend races.

"When I went to the races, I would never have thought that I was witnessing the death of luxury, the passing of the nineteenth century, the end of an era," Chanel once said. She claimed that it was the "last reflections of a baroque style in which the ornate had killed off the figure. . . . Woman was no more than a pretext for riches, for lace, for sable, for chinchilla, for materials that were too precious."

Chanel's trim, boyish body simply didn't fit this "baroque style." And she was more interested in riding horses than in watching them. Rather than dress herself with lace or chinchilla, she wore clothes in which she could look elegant and yet remain practical, such as traditionally male riding costumes and boater hats pulled low to protect against the wind.

The women of the fashionable party that was Royallieu came to admire her style. Knowing she was eager for something more than her courtesan's life, Balsan encouraged Chanel to make her hats for friends. And this is how Coco Chanel got her start—making practical but elegant hats that actually fit women's heads. Eventually, the business grew enough that Balsan permitted Coco to use his Paris apartment as a storefront and studio.

During her time at Royallieu, around when she started her small business, Chanel met the man she would later describe as "the great stroke of luck in my life . . . he shaped me, he knew how to develop what was unique in me, at the cost of everything else." Arthur Edward "Boy" Capel was a self-made Irish aristocrat who was in a relationship with Coco from 1908 through 1918. Unlike most of the men in Balsan's Royallieu set, Capel worked for a living. While he had inherited some wealth from his family, he had also grown a significant business on his own. As Coco fell in love with Boy, she entered a world that suited her sense of who she was, and where idleness was not idolized.

Moreover, Capel supported her. Financially, to be sure, but also with the candour of a caring mentor. During one incident, after Chanel had started making a bit of money, she remembered telling Capel, "Business is wonderful. It's very easy, all I have to do is draw cheques." Capel, who was covering her expenses at the time and maintained her account at the bank, told her: "Yes. That's very good. But you're in debt to the bank. . . . The bank gives you money because I have deposited securities as a guarantee." This pointed response by Boy would initially sting her, but within a year, Chanel had reduced her expenses and become solvent on her own. Capel's comment to Chanel wasn't that of a harsh critic—it was advice that treated Coco as a businesswoman in her own right, and one who deserved support and advice.

By 1910, Coco had left Royallieu, and she and Boy were essentially living together full time in Paris. That same year, Boy subsidized Chanel's move from Balsan's Paris apartment into her first real Paris headquarters. At 21 Rue Cambon, just steps away from what would become the modern Chanel flagship store, she expanded beyond hats and started making clothing. In 1913, with Capel's encouragement, Chanel opened a second storefront in the Normandy resort town of Deauville, where they spent their summers. In the midst of World War I, Boy also helped her to open a third location on the Bay of Biscay, near the Spanish border in the town of Biarritz, an isolated getaway for Europeans who could afford to escape the worst of the horrible war.

Capel helped Chanel expand, finance her operation, and find her first employees, and he introduced her to the social scene that would help her rise. Chanel was a good businesswoman, but from the very beginning, she took on a role as a sort of creative director within her growing business— the role she would insist upon for the remainder of her career. For Coco, that meant making the clothes that she liked, and that were appropriate for the time she was living in. "What did I know about my new profession?" she once asked herself. As ever, she would also provide the answer to her own question:

> Nothing. I didn't even know dressmakers existed. Did I have any idea of the revolution I was about to stir up in clothing? By no means. One world was ending, another was about to be born. I was in the right place; an opportunity beckoned, I took it. I had grown up with this new century: I was therefore the one to be consulted about its sartorial style. What were needed were simplicity, comfort and neatness: unwittingly, I offered all of that. True success is inevitable.

At the outset of the twentieth century, there was some readiness to leave behind an era when elite women were confined, not least because of their burdensome clothes. Chanel was ready—not just to create the clothes that women would wear, but to show how they might live when wearing them.

Cotton-Jersey

In 1914, Chanel told Jean Rodier, a textile producer, that she wanted to buy his entire stock of jersey fabric. He was surprised, but agreed. Rodier had intended for this humble fabric to be used only for undergarments, and even then men found the material "too scratchy." And when Chanel asked him to produce a new stock of the machine-knit material, he refused, citing wartime scarcity and his skepticism that cotton jersey could be sold as high fashion.

Chanel would prove him wrong. By May 1916 in Paris, the "dress of the hour" was "the Chanel embroidered jersey costume." She wasn't the first person to invent a loose dress, but Chanel had managed to redefine Rodier's jersey material as luxurious. Many years later, Karl Lagerfeld, the creative director of Chanel, described her innovation more bluntly: "Jersey was men's underwear material and it was much more shocking in those days because women weren't supposed to know that men wore underwear. And Chanel made dresses from them."

The timing was right for Chanel's seemingly irrational purchase. Chanel made herself into a woman of her times by intuiting shifts in taste before others, and then acting quickly on her intuition. This was the pattern of her success from the outset of her career.

World War I accelerated the forces of history that were already overturning women's fashion. Before Chanel, "Women were full of gussets, garters, corsets, whalebones, plackets, false hair, and brassières." Sometimes dresses were so decadent, two people were required to simply put one on. Chanel recalled, "In 1914 . . . they [women] were bound at the hips, legs, everywhere. . . . Since they ate a great deal, they were stout . . . and didn't want to be, [so] they strapped themselves in. The corset pushed the fat up to the bosom and hid it beneath the dress." Layers upon layers of inconvenience were the norm.

But when World War I broke out, things changed. Across Europe, even elite women had to take jobs while their husbands were away. This necessitated the practical, yet still elegant, clothes that were Chanel's specialty. As a 1931 *New Yorker* article would later explain, "She has put the *apache's* sweater into the Ritz, utilized the ditch-digger's scarf, made chic the white collars and cuffs of the waitress, and put queens into mechanics' tunics."

When Chanel created jersey dresses—which might as well have been undergarments compared to the elaborate dresses of the years prior—she was also reinforcing a new body type. She spoke of this corporal reinvention with nonchalant bluntness: "By inventing the jersey, I liberated the body, I discarded the waist," she said. "I created a new shape; in order to conform to it all my customers, with the help of the war, became slim, 'slim like Coco.' Women came to me to buy their slim figures."

By the end of World War I, she was becoming an icon. As one of her former Biarritz employees recalls of the time: "You had to see her arrive at noon, getting out of her Rolls, a chauffeur and a footman. She looked like a queen." She was the talk of the town in Paris, Deauville, and Biarritz. But she wasn't just glamorous—she was a successful entrepreneur. From the humble beginnings of a hat store in Étienne Balsan's apartment, she now had boutiques in three of France's most fashionable cities. She'd done well enough to purchase a villa with her own money, and was employing around three hundred people. She was also still in a relationship with Boy Capel, who over the course of the war had become an adviser to French prime minister Georges Clemenceau. Socially, Chanel was beginning to mingle with global elites.

The choice to purchase so much cheap cotton-jersey was one of many business decisions Chanel made in the midst of World War I. It's a particularly memorable one because it was so risky, and because it so neatly symbolizes the role Chanel played in crafting the new image of a fashionable woman. And if it had failed, history might not remember Coco. But she was successful, and by 1916, Chanel's dresses were selling for about 7,000 francs (or $3,700 in today's US dollars). The business model itself was built on an image. Whereas the price of a dress was typically based on the quality of its material and the intricacy of its craftsmanship, people willing to pay thousands of dollars for a cotton-jersey dress were now paying a premium for Chanel-designed chic.

Chanel could have settled for being the era's most important designer—and she was most certainly that. But the modern woman needed a symbol, and Chanel readily assumed the mantle. While she was in some ways a private person—no one in her life knew, for instance, the truth of her upbringing—assuming the role of "symbol" meant that her personal, public, and professional lives all melded into a singular Coco. "I didn't go out because I needed to design dresses, I designed dresses precisely because I went out, because I have lived the life of the century, and was the first to do so," she said. "Before me, couturiers hid away, like tailors, at the back of their shops, whereas I lived a modern life, I shared the habits, the tastes and the needs of those whom I dressed."

A Life on Display

The room was decadent. Glossy floors were covered with furs, the furniture was covered with exquisite upholstery, and the "windows were lavishly draped with somewhat moth-eaten leopard skins." Cécile Sorel, one of France's most famous actresses, was hosting a dinner party at her home on

Coco Chanel,
circa 1928.
(PHOTOGRAPH BY FPG/HUTTON ARCHIVE/GETTY IMAGES)

the Seine. Among other luminaries, Misia Sert, leading patroness of the arts in Paris, was in attendance.

Dubbed "the Queen of Paris," Sert was known, among other accolades, for bringing Paris the Ballets Russes, its most famous cultural phenomenon of the new century, and for making the careers of men such as Vincent van Gogh and Igor Stravinsky. At Sorel's dinner, Misia found herself fixated on a "very dark-haired young woman" who "radiated a charm that I found irresistible." Silently sitting across the table was Coco Chanel, the archetype of the style she'd created. One of her own simple dresses elegantly tailored around her athletic, 5´3˝ frame (she typically weighed between 103 and 105 pounds), revealing just a touch of her seasonally bronzed skin and, on this evening in 1916, a particularly beautiful coat.

Following dinner, Misia arranged to sit next to Coco and began what would become a three-decade friendship. While their relationship would later be tinged with cruelty, it started with graciousness. As the evening was ending, Coco noticed that Misia liked her "ravishing fur-trimmed, red velvet coat," so she took it off and offered it to her, a gesture Sert recalled was "so pretty that I found her completely bewitching and thought of nothing but her."

Such apparent graciousness was commonplace for Chanel, for it was good for business to have Paris's trendsetters wearing her clothes, and she handed them out liberally to the right people. Whereas some in her business might maintain an air of scarcity, Chanel's impulse was quite the opposite—the more Cocos, the better. Later in her career, during the rise of the big department store, she was spurned by some of her couturier peers for refusing to pursue lawsuits against downmarket labels selling Chanel knockoffs.

Imitation was not something that could be instructed from her studio at 31 Rue Cambon. Chanel had to live a life worthy of imitation, something no fashion designer had yet done. As Misia wrote in the 1940s,

> Today, when couturiers are not only invited everywhere, but are almost the only people to give lavish parties to which everyone rushes, it is difficult to imagine the vast privilege conferred on Mademoiselle Chanel toward the end of the war [World War I], when the doors of the salons opened for her! It was certainly without precedent and the forerunner of a good many upheavals.

Misia Sert and others were drawn to Chanel for various reasons—Misia credited Chanel's charm, style, and good looks as the qualities that left Misia feeling "bewitched." But as much as people were attracted to her style, Chanel in turn needed men and women like Misia to give her access to a social scene worthy of admiration and imitation. According to Garelick, when Coco met Misia at Sorel's dinner party, Coco "was already glamorous and rich, yet longed for access to the highest levels of artistic society. Misia represented the dazzling apex of this society; she embodied social access." Through Misia, Chanel became intimate with some of the most famous men in the world, a group including the ballet dancer Diaghilev, the composer Stravinsky, and Pablo Picasso. She enchanted each of these men in the same way she had Misia. Picasso once said of Chanel that "she has more sense than any woman in Europe."

Becoming a part of high society was good for Chanel's business in a very literal sense. Through her social connections, Chanel was contracted to make clothes for the ballet, theater, and eventually Hollywood, and she

Coco Chanel with Winston
Churchill and his son Randolph, at
one of the Duke of Westminster's
estates.
(PHOTOGRAPH BY HULTON ARCHIVE/GETTY
IMAGES)

infiltrated both high society and popular culture. But beyond the stunning clothes she made, Coco Chanel the woman adopted a rambling, border-crossing, impeccably well-dressed, upscale bohemian lifestyle from about 1916 until the outbreak of World War II.

And she usually had an interesting man at her side. Though Boy Capel married another woman after World War I, he and Chanel continued to see each other until Boy died in an auto accident in 1919. Between then and the end of World War II, Chanel was involved with several men, including an exiled Russian royal (the aforementioned Romanov), a writer, a musician, the richest man in Europe, and a senior Nazi spy. To be sure, she had a luxurious lifestyle, and not a normal life of set routines. It was a life spent traveling to dinners, parties, and houses across Western Europe. Through all of it, she continued to make clothes.

The longest of these relationships was with Hugh Richard Arthur "Bendor" Grosvenor, the Duke of Westminster, and at the time the richest man in Europe. From 1924 until 1929, Coco held court at the duke's various estates. It's no surprise that during this time, Chanel's designs include wools, tweeds, argyles, and other items inspired by Bendor.

Among the duke's friends was Winston Churchill. He wrote his wife a letter after spending a weekend at one of the duke's châteaus in France in the mid-1920s: "The famous Coco turned up and I took a great fancy to her. A most capable and agreeable woman with the strongest personality Benny has yet been up against. She hunted vigorously all day, motored to Paris after dinner and is today engaged in passing and improving dresses on endless streams of mannequins."

Churchill's commentary on Chanel was just an aside in a letter to his wife, but his observations were trenchant. In a single sentence, he summed up the core of how Chanel passed her times: She at once lived an interesting, vigorous, glamorous, desirous life and also took the painstaking time to make beautiful dresses. If she couldn't be in Paris, then her mannequins— female models who were expected to stand for hours at a stretch as Coco configured dresses around them—came to her.

By 1930, the year after her relationship with Bendor ended, Chanel had successfully built her fashion empire: she paid taxes that year on 120 million French francs and reportedly held 3 million pounds in London. She had 2,400 employees working for her in five different workshops. Despite all the money, all the employees, and the glamorous lifestyle, Chanel continued to personally design all of her clothes. As Churchill noticed, whatever else she was doing, she was always working.

Retirement

In 1936, workers across France went on strike in response to turmoil across Europe. Page one of the *New York Times* from June 19 of that year has a dispatch from Paris, which begins:

> With the same instinct she has shown in making for herself a leading place in the world of fashion, Gabrielle Chanel, well-known dressmaker, has acted boldly in the face of the advance of French socialism. She has offered her business to her employees rather than make a settlement with them regarding wages and hours of labor which, she says, she cannot, under present business conditions, promise to be able to fulfill.

Never one for convention, Chanel offered to sell her entire company to her employees in the face of a strike, but her employees didn't have that sort of capital. Chanel's stores were quickly reopened.

But within three years, Chanel was once again shut down—and this time, the closure seemed permanent. When Germany occupied much of France in 1940, Coco abruptly closed the House of Chanel, leaving 2,500 employees out of work unexpectedly. Coco spent the years of World War II living in Nazi-occupied Paris. To get to her apartment at the Ritz, she had to walk beneath a swastika emblazoned at the front entrance, and through this period she had an affair with a high-ranking Nazi intelligence officer.

In the middle of the war, she also tried to use Aryanization laws to wrest control of Parfums Chanel from the Wertheimer brothers, who had fled France and moved to New York City prior to the German occupation. As Jews, the brothers were barred from owning the French-incorporated Parfums Chanel. Though she had grown rich from their original deal, she harbored resentment over her minority stake in the company that bore her name, and was even more upset that the Wertheimers had opened an American outpost of Parfums Chanel without consulting her. But Chanel lost her gambit. Resourcefully, the brothers had established a well-connected non-Jew as the nominal owner prior to their flight, and eventually won the legal dispute.

Beyond living luxuriously with a high-ranking Nazi official while Europe was at war, Chanel was also involved in a plot to broker peace with Britain on terms as favorable as possible to Germany. According to the details in Garelick's *Mademoiselle*, Chanel even traveled to Berlin to be briefed on the plan. This sort of made-for-the-movies intrigue was unlikely to succeed, and the German officials who approved the mission must have known as much. The scheme, code-named Modellhut (couture or model hat in German), was approved—without Hitler's knowledge—by the chief of German intelligence. The idea was to leverage Chanel's connections to Winston Churchill to establish a back channel between Nazi official Heinrich Himmler and the British prime minister. Predictably, the scheme failed when Churchill didn't reciprocate Chanel's outreach—he likely never even received the letter she sent to him.

No one in France at the time knew about Modellhut, but they did know of Chanel's relationship with an SS officer. As the country was liberated, other French women branded as collaborators faced public humiliation, but Chanel avoided the often violent indignities, having fled France and moved to Switzerland in 1944. It would be another nine years before she returned to work. When that time came, all the people she had crossed eventually welcomed her back into their lives: her employees, the Wertheimers, and her customers.

"There Is Only Mademoiselle"

By 1953, a layer of dust coated Chanel's fourth-floor studio at 31 Rue Cambon. Some four hundred miles away, the seventy-year-old Coco was living in luxurious hotels and her villa in Switzerland. It had been fourteen years since she had shut down her couture house, nine since she had vanished from France altogether.

If the First World War helped build the House of Chanel, World War II disassembled it. From 1939 to 1953, the Paris store sold nothing except perfume. While her flagship on the Place Vendôme remained intact, Coco Chanel, her employees, and her clothes disappeared for over a decade. Yet she would later recall, "Never was I in retirement in my heart."

From afar, Chanel had observed how Parisian fashion had evolved or, in her view, taken a step back. Skeptically, the matriarch of fashion paid particular attention to the young male upstart Christian Dior.

Dior's decadent designs of the late 1940s were a nod to an era of fashion that Chanel had attempted to end. Dior replaced Chanel's knee-length functional dresses with large crinoline-filled skirts, exchanged her chic belts for tight corsets, and sold bulky hats instead of the simpler ones to which Chanel owed her early success. His fashion, unlike Chanel's, was not meant to be replicated.

"It's quite a revolution, dear Christian!" the editor in chief of *Harper's Bazaar* said. "Your dresses have such a new look!" In Chanel's mind, there was nothing "new" about it—Dior's designs were updated replicas of decades-old fashion. "He doesn't dress women," she remarked, "he upholsters them!" Witnessing fashion decline into what she called "a joke," Chanel decided to reopen her studio.

In *Mademoiselle*, Garelick captures the reactions of Chanel employees during Coco's comeback. Though they'd been abruptly fired fourteen years before, Chanel's employees couldn't resist her. "We were all greatly

A Chanel suit circa 1969.
(PHOTOGRAPH BY JAMES ANDANSON/SYGMA VIA
GETTY IMAGES)

excited!" said Manon Ligeour, an employee who began working for Chanel when she was only thirteen. Madame Lucie, Chanel's forewoman before the war, had opened up her own store with other former employees in the years since Chanel had closed. Even she "leapt at the chance to return to Coco and closed up shop."

Chanel had drawn inspiration from the world and people around her. But the studio is where she did the actual work that made her mark, and she worked hard. In a pre–World War II article, *The New Yorker* recalled that "each year" Chanel "tries not only to beat her competitors but to beat herself—much more difficult."

Early on, she had reimagined the sweater, simply by cutting a man's pullover down the middle and attaching buttons to it. Later on, in between yacht rides on the French Riviera, she developed costume jewelry: "Long necklaces made of baroque gemstones . . . where Venetian and Byzantine influences are side by side, with the Duke of Westminster's England and the Grand Duke Dimitri's Russia." She popularized pearls—which cascaded en masse from her neck—and created the "Little Black Dress." Even the color black was not in style before she made it so. "I imposed black; it's still going strong today, for black wipes out everything else around," she once said. The "Chanel Suit"—which was cut right above the knee and was the first to include actual buttonholes for buttons sewn on the jacket—is the model for the modern female suit. Along the way, she had made tweed and jersey fabric beloved; two-toned shoes fashionable; and simple, loose-fitting clothing iconic.

The sheer output of her creativity was possible because she prioritized being in her studio, actually making clothes and accessories (and instructing others to do so), over every other facet of her life. Done with travel, and after returning from her Swiss exile, Coco lived primarily at her two homes in Paris. Both her apartment on the third floor of 31 Rue Cambon and a suite at the Ritz located across the street kept her physically tethered to the fashion house.

The building at 31 Rue Cambon was divided into four floors. The first floor was for selling products, and the second floor a mostly vacant space used for showing collections. The third floor had Chanel's apartment and some office space, and the fourth floor was reserved for her design studio. As one Chanel model remembers it, this was where "skilled hands encrusted silk with hundreds of tiny seed pearls and rhinestone beads, pieced handmade lace panels into chiffon, [and] covered buttons for discreet custom buttonholes with invisible stiches."

There was a hierarchy in Chanel's studio, and Coco was at the top. On the lowest rung were apprentices or seamstresses who aspired to the level of première. Chanel's right-hand woman, the *chef de cabine*, was second in command and oversaw dressmakers and models alike. But Chanel reigned supreme. "In other establishments," Chanel said, "they allow for fifty chefs and sous-chefs. With me, there is only 'Mademoiselle.'"

Whenever Chanel was going to be in the studio, seamstresses were notified. Usually in the afternoon, a phone rang sounding the alarm. An employee sprayed Chanel No. 5 by the door while others began to form a line to greet Coco upon entrance. After passing through the cloud of her own perfume, her virtual lookalike employees—who were required to wear a sort of Chanel uniform ("the same white blouse, beige-and-black Chanel shoes, and a blue or black suit")—might be called out, or even dismissed, if they did not meet her standards.

Princess Odile de Croy, a Chanel model, told Garelick in an interview

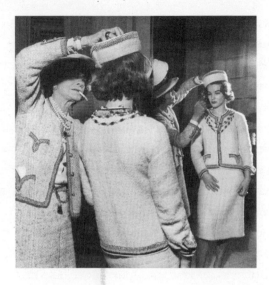

Coco Chanel working
in her studio circa 1960.
(PHOTOGRAPH BY BOTTI/GAMMA-KEYSTONE
VIA GETTY IMAGES)

that "I copied her a lot. . . . I would have never worn something that was not in the Chanel style." Chanel employees were furthermore expected to be just as devoted to the "idea" of Coco Chanel as her customers were—every dress was always designed with her in mind. Later in her life, she told her friend Paul Morand: "'This dress will not sell,' I sometimes tell my staff, 'because it is not me.'"

Chanel, who was never formally trained in fashion design and believed "that no one can tell what a dress looks like either on paper or on a cutting table, or in anything but the material for which it was intended," never used sketches when creating clothes. Instead, she instructed a première to create a "rough form" and pinned designs on live models, making them stand for hours. In another instance she threw "a hairbow back at a seamstress, crying huskily: 'It was better when I pinned it together than when you sewed it!'"

Days spent in the studio were the blistered opposite of Chanel's otherwise plush life. Sometimes she worked for nine hours straight without sitting, pinning models, instructing seamstresses, and shredding their designs right in front of them if they didn't meet her standard. Ann Montgomery, a model for Chanel during her comeback in the 1950s, recalled that it was "difficult to endure the tedious routines of the *cabine*."

While she could be generous as a boss—earlier in life she offered holidays to various employees at her and her lovers' estates—she was also cruel and unpredictable. She often chose favorites, and pitted her employees against one another. She made models stand for hours, criticized her workers' physical appearance, spread rumors, and limited what staff could discuss with her. "I am not the least frivolous. I have a boss's soul. I take everything seriously," Chanel once said. And she was imperious: employees were expected to function on Coco's time. If she decided to have a last-minute dinner or give an impromptu hours-long soliloquy, employees were expected to stay and listen. "She was exhausting," stylist and assistant Lilou Marquand recalled.

And yet when Chanel called upon her employees to return to the now-dusty fourth-floor studio, they came. In the first days and nights of February 1954—leading up to the first Chanel show in fifteen years—a select few of them remained in the studio all night with her along with several models. Coco personally inspected every dress, restlessly meticulous even into her old age. Through long nights, her mannequins would

> . . . make their appearance with all the submissiveness of conscripts. They had to endure interminable fittings without uttering a syllable, knowing only too well that Chanel would have remained deaf to their protests, deaf also to their fatigue and that of the tailors. Again and again Chanel undid a jacket, cutting the stitches of an armhole, which she would then redo, using pins to reposition it point by point, all stuck in with an almost demonic thrust. All the while she remained resolutely indifferent to everything but the creative process, a process that was leading toward perfection.

Her first show, on February 5, 1954, was disastrous. One review in *Le Monde* opined, "God was it ugly!" But across the Atlantic, the *New York Times* claimed, "The spirit of Chanel has made itself widely felt in the creation of the coming fall styles." Her line appealed to what American women wanted: sporty and practical clothes.

Pierre Wertheimer met with Chanel after her February 5 show. It was a seemingly odd visit given how, during World War II, Chanel had fought him for control of Parfums Chanel. Somehow, the pair had gotten over it. "I want to go on . . . and win," Chanel told Wertheimer after the failed opening. He believed she could—on May 24, 1954, he offered to buy out Chanel completely—her logo, her fashion house, everything. In return, he would cover all of Chanel's expenses for the rest of her life, and Coco would retain complete creative control.

While the economic security of a blank check was likely a factor in her old age, the deal was consistent with Coco's priorities. Her lifestyle was important, but she needed control over the things created in her name. Chanel took the deal, and kept making clothes until her death in 1971.

Allure

Surrounded by Swiss mountains and a wintry cold, in 1946 Chanel told her life story to Paul Morand in the glittering St. Moritz Hotel. After their evening talks, Morand took notes on what Chanel had said. After her death he compiled these notes into a book titled *The Allure of Chanel*.

It is a peculiar piece of work, for Morand styles the book as if Chanel herself is writing, despite its being a series of his own recollections. "Nothing was written by me," he wrote in the introduction. "It was all by a ghost, but a ghost who, from beyond the grave, kept up a frantic gallop, her normal pace. Allure, in every sense of the word."

A half century after her death, Coco Chanel was seemingly still alive as the singular icon of the famous company she started as a hat store in 1910. Chanel boutiques are modeled after her apartment at the Ritz, jewelry and perfumes are created with her image in mind, and women still imitate her look and style—albeit less knowingly—by wearing her little black dresses and well-fitted suits.

"I would make a very bad dead person," Morand wrote, as Chanel, to conclude his book. "Because once I was put under, I would grow restless and would think only of returning to earth and starting over again."

ENTREPRENEURIALISM AND EGO

To understand the entrepreneur, you first have to understand the psychology of the juvenile delinquent.

—ABRAHAM ZALEZNIK

The contract granted the budding railroad developer "complete, full, undisturbed, unfettered and unrestricted control and supervision, unhampered and unimpeded by the other parties hereto. . . ." Even compared to the sharp-elbowed tactics for which the titans of America's mighty railways were renowned, it was extreme given that the "other parties hereto" in this case were the would-be magnate's wife and two daughters.

It was a gag contract that in 1948 Walt Disney, a lifelong railroad enthusiast, asked his lawyer to draft setting up the fictional "Walt Disney R.R. Co." It was his unusual way of convincing his family to allow him to build a working railroad at their new home in Holmby Hills, California.

As with other things he cared about so passionately, Walt threw himself headlong into the most exacting details. The locomotive was modeled after the Central Pacific's engine number 173. Walt learned how to work with sheet metal so he could personally construct its headlamp and smokestack, and he had newspapers from the 1880s shrunk to scale and put in the newspaper racks in each car. He blasted a ninety-foot S-curved tunnel into his property to make the ride more intriguing and asked his secretary to shield him from how much the project would cost, ensuring that his only focus was on the quality of the experience. The end result was a perfect one-eighth-size replica steam-engine railroad, named the "Carolwood-Pacific," sputtering around Walt's family home on Carolwood Drive. He loved "donning his coveralls and engineer's cap and transporting his daughters' friends or guests at cocktail parties. . . ."

Whether it was Disney going to such punctilious extremes to entertain guests at his home or Chanel spraying a scented liquid on perfect strangers to gauge their reaction, each of our founders did things on their path to fame that most of us would find odd. And rather than being put off, we often find their behavior intriguing. Each of our founders was eccentric, but their creative and obsessive perfectionism was the upside of personalities that could be equally abrasive.

In part because Disney and Chanel were such unique individuals, they left indelible marks on the brands that still bear their names. As a result, it's tempting to attribute their companies' success to the founders' where-withal. In truth, like many other successful founders, they had the insight and energy to knock over a domino only to get lucky and find it cascade against others.

Chanel emerged at a time when women were bound in uncomfortable corsets and expected to balance twenty-pound ornamental hats atop their heads. Chanel herself admitted the luck of her timing: "I was in the right place; an opportunity beckoned, I took it. I had grown up with this new century: I was therefore the one to be consulted about its sartorial style. What were needed were simplicity, comfort and neatness: unwittingly, I offered all of that."

While Coco Chanel had the right insight at the right time, to take her opportunity she still had to make the clothes. Beginning with a very particular idea—that women at the horse races would prefer to be as comfortable and stylish as she was—she gained the confidence to pursue the ambitious goal to make an entire society of women look and feel like she did.

Disney wanted to change the way a generation entertained itself even before he tasted initial success. His 1937 breakthrough success with *Snow White* was not the payout of a three-year gambit, but instead the culmination of a decade-plus string of innovations in animation. Walt's 1923 film *Alice's Wonderland* pioneered the blending of live acting with cartoon animation. The release of *Steamboat Willie* in 1928 was the first animation to synchronize sound with action. A year later, *The Skeleton Dance* would trumpet this achievement with an entire cartoon of playfully synchronized sound and motion. In 1930, the cartoon *Frolicking Fish* introduced realistically continuous movement for the first time. Two years later, *Flowers and Trees* was released as his first Technicolor cartoon, and the 1937 release of *The Old Mill* was his first use of the revolutionary multi-plane camera.

In retrospect, Disney was laying technological track in front of the three-year project that would put him forever on the map. But it also reveals an ambitious and playful artist emerging at the moment that animation was ripe to be disrupted with the miracles of color and sound. The point is not simply that luck plays a role, as true as that may be. We also have a natural bias for attributing what works out well—in the end—as being the "right" formula for success. Yet such attribution is blind to the role of context and chance in devising such formulae, and can't possibly consider the lessons of the thousands of would-be artists and animators who failed to capture the biographer's spotlight.

Of course, through some combination of luck, skill, and dogged persistence, Disney and Chanel each grew rapidly following their breakout moment. For Disney it was *Snow White* and for Chanel it was her string of successes in the midst and aftermath of World War I. For such successful founders there inevitably comes a stage of growth when the mountain of corporate decisions exceeds the number of minutes in the day. At this point, the creative and innovative genius must learn to rely upon others to sustain the vision, despite the founder's natural and perhaps reasonable conclusion that his or her judgment is indispensable to the company's success.

Disney and Chanel both wrestled with this "Founder's Dilemma," and ultimately decided to spend the preponderance of their time and energy on making things, rather than managing a company. Walt delegated much of the day-to-day to his brother, Roy. Though she fought for control of her company during World War II, Chanel ultimately ceded her business to the Wertheimers. Such entrepreneurs are likely happier in a studio—or garage, workshop, or lab—than a boardroom, just as our two founders were clearly focused on creative excellence above all else.

Disney's most successful projects—*Snow White* and Disneyland, for example—featured Walt in the thick of things, micromanaging to the smallest detail. Chanel lived a glamorous life, but the flip side was bleeding fingers and long hours in her studio, where she is remembered as an imperious presence. In the end, each founder's commitment to creative excellence meant that to work for Disney or Chanel was to have the chance to upend one's industry and build something both new and lasting. Day to day, the same energy that propelled each company's creative excellence could be grating, confounding, and downright insulting.

While Chanel and Disney are quintessential case studies of entrepreneurial leadership, and as much as we can understand their success through the context of timing and their ability to create, we're still left puzzling over the magnetic pull of their often-abrasive personalities. Indeed, the reality of their leadership styles is not something we'd try to teach or mimic.

And while these two leaders might not be able to teach us much about how to lead, they do offer lessons in why we follow. Both Disney and Chanel considered people enablers of their objectives. Neither was inherently uncaring, but they ultimately cared more about the product than about their employees. This is a classic struggle in leadership, known in the military as the dilemma of prioritizing "our mission or our people." For Disney and Chanel, their companies were an enabler, or a vehicle, to building the thing they wanted. And in the end, their people were largely willing to live with that.

If you wanted to upend women's fashion in the early twentieth century, working for Chanel was your best choice. Similarly, if you wanted to upend popular entertainment, you'd end up working for the impractical creative who agonized over the most exacting detail to make sure his model railroad was fun for his guests. And by choosing to work for Disney, you might also have gone on strike over your wages, and your boss might have lambasted you as a result.

We seem willing to follow leaders who put the mission first because we all make trade-offs, and life is rarely simple or idealized. We want to be happy in our work, but athletes also want to win, soldiers want to survive the battle, and businesspeople hope to prosper. That's not to rationalize successful leaders who have a mean streak. It's simply to say that a nice personality is not necessarily required for holding a compelling vision for the future. And when forced to choose, we'll sometimes take a leader's vision over their style. More broadly, if a leader is giving us what we think we need, we don't always care how they get us there.

Four

THE GENIUSES

Towering genius disdains a beaten path.
It seeks regions hitherto unexplored.

—ABRAHAM LINCOLN

D espite the bright summer sun and the cacophony of nearby conversations, I watch intently. The pitcher rocks back, pivots his toe on the
rubber, then lunges toward home plate, his arm flinging itself forward
until his hand releases a five-ounce sphere consisting of a cork center under
almost a mile of tightly wrapped yarn and stitched into white cowhide. The
baseball is traveling slightly over ninety miles per hour.

Roughly fifty-five feet from where the ball leaves the pitcher's outstretched hand, a helmeted batter stands slightly crouched, a thirty-four-
inch-long stick of New York ash lathe-shaped into a wooden bat cocked
behind his head, poised to strike. The hitter's eyes squint slightly—he's
done this many times before.

About .4 seconds later the batter will swing and hit the fastball—or a
thud in the catcher's mitt will indicate that he has not. Within a few feet of
leaving the pitcher's outstretched hand, after only a fraction of a second, the
batter must judge the trajectory (and any spin) of the ball and decide to
swing—beginning the swing when the ball is still only one-half of its way to
the plate—a seemingly impossible challenge.

In this case, a sharp retort, a collective gasp from the crowd, and then a soaring line drive arcs over the left field fence. Another home run. The slugger jogs ceremoniously around the bases, appearing almost nonchalant about his accomplishment.

Watching, I marvel at the feat, not because I don't understand the game, or the act of hitting. I played many years of baseball, batted countless times, and periodically hit the ball. But I never hit like that. I *could never* hit like that. The fact that I've played the game means that I can appreciate the difficulty of the task and it increases my awe of those who master it. For me, it represents a level of skill I can never attain—but can admire. The twenty-three-year-old player never sought a university education, but it still feels as though I'm in the presence of a form of genius. And it garners my respect.

Each of us has varying abilities that can be developed into competencies, but a quantum leap above lies the qualitatively different category of genius. Beyond a useful gift, or natural cleverness, are abilities of stunning skill that separate a genius from the rest of us. In their particular field, whether narrow or broad, geniuses can do what most of us cannot.

But does that make them leaders?

The intersection of genius and leadership is a curious space. Brilliant concepts of philosophy, breakthroughs in science, and the emotional power of great art influence our attitudes and actions, yet the geniuses behind the breakthroughs are often isolated and inscrutable. We are shaped and inspired by men and women with abilities beyond ours, sometimes in ways that are as unintentional as they are unexpected. Here we explore whether genius and leadership have any true connection.

In seeking to examine and compare two individuals of clear genius, we surveyed some familiar names—Leonardo da Vinci, Michelangelo, Benjamin Franklin, and John Stuart Mill—but chose to anchor our exploration of genius and leadership with Albert Einstein. We realized we had to begin with the theoretical physicist whose name we all know, but whose towering achievements and relevance to our lives far outstrip popular awareness or appreciation. The aging Einstein, with unruly hair, bushy mustache, and charmingly rumpled clothes, was the kindly uncle we'd longed for. But his incredible ability to conceive of then-novel but now-famous thought experiments, and to ponder abstractions in space time, creates an intimidating gulf between Einstein and all but a tiny number of brilliant minds.

Far closer to home, and more visceral, is the finger-snapping music of *West Side Story*. We chose to pair its composer, the colorful conductor Leonard Bernstein, who most knew as Lenny, with Einstein, because although an extraordinarily accomplished genius, Bernstein seems all too approachable and human. His natural talents, burnished by a relentless drive, are monumental—but lack the opaque mystery of theoretical physics. We admire Bernstein's gifts, but somehow feel more qualified to judge them.

We respect genius, but unlike the comfort of wealth, or the status of celebrities, we seldom covet the gifts of the genius. They are too rarely bestowed for any of us to feel cheated without them, so we simply gaze on them in curiosity and wonder. And sometimes that gaze intensifies to hold influence over us. So when and how does genius become leadership?

Key Books

- Albrecht Fölsing, *Albert Einstein: A Biography* (New York: Penguin, 1997)
- Walter Isaacson, *Einstein: His Life and Universe* (New York: Simon & Schuster, 2007)
- John S. Rigden, *Einstein 1905: The Standard of Greatness* (Cambridge, MA: Harvard University Press, 2005)
- Humphrey Burton, *Leonard Bernstein* (London: Faber and Faber, 1995)
- Allen Shawn, *Leonard Bernstein: An American Musician* (New Haven, CT: Yale University Press, 2016)

ALBERT EINSTEIN

Paradoxically, as the years passed, the figure of Einstein the man became more and more remote, while that of Einstein the legend came ever nearer to the masses of mankind. They grew to know him not as a universe-maker whose theories they could not hope to understand but as a world citizen, one of the outstanding spiritual leaders of his generation, a symbol of the human spirit and its highest aspirations.

—*NEW YORK TIMES*, APRIL 19, 1955, OBITUARY FOR ALBERT EINSTEIN

Einstein in his Berlin study, the attic from which he "ran"
the Kaiser Wilhelm Institute. (BPK BILDAGENTUR/ART RESOURCE, NY.)

In 1924, Satyendra Nath Bose, a young physicist at the University of Dhaka, sent an unsolicited letter to Albert Einstein. Attaching a paper of his that had just been rejected for publication, he asked a favor of the world's most famous scientist.

> If you think the paper worth publication I shall be grateful if you ar-range for its publication . . . though a complete stranger to you, I do not feel any hesitation in making such a request. Because we are all your pupils though profiting only by your teachings through your writings.

Five thousand miles west of Dhaka, likely while sitting in the attic office of his Berlin apartment, Einstein read the letter from the young man he'd never met. Einstein spent much of his time at home in solitude, alone with his thoughts in a disheveled room filled with books and papers, the walls bare except for prints of Isaac Newton and Michael Faraday. He was alone, but hardly isolated, for Einstein was generally in conversation with some-one. By orders of magnitude, his correspondence was the most prolific of all modern scientists, including some thirty thousand letters in all.

As usual, Einstein was busy when he received Bose's note. He was planning a journey to South America, had been traveling extensively throughout Europe, and had just given his lecture accepting the 1921 Nobel Prize. He was also working out the implications of his general theory of relativity—the confirmation of which, in 1919, had propelled him to international stardom. He had every reason to ignore this correspondence from halfway across the world, but instead Einstein replied to Bose in a handwritten note:

I have translated your paper and submitted it . . . for printing. It constitutes an important advance and I liked it very much. I think, however that your objections to my paper are not correct. . . . Nevertheless, that does not matter. . . . It is a fine advance. With friendly greetings, yours, A. Einstein.

Einstein not only responded to Bose, but also had this newly acquainted colleague's overlooked paper translated so it could be printed in a prominent German journal. Afterward, Bose leveraged Einstein's response to convince his higher-ups to sponsor a two-year trip to Europe, something he had been attempting for years.

"I cannot exactly express how grateful I feel for your encouragement and the interest you have taken in my papers," Bose wrote from Paris in January 1925, during a trip in which he collaborated with many of the world's foremost physicists. "Your first card came at a critical moment, and it has more than any other made this sojourn to Europe possible for me." Einstein had invited Bose into a world of experts, a network where a talented but otherwise isolated scientist could both learn from and also contribute to a conversation that would carry across oceans and centuries.

Their correspondence became one of the most storied collaborations of twentieth-century physics. The two exchanged notes for another thirty years in a partnership that would go on to outlive each correspondent. Among other advances, they had predicted a state of matter called Bose-Einstein condensate that appears at very low temperatures. The existence of the condensate was experimentally confirmed in 1995 by two scientists, who were awarded the Nobel Prize in 2001—nearly seventy-seven years after Bose's first letter.

While ancillary to Einstein's career, their correspondence set a critical course of discovery for Bose and other physicists for the century to come. Einstein didn't respond to Bose merely out of kindness or sympathy, although there is obvious warmth in the exchange. Einstein saw potential in the young man's ideas, and he responded because he thought the collaboration might lead to some deeper understanding of the universe. Einstein's touch gave confidence to Bose, and legitimized the younger physicist.

Their partnership would become legendary, but their correspondence reflected the routine exchange and collaboration required for scientific discovery. Before they became acquainted, both scientists were steeped in centuries of cumulative scientific knowledge. Through the back-and-forth of their correspondence, Bose critiqued Einstein's work and Einstein replied with tweaks and improvements. Between letters, the men were both alone with their work and in conversation with other scientists. This combination of individual insight and collaborative refinement reflect a powerful requirement of innovation.

Of course, not all nodes in a collaborative network are equal. Einstein not only corresponded more than any other scientist of his time, but also established common reference points that enabled discovery by thousands of future physicists he would never meet. In particular, Einstein was at the center of two fundamental revolutions in twentieth-century physics: the theories of relativity and quantum mechanics.

Einstein's theory of relativity was published in two installments: his theory of special relativity in June 1905, and general relativity ten years later. Special relativity updated and corrected Newton's two-hundred-year-old laws of physics by stating that space and time are relative to the motion of an observer, with the shocking implication that things we had come to see as fixed—such as the length of an object—could actually contract and expand. Special relativity was termed "special" because it pertained only to the particular set of circumstances in which the objects of the system are in constant motion relative to one another; in other words, they are not accelerating.

This constraint concerned Einstein, and he immediately sought a generalized version of his theory that would pertain in all cases, hence his quest for a second theory of "general" relativity. Ultimately, his realization of this goal became his crowning achievement, with the similarly revolutionary idea that mass bends space and time. The resulting implication was that what we had come to think of as "gravity" between two objects was really just the acceleration that results when the mass of the objects bends the space and time around them. A common metaphor to visualize general relativity involves heavy balls on an elastic surface, as explained by biographer Walter Isaacson, who asks his reader to "picture what it would be like to roll a bowling ball onto the two-dimensional surface of a trampoline. Then roll some billiard balls. They move toward the bowling ball not because it exerts some mysterious attraction but because of the way it curves the trampoline fabric."

While Einstein is indisputably credited with discovering relativity, many others were more important than Einstein in the development of quantum theory. Nonetheless, quantum theory had its roots in Einstein's March 1905 suggestion that light is made of particles, or energy quanta. Prior to his paper, it was generally accepted that light energy traveled only as a continuous wave. Einstein's then-radical idea was that light is made of discrete particles, or as Bertrand Russell eloquently summarized, light is not a "pail of molasses," but a "bucket of sand." Einstein was eventually proved correct, and particle physics would later identify and name these particles "photons."

In time, Einstein's theories enabled a number of important and more practical technological advances, including lasers, GPS, nuclear power, and atomic energy. More important, Einstein's insights didn't merely enable new technology—they were the pillars on which a new generation of physics was built.

And even for the vast majority of us who do not work with his theories, the weight of his influence still pulls on us. He tops almost any list of famous people—for instance, he was *Time* magazine's "Person of the Twentieth Century." And while his fame is based on how he changed the way we grasp the world, very few people actually understand what he did. The day after his theory of general relativity was confirmed, Einstein cautioned that "there were not more than twelve persons in the world who would understand it." The number has steadily increased, but there are still relatively few people who can truly understand Einstein's impact on science. If

anything, we sit in awe of what he did precisely because we do not understand it. He understood and described a universe that we can't readily
visualize, and while we're forever changed for it, we're even more intrigued
by it.

A Compass, Euclid, and a Violin

Albert Einstein was born on March 14, 1879, in Ulm, Germany, the
first child of Hermann and Pauline Einstein. When Albert was four or
five, Hermann gave him a life-altering gift: a magnetic compass. Later in
life, Einstein called this moment his first experience of "wonder." He was
awed that a needle could move without anything touching it, aware for the
first time that, in his words, "something deeply hidden had to be behind
things."

Einstein would later observe that "this 'wondering' appears to occur
when an experience comes into conflict with a world of concepts already
sufficiently fixed within us." Rather than just sit in amazement, Einstein
was driven to address the conflict and understand the "hidden" hand behind his sense of wonder. As he put it: "the development of this world of
thought is in a certain sense a continuous flight from 'wonder.'"

It's not surprising, then, that Albert moved through boyhood as an au-
todidact. At the age of twelve, he encountered his "second wonder," Euclid,
the founder of plane geometry, during the self-learning he did outside of
school. He was struck that "here were assertions . . . that—by no means
evident—could nevertheless be proved with such certainty that any doubt
appeared to be out of the question. This lucidity and certainty made an
indescribable impression upon me."

His recollections of the compass and Euclid expose some of what motivated Einstein's thinking. Einstein was driven to shine light on the darkness of ambiguity and provide for a more certain world. In his own words,
he had a tendency to "scent out that which might lead to fundamentals and
to turn aside from everything else, from the multitude of things that clutter
up the mind and divert it from the essentials."

Einstein had an itinerant life, moving between German, Italian, Swiss,
and Austrian cities twelve times before he was thirty-five years old, with

several moves when he was just a boy. But wherever he was, Einstein had an ability to find the solitude necessary for deep thought. As his sister, Maja, remembered: "His working method was rather strange: even in . . . company, when there was quite a lot of noise, he could retire to the sofa, pick up pen and paper, precariously balance the inkwell on the backrest, and engross himself in a problem to such an extent that the many-voiced conversation stimulated rather than disturbed him."

By 1895, as a teenager, Einstein was beginning to think mostly about physics. This is the year he sent his uncle Caesar Koch an essay titled "An Investigation of the State of the Ether in the Magnetic Field," and at about this same time, he also began a thought process that would change our understanding of the world. He famously pondered what it would be like to "pursue a beam with the velocity c (velocity of light)." This thought contained within it the paradox that would lead him to the special theory of relativity ten years later.

In pondering these things, he was sustained in part by a gift from his mother. About the same time that Hermann handed him that life-altering compass, Einstein's mother, Pauline, handed him a violin. Whereas his father's compass ignited his inquisitiveness, the violin exposed him to the sheer beauty of music, which would become a source of his most vital friendships. As much as his genius depended on solitude, it was also fueled by kinship.

In 1896, the seventeen-year-old Einstein was admitted to the Swiss Polytechnic in Zurich, where he studied physics. While playing the violin there one Saturday evening, he met Michele Besso, who was six years Einstein's senior and already had a degree in mechanical engineering from the Polytechnic. The two immediately began a conversation about physics, math, philosophy, and music that would go on for sixty years until their deaths, which came within weeks of each other. At the Polytechnic, Einstein was also classmates and friends with Marcel Grossmann, a collaborator for the next forty years, and Mileva Marić, who would become his first wife.

Einstein was twenty-one years old when he graduated from the Polytechnic in July 1900. He'd gotten high marks, and had gained friends in Besso and Grossmann with whom he could have deep conversations. He was falling in love and beginning to think about marrying his "Dolly," Mileva Marić. He was just five months away from publishing his first article in the world's premier physics journal, the *Annalen der Physik*. Surely, he thought, he'd be able to get a post as an assistant at a top university and move on to his doctoral studies. But the reputation he'd earned with professors as a result of the classes he'd skipped made finding a job in academia difficult.

The Bureaucrat

For the next two years, from July 1900 through June 1902, and with the exception of a few stints as a private tutor and substitute teacher, Einstein was an out-of-work college graduate, shuffling between Switzerland and Italy. Einstein and Mileva were vacationing in the Swiss mountains in 1901 when Mileva became pregnant out of wedlock. Albert never met his daughter, Lieserl, who was likely given up for adoption. This was a difficult period, but he nonetheless continued thinking about the paradoxes of nature that were the source of his "wonder." We can gain a glimpse of Einstein's life during this challenging phase in the text of three letters, each sent just one day apart in April 1901.

On April 13, 1901, Einstein's father, Hermann, sent a note to Wilhelm Ostwald, the professor of physical chemistry at Leipzig University. It opens: "Please forgive a father who is so bold as to turn to you, esteemed Herr Professor, in the interest of his son." After explaining Albert's high marks at the Zurich Polytechnic, he goes on to say that his son thinks he has "gone off the tracks with his career" and that "he is oppressed by the thought that he is a burden on us, people of modest means." While Hermann does ask if the Herr Professor needs an assistant, the real purpose of the note is a "humble request to read [Albert's] paper published in the *Annalen der Physik* and to write him, if possible, a few words of encouragement, so that he might recover his joy in living and working." He closes the note by saying that his son has no knowledge of Hermann's actions.

On April 14, 1901, Albert Einstein, now in Italy with his parents, wrote to his university friend Marcel Grossmann in Switzerland. He opens by thanking his friend for helping him look for a job, and finds some levity in his current situation. "All the same," writes Einstein, "I leave no stone unturned and do not give up my sense of humor. . . . God created the don-key and gave him a thick hide." He says that his "musical acquaintances" in Milan "protect me here from getting sour." He then spends a paragraph explaining his current scientific pursuits, concluding with a summation of his philosophy of discovery: "It is a glorious feeling to perceive the unity of a complex of phenomena which appear as completely separate entities to direct sensory observation."

On April 15, 1901, he begins a letter to Mileva Marić, "My dear Doxerl [Dolly], Don't be angry at me for my not following your summons to Logano." After the apology for not being able to get away with her, he spends a paragraph discussing various job prospects. Then, just as the day before, most of the letter is about physics: "As for science, I've got an extremely lucky idea, which will make it possible to apply our theory of molecular forces to gases as well." Einstein met Marić as a fellow physics student, and so their correspondence is, at times, highly technical. Yet the note ends just like any other might between young lovers: "And how are you, dear girl? . . . Tender kisses from your, Albert."

On Saturday, a plea from a pained father for someone to lend a word of encouragement to a son going through a rough patch. On Sunday, a warm note to a friend, thanking him for his help, poking fun at the author's own misfortunes, and finding comfort in the pursuit of understanding nature. On Monday, a note to his girlfriend, mostly discussing physics, with some "tender kisses" thrown in for good measure. Albert Einstein was a young man in love, a little bit off track, but doggedly pursuing his passion for science.

In the letters to Grossmann and Marić, Einstein alluded to a job that Grossmann's father was trying to arrange for him. On June 23, 1902—after two years of unemployment—Einstein began a job as an "Expert III Class" at the Swiss Patent Office in Bern.

While in Bern, Einstein and Marić married in early 1903, and their first son was born in early 1904. Einstein's job as a patent clerk was precisely eight hours a day, six days a week. But he was usually able to finish his work well before closing and spent much of his time in the office thinking about physics.

Upon arriving in Bern, Einstein knew no one, but that would change

*From left to right are Conrad Habicht, Maurice Solovine,
and Einstein circa 1903. The three men founded Bern's Olympia Academy.*

quickly. Most of his life outside the office was organized around physics and friends—and often both at the same time. He continued to submit articles to the *Annalen der Physik*, and was well known enough that by 1904 he became one of sixty-two referees of *Beiblätter zu den Annalen der Physik* (*Supplements to the Annals of Physics*), which carried reviews of papers in other journals and the occasional book review. While no universities would grant him a doctorate on the strength of his published papers, he was inducted into the Naturforschende Gesellschaft in Bern, a gathering of elites who were interested in the sciences. He visited their evening meetings often, but he spoke at them only twice.

Of far more consequence to Einstein's daily life in Bern was the Akademie Olympia, or Olympia Academy. The name was an inside joke—it was nothing more than Einstein and two friends: Maurice Solovine, a Romanian student he'd met while tutoring him, and Conrad Habicht, a doctoral student in mathematics.

The three met regularly in the evenings over simple meals of sausage, cheese, fruit, honey, and tea, and through their discussions kept one another up to date with the latest happenings in the world of physics and broader topics as well. Among many others, they read and discussed the works of physicist Ernst Mach and philosopher David Hume, both of whom Einstein later credited as inspirations for his thinking on relativity.

It was in this spirit of learning mingled with lighthearted friendship that Einstein sent what is perhaps the most remarkable letter in the history of physics in May 1905. He likely wrote it in the patent office or, as he was known to do, with his baby boy perched on his lap in his tiny apartment. To his friend and fellow Olympian Conrad Habicht, Einstein began with some ribbing: "So, what are you up to, you frozen whale, you smoked, dried, canned piece of soul, or whatever else I would like to hurl at your head. . . . Why have you still not sent me your dissertation? Don't you know I am one of the 1½ fellows who would read it with interest and pleasure, you wretched man?" Casually and abruptly, Einstein promises "four papers in return, the first of which I might send you soon." He goes on:

> The paper deals with radiation and the energy properties of light and is very revolutionary, as you will see if you send me your work *first*. The second paper is a determination of the true sizes of atoms from the diffusion and the viscosity of dilute solutions of neutral substances. The third proves that, on the assumption of the molecular theory of heat, bodies on the order of magnitude 1/1000mm, suspended in liquids, must already perform an observable random motion that is produced by thermal motion . . . the fourth paper is only a rough draft at this point, and is an electrodynamics of moving bodies which employs a modification of the theory of space and time; the purely kinematic part of which will surely interest you.

The four papers that Einstein promised, and a fifth that he'd write in the same year, would revolutionize physics and, over time, reshape how humanity interprets nature. In an astounding surge of academic effort, he published all five papers in just six months. But Einstein was still just a Swiss bureaucrat and the only academy he was formally a part of involved eating sausages and cheese with his friends.

"Thank You. I've Completely Solved the Problem."

In 1905, the most prominent German-speaking physicist was Max Planck, who would become the father of quantum mechanics and go on to win a Nobel Prize in 1918. Beyond his personal discoveries, he also had serious institutional authority as president of the Berlin Physical Society, the sole professor of theoretical physics at the University of Berlin, and the editor for theoretical physics of the *Annalen der Physik*. Thus he moderated the fora through which physicists shared, debated, and refined their ideas, and helped to curate the ecosystem that enabled a lowly bureaucrat to submit a paper that would offer the world its most important advances in physics in more than two hundred years.

By 1905, Einstein was also an excellent physicist, and while Planck didn't know Einstein personally at the time, Einstein had submitted many articles to Planck's *Annalen*. Nominally, Einstein was an unknown patent clerk and Planck a famous scientist, but this distinction meant less than one might assume. Planck and his predecessors cultivated an environment where even a patent clerk could mingle with the field's giants, provided his ideas were good enough.

So it was that Planck and the *Annalen* would become the enablers that reviewed and published Einstein's outpouring of work in 1905. In March of that year, Einstein submitted to Planck his paper on light quanta. In May, a paper on the movement of molecules, called Brownian motion. In June, the paper on special relativity, and in September a follow-up, the "$E = mc^2$" paper. Of note, 1905 was also the year Einstein submitted his doctoral thesis to the University of Zurich, which the *Annalen* eventually published in 1906.

Planck disagreed with the science in some of Einstein's papers, but he sent all of them through for publication, and he quickly championed the theory of special relativity. Planck's support brought needed attention to Einstein's disruptive ideas, and Einstein later wrote of Planck that it was in "great measure due to the decisiveness and warmth with which he championed this theory that fellow physicists began so quickly to pay attention to it."

Einstein's paper on special relativity contained within it the solution to the problem of the "ether," which had confounded the physics community for decades. At the time, scientists believed that light traveled as a wave and that, like other waves, light must move through a medium (i.e., sound waves travel through air, ocean waves through water, etc.). Light waves, physicists had thought for centuries, must travel through an imperceptible "ether." In 1887, an experiment had been done to confirm the existence of the ether, but the experiment failed to do so, leaving physicists in search of an explanation. Einstein later credited this search as the seed that would become special relativity, as he was "certain that it was contained in the problem of the optical properties of moving bodies. . . . I tried to find clear experimental evidence for the flow of the ether in the literature but in vain." After a decade of his own persistent thinking, calculating, and conversing, Einstein was the first physicist to get the problem of the ether right.

The breakthrough came in the midst of a conversation with his lifelong friend Michele Besso. In May 1905, in Einstein's words, "I started the conversation with him in the following way: 'Recently I have been working on a difficult problem. Today I come to do battle against that problem with you.' We discussed every aspect of this problem. Then suddenly I understood where the key to this problem lay. Next day I came back to him again and said to him, without even saying hello, 'Thank you. I've completely solved the problem.' An analysis of the concept of time was my solution." Einstein took two seemingly distinct concepts, the propagation of light and our conception of time and, by looking at each with respect to the other, arrived at a transformational breakthrough.

Einstein's insight was that light does not move as a wave through ether, but as a particle through space and time, and that space and time were not absolute—as Newton thought—but relative to the position of an observer. This breakthrough hit him like a thunderbolt, jolting him to submit his special relativity paper only five weeks after the conversation with Besso. But unlike lightning, the discovery was hardly random—it was the manifestation of what many physicists had been discussing for almost two decades. Moreover, Einstein's place on the fringes of academia was of some advantage in finding the insight to solve the problem of the ether by looking at the concept of time, for he was close enough to the problem to understand it, but removed enough to have some freedom from mainstream academia.

Einstein's context—along with his skepticism, imagination, and ability to question the most fundamental pillars of science—was critical to his discovery. For example, the physical and situational context of the patent office, a place filled with clocks, trains, and patents for devices that used signals traveling at the speed of light, was important to his thought process. Einstein himself once conceded that there was "a definite connection between the knowledge acquired at the patent office and the theoretical results."

At some point in the summer of 1905, Einstein sent a follow-on letter to Habicht, the same friend he'd written to just that May promising his five new papers. At the end of the note, Einstein tries to persuade Habicht to visit him: "Keep in mind that besides the eight hours of work, each day also has eight hours for fooling around . . . the value of my time does not weigh heavily these days; there aren't always subjects that are ripe for rumination." This luxury of having time on his hands was unusual for Einstein, who typically worked incessantly. Einstein scholar John Rigden once explained that from the time Einstein submitted his first paper in late 1900 until his death in April 1955, "physics consumed Einstein's waking hours. . . . The day before death stopped his work, he asked that his writing materials be brought to his hospital room. . . ." When Einstein told Habicht that there weren't "always subjects ripe for rumination," he meant that having upended the fundamentals of physics, he was now in search of a new problem worth solving.

It took Einstein another two years to find his next great problem. In the middle of 1907, Johannes Stark, a German physicist and himself a future Nobel laureate, sent a note to Einstein (who was still a patent clerk), asking him to write a monograph on the special theory of relativity in the journal that Stark moderated. At the time, Einstein was "dissatisfied with the special theory of relativity" because it applied only to specific cases where bodies were moving at constant velocities with respect to one another. He wanted to generalize the theory to make it universally applicable. While working on the paper that Stark requested, Einstein said that he "came to realize that all the natural laws except the law of gravity could be discussed within the special theory of relativity." This thought, whose culmination became the general theory of relativity, consumed Einstein for close to the next decade.

Einstein replied to Stark, telling him he'd be "glad to furnish the report . . . that you requested," but he did so with a caveat. In the two years since he'd published his original paper on special relativity, other physicists had begun responding to and expanding upon it. Einstein cautioned Stark that "I must also note that I am not in a position to acquaint myself with *everything* published on this topic, because the library is closed during my free time."

When he wrote his letter to Stark, Einstein had been searching for an academic job for seven years. He was an important and well-known physicist after 1905, but he was still on the fringes of the very field of science he'd just revolutionized. For a while, that had been fruitful for him. The patent office allowed him to dodge the more stifling parts of academia, but he was still able to share his ideas through the *Annalen*, and his closest friends were excellent scientific collaborators. But by 1907, his outsider status was becoming a hindrance to his continued discovery. Einstein needed a job that would pay him to think about physics, not sit in an office in which colleagues would kindly look the other way when he did so.

In 1909, nine years after his academic job search began and four years after he received his doctorate, Einstein finally received a professorship at the University of Zurich. Over the next four years, he and his family moved around Europe, with Einstein taking professorships in Prague and again in Zurich. Finally, in 1913, Max Planck and Walther Nernst, a German chemist, nominated him to the Prussian Academy of Sciences. In his acceptance letter to the Prussian Academy, he wrote:

I am no less grateful to you for offering me a post in your midst in which I can devote myself to scientific work free of any professional obliga-
tions. When I reflect upon the fact that each working day demonstrates to me the weakness of my thinking, then I can only accept the high distinction intended for me with a certain trepidation. But what encouraged me to accept the election was the thought that all that can be

expected of a person is that he devote himself with all his might to a good cause; and I do feel capable of that.

On inducting Einstein into the Prussian Academy, Planck said that Einstein's "real love is the discipline in which a personality most freely unfolds, in which imagination flowers most richly, and in which a scientist can most easily abandon himself to the comfortable feeling that he cannot be easily replaced by another." Einstein's impact on people went well beyond the strength of his intellectual insights.

"More Easily Than in Other Sciences"

The Prussian Academy was a formal institution, and Einstein was an irreverent man. A sort of roundtable of the German intellectual elite that met in person once per week to hear and discuss papers, everyone in the Academy was expected to wear a robe and behave in a dignified manner. Einstein did what was expected of him—he rarely missed a meeting, and respected the norms of the institution—but it's easy to imagine him as the class clown. A few weeks after settling in Berlin, Einstein described the Academy to a friend: "most of the members," he wrote, "restrict themselves to displaying a certain peacock-like grandeur in writing, otherwise they are quite human."

In his inaugural lecture to the Prussian Academy, presented on July 2, 1914, Einstein stood before the fifty or so other men seated in the Western Wing of the Prussian State Library. At thirty-five years old, Einstein was among the youngest in the room. He began his talk with humility: "I ask you to believe in my feelings of gratitude and the assiduousness of my striving, even if the fruits of my efforts may appear to you as meager ones." For the rest of the lecture, Einstein focused on how he conceived of theoretical physics, and argued for generalizing his special theory of relativity— outlining the problem he'd been working on since he sent his letter back to Johannes Stark seven years earlier, in 1907.

Planck, as secretary of the Academy's physical-mathematical "class," delivered the public reply to Einstein's inaugural lecture and began by praising him but went on to say that he "runs the risk of occasionally losing himself in dark regions and unexpectedly encountering hard contradic-

Einstein, now formally a part of the Academy, joins the other great physicists of the time at the 1911 Solvay Conference. Seated from left to right are Walther Nernst, Marcel Brillouin, Ernest Solvay (whose photo was added after the original picture was taken), Hendrik Antoon Lorentz, Emil Warburg, Jean-Baptiste Perrin, Wilhelm Wien, Marie Skłodowska-Curie, and Henri Poincaré. Standing from left to right are Robert Goldschmidt, Max Planck, Heinrich Rubens, Arnold Sommerfeld, Frederick Lindemann, Maurice de Broglie, Martin Knudsen, Friedrich Hasenöhrl, Georges Hostelet, Édouard Herzen, James Jeans, Ernest Rutherford, Heike Kamerlingh Onnes, Einstein, and Paul Langevin.

tion." Planck then said that he "could not resist the temptation" to argue that the special theory of relativity did not, in fact, need to be generalized. Planck dissented from Einstein's most important new ideas at the very moment he was sponsoring Einstein's induction into the Prussian Academy. As Planck continued in his response to Einstein's inaugural lecture, "Not without some pride [in physics] . . . more easily than in other sciences, the sharpest factual differences can be carried out with personal high esteem and cordial friendship."

Einstein had finally been baptized into the very establishment he had been trying to break into since his young days as a poor college graduate. Whereas once that community had accommodated his outsider status, now, as an insider, there was no expectation that Einstein change his ways. Einstein was modest, but he was always confident in his ideas, even when they ran counter to the status quo. Crucially, he was accepted as a peer of those who set the status quo, and was respected—and at times, revered—as someone who had original and oppositional insights. As long as he spoke his mind and communicated clearly, Einstein could be a leader in his community while still being himself. That said, Einstein was never an institutional figurehead. His leadership was interpersonal: it involved visiting, corresponding, writing, conversing, traveling, and communicating. In countless conversations, dozens of papers, and thousands of letters, he reframed how his colleagues understood the world. They, in turn, helped him to advance his own thinking.

"In the Service of This Problem"

Einstein had written his paper on special relativity in a mad rush of five weeks after ten years of hard work. Similarly, from 1907 through 1915, the focus of Einstein's pursuit was the general theory of relativity, and it was a long road of fits and starts that ended quickly and dramatically, and one that again required both solitude and kinship along the way.

He had conceived of the original insight that led to the theory while writing the article that Johannes Stark had requested from him in 1907. Around the same time, he conceived of another of his famous "thought experiments." As Einstein himself recounted: "The breakthrough came suddenly one day. I was sitting on a chair in my patent office in Bern. Suddenly a thought struck me: If a man falls freely, he would not feel his weight. I was taken aback. This simple thought experiment made a deep impression on me. This led me to the theory of gravity." The thought experiment suggested to Einstein that acceleration and gravitation were indistinguishable, an insight made possible only from the imaginary point of view of thinking about falling.

The central insight in this thought experiment was that he had to incorporate gravity and acceleration into his special theory of relativity. But as Einstein remembers of this day in 1907, "I could not solve this problem completely at that time. It took me eight more years until I finally obtained the complete solution. During these years I obtained partial answers."

While there are similarities in how Einstein arrived at both the special

and general theories of relativity—the thought experiments, intense solitude coupled with lively collaboration, a singular and relentless focus on
the essentials, and years-long persistence—the fact that he now had an academic job enlarged the cast of characters with whom Einstein could interact, and the sheer time he had to focus on physics. From 1905 through 1915,
he developed a much wider network than the ad hoc collaborators he'd
brought together earlier in his career. Old friends—particularly Michele
Besso, Marcel Grossmann, and Conrad Habicht—were very helpful to
Einstein in arriving at the general theory of relativity. But so too were a
wider set of new colleagues—scientific greats like Hendrik Lorentz, Heinrich Zangger, Arnold Sommerfeld, Paul Ehrenfest, and David Hilbert.

Einstein described the path to general relativity as a "chain of wrong
tracks, which nevertheless did gradually lead closer to the objective." One
such wrong track involved an experiment that might prove his theory. In
1911, he published "On the Influence of Gravitation on the Propagation of
Light" in the *Annalen*. At the outset of the paper, he wrote, "I have now
come to realize that one of the most important consequences of [my] analysis is accessible to experimental test. In particular, it turns out that . . . rays
of light passing near the sun experience a deflection by its gravitational
field." In the paper, Einstein predicted that "a ray of light traveling past the
sun would undergo a deflection amounting to . . . 0.83 seconds of arc," and
concluded that "it is greatly desired that astronomers take up the question
broached here." It was possible to measure the deflection of light around
the sun by taking photographs of a total solar eclipse. A couple experiments were planned in Russia during the upcoming 1914 solar eclipse, but
these experiments were scuttled by the outbreak of World War I.

This was actually a lucky break for Einstein. Had those experiments
occurred, Einstein's original calculations would have been shown to be
wrong. Eventually, his field equations (correctly) predicted that the sun
would deflect light by 1.7 seconds of arc. The discrepancy was caused by
another "wrong track." Einstein needed a different conception of geometry
from what he had available to him. He said that "describing the physical
laws without reference to geometry is similar to describing thought without words." He needed a new form of non-Euclidean geometry recently
theorized by mathematicians.

To learn this complex math, Einstein relied on his old friend Marcel Grossmann. Einstein fondly remembered his old friend's reaction to the call for help: "Instantly he was all afire, even though, as a true mathematician, he had a somewhat skeptical attitude to physics." He and Grossmann wrote a paper in 1913 whose calculations were wrong, but by that time Einstein was on the right track. "After two years of struggle," from 1913 to 1915, years he spent traveling extensively to collaborate with other colleagues, he wrote, "I found that I had made mistakes in my calculations. I went back to the original equation using invariance theory and tried to construct the correct equations. In two weeks the correct equations appeared in front of me!" He announced his general theory of relativity in a series of lectures on four consecutive Thursdays in Berlin, in November 1915.

By early 1916, Einstein was refining his recently completed general relativity theory. And, as usual, he was warmly corresponding with close friends, commingling science and interpersonal intimacy. On January 17, he penned a letter to Hendrik Lorentz, a Nobel laureate and a father figure to Einstein, and a man he'd grown to love. In his note, Einstein spent a page going through the problems with his field equations of gravitation. The physics done with, as usual, he concluded the note with warmth. "In thanking you again for your burning interest and even more for your intention to place your efforts in the service of this problem, I remain with heartiest greetings to you and yours, in friendship, yours truly."

Over the previous twenty years, the most productive of his life, dozens of people helped Einstein arrive at special and then general relativity. He was a leader precisely because his mode of thinking inspired men like Lorentz to work with him. Einstein articulated problems worthy of the service of the world's greatest scientists.

"My Name . . . Can Be of Benefit to the Cause"

In November 1952, David Ben-Gurion, prime minister of the newly created state of Israel, sat across from his assistant drinking a cup of coffee. Chaim Weizmann, Israel's first president, had died earlier in the week, and under public pressure Ben-Gurion had offered the post to the most famous Jew in the world, the seventy-three-year-old Albert Einstein, by then retired and living in Princeton, New Jersey. "Tell me what to do if he says yes!" Ben-Gurion pleaded with his assistant. "I've had to offer the post to him because it's impossible not to. But if he accepts we're in for trouble."

Thankfully for Ben-Gurion, Einstein wrote in a letter to Israel's ambassador to the United States, "I am deeply moved by the offer from our state [of] Israel, and at once saddened and ashamed that I cannot accept it. All my life I have dealt with objective matters, hence I lack both the natural aptitude and the experience to deal properly with people and to exercise official functions." In a letter to a friend, he was less formal: "The offer from my Israeli brethren moved me deeply. But I declined straight away with genuine regret. Although many a rebel has become a bigwig, I couldn't make myself do that."

Once he became famous for his physics, Einstein was asked to be a leader for many causes. And while he didn't accept the offer to become president of Israel, over the course of his life Einstein did use his fame in support of other efforts.

We can point to the day Einstein became famous. On November 6, 1919, the Royal Society of London hosted an event where it announced that British scientists, using Einstein's 1915 calculations, had confirmed that the sun deflected light by a measure of 1.7 seconds of arc. The general theory of relativity had been experimentally confirmed.

On November 7, the *Times* of London ran the headline: REVOLUTION IN SCIENCE; NEW THEORY OF THE UNIVERSE: NEWTONIAN IDEAS OVERTHROWN. Three days later, on the first column of the first page, the *New York Times* had a six-bar headline: LIGHTS ALL ASKEW IN THE HEAVENS, MEN OF SCIENCE MORE OR LESS AGOG OVER RESULTS OF ECLIPSE OBSERVATIONS. EINSTEIN THEORY TRIUMPHS. STARS NOT WHERE THEY SEEMED OR WERE CALCULATED TO BE, BUT NOBODY NEED WORRY. A BOOK FOR 12 WISE MEN. NO MORE IN ALL THE WORLD COULD COMPREHEND IT, SAID EINSTEIN WHEN HIS DARING PUBLISHERS ACCEPTED IT.

Einstein soon became a household name. After November 1919, his fame made him popularly influential. Einstein neither loved the spotlight nor loathed it, but he understood its necessity, and that his fame had broadened his influence and meant that people would ask him to champion their causes. Einstein didn't say yes to everyone, but neither was he afraid of being politically outspoken, even when it might have threatened his career. He'd had a rather public political disagreement with his German colleagues dating back to the outbreak of World War I.

Barely a month after the 1919 eclipse experiment, Einstein had been invited to participate in a meeting about the founding of Hebrew University. He wrote about it to his old friend Michele Besso: "I believe that this undertaking deserves energetic collaboration. The reason I am going to attend is not that I think that I am especially well qualified, but because my name, in high favor since the English solar eclipse expeditions, can be of benefit to the cause by encouraging the lukewarm kinsmen."

Two years later, in the spring of 1921, Einstein endeavored to raise money for the same cause on his first trip to the United States, stopping to give some lectures in England along the way. He wrote to Maurice Solovine, his friend from twenty years prior in Bern's Olympia Academy, saying: "I am not keen on going to America, but am just doing it on behalf of the Zionists, who have to beg for dollars for the educational institutions in Jerusalem, for which I must serve as famed bigwig." This trip caused conflict with his German colleagues. Fritz Haber, a chemist and German Jew who had converted to Christianity and developed chemical weapons for Germany in World War I, wrote to Einstein: "For the whole world you are today the most important of all German Jews. If at this moment you ostensibly fraternize with Englishmen and their friends, then people here at home will regard this as evidence of the disloyalty of Jews. . . ."

Einstein replied the same day he got Haber's note, politely but firmly telling him he'd be going on the trip. Mostly, Einstein was exceedingly courteous, but he could also be brutally straightforward: "If scholars would take their profession more seriously than their political passions, they would guide their actions more according to cultural aspects than political ones."

Einstein eventually renounced his longtime pacifism only in response to the rise of Adolf Hitler. The Nazis seized power on January 30, 1933, and the outspoken Jew could no longer safely remain in the country that had been his home for almost the last twenty years.

By 1933, he'd been to America a handful of times to lecture and conduct research, and he made the transatlantic voyage for the last time that

October. Einstein, now fifty-four years old, was leaving Europe behind, and with it the most productive years of his life.

"A Kind of Idol"

One hobby Einstein took with him from Germany to the United States was sailing. In the summer of 1939, he was vacationing on Long Island's North Fork, where he spent much of his time bobbing across the Little Peconic Bay in his fifteen-foot sailboat, *Tinef*—a Yiddish word meaning "worthless" or "junk." While he loved the peace of the water, he was not a gifted sailor. Even seventy years after his vacation there, dozens of locals in the town of Cutchogue, New York, still retold stories about rescuing Einstein as he struggled in his little boat.

In a photo taken that summer, Einstein is sitting on the edge of his boat adjacent to the bay, his puffy silver hair whipped by the wind half a foot above his forehead and to the right of his gently smiling face, the lips concealed by his bushy mustache. He's wearing a lightweight, open-collared white golf shirt, and blue shorts with white piping up the seam. On his feet are cream-colored women's sandals that had been sold to him by David Rothman, the brown-suited man sitting to Einstein's right in the photo.

David Rothman owned Rothman's Department Store. At the outset of his vacation, Einstein was looking for some sandals to wear on the beach. When Einstein had walked into the store looking for footwear, Rothman thought the famous sixty-year-old who spoke heavily accented English was looking for "sundials." Einstein cleared up the misunderstanding by pointing at his feet, and didn't seem to care that Rothman's carried only sandals for women. The two struck up a friendship when Einstein complimented the music playing in Rothman's store, and over the course of the summer the two met weekly to play the violin together.

That same summer, two emigré Hungarian scientists, Leo Szilard and Eugene Wigner, tracked Einstein down on Long Island. They warned Einstein about new work that made a nuclear chain reaction—and therefore nuclear weapons—possible. And they persuaded Einstein to send a letter to President Franklin D. Roosevelt explaining the direness of the situation. The final letter was drafted by Szilard and one of the president's advisers before Einstein signed it. The note warned how destructive nuclear

Einstein sitting next to his friend and erstwhile shoe salesman David Rothman on Long Island in the summer of 1939. That same summer, two other scientists found Einstein during his vacation, notified him about atomic weapons, and recruited him to send a letter about the weapons' potential to President Roosevelt.
(COURTESY OF THE SOUTHOLD HISTORICAL SOCIETY, SOUTHOLD, NEW YORK)

weapons could be and cautioned that German scientists were already trying to develop such a weapon. The note is the first record of the president's learning about the possibility of nuclear weapons. This and many other efforts led to the eventual creation of the Manhattan Project to develop the first atomic weapon. Einstein was not involved in that project and did not even learn of its existence until it was already well under way.

The seemingly contradictory combinations of eccentricity and approachability, of profundity and simplicity, are part of what made Einstein an intriguing figure to locals in Cutchogue, New York, and to Americans more broadly. And to an esoteric scientist like Szilard, Einstein's fame made him the perfect person to attract the attention of someone like the president of the United States. Much like his relationship to the Manhattan Project, for the last two decades of his life Einstein had to cope with being more famous than relevant. During this time Einstein played a role in physics, but he was no longer as central to ongoing discovery as he once was.

From 1933 until his death in 1955, Einstein lived in Princeton, New Jersey, taking over a post at the Institute for Advanced Studies. He occasionally lectured, but only when he wanted to. By the time he'd gotten to Princeton, much of physics depended on ideas that Einstein had helped to advance. Ironically, Einstein spent the last few decades of his life in tension with quantum physics, one of the very revolutions in physics that he had helped to enable. Einstein's ideas, in other words, were living a life of their own, quite apart from the man himself.

He'd always chosen to pursue fundamental problems to which there were not clear answers. He was accustomed to—and comfortable with—changing course along the way in pursuit of those answers. But he didn't change his essential goal. This mix of dogged persistence with respect to ends and openness to compromise with respect to means is a large part of what helped Einstein arrive at the general theory of relativity. That same approach meant he took his last breath in the pursuit of improving upon that theory. It also meant that by the end of his life, Einstein had become less of an active leader in the physics community and more of a self-described "petrified object," deeply respected and sought after for his past contributions, but viewed as out of step with the latest advances in the field.

In 1925, a group of scientists advanced the theory of quantum mechanics, which describes the interactions between the universe's smallest particles. Whereas the general theory of relativity is predictive, in quantum mechanics, the extent of what is knowable is only probabilistic. Einstein never disagreed with the logic of quantum mechanics, he just felt there was something more profound—more fundamental—behind things. As early as 1926, Einstein wrote to his friend Max Born, one of the founders of quantum mechanics: "Quantum mechanics is certainly imposing. But an inner voice tells me that it is not yet the real thing. The theory says a lot, but does not really bring us closer to the secret of the 'old one.' I, at any rate, am convinced that *He* is not playing dice." The same Max Born had earlier written that "the starting point of his considerations was a 'remark by Einstein on the relation between [a] wavefield and light quanta.'" Einstein therefore ended up in fundamental disagreement with an idea that he had helped spawn in the first place.

Because Einstein believed in nature's rationality and fundamental simplicity, he spent most of the last thirty years of his life unsuccessfully trying to bridge quantum mechanics with his theory of relativity, essentially searching for a "unified field theory" or a "theory of everything" that would tie together all of the universe's physical forces. During those thirty years, the scientific community, while maintaining great respect for Einstein's pursuit, mostly moved on without him.

While he became less important in the day-to-day scientific community, he was more popular than ever. The Einstein of 1933–55 is the man in the modern popular imagination: fuzzy slippers, disheveled hair, and no socks. It is not entirely inaccurate to remember Einstein as this stereotype, as the politically outspoken old man writing equations on scraps of paper.

He was, in fact, working on the unified field theory until the day he died in April 1955, and he did, in fact, remain politically outspoken. But this public view must be balanced with a more private image of the old man in his study at 112 Mercer Street, occasionally receiving guests, and always writing lovely letters. And in many of these letters, he mocked his own irrelevance, once calling himself a "petrefact," but one who never ceased to "sing his lonely old song." And there were letters where he comfortably described his "attitude towards the simple life," such as in a note to Max Born sent in April 1949: "I simply enjoy giving more than receiving, do not take myself nor the doings of the masses seriously, am not ashamed of my weaknesses and vices, and naturally take things as they come with equanimity and humor. Many people are like this, and I really cannot understand why I have been made into a kind of idol."

Or he would write lines eulogizing lifelong friends, as he did to the surviving family of Michele Besso, who died only weeks before Einstein in 1955: "Now he has preceded me a little by parting from this strange world. This means nothing. To us believing physicists the distinction between past, present, and future has only the significance of a stubborn illusion."

Einstein died quietly in 1955, five decades after rocking the scientific world with his special theory of relativity and other breakthrough concepts. But his image remains: the lovably disheveled genius lost in silent contemplation of how the world works—and why. His genius and the consequences of his efforts are undeniably real. But too often we miss the relationships that shaped and supported him. In the end, the magic of Einstein's leadership wasn't only his ability to run alongside waves of light, but his openness to having friends occasionally guide him.

LEONARD BERNSTEIN

My job is an educational mission.

—LEONARD BERNSTEIN

The front page of the November 15, 1943, edition of the *New York Times* was crammed with reports of the Second Great War. The United States, a country that Adolf Hitler had dismissed as "the mongrel nation," was emerging as the preeminent power that would lead in establishing a new postwar order. In the soon-to-be ascendant nation, America's cultural scene was brimming with the sense of a great awakening.

Nestled between the front-page articles detailing the gory matters of war, there was a single, comparatively pedestrian headline, YOUNG AIDE LEADS PHILHARMONIC, STEPS IN WHEN BRUNO WALTER IS ILL. Handsome, energetic, and abundantly confident, twenty-five-year-old Leonard Bernstein had his lucky break.

The previous evening, Bernstein had stepped onto the stage of Carnegie Hall, one of the great testaments to New York masonry and philanthropy, whose more than one thousand seats held some of the city's best-heeled classical music aficionados. The New York Philharmonic, fast becoming one of the world's most prestigious orchestras, had found a homegrown star conductor to call its own.

While in his later years fuller-faced and classically handsome, at twenty-five Bernstein, or "Lenny" as he was fondly known, still had the look of the Ivy League undergraduate about him, scrawny but impeccably dressed. The "Harvard accent" he had picked up in college removed any impressions of his middle-class Bostonian immigrant roots, and gave him a Gatsby-like air. In time, Bernstein's critics would say that he became better known for his aura than his music.

The audience was captivated by this fresh-faced boy wonder. As a New York Philharmonic musical assistant, Bernstein was expected to have a deep familiarity with the musical scores that he might be called upon to

THE PHILHARMONIC-SYMPHONY SOCIETY
1842   OF NEW YORK   1878
CONSOLIDATED 1928
ARTUR RODZINSKI, Musical Director

1943   ONE HUNDRED SECOND SEASON   1944

CARNEGIE HALL
SUNDAY AFTERNOON, NOVEMBER 14, 1943, AT 3:00
4025th Concert

Under the Direction of
~~BRUNO WALTER~~
LEONARD BERNSTEIN   Substitute

PROGRAM

SCHUMANN   Overture to "Manfred," Op. 115

MIKLOS ROZSA   Theme, Variations and Finale, Op. 13

INTERMISSION

STRAUSS   "Don Quixote" (Introduction, Theme with
Variations and Finale) ; Fantastic Variations on
a Theme of Knightly Character, Op. 35
Solo 'Cello: JOSEPH SCHUSTER
Solo Viola: WILLIAM LINCER

WAGNER   Prelude to "Die Meistersinger"

ARTHUR JUDSON, Manager   BRUNO ZIRATO, Associate Manager
THE STEINWAY is the Official Piano of The Philharmonic-Symphony Society
COLUMBIA AND VICTOR RECORDS

ORCHESTRA PENSION FUND—It is requested that subscribers who are unable to
use their tickets kindly return them to the Philharmonic-Symphony Offices, 113 W. 57th
St., or to the Box Office, Carnegie Hall, at their choice either to be sold for the benefit
of the Orchestra Pension Fund, or given to the uniformed men through the local
organizations instituted for this purpose. All tickets received will be acknowledged.
"Buy War Bonds and Stamps"

Leonard Bernstein's subsitute debut at the New York
Philharmonic on November 14, 1943.

conduct. Buttressing this profound familiarity, Bernstein had a vivacious personality, flair, and a natural enjoyment in interpreting music.

The *Times* reviewer lingered on young Lenny's flamboyant conducting style: "He was remarkably free of his score, which he followed confidently but without ever burying his nose in it. . . . He conducted without a baton, justifying this by his instinctively expressive use of his hands and a bodily plastic which if not always conservative, was to the point, alive and expressive of the music."

A subsequent editorial in the same paper added to this ringing endorsement of the performance: "Mr. Bernstein had to have something approaching genius to make full use of his opportunity. . . . It's a good American success story. The warm friendly triumph of it filled Carnegie Hall and spread far over the airwaves." And the tabloids were just as enamored. As New York's

Daily News put it, Bernstein's debut was "an opportunity like a shoe-string catch in mid-field. Make it and you're a hero. Muff it and you're a dope."

Bernstein was an overnight sensation in part because he was home-grown, a symbol of American talent in a field that had, until then, been staunchly European. The European powers, which had struggled endlessly for military and cultural supremacy, had their unique musical cultures. It was fitting that the United States should develop its own.

Looking to cultivate the arts, the New Deal instigated a Federal Music Project, which at its peak funded 125 orchestras, 135 bands, and 32 choral and operatic units across the country. This American venture was also served through transatlantic cultural interchange. Since 1937, Italian Arturo Toscanini was the most famous of the many musicians who exited war-torn Europe for a new life in America. He headed up the NBC Orchestra, with weekly performances broadcast live across the nation on radio. In the decades before the war, a nascent American style of classical music composition had been given momentum by Bernstein's mentor, Aaron Copland, whose score *Fanfare for the Common Man* (1942) became ingrained in the national psyche.

Leonard Bernstein stepped onto the podium in 1943 as the conductor who could give this classical music upswing a public face. It was a position he was well aware he might be called on to fill, writing to a friend four years before his debut: "The Big Boys [like Copland] (and thank God they're rooting for me) have it all decided that I am to become America's Great Conductor. They need an Apostle for their music."

"Closest Thing to Love Itself"

One of Bernstein's less favorable reviewers wrote of his debut that "some of the flares of temperament . . . might fruitfully be modified and the stamping of the foot should be avoided." But Lenny never took the advice of those who told him to "tone down" his conducting, and the foot-stomping became a well-known feature of the Bernstein house style. Nearly fifty years later, in 1989, Bernstein would conduct a special gala concert in Berlin, in celebration of the fall of the Berlin Wall. In the recording, Bernstein can be heard stomping his foot at moments of crescendo.

By 1943 the orchestral conductor, especially in prestigious orchestras like the New York Philharmonic, had become the most prominent leadership role in the world of classical music. It was expected that conductors' personalities should fill the stage. When Bernstein arrived on the scene with the charisma required to make the enjoyment of classical music a cultural norm, he became a leader in the classical music world and, with time, of American high culture.

Understanding how the conductor's leadership role had developed so that a man like Bernstein could fill it, we must first cross an ocean, turn back the clocks a century, and revisit the German city of Leipzig's concert hall, where in 1835 the great Felix Mendelssohn was conducting Bach's *St. Matthew Passion*.

Whereas today we are accustomed to the sight of an impassioned conductor controlling the orchestra, in Mendelssohn's time such behavior would have been deemed wholly inappropriate. In fact, the conductor was hardly the "leader" of the orchestra in any obvious sense. It was not an individual position, but a role performed in rotation with other philharmonic society members. It would have been considered rude for him to have his body turned away from the audience. He might beat to the first twenty or so bars of music, but after that his presence onstage was largely superfluous. Instead, he periodically joined in with the audience in applause, and was largely a spectator appreciating the quality of the music.

Leadership in the nineteenth-century orchestra did not reside with the conductor, but was a responsibility distributed across the entire assemblage. The German composer Robert Schumann, who attended Mendelssohn's 1835 performance, wrote of the conductor's diminutive role before concluding, "the orchestra should stand as a republic over which no higher authority should be recognized."

The baton, the iconic symbol of the conductor's authority, only emerged over time. It was introduced in Germany in the 1820s, and then taken up gradually throughout Europe, and was used to help musicians keep in time in larger concert halls and to more complex music. This was partly a matter of physics: the larger halls produced an echo effect that meant players had to ignore the sound of the music and instead look to the conductor's rhythmic baton to achieve unity. While useful, the baton was nonetheless deemed by instrumentalists to be an outrageous power grab by the conductor, who sought increasing authority.

In an attempt to level class signifiers in Soviet Russia, a new system of artistic production developed, whereby "delegates" from each section of the orchestra would attend a general committee to make certain decisions over how a piece of music should be interpreted. Still, the baton was symbolic of a broader trend: it was now the conductor's place to impose his personal interpretation on the musical score. All eyes, audiences' and instrumentalists' alike, were now on the conductor, firmly seen as leader of the flock.

By Bernstein's era, the conductor was expected to be the final arbiter of taste, and the expressive centerpiece of the performance. Still, compared to other conductors, Lenny's onstage bravado and profound emotional intensity were seen by some as overplaying what it means to lose yourself in the music. In a public lecture, he said the true conductor was one who had

great sensitivity to the flow of time . . . a kind of sculptor whose element is time instead of marble. . . . He must judge the largest rhythms, the whole phraseology of the work. He must conquer the form of a piece not only in the sense of form as a mold, but form in its deepest sense, knowing and controlling where the music relaxes, where it begins to accumulate tension, where the greatest tension is reached, where it must ease up to gather strength for the next lap, where it unloads that strength.

The modern conductor has become something of a storyteller. His facial expressions, hidden to most audiences, convey his relationship with the musical moment, and his instructions to individual players. Bodily movements do the same: they anticipate the sound of the music, bringing its story alive to an audience. For Bernstein, the story had to be communicated in all of its agony and ecstasy. He is memorialized in his *New York Times* obituary as "in moments of excitement, [leaving] the podium entirely . . . rising like a rocket, arms flung aloft in indication of triumphal climax."

Bernstein's style was instinctual. He once explained what the relationship with players felt like:

Finally, the great conductor must not only make his orchestra play, he must make them want to play. He must exalt them, lift them, start their adrenalin[e] pouring, either through cajoling or demanding or raging.

But however he does it, he must make the orchestra love the music as he loves it. It is not so much imposing his will on them like a dictator; it is more like projecting his feelings around him so that they reach the last man in the second violin section.

Successful conducting, for Bernstein, involved creating a feeling shared but also owned:

> . . . when one hundred men share his feelings, exactly, simultaneously, responding as one to each rise and fall of the music, to each point of arrival and departure, to each little inner pulse—then there is a human identity of feeling that has no equal elsewhere. It is the closest thing I know to love itself. On this current of love the conductor can communicate at the deepest levels with his players, and ultimately with his audience.

Lenny became known as a serial seducer. From his New York Philharmonic debut onward, Bernstein cultivated career-long relationships with American and international orchestras and their audiences. He was a tireless socialite and venerated as a genius who could turn his mind to anything. His looks certainly helped, and he had a magnetizing presence. In addition, his talent, charm, and the patronage he received from leading musicians like Aaron Copland helped him win his early success. Biographer Humphrey Burton wrote that Bernstein "replaced the received image of the conductor as a remote foreign autocrat with a self-portrait of the maestro as a young American, a jazz-loving, wise-cracking, boogie-playing, hat-spurning, self-deprecating fellow, still boyishly bewildered by his success." He was a rock star genius who happened to be a classical musician.

This jocular exterior masked a deeper, darker introspectiveness. From his early triumphs at the New York Philharmonic, it was partly the glimpse of this conflicted inner genius that made audiences and orchestras alike fall in love with Leonard Bernstein. A musical acquaintance who had just watched Lenny conduct sent him a "personality analysis," concluding that he was a "genius" who "is completely concentrated in his career. . . . This man has great ego-maniacal tendencies and will often go to bizarre ends to gain a point."

Finding Fame

In 1949, a film version of the hit 1944 Broadway musical *On the Town* was released, with leading roles played by eminent stars of classical Hollywood including Gene Kelly, Frank Sinatra, and Betty Garrett. There were an increasing number of classical musicians who collaborated in Hollywood productions, but Bernstein was unique in that he was treated like a fellow cast member in celebrity culture. His early work in musical theater, like *Fancy Free*, and later achievements, such as *West Side Story*, saw him embrace popular culture at the very same time that he was reaching his ascendancy in the classical music world.

On the Town depicts a raucous twenty-four hours of sightseeing and botched womanizing in New York City, as three sailors, Ozzie, Chip, and Gabey, enjoy a day's shore leave. Famous tunes composed by Bernstein, such as "New York, New York," convey the trio's excitement as they experience the heaving metropolis.

However, when it came to the 1949 Hollywood adaptation, Bernstein lost creative and directorial control. Along with standard chopping and changing, there were more crucial differences in the film's reinterpretation of the Broadway classic. First, in the film version, Bernstein's music—one of the first scores produced by an acknowledged American symphonist—was significantly cut. And where the stage version had been one of the earliest major Broadway productions to see a desegregated ensemble cast (i.e., one containing both whites and people of color) dancing with and touching one another onstage, the Hollywood film whitewashed this racially progressive element. Unlike the film, Bernstein and his collaborators' stage version of *On the Town* had expressly political aims. Notably, whereas in 1944 the US military remained segregated, in the play, black men donned Navy uniforms and performed alongside white sailors. So too in the play version, black and white dockworkers and a black policeman provided a glimpse of what a desegregated world might look like.

The earlier stage version had been delivered through a tight network of New York theatrical personalities, including Bernstein's lifelong friend Jerome Robbins, with whom Bernstein would later collaborate in the watershed *West Side Story*. One dancer told of the excitement of having Lenny attend *On the Town* rehearsals: "In bursts this flying apparition with his coat draped over his shoulders as a cape and his hair flying. 'Hello everybody,' he said . . . all us little kids were just struck dumb with admiration and love. . . . We would have gladly gone under trains for Jerry [Robbins] and Lenny because they were both geniuses."

Despite the inevitable frustrations of the creative process, Lenny adored composing for Broadway, and would later return to musical theater. He never wrote a piece as celebrated as Copland's *Fanfare for the Common Man*, perhaps in part because unlike for Broadway, composing symphonies is a solitary vocation, and Bernstein was a naturally collaborative worker. And even for the composer of stunning classical music, popular reception is hard to come by. Composing for Broadway, meanwhile, was highly collaborative, involving artists from a number of fields. Bernstein created the music, but there was also a play director, scriptwriter, actors, dancers, and many others involved. For Lenny, the output was more satisfactory because he could see it, talk about it, and improve on it with these collaborators. Broadway also brought with it more tangible returns, both financially and in terms of public reception.

But according to his mentors, this indulgence in musical theater was costing him precious time. In the wake of his serendipitous debut with the Philharmonic, Lenny had quickly become the hot ticket as a conductor of classical music. Criticism of his Broadway stints came in the form of a stern talking-to from his two most ardent mentors, composer Aaron Copland and conductor Serge Koussevitzky. Musical theater was seen as a frivolous diversion for Bernstein's naturally distracted mind. After watching the opening night of *On the Town*, Bernstein reports of Koussevitzky's reaction: "He was furious with me. He gave me a three-hour lecture the next day on the way I was going." One critic summed up the conundrum facing Bernstein at the time: "Leonard Bernstein would be a delightful conductor if he could ever forget . . . that he is being considered by Warner Brothers to be a potential film star." The world of classical music operates on a system

Leonard Bernstein conducting
a rehearsal at Carnegie Hall,
New York City, circa 1947.
(PHOTOGRAPH BY WILLIAM P. GOTTLIEB/IRA
AND LEONORE S. GERSHWIN FUND
COLLECTION, MUSIC DIVISION, LIBRARY OF
CONGRESS/GETTY IMAGES)

of patronage, and at this early stage of his career, Bernstein could not afford, nor would he have wanted, to lose these patrons.

Bernstein enjoyed blending the worlds of high culture and popular celebrity, but for now, he followed the cue of the patrons who had done so
much to help him find fame in higher-brow classical music. Leading fourteen different American orchestras as guest conductor in 1945 alone, he was
being coached for the role of music director of one of America's "Big Five"
orchestras. So, at least temporarily, he left Broadway. As he said, "I've done
that now. I like to do everything once, just to see what it feels like." This
was precisely part of his trouble: an insatiable desire to do everything not
just once, but *at once.*

Energy of the Jungle

"Astounding, demonic gifts," German critics lauded in May 1948, as
Bernstein concluded the first visit of an American conductor to Munich
since the end of the war. He had had some understandable reservations
about going to former Nazi heartlands and east of the Iron Curtain to
conduct. The dark ambiguities of leading some of these orchestras
remained—"fabulous, filthy, Nazi, exciting," as Lenny wrote to one friend
of the experience. Bernstein's name had crossed the Atlantic, and as in

America, he seemed a natural at developing the relationships necessary to book European tours with the continent's many orchestras.

In painful contrast to the grand, if run-down, environs of Central Europe's gilded concert venues, Lenny also took the opportunity to play in the squalid environs of remaining Jews who were, as he bitingly put it, "rotting in the [refugee] camps." The Jewish Representative Orchestra that he led, made up of surviving musicians of the liberated concentration camp Dachau, played to upward of five thousand refugees at each performance. "[I] cried my heart out," Lenny wrote.

Using classical music as a tool for both reconciliation and therapy was an about-turn, given the darker role it had played in the Second World War. All of the Allied and Axis powers had, in their own ways, found sounds to drown out the noise of war. Hitler had courted an array of musicians and conductors, seeing excellence in classical music as an endpoint of German supremacy. Hauntingly, at Auschwitz, conductor-composer Gustav Mahler's niece, Alma Rosé, directed a women's orchestra that regularly played Strauss, Beethoven, and Schumann to prisoners and SS officers. In Russia, the blaring out of Shostakovich's Symphony No. 7 in Nazi-besieged Leningrad (now St. Petersburg) was a classic use of psychological warfare. The Second World War had reverberated with the eerie sound of musical discipline.

Lenny's tours in Europe, in contrast, invoked the freshness and confidence of a victorious America. He became an arm of cultural diplomacy in a beleaguered continent. Amazingly, in these former Nazi strongholds, which had more than a trace of residual anti-Semitism, Bernstein was still able to steal the show. He was carried through the streets on the shoulders of fans after his May 9, 1948, performance in Munich. Then, after an audience had "stamped and shouted" in appreciation in Budapest, he was given the same rapturous public congratulation, where a singing review read: "This young genius brings to the surface the tremendous power and elementary energy of the jungle. . . . His virtuosity is not an end in itself. He inspires the orchestra to a performance without precedent."

In the days after these performances, the state of Israel was officially proclaimed, and Israel's formal recognition as the Jewish homeland was a moment held dear to Lenny, who at this time even considered settling there. The young Palestine Symphony Orchestra had first invited Lenny to travel to Palestine to conduct in November 1945, but they could not afford to cover his travel. It was nearly two years before Lenny could get there, but he loved it so much that he made it a regular destination, and he developed a lifelong relationship with the orchestra.

When he was conducting in Palestine, the intertwining of proud high culture and violence was even more marked than on his European tour. In many ways, the Palestine Symphony Orchestra—renamed the Israel Philharmonic Orchestra—was something of a spiritual home. Here, the young institution was filled with proud young Jews interested in their cultural heritage, broader questions of faith, and keeping alive their links with European traditions like classical music. Bernstein, himself a proud Jewish Bostonian, was also perennially interested in such matters. He spoke to the *Palestine Post* of the audiences who soaked up the sound of the performances he conducted: "They rise with the crescendo and sink down with the decrescendi. . . . They are like a barometer—there is nothing more subtle."

Bernstein would soon turn down the position of music director of the Israel Philharmonic Orchestra with a rare self-awareness, stating "I can't do everything." If not everything, he was nearly everywhere, though. In Europe, the Americas, the Middle East, and beyond, Bernstein was developing lifelong relationships. Each performance said something about Bernstein's specific relationship with individuals or groups of people. Collectively, they reflect the extent of what Bernstein had achieved, and what the world had asked of him.

A New Director, a New People, and a New Music

"I'm all for snobbism," Felicia Bernstein told a *New York Times* journalist, as she posed in sumptuous clothing from an upmarket New York City fashion house. The photographs of Mrs. Bernstein appeared in a half-page spread in the days before her husband's opening night on October 2, 1958, as music director of the New York Philharmonic, the first American-born citizen to hold that position in its history. In one, she wore a "softly tailored suit of ruby wool," appropriate, readers were told, for afternoon performances. In the other photograph, a more regal Felicia posed in what was termed a "first night" formal "gown of blue cut velvet."

Lenny had married Felicia Montealegre, a famous Chilean actress, on September 9, 1951. The couple had been engaged on and off for several years, and while their marriage started out as something of a compromise, the pair fell deeply in love, and in time Felicia became Lenny's north star. While on honeymoon, he reflected with friends what being married to him must feel like. The answer, he unnervingly concluded, "depends on what security she will manage to feel in a marriage contracted in insecurity. We hope and pray and we wait." Happily, Felicia was pregnant with their first child, a girl they named Jamie, after an extended three-month honeymoon, and the couple went on to have two more children, Alexander and Nina. For all the later complexities of the marriage, Lenny loved being a family man, a father, and a husband.

Felicia's October 1958 appearance in the *Times*'s pages was part of a publicity campaign to drum up attendance at the New York Philharmonic by younger, fashionable New Yorkers—wealthier and trendy "twentieth-century minded" people whom Lenny had enjoyed performing for before. For instance, New York socialite Elsa Maxwell called Bernstein's opening night "the most socially important affair of this or any season." Felicia spoke of there being "a lot of new life in the symphony," and getting young, wealthy New Yorkers to go would mean that "some people may attend to show off their mink, find they enjoy the music and become devoted to the Philharmonic."

Bernstein had as late as 1955 told journalists that "I have never wanted an orchestra of my own because immediately I'd become bogged down. I might be able to compose symphonies but I'd never be able to do theater work." Opting to do so two years after this statement, he admitted at a press conference, "We're getting old, you know." Bernstein sought respite from the grind of national and international travel that was involved in being one of the world's most celebrated guest conductors. "We just don't have the energy we had at twenty. One begins to center on certain things."

In any case, the Bernsteins had a curious definition of "[settling] down to a single job," as Felicia put it, given that the many responsibilities involved in Lenny's new position—and the countless other projects he involved himself in—were mammoth.

He signed on as music director with a commitment to conducting sixteen weeks each year. Where his predecessor had conducted an annual average of 131 concerts during his 1951–57 tenure, Bernstein's first five years saw an increase to 165 concerts per annum, and the second five years he was at the helm that increased to 192 each year. In addition, the Philharmonic recorded, Bernstein "plans the format for each season; determines the general content of the programs; selects and co-ordinates guest conductors and soloists; handles orchestral personnel problems; studies scores; and plans concert tours including selecting artists and programs for tours." It was a role that meant both leading an orchestra of elite musicians, but also leading a venerable institution, with the manifold personnel and administrative challenges involved in that. He had that entire institution supporting him, but Lenny was there to lead and craft it.

Alongside Felicia's promotion of the Philharmonic as a venue for high society fashionistas, Lenny also implemented several of his own personal aesthetic changes, including modern new uniforms and a regular, more casual series of "Preview Concerts." Moreover, on his Israel tour, a bad back had seen Bernstein take to using a baton, concluding that doing so would "add ten years to his career." From this point forward, after eighteen years of gesturing with his hands, he used custom batons sourced from a musician based in Bayside, Queens—always seventeen inches long, whittled from birch, and capped with a pear-shaped ball of cork (at his death in 1990, he was buried with one of them). This did nothing to change his flamboyant style: *The New Yorker* compared his conducting, freshly armed with this new implement, to a Byzantine monk frantically shaking martinis.

For Lenny, this was about cultivating America's artistic soul. Before his arrival, Lenny had noted a lack of discipline in the New York Philharmonic orchestra: "a raggedness, a lack of ensemble, of precision, of intonation." Bernstein's leadership brought in a renewed focus on learning, not just for audiences, but for the elite orchestra too. "My job is an educational mission," he told the *New York Times*.

Members of the orchestra found themselves spending hours a day revisiting the nuts and bolts of music they thought they already knew like the back of their hands. Paying close attention to anything from breaths to pauses to irksome quirks in the score ended up giving a freshness to what the

instrumentalists had otherwise been playing on repeat, with little differen-
tiation, for most of their professional lives. Because Bernstein was happily
still learning too, this created a leveling dynamic in which, as his biographer
puts it, "He was one of them and yet demonstrably he was their master."

Soon Lenny's gifts as a teacher were brought into the public eye, and
made Bernstein a household name across the country, through two televised series he presented, *Omnibus* (1954–61) and the *Young People's Concerts* (1958–72). *Omnibus*, a program for adults, opened up the closed shop
of the classical music world to novices, attempting to respond to audiences'
simple but commonplace intrigues on musical topics.

The first show, on Beethoven's Fifth Symphony, aired on CBS on November 14, 1954, and aimed to give audiences a layperson's insight into just how
Beethoven had come to pen a work of such historic magnitude. A natural
public performer, Lenny gave some insight into how he—and Beethoven—
approached the art of composition: "the composer . . . leaves [one] at the
finish with the feeling that something is right in the world, that checks
throughout, something that follows its own law consistently, something we
can trust, that will never let us down."

The subsequent *Young People's Concerts* were designed for children, and
aimed to introduce a new generation of Americans to classical music. These
concerts showed Bernstein at his didactic best, and elucidated his entire thinking on music. Each evening was attended by thousands of young children,
who were occasionally captured on camera with jaws wide open in amazement, or with faces beaming at a Lenny joke or his rendition of a popular
musical piece. The program became a staple for young American musicians,
and many successful professionals of the following generation spoke of the
Young People's Concerts as the source of their musical inspiration when growing up. Lenny was a born communicator, and he could understand the way a
curious child's mind works just as well as he could one of his disciplined in-
strumentalist's.

These episodes would deliberately cut across all genres of music, from
jazz to classical. Indeed, Bernstein had been thinking about how to combine utterly different kinds of music since his college days. Then, at age
twenty, he had written of how America's racial history, combined with a

unique nationalism that had been developing since the beginning of the twentieth century, was creating a unique moment for American music. Jazz was at the heart of this emergent music culture.

In an argument well ahead of Ivy League social discourse, he had discussed how music could help translate what he called the "material" conditions of America's "racial elements" into "spiritual" or artistic conditions: "These elements are soluble, adaptible [sic]; in heterogeneous America it is the delicate balancing of them which determines the composer's particular, personal Americanism." The three main cultural influences, Bernstein believed, were those of African Americans, who had created jazz, New Englanders ("the greater-British races [which] form the racial and social backbone of the country"), and the composer's individual heritage. He had concluded that "the confluence of these three streams has become the mighty American river which is now, for the first time, pouring its fulness [sic]—a genuinely indigenous contribution—into the sea of world music."

Lenny believed that these ideas would come to have real effects on musical culture. But many of them were left unrealized, in part because he could not settle on the sort of career that would enable him to make the kind of music whose form seems to have come from deep within him. It was his greatest ambition, but the source of lifelong personal frustration, that he would not become the greatest tributary flowing into this "mighty American river." This conflicted "double life" also affected his personal relationships. He wrote to his sister:

> My world changes from one of abstractions and public-hungry performance to one of reality, a world of creativity . . . travel and rest and love and warmth and intimacy . . . how through I am with the conducting-performer life . . . and how ready I am for inner living, which means composing and Felicia.

After fifteen years of relative hiatus from composing new work since *West Side Story* (1957), Bernstein tried to reconcile many of these inner divisions and ideas about music in a new creative masterpiece.

Mass

Mass: A Theatre Piece for Singers, Players and Dancers was a musical extravaganza to commemorate the life of America's first Catholic president, John F. Kennedy, and also the piece commissioned for the 1971 grand opening of a new institution named after him, the Kennedy Center for the Performing Arts in Washington, DC. A longtime friend and confidant of the Kennedys, and by the 1970s the nation's most celebrated musical genius, Bernstein was the natural choice for the new commission.

Composing *Mass* was always about finding the right ending. It was something between a celebration and a memorial, intended to provide symbolic closure but also a more literal grand opening. At least in public, Lenny was a "glass half-full" person, and that was reflected in many of his most important creative decisions. Ending the work on a note of fuzzy fulfillment might have seemed disingenuous to some, but many audiences expect a happy ending; Lenny wanted one too.

Bernstein's piece delivered a combination of jazz, rock, symphonic-classical style, and Broadway. Somewhere between a musical, a festival, and a symphony, it was Lenny's most original work, and its hybrid nature harked back to the ideas of his Harvard thesis, exploring different "streams" or genres of music "sneaking into" one another. It was trying to produce music unique to American conditions. Lenny commented that "I feel it's a work I've been writing all my life." While jarring to some, the work is eminently American, and uniquely Bernstein.

With its religious underpinnings, Bernstein's *Mass* follows the story of a central character called the Celebrant, the priestly leader of the *Mass*, who hopes for world peace, and yet who is struck down by wayward followers and goes insane in the process. Given the dedication of the work, many saw the story (less the insanity) as analogous to the lost promise of President Kennedy, and the fraught foreign policy of the decades after his death.*

It was a work shrouded in political controversy. Where Bernstein had

*Bernstein himself also identified with the Celebrant protagonist, telling an interviewer that "*Mass* follows three years of despair, since Russian tanks invaded Prague [in August 1968]. When I'm writing, my first impulse is to communicate. So I stand for the audience. So the Celebrant is an extension of my thought."

been a kind of "court musician" to the Kennedy White House, under President Nixon, Lenny and Felicia—overt in their left-wing leanings—fell out of favor, and FBI investigations concerning their political activities were ramped up. Lenny's chief musical assistant for *Mass* recalls him (apparently only half jokingly) proposing an ending in which the Celebrant, mad and half naked, slams the door of the Kennedy Center and shouts "Fu*k you and your War," with "the cast spread about the stage, and the audience, Nixon and the entire Congress of the United States, left sitting there, abandoned, stunned. And that's how the piece ends."

Nixon was told in advance by the FBI that he should not attend the *Mass* premiere in case its Latin lyrics contained anti-administration messaging to which he might find himself unwittingly applauding. That same musical assistant (again, perhaps only half jokingly) later mooted that his private conversation with Bernstein about the ending must have been wiretapped, given the subsequent political fallout. A White House tape of a conversation between President Nixon and his chief of staff, H. R. Haldeman, reflects the suspicion Bernstein's creation was held in by the administration:

Haldeman: The reason you should not go to the other [opening] . . . is that [it's] this *Mass*, written by Leonard Bernstein . . .
Nixon: Oh sh*t, I know him.
Haldeman: . . . which is very, very bad . . . it has some political overtones to it . . . a sort of everything's-gone-wrong kind of thing . . . and it would be very inappropriate for the President to attend.

Based on the final output, these concerns ended up being overblown, but Nixon did not attend the premiere, and instead gave his box to Jacqueline Kennedy, by then Mrs. Aristotle Onassis.* Still, while no curses were thrown at the president or congressmen, finding the right ending to *Mass* presented a great challenge to Bernstein.

Staging the work was a masterpiece in coordination alone, with more

---

*For personal reasons, Mrs. Onassis waited until a June 1972 revival to watch *Mass*, after which she sent Lenny a photograph of the two of them, signed with the personal inscription: "Lenny—I loved it, yes I did and I love you too—Thank you so much for making *Mass* so beautiful."

than two hundred performers involved in the final production. From the Berkshire (Massachusetts) Boys' Choir (who learned their parts at their summer camp) to the seventy-eight dancers, singers, and musicians (who convened daily in New York), pulling it together for the final show in Washington reflected Bernstein's ability to combine diverse artistic talent and his instinctive love of extensive collaboration. Some questioned why he and his Jewish colleagues would be interested in basing a major work around the Catholic Mass. Reflecting on this, Lenny referred to his working on the piece as "inevitable," and given his propensity to entertain heterogeneity and live in ambiguities, it is not difficult to see why.

Despite the phenomenal pooling of talent, Bernstein kept to himself both the penultimate and last scenes of the work. In fact, his many other commitments meant that he was still hurriedly finishing the scenes as cast members convened in Washington for final rehearsals at the end of a frantic summer of collaboration. The cast did not know what would happen at its climax, nor did they have a true sense of how all the parts would come together. Eventually, he offered up his handiwork to the cast. The penultimate song, "Fraction: 'Things Get Broken,'" sees the cast sing in despair, angrily directing their frustrations at their leader, the assailed Celebrant:

> We're fed up with your heavenly silence,
> And we only get action with violence,
> So if we can't have the world we desire,
> Lord, we'll have to set this one on fire!
> Dona nobis, Dona nobis.

The Celebrant goes into a crazed frenzy at his followers' demands and threats, and ends by babbling in Latin, Hebrew, and English, before exiting the stage, leaving his followers splayed across the floor. His earlier cries, "PA . . . CEM! PA . . . CEM!! PA . . . CEM!!!" (Peace! Peace!), had fallen on deaf ears. It reflected something of both Lenny's inner despair at world events like the Vietnam War and the bloody end President Kennedy had met.

But again, Bernstein did not wish to finish on such a sorry note. At last, in the days before the first performance, he shared with his team his final piece, appropriately named "Secret Songs," which, as his musical assistant records, "breathed a bereft, leaderless, and fractured community back into life." There was no angst at contemporary politics; instead, *Mass* concludes on a message of hope. Recalling these final, frantic rehearsals, his assistant, who was also booked to conduct the premiere (and therefore whose knowledge of the score was especially paramount), wrote: "In retrospect I realize that this manipulation of the company [giving the final pieces to them just beforehand] was Bernstein's way of protecting his message from the inevitable criticism of the pessimists . . . of this world."

Coming after the apocalyptic "Fraction," the final words of *Mass* occurred as the lights dimmed, and Bernstein's voice rang across the auditorium: "The Mass is ended; go in peace." This was Lenny's creative apex, one that came after nearly fifteen years of writing very little music. It was flamboyant and messy, and partly because of Bernstein's celebrity status at this stage, his collaborators were unable to tame his extravagance and tendency toward percolating—rather than penning—creative thought. But the final product was still brilliant. *Mass* carried with it Lenny's innate sense of hope for humankind, and it was his musical gift to the world.

The project's completion was cathartic for all involved. But as this great musical, creative, and symbolic synthesis occurred, Lenny's private life intruded.

Reflections on a Life

By the time of *Mass*, Bernstein had retired from his role as music director of the New York Philharmonic, drawing to a close a long and successful ten-year tenure. It was the most important relationship of his life. Twenty-five years since his debut, he had conducted more than eight hundred concerts as music director, of which thirty-six had been world premieres. His parting gift from players in May 1969 was a silver and gold mezuzah, a symbol of faith for Jews and often fixed to the doorposts of their homes. It was their way of telling Lenny that the New York Philharmonic would always be his home.

Bernstein had accepted the directorship on the grounds that he wanted to settle down into a steady rhythm for his work and well-being's sake. His leadership position had allowed him little respite—in fact, his routine had been punishing—but it had kept him grounded and with a home base.

After working on *Mass*, the last six or seven years of Lenny and Felicia's life together were not entirely happy ones. He met Tom Cothran, a music director of a Los Angeles radio station. The pair fell in love, and Cothran quickly became part of the Bernstein inner circle. The relationship was both sexual and professional. With some hiatuses, it would continue through to Felicia's death from lung cancer in 1978.

The affair became particularly divisive to the Bernstein family from 1975 onward, and caused Lenny and Felicia to separate in July 1976. Lenny had had affairs along the way, but that he had fallen in love with Cothran was a step too far for Felicia.

As he moved from hotel to hotel, Lenny's falling-out with the woman who had given him much of his stability in the previous decades unanchored him. When conducting, he was more often seen to miss the mark in his usually faultless technical delivery. But the personal turmoil seems if anything to have helped him keep his attention on the world of music-making, the focus of work becoming a welcome distraction.

Within a year of this public fallout, Lenny and Felicia had rekindled their relationship. Felicia was now ill, and soon diagnosed with lung cancer, and died within twelve months. Her death may have brought Lenny greater personal freedom, but that freedom did not bring self-fulfillment.

Instead, he became possessed by the idea that he had caused Felicia's death, and became an at times melancholy, and increasingly difficult, person. Being a leader of the arts world did not give him the most private of mourning periods. Just two months after Felicia's passing, at a fund-raiser where he was guest of honor, a speaker pronounced to a huge crowd of friends, colleagues, and family: "Leonard Bernstein will have to live with the memories of their many good times and also with those of the last horrible months. Perhaps he will become the wiser for it, and these memories will lead him to create even greater things." Lenny later referred to this as "the most horrible night of my life."

THE FINAL TWELVE YEARS of Lenny's magisterial career felt to him like a race against time. To one interviewer, he said: "I don't mind that I'm aged, that my hair is white, that there are lines in my face. What I mind is the terrible sense that there isn't much time."

Despite all his achievements, Bernstein remained sensitive to questions about legacy. He feared that the only work of his that would be celebrated posthumously was *West Side Story*. In itself, this was a genre-defining work. According to Ruth Leon, who knew him during his later career, "His masterpiece is *West Side Story*, which he never accepted or believed.... But after you write *West Side Story*, nothing else really matters."

But as the 1980s marched on, and despite his anxieties, it did not seem that he could give up his insatiable desire to continue with international conducting tours. An enormous commitment of time and energy, his addiction to conducting compromised his ability to finish new compositions. Even after booking out 1981 as a sabbatical year, he ended up spending nearly half of it on the road.

In May 1983, a cutting lead article in *Harper's* concluded that Lenny was more interested in applause than permanence. It probed: "It was a career that could have transformed American music. What in our culture and in himself led our most gifted musician to squander it?" Lenny became frazzled about what projects he should now turn his attention to. It was a tension that he never fully reconciled, and he later said, "I can't myself decide whether I have achieved everything, or a portion, or a fraction." In an interview, Leon said: "I believe Lenny died a disappointed man because he knew how good a pianist he was. He knew how good a conductor he was. He knew how good a teacher he was. But all he ever wanted was to be Aaron Copland, and he was never going to be that."

In these last years, Lenny left a special imprint as an educator. Geniuses tend to be remembered for the originality of their work, but late Bernstein's greatest impact was educating a new generation in the musical canon and in helping them unlock their artistic potential. In 1990, with just months left to live, he said: "I want to devote most of the remaining energy and time the Lord grants me to education."

Teaching a trainee musician is not simply a case of telling them how to play a note or wave a baton most effectively. It is a more relational, tactile skill, taking vast time and energy from teacher, student, and patient orchestra. Teaching each piece is iterative, relies on deep personal knowledge from teacher and student, and a willingness from both to appreciate the intricacies of musical history. It is instructional only in the most dynamic and interpersonal sense of that word. Bernstein pointed to the subtleties of this kind of teaching in an interview a year before his death:

> Everything I do is to the orchestra—what the audience sees from their side is their business. I can't be responsible for that. I don't plan gestures, I've never rehearsed in the mirror. And when my students ask me what they should do to get an orchestra to play the way I did, I can't tell them—I have to ask them what I did. . . . I just advise them to look at the score and make it come alive.

So it was fitting that Lenny should conduct his last performances at America's premier musical education establishment, Tanglewood, in the Berkshire hills of western Massachusetts. It was the fiftieth anniversary of the music school, the one to which Lenny had given the most time. No video recording of this performance was made, but a sound recording was later released. During the final piece in the program, Beethoven's Seventh Symphony, the recording is not able to convey the physical and mental strain Lenny was under.

While, as always, smartly turned out in his staple summer white jacket and black bow tie (one he had worn for years—while that night it was raining, Tanglewood's summer festivals were said to bring sunny "Bernstein weather"), he was now a frail man, hunched over, with grayish skin, and unable to conduct with hands much above his waist. The members of the Boston Symphony Orchestra—who aside from those of the New York Philharmonic were Lenny's closest classical colleagues— were so familiar with Lenny leading them that they could by this time almost totally rely on the penetrating flits of his eyes as they moved across the different orchestra sections.

Lenny, conducting the Boston Symphony Orchestra at the climax of Mahler's Resurrection Symphony, again at Tanglewood, in 1970.
(BETTMANN/CONTRIBUTOR)

But in the third movement of Beethoven's Seventh, with his ninety-one-year-old mother and children watching anxiously in the audience, Lenny, ashen, was seized by a coughing fit, propping himself up against the back of the podium and gasping for breath.

His hands wrapped around a red handkerchief to contain the noise; his arm movements halted. Eye contact with the players was broken. But the BSO, true to form, played on. The brass instruments trumpeted with renewed determination, acting as a triumphal tribute to the man who had led them with such vitality for forty-seven years. He had taught them well; and they played on, leaderless.

For the fourth and final movement, the players willed him back into position. Agonizingly, Lenny found the breath and energy to lead on. As the symphony came to an end, some in the audience may have guessed that this would be the last ovation they would give to Leonard Bernstein.

No matter. As the crowd rose in unison from their seats, Lenny and his orchestra remained in their solemn gaze. Silently facing one other, the maestro and his loyal players continued, the music now just etched in memory, to explore those intricate, often unspoken webs of being and belonging of which we are all a part.

THE GENIUS NEXT DOOR

Lenny was like everyone else only more so, but nobody else was like him.
—NED ROREM

In a 1944 *New York Times* interview, Albert Einstein asked, "Why is it that nobody understands me, and everybody likes me?" The question was quintessentially Einsteinian, for it probed his own paradox. Einstein's theories sat beyond most people's comprehension and yet, the older he grew, the more his persona was humanized. After all, he became estranged from his first wife and married his cousin, was famous for forgetting routine things, and had a disheveled manner that belied his brilliance. Einstein was at once inaccessible and intimately relatable.

Forty-six years later, the week after Leonard Bernstein's death, the *New York Times* ran a series of remembrances "by his friends." One friend, the composer Ned Rorem, was besieged by media calls asking "So what was he really like?" Among other descriptions, Rorem replied that "he had, and forever retained, a biblical look, handsome and nervy as the shepherd David who would soon be king. . . ." But his more telling testimonial was that "Lenny was like everyone else only more so, but nobody else was like him." Like Einstein, Bernstein seemed both among us and beyond us.

For both of them, their mark on history cut far deeper than the edge of their genius, but it is difficult to put a finger on why. Did Bernstein's undeniable confidence and attractiveness play a role in his rise? Would Einstein have become the world's most famous person if not for his endearing eccentricity and affability? There was more to their genius than intelligence, just as there was more to their leadership than their genius.

We tend to see both leadership and genius as within an individual, rather than coming from a system. The popular idea of Einstein as a "lone genius" is appealing but inaccurate. It's telling that Einstein's correspondence is so prolific—he had a network of collaborators that proved critical to his achievement, and his genius was only made whole through the coupling of his legendary, solitary reflection with his lesser-known interpersonal collaboration.

As we read through Einstein's letters, it was difficult for us to parse through the physics that dominates so much of his correspondence. But it was easy for us to grasp his wry wit (he opens the most impressive letter in the history of physics by calling his friend Conrad Habicht a "smoked, dried, canned piece of soul"), and to feel the joy exuding from his words when exchanging ideas with other scientists. We were left with the impression that while other physicists corresponded with Einstein because he made the most fundamental physical discoveries of his time, they also genuinely enjoyed their back-and-forth for its own sake.

Bernstein, on the other hand, was known for his social and gregarious nature, but was made whole by his lesser-known need for solitude. Bernstein understood that while he was capable of being an extroverted performer as a conductor, his role as a composer was as "an introspective person, with a stronger inner life. . . ." He once told NBC News that he had come to regret spending too much time conducting and not enough energy composing, realizing: "I have to be both—that's where the strain comes in almost to a schizophrenic degree."

This duality of collaboration and solitude cuts against our simple narrative of genius. It is tempting to distill both Bernstein and Einstein down to their dominant reputations, with Lenny as the archetypal extrovert who thrived on collaboration and shunned isolation and Einstein as his polar opposite. But the true depth of genius requires both individual skill and the feedback and challenge of collaboration to be made whole. These men may have seemed to contain their genius within themselves, but as with leadership, when we look closely, we see that their individual achievements are also inseparable from collective interaction within a system.

For instance, Einstein extended his field's frontiers, and set the agendas for generations of scientists still coping with the implications of his insights to this day. But it is also the case that without the field of physics—and its centuries of stored knowledge and institutions designed to exchange ideas—an Einstein wouldn't have been possible in the first place.

All of this speaks to how the concept of genius is comparable to the concept of leadership, but we are still left with the question: How did their genius become leadership?

It is not enough to put them into a category like "thought leadership" and be done with it, for their influence transcended their academic fields. And while both our geniuses were deeply influential in their fields, neither was a leader in the traditional sense. Einstein was the most cited physicist of the twentieth century, but he was never at the top of an organizational chart, and he evaded the distraction of formal leadership roles. Bernstein, by contrast, managed one of the most important institutions in classical music—the New York Philharmonic. But his influence extended well beyond the limits of institutional authority, shaping the world's expectations of music and what a conductor was supposed to be. In both cases, they each grew to have profound influence with surprisingly little formal authority.

It is also not enough to chalk up their leadership to the fame that grew from their achievements and performance. They were each virtuosos of their respective crafts, but their influence went well beyond the fame that came from technical mastery in their fields. For instance, their respective mentors Aaron Copland and Max Planck were comparable in the depth of their genius, and even in their influence within their fields, but not in the way that Bernstein and Einstein became social leaders on a grander scale.

What made Einstein and Bernstein different as leaders was their ability to connect their genius with a broad followership. By its very nature, genius is inaccessible, and must be made accessible to be popularly relevant. Connecting with others not only made their genius possible, it is also what made their genius popularly relevant.

Most groups select leaders with only *slightly* above-average intelligence, presumably because they find it difficult to relate to those with exceptional intelligence. Followers desire competence and intelligence in their leaders, but also want them to remain relatable. This is why the relationship between leadership and genius is so curious. While leaders are generally intelligent, *exceptionally* intelligent people are actually *less likely* to emerge as leaders.

While Bernstein's and Einstein's technical mastery brought them an audience, each needed ways to connect that audience with their genius for their influence to find its special breadth. As much as their achievements, it was Bernstein's and Einstein's openness to the world that connected their esoteric achievements to a popular audience.

Once we are connected with genius, it becomes doubly powerful, for its aura of sense-making provides valuable understanding, while at the same time the tension of gaining access to something that's seemingly inaccessible evokes a sense of awe. This coupling, of understanding and awe, or of clarity and bewilderment, is a powerful form of informal and noncoercive leadership. More simply put, we often want our leaders to be like us, but also something more.

Both Einstein and Bernstein benefited from this human tendency to be drawn into the space between understanding and wonder, to affix one's gaze on those who are somehow both among us and beyond us. This is the animating power of genius, whereby we feel more alive in its presence.

All of this holds up the idea that we turn to geniuses and leaders less for what they produce, or even for what they've achieved, and more for the sense of meaning they offer. We may not want our leaders to be geniuses, because we want them to be relatable. But when we encounter a genius who is somehow made relatable, we are often captivated by and allow for that genius to emerge as a leader. This accessible inaccessibility provides for an invigorating sense of renewal by stretching boundaries and making space for new possibility.

When the disheveled and intimately relatable Albert Einstein stood before us and asked in plain language, "Why is it that nobody understands me, and everybody likes me?," the answer could well have been "Precisely."

Five

THE ZEALOTS

It is the certainty that they possess the truth that makes men cruel.

—ANATOLE FRANCE

B lurred by the scratched plastic window of the helicopter, and barely illuminated by the dull early morning light, the distinctive terrain nonetheless told a story. Perched above the Judean Desert and overlooking the Dead Sea, Masada is a natural fortress. But on the terrain surrounding Masada, the still extant outlines of a besieging Roman legion's campsite and the huge ramp they constructed to breach the mountaintop refuge, were clear reminders of how it ended in 73 CE.

After we landed, amid the hallowed ruins that have come to symbolize unwavering commitment, our Israeli counterparts reviewed the history of the splinter element from the Zealot political movement that furiously fought to defend Masada, and then ultimately committed mass suicide in their mountain fortress to avoid surrender. This 2006 military exchange trip was more than simple sightseeing; with little attempt at subtlety, the Israelis were communicating their own resolve against the many foes who still threatened them.

The willingness of these Zealots to murder their families, and then themselves, to prevent subjugation has made the name of their movement synonymous with absolute, seemingly unreasonable, commitment to an idea or cause. The modern moniker "zealot" can imply the erasure of conventional boundaries of behavior, where anything is justified in support of the goal. And leaders who inspire others to seemingly irrational commitment are a special breed that can generate hurricanelike winds of disruption and change.

As we examined the role of zealots in leadership, we found they need not dress, act, or even think alike. They can be vastly different in education, experience, demeanor, and ultimate effectiveness. They need only to share an absolutism in pursuit of their objective.

In seeking ideologically driven leaders to profile and compare, we considered a range of figures from the pre–Civil War abolitionist John Brown to ardent revolutionaries like Ho Chi Minh. Even the Reverend Jim Jones, who inspired more than nine hundred of his followers to "drink the Kool-Aid" laced with poison, was considered. Unwavering commitment to a cause was a prerequisite, but ultimately our search narrowed to individuals whose passion led them to extreme actions.

For many, the Frenchman Maximilien Robespierre, now more than two centuries dead, is a two-dimensional character who ruled over the chaos of revolutionary France with the guillotine. By contrast, the Jordanian Ahmad Fadeel Nazal al-Khalayleh (aka Abu Musab al-Zarqawi), the founder and leader of Al-Qaeda in Iraq, against whom we waged a bitter, blood-soaked campaign, seems to fit the context of our times. We reviled Zarqawi's tactics, but we came to grudgingly respect his effectiveness and commitment. And as we studied Robespierre in history and Zarqawi in hindsight, the very real complexity of these leaders came into focus.

Robespierre and Zarqawi, born 208 years and a continent apart, would likely have been uneasy colleagues. The vast differences in how they looked, how they learned, and ultimately how they led obscure the fundamental reality that they shared a dogged, fanatical sense of devotion to their cause. Each would kill—Robespierre with a pen from afar, Zarqawi with a knife up close—and both became renowned for their willingness to spill blood.

Their similarities go beyond their association with death. Each led differently, but both inspired and guided disruptive movements that demanded more than mindless fanaticism or simple violence. The reclusive Robespierre toiled nightly producing speeches he would deliver, while Zarqawi affected the garb and exaggerated demeanor of a hardened warrior. Robespierre's vision to shape France into a truly virtuous state was as fancifully unrealistic as Zarqawi's desire to establish a strictly fundamentalist Islamic caliphate was frightening. But each man displayed a genuine—and ultimately horrifying—consistency.

The zealots we profile frustrate the archetype of a "textbook" leader. But they're a vital focus of any leadership study, because they lay bare the idea that leadership is a feedback loop more than a top-down process. Propelled by underlying chaos, their followers craved the magnetism that came to define Robespierre and Zarqawi. The feedback loop that propelled these zealots sheds light on a crucial question: How does leadership help take people to dark places?

Key Books

- Peter McPhee, *Robespierre: A Revolutionary Life* (New Haven, CT: Yale University Press, 2012)
- Ruth Scurr, *Fatal Purity: Robespierre and the French Revolution* (New York: Henry Holt and Company, 2006)
- Joby Warrick, *Black Flags: The Rise of ISIS* (New York: Anchor Books, 2016)

MAXIMILIEN ROBESPIERRE

What scares me, gentlemen, is precisely that which seems to reassure everyone else. Here I need you to hear me out. I say once again, what scares me is what reassures all the others: it is that since this morning all our enemies speak the same language as us. . . . Look about you, share my fear, and consider how all now wear the same mask of patriotism.

—ROBESPIERRE, JUNE 1791

A hailstorm swept France in July 1788, destroying most of the ripening harvest of grain, raising fears of economic collapse, and precipitating the political crisis that would lead to the Revolution. The storm had been long brewing. The French king, Louis XVI, his government coffers empty from ineffective taxation, support of foreign wars (including the American Revolution), and profligacy, found himself increasingly unable to govern. Within a year, the Revolution would begin. In four, the king and his family would be under house arrest. And in five, the royals would be dead, along with hundreds of thousands of their countrymen. The Revolution that ended 805 years of French monarchy called for a new, idealistic approach to governance. After a full decade of turmoil, France would emerge with a new leader, general, and later emperor, Napoleon Bonaparte.

Prior to the Revolution, in ancien régime (literally "old order") France, society was divided into three so-called estates, the First Estate being the clergy, the Second being the nobility, and the Third comprising everyone else. The most widely circulated pamphlet of winter 1788, "What Is the Third Estate?," answered its title's question unequivocally: "Everything. What has it been until now in the public order? Nothing. What does it want to be? Something." Under pressure from the mounting political and economic crisis, the king called the Estates General, an occasional deliberative body of France's three estates. It convened in Versailles, ten miles outside of Paris, on May 5, 1789, widely regarded as the first day of the French Revolution. After a lengthy electoral process, Maximilien de Robespierre was selected as one of eight Third Estate deputies from his home province, Artois.

On June 6, 1789, a month after the Estates General had begun, Robespierre, an unremarkable thirty-one-year-old lawyer from an unimportant province in the north, came to the podium without notes, dressed in one of the three waistcoats he'd taken with him to Versailles. On the dais, the short, bespectacled man trembled in front of his audience. His face twitched with a violence that contorted his eyes. He spoke softly but severely to the 645 other delegates of his Third Estate, many of whom were milling about the room, hardly paying attention. Though he would make thousands of speeches in the next five years, the soft-spoken Robespierre would never become a good orator. It's unlikely most of his colleagues could even hear him.

But those who could hear him listened to a blistering attack on an archbishop who had come to the then-separate convening of Third Estate delegates and asked them to do something for France's poor. The upstart Robespierre's sharp retort: "Let the bishops ... sell their coaches and horses and give that to the poor." The line was representative of Robespierre's words at their best: sharp, quotable, and clarifying. How dare an entitled man from either of the two privileged estates ask for something from the poor? This was only his second speech at the Estates General, and one of the last he would deliver unscripted. Many of his fellow deputies didn't yet know who he was, but his words distinguished him. He began to speak more often, becoming a spokesman of the left at a moment, and in an environment, when that kind of role equated to leadership.

He developed such a strong will over the first three decades of his life, one result of an unlikely rise to prominence. The men who came to Versailles had varying degrees of prestige and power and, at the outset, Robespierre was a relatively unknown representative from Arras. But there was a dais where deputies were given the opportunity to speak. And so Maximilien Robespierre did what came naturally to him: he spoke. And when he spoke, he took sides.

Over the first three decades of his life, he'd developed a strong will, one result of an unlikely rise to prominence. In 1758, he was born into a minor scandal in Arras, the provincial capital of Artois: his parents hadn't married yet when his mother became pregnant. Maximilien's mother died when he was just six, and his father left the family immediately after her death, never to return. Despite being raised an orphan, he did well enough in his parish school that at eleven years old he was awarded one of four local scholarships to attend the most prestigious school in France, the Lycée Louis-le-Grand, in Paris. It was at Louis-le-Grand that he first was introduced to Enlightenment ideals: liberty, equality, the fundamental goodness of man, and the basic idea that men were capable of governing themselves. He would go on to symbolize these ideals during the course of Revolution, but first, as a boy in Paris, he soaked up the writings of Jean-Jacques Rousseau, despite his books having been banned at Louis-le-Grand for their antimonarchist motifs.

In defending these ideals he was quite comfortable offending people—a habit cultivated in his youth and sharpened by his years as a lawyer in Arras. By the time the Estates General convened, Robespierre was confident in his worldview. As a result, he wasn't cautious with his words. While he wasn't a skilled orator, he spoke more than his peers and he was unequivocal. To aristocrats, this sickly man from the provinces was an easy target of mockery. According to one Third Estate colleague, Robespierre was "too verbose, he doesn't know how to stop; but he has depths of eloquence and acerbity which will make him stand out from the crowd."

Events were unfolding quickly, and king and court were ill disposed to handle them. Most famously, on July 14, 1789, a mob stormed the four-hundred-year-old fortress-turned-prison Bastille Saint-Antoine after a series of monarchical missteps. The Bastille was mostly empty when it was stormed, but it was still a symbol of tyrranical injustice. Robespierre had nothing to do with the day's events, and was appalled by the gore. Rioting citizens had killed the fortress commander and then carried his head around Paris on a pike. But he did benefit from the turn to violence. More so than other delegates, by the time of the Bastille, Robespierre was on record in strong opposition to the prevailing order. When the people of Paris rose up, Robespierre was there at the ready to represent, and help shepherd, popular sentiment.

Three days after the uprising, 100 of the 646 Third Estate delegates joined the king on a public procession to Paris, a ceremony meant to symbolize the crown joining itself to the people. Robespierre was among those chosen for this honor. Two months into the Revolution, with an ear and an eye for the wave of popular sentiment, Robespierre had already set himself apart.

For the next two years, after the government officially moved to Paris in the fall of 1789, Robespierre spoke incessantly. In the first eight months of the Revolution, he made 38 speeches, and between 1789 and 1791, he gave 276 speeches in the National Assembly, the twentieth most of all delegates.

Often, Robespierre and other delegates' reference point when speaking was the August 1789 Declaration of the Rights of Man and of the Citizen, a document as foundational to the French Revolution as the Declaration of Independence had been to the American Revolution a decade earlier. Based in the Enlightenment ideals of thinkers like Rousseau, it invited the French people for the first time to participate in a government designed to preserve the "natural and imprescriptible rights of man," rights including "liberty, property, security, and resistance to oppression."

While the Declaration nominally affirmed everyone's natural rights, it was not a playbook. Fundamental questions were left up for debate: If everyone was an equal citizen in the new France, for instance, would everyone therefore be able to exercise full political rights? Robespierre took an expansive and literal view of what was laid out in the Declaration. As he explained just two weeks after the Declaration's passage in the National Assembly,* when the Assembly was embroiled in a debate over whether the king should have veto power (Robespierre was arguing against any veto): "All men are capable, by their very nature, of governing themselves through their own will; all men united in a political body, that is to say the Nation, therefore have the same right."

Robespierre's speechmaking didn't end when the Assembly closed down every afternoon. Now in Paris, in the evenings he began building his name and asserting his authority across France through a network called the Jacobin Club. The club firmed up his role as a spokesperson of the Revolution's left flank, and came to be the source of all his friendships.

The Jacobins, a society of left-leaning politicians, most of whom were also deputies in the Assembly, gave men with ideas like Robespierre's an outlet and platform. Across France, citizens, especially Third Estate elites, began getting together at cafés, tennis courts, churches, and any other building that could house them. People were understandably excited to talk about the upheavals changing their everyday lives. They could now openly discuss emerging ideas and the rapidly unfolding turn of events. Eventually, these groups sought affiliation with the main revolutionary club in Paris. Formally titled "Societies of the Friends of the Constitution," the clubs and their members were more commonly referred to as the Jacobins, because the Paris club, referred to as the "mother society," convened in an old Jacobin monastery. Among various other functions, these clubs printed and distributed their members' speeches to affiliates throughout the country.

---

* In June 1789, the Estates General's representative body became known as the National Assembly.

The Paris Jacobin Club formed an important part of the rhythm of Robespierre's life. On a typical day in 1791, he spent the morning through the early afternoon in the National Assembly, where he conferred with co-partisans and harangued the conservative opposition. In the evenings he was surrounded by the same co-partisans at the Jacobin. Later, he drafted speeches in the home of Maurice Duplay, a carpenter and devout Jacobin from whom Robespierre rented a single second-floor room for most of the Revolution.

Robespierre was emerging as a radical member of the National Assembly, and established himself as a leader among the Jacobins—by 1790, he had been elected as the club's president for the first time. As the Revolution accelerated, unfolding as a series of political responses to unpredictable events, Robespierre's role landed him at the fore of both organizations.

The Incorruptible: 1791

King Louis, his wife Marie Antoinette, and their children were forcibly relocated to Paris in October 1789. The king held nominal power while the royal family was functionally under house arrest in the Tuileries, their palace in the capital. After almost two years in this tenuous position, on June 20, 1791, the thirty-six-year-old King Louis XVI and his family attempted to flee the country to join a monarchist army on France's eastern border.

The coach departed Paris's city gate near midnight carrying a visiting Russian aristocrat and her children, accompanied by their governess and a valet. In reality, the aristocrat was herself the governess, and the woman ostensibly caring for the children was their mother, thirty-five-year-old Marie Antoinette, France's Austrian-born queen consort who had once been dubbed "Madam Deficit" for her profligate spending. The valet, disguised in common clothing, was her husband, Louis XVI.

The heavy wagon was drawn by six powerful horses but quickly fell behind the elaborate escape plan's schedule. Detained less than twenty-four hours after they left, the royal family found their ruse ended when an elderly Frenchman who had once worked at Versailles was brought in and instinctively cocked his knee in deference to the royal couple. The family was returned to Paris.

For the first time in the Revolution, many delegates who had insisted the king was a vital part of the new France were now openly criticizing him. That night, Robespierre spoke to the Jacobin. He could have used the moment to convince new allies, or to solidify his club's opposition to the king. Instead, he impugned those who were only now questioning the fitness of the monarch. "What scares me, gentlemen," he insisted, "is precisely that which seems to reassure everyone else. Here I need you to hear me out. I say once again, what scares me is what reassures all the others: it is that since this morning all our enemies speak the same language as us. . . . Look about you, share my fear, and consider how all now wear the same mask of patriotism."

Convinced of his own righteousness, he accused other revolutionaries of dissembling. While some were now wearing a "mask of patriotism," Robespierre was sure he required no costume. The night of the king's capture, in response to his speech, all eight hundred men crammed into the Paris Jacobin Club swore an oath to defend Robespierre's life. The lawyer from Arras, now an unwavering, outraged advocate for a new France, had become a star of the Revolution.

After an initial outburst of anger, most of the National Assembly remained wary. Some genuinely wanted the king and the people to share power, while others were simply unsure what the future might look like in France without a king, or were fearful of what sort of violent retribution he and his supporters might carry out as his divine role was called increasingly into question.

Fearing the potential chaos of uncharted political waters and anxious for compromise, all but about thirty of its members left the Jacobin Club to join another society whose aim was to negotiate with the king and bring about immediate constitutional order. And in the fall of 1791, France took a cautious course of establishing itself as a constitutional monarchy, where the king and legislature shared power. But Robespierre stood firm in the Jacobins when others fled, and used his platform to unceasingly condemn the king and his supporters. The political outcome seemed a victory for his rivals, but with time Robespierre would win the battle of public sentiment. Robespierre's incessant confidence in the Revolution, and in himself, reassured a people scared to see the only source of authority they'd ever known called into question.

Once constitutional order was salvaged, many of Robespierre's colleagues rejoined the antimonarchist stance from which Robespierre had never wavered. Within months, the Jacobins' numbers soared back up to around eight hundred. Robespierre had been intransigent even when abandoned by more than 95 percent of his fellow Jacobins, and the gambit gave him tremendous credibility. But his stance had not been a political calculation. His actions had simply aligned with his values. Robespierre's willingness to stand against the prevailing tide, or perhaps his natural aversion to compromise, secured his position as a leader in the Revolution. One scholar suggests that Robespierre's "early isolation helped give him a sense of a rare stormy destiny."

Although his dogmatic opposition did not immediately topple the king, Robespierre was already a revolutionary hero. He had become the symbol of what it was to be for the Revolution, and against everything else. On September 30, 1791, the day the National Assembly ended, and the day before France instituted its new constitutional monarchy, the citizens of Paris hailed Robespierre on the streets, cheering him with his nickname: "Long live the deputies without stain! Long live the Incorruptible!" In a Revolution based on complicated ideas, Robespierre offered people clarity, excitement, and, above all—representation.

The Revolution became a violent, frightening journey into the unknown for a nation that had long been settled in a known misery. As it lurched forward, tentative and uncertain, Robespierre was an icon of authenticity, one whose words were a confirming touchstone in unfamiliar times.

The Spokesman: 1792

In late 1791 and early 1792, the central question animating the day-to-day of the Revolution was whether or not France should go to war. Most of the

A portrait, circa 1791, depicting Robespierre where
he spent much of his time—at his desk.

Legislative Assembly, most of the population, and a large faction of Jacobins
wanted war to protect the Revolution's gains. Robespierre led the antiwar
faction, arguing that foreign war was a monarchist trick to stanch the Revo-
lution by reasserting the authority of the king. Robespierre lost the debate,
and France declared war against Austria in April 1792. That summer,
French casualties mounted, especially after Prussia joined the war on the
Austrian side.

Under pressure, the monarchy broke. On August 10, 1792, a joint force
of national guardsmen and sans-culottes—poor Parisian peasants (the
term laterally means "without breeches")—stormed the Tuileries Palace,
massacred 600 Swiss Guards, and overthrew King Louis XVI. Within
a month, France was controlled by an elected National Convention, and

*on September 21, 1792, the Convention declared France a republic. After
805 years, the French monarchy was no more. New leaders would fill
the void.*

The question "Who leads?" loomed over the capital city. Jérôme Pétion,
the mayor of Paris, had called for the citizens of his city's forty-eight sections to be armed with pikes—a weapon that had become symbolic after its
use in the storming of the Bastille. In honor of the weapon, one section of
the city even renamed itself "Les Piques." The sans-culottes were now a
popular militia with opaque authority.

Every day, more and more *fédéres*, or "federals," were entering Paris,
with the greatest number from Marseilles. Nominally, these 20,000
troops—which supplemented national guardsmen already in Paris—were
there to celebrate the anniversary of the Bastille and receive training before
heading to the front. In reality, their station in the capital was a matter of
debate. Some saw their presence as a ploy to calm down the pike-wielding
Parisians and protect France's tenuous constitutional monarchy; others
saw them as a better-equipped version of the sans-culottes, whose purpose
was to menace the king and his allies.

Confined to house arrest at the Tuileries Palace, the king and his family
had several thousand national guardsmen and a 600-person Swiss Guard
whose sole purpose was to protect the royal family.

In Paris's highly charged atmosphere, various factions carried on a debate about how France should be governed. While opinions ranged from a
constitutional monarchy to a pure republic, of more immediate concern
was how to deal with the reality of the presence of so many armed men in
the city.

Robespierre was not convinced that either a constitutional monarchy or
a republic was best for France—as ever, what he cared about above all was
fidelity to the Revolution's ideals. In his own words: "I would rather see a
popular representative assembly and free and respected citizens with a king
than a People enslaved and degraded under the whip of an aristocratic senate and a dictator. . . . Does the solution to the great social problem reside in
the term *republic* or *monarchy*?" And on the more practical question,
Robespierre was ardently against the presence of *fédéres* in Paris. He

thought they were there to keep watch over the sans-culottes, rather than to celebrate the Bastille or even to keep the king in check.

But Robespierre's role wasn't one that required him to devise particular policy solutions. What mattered was that he was the symbol of opposition to the ancien régime, and that he was for the people and the Revolution. To a meeting of the Jacobins that April, Robespierre was unequivocal: "I am neither the messenger, nor the mediator, nor the tribune, nor the defender of the people; I am of the people myself."

Robespierre viewed each issue presented to the unsettled nation through a simple, clarifying filter, with his role being to distill the murky sediment of counterrevolution: Does this serve the interests of the new way and the people, or the old way with its unjust and unaccountable institutions? He thought the ongoing war with Austria and Prussia, for instance, could stifle revolutionary progress, so he was skeptical of it. "I do not trust the generals," said Robespierre; "most of them are nostalgic for the old order."

Hysteria accelerated as the joint Prussian-Austrian army crushed French troops and made steady progress toward the capital, where their aim was to reassert the authority of King Louis and prevent the virus of revolution from infecting all of Europe. These counterrevolutionary aggressors further deteriorated the king's standing among the people. At the end of July, one of the Paris sections published an address to the capital's citizens, arguing that "the most sacred duty and the most cherished law is to forget the law to save the *patrie* . . . let us all unite to declare the fall of this cruel king, let us say with one accord, Louis XVI is no longer king of the French."

In response, these Parisians received a written warning from the commander of the Prussian Army, who admonished: "The city of Paris and all its inhabitants without distinction shall be required to submit at once and without delay to the king . . . or face military execution and complete destruction." The French Revolution, in all its complexity, had now been boiled down to a struggle between the old way as embodied by the king and his family, and a new way, reflecting the discontent of the people in Paris, and most crisply exemplified by the iron will of Robespierre.

Robespierre had been skeptical of the *fédéres*. But he described where

public sentiment was, or anticipated where it was headed, more often than
he inspired it to go in a new direction. So by the end of July, his thinking
on the *fédérés* had changed, and his position was clear. In a letter to a friend
in Arras about the troops streaming into the capital, he wrote: "French
Brutuses are now in Paris. If they leave it without saving the fatherland, all
is lost." Robespierre joined an "Insurrectionary Commune," which replaced the sitting municipal government. The Commune had three delegates from each of Paris's forty-eight sections, and was now giving orders
to a joint force of *fédérés* and sans-culottes.

By the evening of August 9, 1792, bells were ringing in Paris: the insurrection was happening. The Marquis de Mandat, commander of the French
National Guard, caught between obeying the municipal Commune and the
formal government of France, was summoned to the Commune's headquarters at the Hôtel de Ville. There the insurrectionary government's
leadership chastised Mandat for refusing their orders to withdraw his
troops from the Tuileries Palace, where he was helping to defend Louis and
the rest of the royal family. Following the meeting, the Marquis was murdered as he descended the steps of the Hôtel de Ville.

The mob advanced to the Tuileries, where the royal family was locked
in a cell for protection. With Mandat's national guardsmen having melted
away, only the king's 600 Swiss Guards remained to defend the palace. By
the afternoon of the tenth, all 600 had been massacred—their limbs torn
from their bodies and their remaining bits and pieces carted through
town and thrown into makeshift bonfires.

The night that France's monarchy fell, Robespierre was not fighting
bravely alongside the Revolution's makeshift army of peasants and *fédérés*.
He was safely perched on the dais at the Jacobin Club. As thousands fought
and many died, the world outside his cocoon in disarray, Robespierre as
usual spent the day writing and talking. His speech that night, given to the
hundreds crammed into the Jacobins' old monastery, described the overthrow of the monarchy as a logical progression of the people's self-will. He
explained how that will had been realized three years earlier at the storming of the Bastille—and that the unfolding violence was a necessary fact of
revolution:

In 1789 the people of Paris raised themselves tumultuously to repel the attacks of the court, to free themselves of the old despotism more than to conquer liberty, the idea of which was still confused, its principles unknown. All passions concurred in the insurrection and the signal it gave to the whole of France.

In 1792 they have raised themselves with imposing courage to avenge the fundamental laws of their violated liberty, the infidel mandatories who sought to enslave once again the imprescriptible rights of humanity. They have put into action the principles proclaimed three years ago by their first representatives; they have exercised their recognized sovereignty and deployed its power and its justice to assure their safety and happiness. . . .

He then reassured the people of their fidelity to the tenets of the Declaration: "The solemnity with which they proceeded in this great act was as sublime as their motives and object."

Since he'd been carried out of the National Assembly ten months earlier, Robespierre the Incorruptible had had no formal role in the national government.* That didn't matter so much: by August 1792, only about a quarter of the legislature's eight hundred deputies were actively governing. Most of them were rightly afraid for their own safety, and so ceded authority to makeshift bodies like the Commune. So while Robespierre had not been legislating, he was still influential. From his Paris apartment, he had begun publishing his own newspaper, the *Défenseur de la Constitution*, a weekly publication that usually exceeded fifty pages in length, and was mostly written by Robespierre's own hand. He'd also continued his long nights of speechmaking, usually in the Jacobin Club.

The Revolution continued to unfold as a series of crises: foreign war, civil conflict, the royal family's pending trial, and a plethora of political scandals and distortive hearsay. For his part, Robespierre was not expected to participate in these often bloody eruptions as they peaked and troughed

---

* Robespierre had lobbied successfully for a law prohibiting delegates of the National Assembly from serving in the new government's legislature, the Legislative Assembly.

The Paris Jacobin Club, January 1792. Robespierre stood opposed to many members of his club early in the Revolution, but what initially was viewed as poor judgment came to be understood as authenticity. The Jacobins disseminated Robespierre's words across France, securing his standing as a national figure.
(PROVIDED BY THE STANFORD UNIVERSITY LIBRARIES)

on the streets. But through his pointed commentary, he offered the people of France a clear, simple vision for what was possible. He was not expected to make choices, but to frame and guide the choices that others—with far more blood on their hands—would have to make.

In a process that had been playing out for more than two years, the "mother society" in Paris bundled up Robespierre's speeches and sent them to the hundreds of Jacobin Clubs operating across France. From Marseille in the south to Arras in the north, and in thousands of little villages and large cities in between, if citizens wanted to know what was happening in Paris, the local Jacobin Club was the best source of information. While few would meet the Incorruptible in the flesh, the interconnected tissue of clubs in the new republic of letters allowed every Frenchman to know who

Robespierre was, and what he was thinking, on nearly a daily basis. It was in his room, and not in the legislative chambers, that he crafted a narrative for revolutionary France.

The Catechism: 1793

The fall of the French monarchy set in motion a chain of events that consolidated Robespierre's power. After the king's overthrow, France elected a new legislature, called the National Convention. Robespierre was elected as a delegate of both Paris and his hometown of Arras, but chose to represent Paris. Shortly thereafter, on September 21, 1792, France declared itself a republic.

Then, by a one-vote margin, the Convention voted to execute the king, who was beheaded on January 21, 1793. In the fallout from the king's execution, the Convention broke down into factionalism. Four months after the king's head was lopped off in front of a Paris crowd, France was still raging: civil war in the west; wars with foreign opponents on all fronts; a constant threat of counterrevolution everywhere; thousands of sans-culottes in Paris threatening to bend the Convention to their collective will; and within the Convention, an atmosphere where being denounced one day could lead to a delegate's execution the next.

On May 10, 1793, the National Convention moved into the former theater at the Tuileries Palace. Here, hundreds of seats were arrayed in a semicircle around a rostrum, with the Paris deputies stacked against the uppermost section of the rear wall—a part of the Convention that came to be known as "The Mountain." At its summit sat the factional leader, Maximilien Robespierre.

In the midst of the chaos, the Convention increasingly centralized the management of revolutionary France. The most important of several committees was the Committee of Public Safety, which supervised investigations, surveillance, military affairs, and other important matters of policy. The Committee also oversaw the Revolutionary Tribunal, a twelve-person body responsible for hearing cases referred by the Convention and doling out punishment. As conditions in France unraveled from 1793 to 1794, and in an attempt to secure the Revolution's gains, the Tribunal oversaw an increasing number of cases for increasingly minor crimes, conviction for which required ever lower burdens of proof. This devolution of France's already shaky system of justice is known as the Reign of Terror. During this period, as many as forty thousand Frenchmen were executed. Robespierre was not the Terror's architect—though, like many other politicians, he did help create the conditions that wrought its devastating impact.

The Convention broke down into factions at the same time as the day-to-day management of France was delegated to the Committee of Public Safety, and as justice was delegated to the Revolutionary Tribunal. As such, the political stakes were high. Winning in the Convention meant control of the country; losing often meant accusation, banishment, and even decapitation.

When he was alive, King Louis XVI had spent most of his life isolated from his 20 million French subjects, surrounded as he was by the most ornate royal court in the world. As his own authority became more centralized, Robespierre isolated himself in his own republican court: his second-story apartment in Paris.

That's where he sat on the evening of July 26, 1793, the night before he assumed his position on the Committee of Public Safety—a role that gave him executive authority for the first time in the Revolution. Other political leaders would prepare for such an occasion by consulting, or perhaps celebrating, with others. Instead, Robespierre spent the evening alone, writing—the single activity that took up the preponderance of his time for the last five years of his life. In his personal notebook, he spent the night drafting his "Catechism."

In the diary entry, he wondered what was necessary to achieve the Revolution's ultimate aim of a virtuous society. And he labored over it. On the original page, still extant, there are a handful of strike-throughs. These clarifications were the only check on Robespierre's agenda. The vision of France's most powerful man went from that man's mind, to the paper in front of him, and eventually out of his mouth in a multitude of speeches, and then affected the lives of millions—and certainly the thousands who died in the Terror. That night, Robespierre wrote to himself:

What is our aim?

It is the use of the constitution to benefit the people.

Who is likely to oppose us?

The rich and the corrupt.

What methods will they employ?

Slander and hypocrisy.

What factors will encourage the use of such means?

The ignorance of the sans-culottes.

The people must therefore be instructed.

What are the obstacles to their enlightenment?

The paid journalists who mislead the people every day by shameless
   distortions.

What conclusion follows?

That we ought to proscribe these writers as the most dangerous
   enemies of the country and to circulate an abundance of good
   literature.

The people—what other obstacle is there to their instruction?

Their destitution.

When then will the people be educated?

When they have enough bread to eat, when the rich and the government stop bribing treacherous pens and tongues to deceive them
   and instead identify their own interests with those of the people.

When will this be?

Never.

Continuing, Robespierre suggested that the war was one of the biggest obstacles to freedom and called for the punishment of all who had been involved with it. The only thing necessary to make this happen? "A single will."

Writing in isolation, there was no one to temper Robespierre's impulses. Nor would he have wanted that. His authority, after all, came from the widespread perception that he held a purist's fidelity to the ideals of 1789. To the people of France, and especially in his own mind, Robespierre *was* the Revolution.

As the head of The Mountain, Robespierre was explicitly selected for the Committee of Public Safety for his leadership, rather than his mastery of specific issues. Peter McPhee, a modern authority on Robespierre, notes: "Whereas other members of the Committee were usually chosen because of particular expertise, Robespierre was effectively a member without a portfolio, chosen by the Convention because of his experience, standing, and popularity." Robespierre was expected to set the tone for France's most important administrative body.

His Catechism guided him in doing so. The diary entry of July 26, 1793, represented the most honest manifestation of ideas that Robespierre first encountered in the 1770s at Louis-le-Grand, buoyed his rise to prominence through the 1780s in Arras, and that the Revolution had now focused. Those same ideas, predictably, led to a subsequent speech, one for which history now remembers him best.

On February 5, 1794, in the National Convention, Robespierre delivered "A Report on the Principles of Political Morality That Should Guide the Convention in the Interior Administration of the Republic." History remembers the speech as "Virtue and Terror." After beginning with a florid description of what he meant by a virtuous republic, Robespierre described the means that were sufficient for achieving that aim.

> If the basis of popular government in peacetime is virtue, its basis in a time of revolution is both virtue and terror—virtue, without which terror is disastrous, and terror, without which virtue has no power. . . . Terror is merely justice, prompt, severe, and inflexible. It is therefore an emanation of virtue and results from the application of democracy to the most pressing needs of the country.

What is striking about Robespierre's Catechism, his February 1794 speech, and all of his speeches from 1789 onward was their remarkable integrity to the Rousseau-inspired ideas he'd been thinking about since his school days. Most effective political leaders are forced to compromise, or at least adapt, their ideals. Robespierre had the opportunity to meet a revolution where he could be effective, at least for a while, by being uncompromising.

Surely understanding the sources of his leadership, Robespierre didn't just speak about purity and authenticity. He intentionally structured his life so that others might perceive his incorruptibility.

Jacques Pierre Brissot and Jean-Marie Roland were two revolutionaries who had been allies of Robespierre in the Jacobins before going on to lead what was called the Girondin faction. Both died when the Girondins were swept out of office by Robespierre in 1793. The locus of power for the Girondins was a series of salons and dinners put on by Madame Jeanne Manon Roland, who was herself beheaded shortly before her husband committed suicide. Prior to his split with Roland and Brissot, Robespierre had in fact attended some of these dinners himself, and had developed a rich correspondence with Madame Roland. But increasingly, Robespierre's leadership of the Jacobins meant drafting speeches in his room with a small cast of close friends, and then espousing his ideology at the club.

Dinners like Madame Roland's could have surrounded Robespierre with other people in idle chitchat, humanized the Revolution, and perhaps tempered his thinking. But Robespierre's habits did not allow for such subtlety—or normalcy. In fact, the severity of his isolation contributed to his popular aura of incorruptibility, and secured his place as a leader. Everyone *knew* that the most powerful man in France lived in a simple, second-story apartment rented from a carpenter, and hadn't profited from his political rise. His motives must have been pure.

As 1794 dragged on, however, the Revolution took Robespierre out of his room and placed him front and center. That this deeply private man both had to and tried to play an increasingly public role would become his undoing.

The Priest: 1794

In April 1794, Robespierre was engaged in a political struggle with former allies. He had his erstwhile compatriots expelled from the Convention, and they were executed as a result. As was often the case after periods of great strife, for the rest of that month, Robespierre confined himself to his room. Emerging on May 7, he gave what one biographer has called "the most revealing document Robespierre has left to posterity." It was his vision for a new national religion, the Cult of the Supreme Being, a belief system based in revolutionary ideals.

Robespierre's first official public appearance of the Revolution was on June 4, 1794, when he presided over the Festival of the Supreme Being. The following month, he was executed.

In 1793 and 1794, the heroes of the Revolution attempted to fill the vacuum left by the abolition of so many of France's institutions. They renamed months on the calendar after pastoral motifs—*Vendemiaire,* or "grape harvest," was the first month of the fall, and *Prairial,* or "meadow," was the first month of the spring. They also attempted to create a religion based on revolutionary ideals, with Robespierre disappearing for much of May 1794 to develop a vision for the new belief system.

That's how Robespierre came to preside over the Festival of the Supreme Being on June 4, 1794. He watched the opening ceremonies from a window in the Tuileries. He could see the roses that had been arranged all over the

Pierre-Antoine Demachy's rendering of the Festival of the Supreme Being. The "Mountain" where Robespierre sat can be seen in the background, with the "Tree of Liberty" planted on top.

capital, with young women in white dresses carrying baskets of fruit lining the Seine. He listened from above as a choir of 2,400 Parisian citizens sang patriotic songs, to include the new "Hymn of the Supreme Being."

Robespierre came down from his perch dressed in a resplendent sky-blue coat, a tricolor sash across his chest, and gave a speech in the garden of the former royal palace. Five years after the Estates General had convened, this was the first official public speech of his revolutionary career. He then led a procession through the heart of Paris. At the end of the march, there was a plaster "Mountain" under a "Tree of Liberty" that towered over the crowd, from where Robespierre watched the afternoon's celebrations. At the end of the day's ceremonies, Robespierre descended to cheers and gave a final address: "Being of Beings! Did the day of Creation itself," he asked, "shine with a light more agreeable in thy sight than that day on which, bursting the yoke of crime and error, this nation appeared in thy sight in an attitude worthy of thy regard and its destinies?"

The French people had strong, and contradictory, reactions to the Festival. The Convention received 1,235 letters about it. In Paris, while every member of the Convention attended, they, too, were deeply divided. Some deputies laughed at Robespierre, while others grew suspicious that he had become a tyrant. In Nay, a small town in the Pyrenees Mountains near France's southwestern border, the local Jacobin Club decreed that there would be a reading from one of Robespierre's speeches every evening. But when the Jacobin Club in Montignac, about 175 miles north of Nay, read Robespierre's speech on the Supreme Being, the local club's president had to adjourn the meeting because so many members had left out of boredom midway through. Not everyone agreed with the new religion; the problem for Robespierre was that everyone saw him as its mastermind.

The Cult of the Supreme Being brought with it the motifs of liberty, justice, and republican *vertu*, the exact qualities that Robespierre claimed to personify. Back in 1792, one of his enemies described Robespierre's leadership in religious terms:

> This revolution of ours is a religion, and Robespierre is leading a sect therein. He is a priest at the head of his worshippers. . . . Robespierre

preaches, Robespierre censures; he is furious, grave, melancholy, exalted—all coldly; his thoughts flow regularly, his habits are regular, he thunders against the rich and the great; he lives on next to nothing; he has no necessities. He has but one mission—to speak—and he speaks unceasingly; he creates disciples . . . he talks of God and Providence . . . he is a priest and will never be other than a priest.

With the distance of more than two centuries, a sympathetic view might hold that Robespierre was the symbol of a revolution that inevitably became violent, that he was a spokesperson with enough backbone to stand up for his beliefs, and that neither of these qualities was useful in governing. Such leadership is valuable only in particular moments. By 1794, France was simply tired of the killing, the paranoia that rippled through the streets, and the ever-deferred reality of a virtuous republic. And the wars that had provided the rationale for revolutionary government had, in spite of the country's internal frictions, turned in France's favor, especially after a major victory at the Battle of Fleurus on June 26.

That same summer, precisely because they felt that the Revolution's aims weren't yet secure, Robespierre and his allies made the Terror even more efficient in its deadliness. In the week leading up to the Festival of the Supreme Being, 119 citizens were executed in Paris. That week, the guillotine itself had to be moved to the edges of the capital, because the blood pooling beneath the apparatus had begun to pollute the city's water.

On May 25, 1794, a young woman was caught trying to assassinate Robespierre with two small knives, only two days after a separate attempt had been made on the life of another revolutionary leader. In the wake of these assassination attempts, and only two days after the Festival of the Supreme Being, the National Convention, under Robespierre's leadership, passed the statutes of 22 Prairial. By these laws, crimes like "spreading false news," "slandering patriotism," and "depraving morals, corrupting the public conscience and impairing the purity and energy of the revolutionary government" could be referred to the Revolutionary Tribunal. No witnesses were allowed to be called, and the accused had no right to legal representation.

With these new mechanisms of justice, from June 18 to July 26, 1794, more than nine hundred people were convicted and beheaded by the Revolutionary Tribunal in Paris—the bloodiest such stretch of the entire Revolution. The man who has come to symbolize this violence, and was responsible for much of its animating force, wasn't in the crowds as a witness. Nor did he participate in the hearings, or sign but a handful of the arrest warrants in those thirty-eight days. As ever, Maximilien Robespierre spent most of this time alone in his room.

Immediately after the Festival of the Supreme Being, Robespierre had gone into isolation. Occasionally he was visited by an ever-contracting group of friends. Between June 18 and July 26, he never appeared in the National Convention, he attended the Committee of Public Safety only twice, and between June 11 and July 9, he went to the Jacobins only two times.

His seclusion, though it was born of exhaustion, no longer added to the mystique that made him a leader. Now it fueled suspicion that he was scheming to become a tyrant. His enemies, in fact, made up stories about his character. He was accused of being a drunk, a libertine, and generally driven by ambition instead of virtue.

Finally, when he emerged from his room on July 26, 1794, Robespierre entered a National Convention gripped by fear. That summer, many delegates had stopped sleeping in their own homes, for fear of being detained in the middle of the night.

Robespierre had spent the previous three days writing what was a two-hour speech for his return to the Convention floor. The speech itself was typical Robespierre: he praised the Supreme Being, defended himself against charges of tyranny, and accused certain members of the Convention of conspiring against him. Normally, after a member of the Convention as important as Robespierre gave such a substantial talk, it was praised on the floor, then printed and prepared for distribution. To Robespierre's surprise, the Convention moved to have the speech forwarded to the Committees for Public Safety and General Security. "What!" he exclaimed. "My speech is to be sent to be examined by the very deputies I accuse!"

The next morning, Robespierre and his accusers all reentered the Convention floor after a long night of scheming. It's a strange thing to ponder:

opposing lawmakers calmly but nervously entering a meeting hall, sure that one side or the other would not be alive for another day.

Neither luck nor the sway of the room was on Robespierre's side: one of his enemies happened to be the Convention president at the time, and so had control over who could keep the floor. Though Robespierre's ally Louis Antoine de Saint-Just took the podium first, he was prevented from speaking. Then Robespierre rushed forward to the dais, but each time he tried to take the floor he was shouted down. Three years earlier, he'd been hailed on the streets of Paris with "Long Live the Incorruptible!" Now he was met with a chorus of "Down with the tyrant!" Robespierre and four of his allies were promptly arrested on the Convention floor, prey to the very rules that had propelled their Revolution.

When the Paris Commune heard of the day's events, they rang the tocsin just as they had the evening the king fell two years before, and by 1:00 a.m. on July 28, Robespierre and his allies thought they might have a chance. City jails refused to take them in, and the condemned men went to the Commune's headquarters at the Hôtel de Ville, in anticipation of an insurrection that never came. Despite the ringing of the bell, only thirteen of the city's forty-eight sections were prepared to fight for Robespierre. Other sections remained at home, and some even took to the streets in support of the Convention.

At the Hôtel de Ville, one of Robespierre's allies had handed him a pistol. As French troops burst in to arrest the six outlaws, Robespierre attempted suicide, shattering his lower left jaw with an ill-aimed shot. He was carried to the Tuileries Palace on a makeshift stretcher, his head propped up on a sack of bread, a pistol bag absorbing the blood from his wound and holding together his jaw. At some point early in the morning, a surgeon dressed the wound.

For his execution that day, the guillotine was returned to the center of Paris. Thousands watched as Robespierre and twenty-one of his allies were wheeled through the streets in crude carts. He was wearing the same sky-blue coat he'd worn six weeks before at the Festival of the Supreme Being. Just before placing Robespierre head under the blade, the executioner ripped the bandage from his face, and the Incorruptible let out a violent scream.

Large-scale executions mostly stopped with Robespierre's death. The people of France were ready for constitutional order, and so, in the words of one of Robespierre's erstwhile Jacobin allies, his death "had become a necessity."

ABU MUSAB AL-ZARQAWI

What can you say to a man who tells you he prefers obeying God rather than men, and that as a result he's certain he'll go to heaven if he cuts your throat?
—VOLTAIRE

As it was for those who perished under the guillotine's blade in Paris, this victim's intimate moment of death was brutally public. But instead of simply ending with a raucous cheer from a crowd, Nick Berg's beheading, captured in a carefully choreographed video, was replayed millions of times in response to the click of a computer mouse. Online reactions ranged from horror to jubilance as a hooded executioner stood behind the seated Berg and, after a short statement, produced an oversized knife, pushed Berg to the side and sawed into his struggling hostage's neck. The gruesome recording surfaced on the internet on May 10, 2004. Two days earlier, American soldiers found Berg's body hanging from a highway overpass, his head lying on the ground beneath him.

The beheading of Berg, a radio-tower repairman from Pennsylvania, was the first in a wave of similar gruesome videotaped stunts that followed. These violent images of a Westerner in an orange jumpsuit awaiting his death are now far too common. But circa 2004, this tactic was relatively new. The beheading of captured victims was not original, but posting the gruesome video for the world to see on the internet was nearly unprecedented. It intentionally sought, and received, a reaction. Jihadis in Iraq and across the world saw an inspirational leader practicing what he'd preached.

I watched the ritual killing at a small base of our Special Operations Task Force outside Baghdad, my fist unconsciously tightening in rage and frustration. Predictably, the operators in our team vowed to identify and capture or kill every one of the six terrorists who stood witness to the murder. We suspected, and soon confirmed, that the man who coldly took Nick

Berg's life was the Jordanian terrorist Ahmad Fadeel Nazal al-Khalayleh, more popularly known as Abu Musab al-Zarqawi. We quickly labeled our foe a psychopath and began our own zealous pursuit.

As soldiers, our reactions were natural, but the eventual response of Berg's father was more surprising. In an interview conducted years later in the aftermath of Zarqawi's death, Michael Berg characterized Zarqawi as a "political figure" caught up in a cycle of vengeful violence. This is a notable perspective for a man to have on his son's murderer: Zarqawi was a passionate actor with an ideological agenda.

By the time we killed Zarqawi two years after Nick Berg's death, he had not only become the zealot at the heart of the global jihadist movement, but he had helped catalyze an unthinkably bloody civil war in Iraq. In doing so, Zarqawi would prove himself an unlikely, but exceptionally effective leader whose legacy excited a generation of followers.

Tattoo

Roughly a decade before Berg's death, prison guards somehow missed the razor blade hidden in the folds of a visitor's clothing at Swaqa, the largest prison in Jordan's notorious penal system. Given the prisoner the visitor was going to see, the guards should have been more thorough.

In the mid-1990s, Jordan's most worrisome domestic threats were regional Islamist extremists who hated the monarchy for its perceived appeasement of the West and Israel. Although the extremists had been spectacularly, almost comically, unsuccessful on the outside, inside the prison walls they had a frustrating ability to sway the minds of others—even those meant to guard them. On this day, the prisoner—the thirtyish Zarqawi—had a more pressing matter on his mind. After a friendly embrace, Zarqawi's visitor set out to do what Zarqawi had requested. Peeling back his right sleeve, Zarqawi revealed a tattoo of an anchor on his forearm.

The ink was more than just a colorful remnant of his thuggish youth. Fired by religious zeal, Zarqawi despised the tattoo because his newfound creed forbade it—it was *haram*. Zarqawi had already tried, unsuccessfully, to scrub the embarrassing ink away with household bleach. The smuggled razor blade would be his latest attempt to be rid of it.

Zarqawi sat patiently as his relative used the blade against his bared skin—holding still as long, bloody slices were cut into his forearm around the anchor. His skin was flayed in successive sheets until most of the image had been scraped away. When finished, the visitor used makeshift sutures to bind the gash shut. Satisfied, Zarqawi rolled down his sleeve and returned to his cell block.

The anchor tattoo that Zarqawi had sliced off represented a prior life of vice and underachievement he was eager to be rid of.

BORN IN 1966 AS Ahmad Fadeel Nazal al-Khalayleh in Zarqa, Jordan, a dusty, hardscrabble industrial town about twenty-five kilometers from the cosmopolitan capital of Amman, this stocky boy was unremarkable apart from a lack of interest in school, a propensity for periodic violence, and a notably short temper.

Fretting over her son's aimlessness, Zarqawi's doting mother convinced him as a young man to attend classes at a local mosque. The imams there soon went beyond raising money for the mujahedeen fighting the Soviets in Afghanistan—they also asked for recruits. Zarqawi, having unexpectedly taken to Islam and gorged himself on propaganda about the anti-Soviet fight, volunteered.

By the time Zarqawi reached the southern border of Afghanistan in the spring of 1989—still going by his birth name of Ahmad—he had missed the war. Only a few weeks earlier, the last Russian soldiers had marched across the Friendship Bridge into Uzbekistan, ending their country's decade-long occupation. Fighting continued between the beleaguered Communist government the Soviets left behind and the mujahedeen. Intra-mujahed strife followed soon thereafter. But the great jihad of this era—an epochal, ultimately triumphant struggle against a godless Communist superpower—was over.

A mujahedeen propaganda organ soon put Zarqawi to work writing glowing profiles of various jihadists. Traveling around Afghanistan to interview war heroes and write about their exploits was an awkward task for the young Jordanian with a tenuous (though exuberant) grasp of his own religion and a lack of combat experience. His reputation as a street thug preceded him, and Zarqawi likely felt insecure around the veteran foreign jihadists. According to a peer at the time, even in the Afghan desert sun, Zarqawi wore long sleeves to hide his *haram* tattoos.

By 1991, Zarqawi had found opportunities to prove himself. Two years after the Soviet withdrawal, the Islamist factions assaulted government-held areas in Paktia and Khost, two mountainous provinces bordering Pakistan. In these skirmishes, his comrades remembered, Zarqawi fought with abandon, becoming known for "bravery bordering on foolhardiness." He would carry this impetuousness to what he saw as his next battlefield: Jordan.

Zarqawi and a cohort of fellow Jordanians returned home in 1993, certain that the mujahedeen's victory over the Soviets was a miracle from Allah. They quickly became bent on replacing the Jordanian Hashemite monarchy—and the Western lifestyle it tolerated—with a fundamentalist regime and pious Islamic society. Zarqawi sought out an acquaintance from Afghanistan named Abu Muhammad al-Maqdisi, an established Islamic cleric and writer whose teachings had gained favor among veterans of the Afghan war. They settled on a name—Bay'at al-Imam, or "Oath of Allegiance to the Prayer Leader"—and started by distributing pamphlets of Maqdisi's sermons.

Zarqawi had ambitious and more violent designs for the group, but despite his experience in Afghanistan, he, as yet, displayed little talent for leading. Bay'at al-Imam's early attempts at terrorism were almost farcically clumsy. In one operation, the group dispatched a man to bomb a Jordanian pornographic theater. But upon seeing the film on screen he became transfixed by the scene, sat down, and forgot about the bomb beneath his chair. It blew his legs off, hurt no one else, and landed him in jail.

After a shooting attack by a Jewish extremist in the West Bank in February 1994, Zarqawi saw a chance to make a daring reprisal against Israel. With weapons Maqdisi had concealed in his home, Zarqawi hatched a plan to attack an Israeli guard post on the Jordanian border. The group's plotting, however, was too blundering to escape the notice of Jordan's intelligence service—the Mukhabarat—and its ubiquitous informants.

The agents sniffed out the scheme and arrested Zarqawi and his fellow plotters.

Zarqawi and Maqdisi landed in Swaqa with lengthy prison sentences.

THE JORDANIAN GOVERNMENT EVENTUALLY moved the group from Swaqa to a different prison in the Ard As Sawwan desert named al-Jafr. Closed in 1979 after housing political prisoners, one wing of al-Jafr's decrepit facility was reopened in 1998 in an effort to segregate particular extremists, including Zarqawi and Maqdisi, considered too dangerous to mix with other inmates.

Inside this desolate place, Zarqawi's enthusiasm for Islam hardened into a brutish, reductionist zealotry. For a poor boy from Zarqa, effective education in Islamic jurisprudence or literacy in classic Arabic would have been inaccessible. Even at his local mosque prior to traveling to Afghanistan, Zarqawi, a high school dropout, would have been intimidated by the imams who had dedicated the better part of their lives not just to study of the Quran and archaic forms of Arabic, but also to debating complex aspects of Islamic vocation.

The Islam that Maqdisi taught in the confines of prison was easier to digest. It was grounded in Salafism, a puritanical strand of Islam that holds that the most righteous way of life is that of Muhammad and his companions, the *salaf*. It has the appeal of a simplistic dogma, especially relative to alternative Islamic theologies. For Salafists, whatever the companions of the Prophet did is allowed in society. Otherwise, it is prohibited. Ingrained in this ideology is a hard-line understanding of monotheism, which interprets any behavior that appears even subtly worshipful of anything other than Allah—even Islamic saints—as idolatrous.

Zarqawi's mind latched on to the simplicity of Maqdisi's hard-line teachings. He began memorizing the Quran and applied it as literally as he could to his daily life. Zarqawi took to wearing a *shalwar khameez* over his immodest prison uniform and made especially pious gestures toward his fellow prisoners—he helped doctors administer medication and personally bathed the amputee who had failed to blow up the adult theater. He enforced Maqdisi's doctrine within the prison, forbidding fellow inmates

A mugshot of Zarqawi as a jihadist on the rise. Though initially a wayward youth, Zarqawi was eventually exposed to Salafism and its extremist doctrine. These provided him with an outlet for his natural propensity for violence and gave him an ideological structure to buy into.
(AFP/GETTY IMAGES)

from watching what he deemed heretical TV programs, even covering the screen with a cloth to prevent unveiled females from being visible to prisoners.

Through enforcing, and practicing, these restrictions, Zarqawi happened upon a key to his future leadership of jihadis. Namely, he could outperform any of his peers in outward displays of piety, and they would follow him for it. Indeed, the true power of Zarqawi's removal of the anchor tattoo lay in the overt commitment it broadcast. He ensured that fellow prisoners had seen his effort to scrub away the tattoo with bleach, and when they saw the razor's wound, it was not simply an act of devotion. It was *leadership by example*, exactly how most soldiers are taught to lead. By his actions, Zarqawi was not only the most pious of their kind, but the toughest.

As Zarqawi gained greater following and confidence within al-Jafr's walls, he and Maqdisi's divergent personalities began to manifest. Whereas the genteel Maqdisi became reclusive, focusing on publishing his theological tracts, Zarqawi strengthened bonds with his cellmates. Maqdisi preached on Salafist theory while Zarqawi confidently enforced—often brutally—the doctrinal precepts he cared about. Gone was the insecurity he had felt among the mujahedeen in Afghanistan in 1989, replaced by an affirmed self-righteousness. Fostered in the Jordanian prison system, this self-certainty caused him to ignore criticism from peer jihadis with a more nuanced understanding of their faith.

In 1999, the death of Jordan's King Hussein, and the subsequent coronation of his son, was marked by a commemorative release of prisoners by the government, and Zarqawi's name was included on the list. For Zarqawi it was fortuitous, but for the region it was an unfortunate and momentous mistake.

When Zarqawi left al-Jafr, he had undergone a prison experience crucially different from that of many of the jihadists' before him. Ayman al-Zawahiri, Osama bin Laden's longtime deputy and (as of 2018) the leader of al-Qaeda, had endured a more common crucible. Where Zarqawi ended up effectively running daily life in the prison, Zawahiri had eventually succumbed to repeated brutal torture by the authorities who had incarcerated him. Broken, he informed on his jihadist accomplices and helped Egyptian authorities scoop up one of his comrades in a sting. The experience left Zawahiri consumed with a shame that fueled a lifetime of rage toward Egypt and its American backers—the ordeal shaped his strategic thinking for years to come.

Zarqawi left al-Jafr with no such humiliation. Far from being broken, Zarqawi exited prison wholly affirmed. After a wasted youth, a criminal adolescence, and an incompetent attempt at terrorism, Zarqawi had finally found in prison something he was good at: leading jihadists. Moreover, to Zarqawi, his serendipitous freedom a few years into a fifteen-year term was not mere luck. Allah, it must have seemed, had big expectations for him.

Fittingly, by the time a Jordanian government van dropped him off on a street corner in Amman a free man in 1999, the improvised sutures on Zarqawi's forearm had long disappeared. His sliced flesh had scarred over.

"Outlier"

Bespectacled and seated behind a placard reading UNITED STATES, Secretary of State Colin Powell made a case for international action against

Iraq. It was February 5, 2003, and from the United Nations' New York headquarters he held the attention of a rapt international community. Over the course of an hour, Powell contended—through dramatic language and imagery—that Saddam Hussein's government was not only sheltering weapons of mass destruction but also extremists capable of wreaking great harm upon the world.

Folding his hands as he approached the end of his speech, Powell informed the international community that "Iraq today harbors a deadly terrorist network headed by Abu Musab al-Zarqawi, an associate and collaborator of Usama bin Laden and his al-Qaeda lieutenants." Because of the gravity of the occasion, as well as Powell's credibility, his emphasis on Zarqawi's name twenty more times in the speech was a resounding pronouncement of Zarqawi's significance as a terrorist leader.

But just over three years earlier, Osama bin Laden had dismissed Zarqawi as an insignificant thug. By late 1999, Zarqawi had become confident in his worldview and capability as a jihadi leader. Having embraced Salafist principles within the confines of Swaqa and al-Jafr and won the loyalty of the men imprisoned with him, Zarqawi now had purpose. Freed through happenstance from prison, Zarqawi fled Jordan for Afghanistan—seeking admittance to the exclusive inner circle of bin Laden's al-Qaeda.

From its haven in Taliban-controlled Afghanistan, al-Qaeda had established itself as a premier terror organization by the late 1990s. Although it had yet to achieve its greatest notoriety, by the time of Zarqawi's arrival it had successfully organized terror attacks from afar—most notably the 1998 bombings of American embassies in Kenya and Tanzania. In seeking out al-Qaeda's central leadership, Zarqawi was effectively making a bid for acceptance as a professional jihadist.

But it seems he made a poor impression, for Zarqawi clashed with al-Qaeda's senior leadership. Though both parties fell within the Salafi tradition—believing in the need to live exactly as the Prophet Muhammad had in the seventh century—the contrasts between their personalities, and the distinctions in their understanding of jihadi strategy, couldn't have been more pronounced. While al-Qaeda's bin Laden was formally educated, and steeped in theological nuance, Zarqawi was a high school dropout, and would have been hard-pressed to cite spiritual doctrine that supported his

The United States' public case for international action against Iraq—formally presented in the United Nations by Colin Powell, on behalf of the Bush administration—rested in part on supposed ties between the Hussein regime and Zarqawi. Despite being proved inaccurate, such allegations heightened Zarqawi's profile in extremist circles.

zealotry. When Zarqawi attempted to convince al-Qaeda of the need to target regional Shi'ite populations rather than just Western targets, bin Laden was alarmed by his ardent willingness to kill fellow Muslims. Besides, Zarqawi had never participated in a successful jihadi operation.

It's unclear if bin Laden and Zarqawi ever met in person, but whether on his own or through a proxy, the head of al-Qaeda made a decision to dismiss the underqualified and, perhaps, overconfident aspirant.

Rejected by bin Laden, Zarqawi's trajectory seemed to have stalled, and his jihadi career might well have ended were it not for an influential al-Qaeda member named Saif al-Adel. Al-Adel, a former Special Forces officer in the Egyptian Army, remains a mysterious (and still at large) figure to this day. Apparently, after meeting the opinionated Jordanian during his initial visit, al-Adel agreed with bin Laden's verdict that Zarqawi was unsuitable for formal inclusion in al-Qaeda. Nevertheless, al-Adel valued Zarqawi's potential as a recruiter and trainer of aspiring Levantine jihadis. As al-Adel put it: "How could we abandon such an opportunity to be in Palestine and Jordan?"

Al-Qaeda offered Zarqawi some seed money—estimates of the exact amount vary wildly—to open and operate an independent training camp for foreign fighters in Afghanistan in 2000. Zarqawi accepted.

Zarqawi's camp was in the expansive western province of Herat. The group was often called al-Tawhid wa al-Jihad ("Unity and Jihad"), but also began going by Jund al-Sham ("Soldiers of the Levant"). The camp would become a microcosm in which Zarqawi would hone his leadership.

The Herat camp wasn't much to behold at first. All it needed to get off the ground was "a patch of land, a couple of chin-up bars, and guys running around with AK-47s." Since simplicity was a facet of the Prophet Muhammad's lifestyle, it was fitting that Zarqawi's Jund al-Sham exist that way too.

A few of the early camp recruits became key leaders for Zarqawi, eventually fighting and dying with him in Iraq. These Levantine lieutenants—from explosives expert Nidal Mohammad al-Arabi to dentist-turned-operations chief Abu al-Ghadiya—were bound together through their shared loyalty to Zarqawi, who in turn increasingly saw himself as a historic holy warrior. As he ran the day-to-day training of his men in Herat, Zarqawi slowly overcame the semi-illiteracy of his past, reading biographies of Islamic military heroes like the twelfth-century Nur ad-Din, and attempting to draw comparisons between himself and them.

While Maqdisi—Zarqawi's original ideological mentor—was thousands of miles away, he was present in Herat through the ideas he had taught the camp's leader. The military camp was also a functional (if small) Salafi society. Zarqawi took a second wife, a thirteen-year-old girl and the daughter of one of the Palestinian members of the camp. The potent mix of theology and military training dragged Maqdisi's simple Islamic ideas into the realm of practice.

When Saif al-Adel visited the camp, he found the fighters and their families engaged by a "cultural program focused on religious education, learning the Koran by heart, and studying history and geography." The ever-growing band of trainees, wives, and children practiced the straightforward Islam that their Jordanian emir had learned in al-Jafr. All the while, Zarqawi exemplified pure piety. According to a former associate at the camp: "I never heard him praise anyone apart from the Prophet, this was Abu Mo'sab's [*sic*] character."

The base soon became less ramshackle, and the wives of jihadis worked in the kitchens producing Levantine food for the hundreds of people who lived there. Jordanian officials later claimed that Herat was Zarqawi's "turning point . . . the beginning of what he is now. He had command responsibilities for the first time." He reportedly took to calling himself the "Emir of Sham." By the time of America's 2001 intervention in Afghanistan, around three thousand people inhabited Jund al-Sham's camp.

The camp's growth—fueled by Zarqawi's sometimes manic mix of charisma and piety—proved enough of his leadership abilities that al-Qaeda's central leadership approached Zarqawi again, asking him to swear *ba'yat* (or pledge allegiance). Had Zarqawi acceded, formal inclusion in al-Qaeda's senior ranks was likely.

Yet each of the five times he was asked to swear *ba'yat*, Zarqawi refused. He had risen, and would continue to lead, in opposition to al-Qaeda's central leadership.

After the Twin Towers were brought down, America descended upon al-Qaeda and the Taliban with fury. But as US troops entered Herat Province, the trainees were gone. They had been dispersed to the winds of jihad, carried either to death in Kandahar, battle in Tora Bora, detention in Iran, or—in the case of Zarqawi and his senior aides—shelter in the remote reaches of Iraqi Kurdistan.

It was Zarqawi's presence in Iraq that Powell cited years later as evidence of Saddam Hussein's complicity with al-Qaeda. As a result, America would soon once more come to Zarqawi's doorstep, and he would be ready for it.

The United States and its allies—the "Coalition"—invaded Iraq in March 2003, quickly toppling the Iraqi Army and sending former dictator Saddam Hussein into hiding. By that summer, what would eventually become an insurgency was still inchoate and a smattering of disparate individuals and groups, each potentially willing to fight the Coalition, but unsure exactly what that meant or how to do it.

Already confident in his worldview, and with the resources and know-how to act quickly, Zarqawi stepped into the void. Though he didn't immediately claim credit for either attack, Zarqawi directed the bombings of both the Jordanian embassy and the UN headquarters in Baghdad in August 2003—killing dozens and injuring hundreds. The insurgency in Iraq was never a single entity. But in 2003, Zarqawi's swiftness of action gave the insurgency some shape. For Iraqis and others who resented the Western military presence on Iraqi soil, these early attacks had a certain magnetism, their spectacular violence attracting them to the man who'd engineered them.

By the following spring, Zarqawi was no longer just an attractive force to would-be jihadis, but an on-the-ground commander of a committed resistance.

Fallujah

On the segment of the "Sunni Triangle" that stretched from Baghdad to Ramadi, Fallujah marked a strategic midpoint. The desert city and the Sunnis who lived there had a reputation for being tough, industrious, and hard-bitten. Saddam Hussein had delicately managed the city for decades, carefully appeasing the powerful tribal interests that dominated political life there. Many of his Ba'athist military officers and civil servants had been drawn from those tribes—men who, after the Coalition's de-Ba'athification policies* took effect, began returning to the dusty city resentful and unemployed. In early 2004, with the exact contours of the Coalition's occupation still taking shape, Fallujah was a powder keg waiting to explode.

On March 31, it did. Four contractors working for the American private security firm Blackwater were escorting supply trucks to a military base west of the city. As their unarmored vehicles returned through the inner streets of Fallujah, an armed mob shot the contractors dead in their cars, their corpses dragged through the streets before being hung from a bridge over the Euphrates River.

---

* The Coalition removed members of Saddam Hussein's Ba'ath party from all of its official offices. Many analysts argue that this decision fueled the insurgency and deprived the new Iraqi government of needed expertise.

The United States responded with overwhelming military force, intending to send a message to the country's developing insurgency through dramatic action. Yet soon the Marine-led offensive was mired in plodding urban combat that bore no resemblance to the comparatively rapid conventional action that had characterized Iraq's capture the year before. News of heavy fighting and civilian casualties in this "First Battle of Fallujah" spread through Iraq and the watching world like wildfire, and by April 9, the Marines were ordered to halt their offensive.

It was a moment of doubt for the United States and the coalition it led in Iraq. After over a year of occupation, stability appeared further from reach than ever. Conflicting impulses to either reduce the foreign military presence or double down with more force buffeted decision makers in Washington, DC. The desired outcome of a secure, democratic Iraq was clear, yet the pathway to it was becoming yet more muddled. As a result, the Coalition's short-term actions were tentative and uncertain.

Zarqawi suffered from no such ambivalence. With the Marines pulled back to the edge of the city, fighters began to fortify Fallujah against future action by the Coalition—and unbeknownst to most of the Americans, Zarqawi and his men were among them. About four months earlier, Zarqawi had released an audiotape calling on Muslims from across the Arab world to come fight the American infidels in Iraq. Now in the heart of this fight, Zarqawi took advantage of opportunities emerging in Fallujah. Zarqawi, his old hands from Jund al-Sham, and new fighters who came to Iraq from across the Muslim world began to coalesce power within the city.

The Marine presence outside Fallujah didn't stop Zarqawi from slipping in early one July morning, as he had done countless times throughout 2004. Driving a white sedan as it cruised down the poorly paved streets of the Jolan district in the city's northwest, he passed the disorganized messes of auto body shops, restaurants, and residences. Months of violence had left structures crumbled and walls pockmarked by bullets. The car pulled up alongside a building—a safe house for some of the foreign fighters Zarqawi's network had helped bring to the city.

Men like the one Zarqawi was there to meet that day had embedded themselves in Fallujah's splintering society. Some brought military training or knowledge about explosives. Others had experience on the battlefields of jihad from Afghanistan to Chechnya. Now these jihadists fused with local actors—tribal leaders outraged by the spasmodic violence of the American presence or frustrated former Ba'athist officials. These groups acted symbiotically. Locals swelled jihadi ranks, while foreign fighter networks like Zarqawi's could control the vast flows of materials, suicide bombers, cash, and violence that propelled the insurgency. In the presence of these foreign agents, the defiant people of Fallujah saw their trash-strewn streets become laced with daisy-chained IEDs, their neighborhoods concealing horrific torture chambers for captured Shi'ites, police officers, and spies.

Zarqawi's car idled in the street ever so briefly. A man walked purposefully out from a nearby house and got in. As Zarqawi drove onward, he greeted the man, quoted the Quran, and asked about the state of Fallujah's defenses and supplies in the district. When the conversation finished, the sedan cut into traffic in a crowded market district. The associate hopped out at a predesignated spot and blended away into the city throng. By nightfall, Zarqawi slipped back north out of Fallujah to one of his many safe houses in the sprawling farmland countryside.

In the days before his al-Qaeda in Iraq (AQI) became dominant within the insurgency, Zarqawi led by fighting alongside, influencing, and supporting anyone who could create trouble for the government and the Coalition. In visits to small cells of insurgents throughout the city, Zarqawi would dress in black and wear running shoes, recite jihadist poetry, and sing songs with the fighters. This hands-on leadership—starkly different from the taped encouragements put out at a distance by al-Qaeda's senior officers-in-hiding—helped him create a mystique among the fighters on the ground in the thick of jihad. He was real, he was committed, and he was there.

Zarqawi subsequently began issuing more and more propaganda, deftly leveraging the increasing power of the internet. In an era when bin Laden's biannual taped messages were couriered via donkey for the world to hear, there was something exceptional about Zarqawi's technology-enabled approach to disseminating his message. On May 13, he released news that his organization had formally merged with an Iraq-based group of mujahe-

Zarqawi as he appeared in a 2006 propaganda video—dressed in black, relaxing next to an American assault rifle and holding court among jihadi fighters in Iraq. In between the First and Second Battles of Fallujah, this became Zarqawi's image in extremist circles as he toured their battlefields: charismatic, hands-on, and dedicated to their mutual cause.
(PHOTOGRAPH BY DOD VIA GETTY IMAGES)

deen Salafists. By the time Fallujah was at a standstill, and foreign fighters roamed its streets with impunity, Zarqawi was a household name in these circles, and the acknowledged leader of a nationwide network of bomb makers, safe house operators, and veteran soldiers.

The foreign fighters brought with them the violent ideology of Zarqawi and ran the town with brutality. Liquor sellers were flogged in the streets next to barbers who had the audacity to shave men's beards. In basements throughout the city, Shi'ites and suspected government sympathizers were electrocuted, dismembered, and beheaded. The barbarity associated with ISIS in 2018 has its origins in these horrific scenes, and Fallujah marked a place Zarqawi was able to act on his genocidal urges against Shi'ite Muslims.

Zarqawi personally participated in this carnage, which was becoming more common throughout the country. It was in a Fallujah building that Zarqawi had decapitated Nicholas Berg on May 7, 2004, and it was his networks that were pioneering the use of suicide bombers against targets across the country. From devastating attacks on Shi'ite pilgrims to truck bombings in Basra, violence and sectarian tension swelled across Iraq, much of it engineered by the seemingly omnipresent Zarqawi.

From their distant hiding places in Pakistan, bin Laden and Zawahiri watched with growing alarm. They had reasons for concern. Zarqawi's reputation as an al-Qaeda–linked terrorist forced uncomfortable associations between his actions and their brand. Televised beheadings (like Berg's) and suicide attacks on Shi'ites represented a level of melodramatic violence with which al-Qaeda's senior leadership wanted no association. Intercepted writings between Zawahiri and Zarqawi reveal attempts by al-Qaeda in 2005 to discourage Zarqawi's satellite group from indulging in these types of divisive spectacles. In one letter, Zawahiri recommended that "the mujahed movement must avoid any action that the masses do not understand or approve," and argued that killing captives with a bullet was a more practical method of execution than beheading.

Moreover, the means through which Zarqawi propagated violence in the country conflicted with established jihadist creed. His normalization of suicide bombing—often against fellow Muslims—was particularly enraging to many in his spiritual family. Zarqawi's jail-time mentor, Maqdisi, publicly severed ties with him over the practice.

And yet al-Qaeda's senior leaders faced a dilemma regarding Zarqawi's actions. For current and potential jihadis, the contrasts between Zarqawi's hands-on, horrifically zealous leadership and al-Qaeda's more cautious approach was coming into ever sharper focus. For those close to the killing, moderation was not a compelling battle cry. Zarqawi's call for decisive, unrestrained action resonated.

When Zarqawi's network began to produce violent results against both Americans and Iraqi civilians, it gave an appearance of progress and achievement. While bin Laden and Zawahiri hid from American reprisals, Zarqawi remained in the thick of fighting against those whom Salafist creed dictated were heretics. Thus, despite al-Qaeda's hesitance to accept Zarqawi's methodology and worldview, there was political pressure to embrace him.

As Marine forces initiated the Second Battle of Fallujah in November

2004—eventually retaking the fortified city after weeks of bloody fighting—al-Qaeda had decided to revisit its relationship with Zarqawi.

In an audio recording released to the public that December, bin Laden declared that his "mujahed brother Abu Musab al-Zarqawi is the emir of the al-Qaeda for Jihad Organization in the Land of the Two Rivers." Coalition forces would come to refer to Zarqawi's rebranded organization as "Al-Qaeda in Iraq." With this new mantle, the self-proclaimed "sheikh of the slaughterers" was empowered to act on his genocidal vision for the region around him.

He would incite and direct carnage for almost two more years.

Endgame

On May 31, 2006, Baghdad was boiling. Temperatures reached 111 degrees. Exposed metal was too hot to touch, and the wind from the open doors of a low-flying MH-60 helicopter felt like a blast furnace. US soldiers and Iraqi police officers recovered at least twenty-two bodies that had been "burned, blindfolded, handcuffed, thrown in to a river or dumped near a pediatric hospital." A separate roadside bomb killed a pregnant woman, and six local police officers were injured in two subsequent blasts.

By then, such bloodshed was the norm—both for the city and its country. In the nearby city of Baqubah, the severed heads of Sunnis were found packaged in banana crates. Nearly simultaneously, a market in the coastal metropolis of Basra was struck by a truck bombing that maimed scores. Between February 2006 and July 2007, Baghdad's morgue alone collected a monthly average of more than fourteen hundred civilian corpses in various states of disfigurement. Sunni and Shi'ite death squads roamed Iraqi streets at all hours.

It was brutal civil war. Many militias, insurgent cells, and terrorist organizations were actively participating in the carnage, but al-Qaeda in Iraq had worked the hardest, and done the most, to bring about this dystopian state of affairs. Zarqawi had reasoned that general chaos was the surest path to creating a home for his vision of a caliphate in Iraq. So AQI became an accelerant in an already-raging conflict.

By 2005, AQI comprised several local cells across Iraq, each of which was expected to act independently. Within each cell, AQI deployed specialists in things like bomb making and fighter recruitment. And the group had the infrastructure to surge resources where they were needed, including logistics pipelines to connect independent cells and explosives factories to assemble car bombs. A handful of Zarqawi's senior lieutenants from Herat oversaw the administration of these facilities, while the man himself shuttled among his various cells, typically traveling alone, reportedly passing through Coalition checkpoints in a variety of disguises. His battlefield circulation helped him maintain a legendary Robin Hood–like persona among AQI's fighters—a reputation that was heightened by his confounding ability to evade US efforts to target him.

While he visited AQI cells, he didn't command them in any functional sense—at this point in the war, AQI was carrying out dozens of attacks every day, and Zarqawi could not have been aware of each of them. Key to the group's success was its ability to act rapidly within a broad intent, and without needing to wait for orders from above. Because American forces were pursuing Zarqawi so closely by 2006, he couldn't direct operations—a more hands-off leadership style was the only path available to him. Zarqawi evolved, and was effective even when the instinctively hands-on Jordanian had to become a more mythic figure.

In Baghdad, AQI's operational strategy was straightforward. From intercepted maps, Coalition forces learned that AQI had divided the suburbs around the capital into distinct "belts" that it aimed to control. Though openly seizing and holding territory within the capital city was impractical in the midst of the American occupation, maintaining shadowy control over bases of power in surrounding areas was all too achievable.

Instead of directly commanding fighters, Zarqawi enforced adherence to a fundamental strategic insight: AQI's aims would be best served by stoking sectarian conflict. Zarqawi's opinion of Shi'ites had long been clear. Soon after the Coalition invasion, he'd written that Shi'ites were "the insurmountable obstacle, the crafty and malicious scorpion, the spying enemy, and the penetrating venom . . . the looming danger." By continually emphasizing that Shi'ites posed a danger to Iraqi Sunnis (a narrative unwittingly affirmed by the Coalition's de-Ba'athification process), Zarqawi cast himself as an outspoken defender of his sect. And by launching bloody attacks against Shi'ites, Zarqawi provoked violent retaliation—thus confirming his own prediction that Shi'ites were dangerous. Zarqawi was like a professional firefighter who was an arsonist by night.

Zarqawi's early attacks in Iraq were devastating, but their initial pattern didn't clearly indicate a sectarian agenda. As the conflict drew on, however, AQI struck the most hallowed Shi'ite sites in Iraq. These bombings were often planned to occur on holy days like Ashura, when the message they sent would be unmistakable and the human toll maximized. Eventually, even the fear of such attacks would have fatal consequences.

ON AUGUST 31, 2005, pilgrims massed at the Kadhimiya shrine of Shi'ite imam Musa Kadhim began to whisper. That morning, there had been a brief mortar attack. Surely something worse was in the works from Zarqawi's men. Soon the chatter turned to speculation, which warped further into erroneous confirmation: a suicide bomber was in the crowd. Panic ensued, and thousands of worshippers stampeded over a bridge out of the area, killing nearly one thousand of their own in the frenzied rush to escape. No bomber was ever detected, but the simple *fear* of one caused more lives to be lost that day than any other in the Iraq War.

The final breaking point occurred in February 2006, when men dressed as Iraqi security forces infiltrated and destroyed one of the holiest sites of Shi'a Islam, the al-Askari shrine in Samarra. Within hours, Shi'ite militias were retaliating against Sunni neighborhoods and mosques around the country.

IN JUNE 2006, after an intense effort to follow his spiritual adviser, American forces located and dropped two 500-pound bombs on a house occupied by Zarqawi. Despite the tremendous size of the subsequent explosions, when a helicopter-borne special operations team arrived minutes later, the terrorist leader was still alive. He died as an American medic attempted to save him. The US invasion both fueled his brand of leadership and then also snuffed it out.

*The al-Askari shrine is among the holiest sites in Shi'a Islam, and the bombing
attack against it in 2006 proved to be a watershed moment in Iraq's emerging
sectarian war. Its shattered golden dome proved symbolic of the
Coalition's fractured hopes for peace in the country.*

Although his death was a significant blow to al-Qaeda in Iraq, Abu
Musab al-Zarqawi had largely accomplished what he set out to do. Iraq's
civil strife had deteriorated to become self-sustaining and sectarian war
continued—in the year following his death, more civilians died in Iraq
than when he'd been alive to oversee the violence. Zarqawi never achieved
his goal while living, but he had set the stage for ISIS to coopt his style a
decade later as the group swept across parts of Iraq and Syria in an
attempt to establish the caliphate. The zealot was dead, but his project
lived on.

THE CYCLIC LURE OF CONVICTION

Hitler responds to the vibration of the human heart with the delicacy of a
seismograph . . . enabling him to act as a loudspeaker proclaiming the
most secret desires, the least admissible instincts, the sufferings,
and personal revolts of a whole nation. . . .
—OTTO STRASSER (AN OPPONENT OF HITLER'S WITHIN THE NAZI PARTY)

The first statue of Robespierre was erected in November 1918 in the center of Moscow, of all places. Vladimir Lenin was eager for the statue, commissioned to commemorate the Bolshevik Party's first year in power, to be completed, so its construction was hurried and the concrete was flawed. After several days of rain, cracks appeared, and the icon collapsed overnight into a pile of rubble, never to be rebuilt.

There is not a single prominent statue anywhere to memorialize either Zarqawi or Robespierre, which is both ironic and unsurprising. Ironic because they are the quintessential leaders-as-symbol, the kind of leadership that emerges when an ideology and a person become inseparable. But unsurprising because each of their revolutions ultimately failed, and both were extremists; the very vehemence that made them effective leaders also makes them difficult to celebrate.

These zealots are also difficult to compare as leaders. Robespierre is remembered as a speechmaker, and Zarqawi as a fighter. Robespierre influenced with his words, whereas Zarqawi learned to read and write only late in life. Robespierre found his leadership-by-ideology in schooling and among the elite. Zarqawi found his in prison. All of this highlights that there's no formula for becoming a zealot, and that *how* an extreme ideology translates to leadership remains dependent on the circumstances available to that leader and to that leader's particular situation.

The strongest point of comparison is their association with violence. For Robespierre, killing was necessary for the end state, but he had no stomach for the carnage and kept it at arm's length—indeed, he only rarely signed execution orders himself. For Zarqawi, it was important that he was hands-on with his violence. For both, and however tragic, immoral, and nonetheless effective, their public willingness to take life re-inforced the depth of their commitment and fueled their cause, at least to a point.

They didn't so much cause all this violence on their own as they helped to focus existing passion to force things in a direction they were already going. Like all leaders, they were part of a system, and their leadership was inseparable from the rest of that system.

Moreover, their leadership was less in what they did and more in how they were framed relative to others. They were extreme not just in an abso-lute sense, but in contrast to their contemporaries. Robespierre took un-popular rhetorical stands (opposing war, for instance) that set him apart from his revolutionary colleagues. Zarqawi was willing to go to extremes to bring about his caliphate, distinguishing him from al-Qaeda's leader-ship, who were themselves in hiding and far from the fight. For each, their willingness to stand apart conveyed a powerful sense of purity and direc-tion to their followers.

It is not a coincidence that each of these men led for less than five years, and then died a violent death. Zealots serve a special and powerful purpose, but their sort of leadership can be cyclical and short-lived. The better they play their role, the less tolerable the environment becomes. Like flames that consume all available oxygen and fuel, Zarqawi and Robespierre became the agents of their own destruction. And because their leadership was tied to their ideological purity, compromise wasn't an option. Zealots become corseted by their own followers' expectations.

While we can understand their short shelf life, it remains difficult to explain and awkward to rationalize the zealot's effectiveness as a leader. As with both Robespierre and Zarqawi, grudging respect, and often admira-tion, is given to the totally committed. If we agree with their cause, we of-ten find ourselves full-throated advocates for a zealous leader, despite the fact that their approach may be difficult to defend. Robespierre and Zar-qawi overcame this tension by allowing their followers to feel completely in touch with an important idea.

These zealots were particularly useful in a period of chaos, when their uncompromising nature and straightforward ideology offered followers both stability and energy. There was no uncertainty about where they stood, and that provided for a meaningful sense of direction—they were clarifying and comforting. Zarqawi, for instance, was the first insurgent to launch massive suicide attacks in the wake of the US invasion of Iraq. Similarly, Robespierre began to build his reputation as the Incorruptible nearly as soon as he arrived at the Estates General. Each was able to act quickly and decisively. As a result, even to their opponents, these zealots were a benchmark, helping myriad players to define where they stood.

That straightforwardness left an impression on the leader of Russia's Bolshevik Party, who praised his short-lived statue of Robespierre for capturing the revolutionary hero's "decisiveness." In his own age of turmoil, Lenin recognized the power of a zealot as a potent symbol of clarity.

Six

THE HEROES

This is the West, sir.
When the legend becomes fact, print the legend.

—FROM THE FILM
THE MAN WHO SHOT LIBERTY VALANCE

Periodically, while crossing the Yale campus, I pass a statue outside
Connecticut Hall, where young Nathan Hale resided before graduat-
ing in 1773 at the age of eighteen to become a teacher. Dedicated in
1914, the bronze likeness celebrates the selfless courage of the Continental
Army first lieutenant who in September 1776 volunteered to spy on British
forces in and around New York City and was captured and hanged. Famously, his final words are remembered as: "I regret that I have but one life
to lose for my country."

His example of intrepidity and selfless sacrifice have inspired generations since.

The story is largely true. Nathan Hale did, in fact, courageously step
forward to gather information behind enemy lines, and accounts of his execution indicate he conducted himself with impressive composure—no
small task for a twenty-one-year-old with little background and zero training for the task he undertook, and likely only a hazy appreciation of the
enormous risks associated with it.

Unfortunately, in the nine days between infiltrating the British-
controlled city and his apprehension, Hale apparently accomplished little.

His most significant contribution ultimately lay in his conduct as a condemned prisoner.

And disturbingly, some accounts credit Major Robert Rogers, a hero of the French and Indian War and founder of the American Rangers, a unit in which I served two centuries later, with entrapping the novice secret agent. Not surprisingly, Rogers's decision to align with the British against the Revolution is rarely discussed in the history of the Ranger Regiment.

Even Hale's iconic last words may not be true. Accounts vary, and so we are left to speculate. But it doesn't really matter. The statues of heroic young Nathan Hale at Yale, Hartford, New York City, and the dormitories, barracks, schools, and United States Navy submarine that carry his name all honor the idea more than the man. They are the hopeful gesture that in honoring the concept, we encourage the ethos and behavior in those who follow.

While the terms "hero" and "leader" are not synonymous, heroes often serve as useful models of courage, stoicism, and sacrifice. And although not all heroes seek or accept the mantle of leadership, the example they set, and the inspiration it provides, can be noteworthy. We search for heroism, and where it suits us, we celebrate it. Where genuine heroes are not apparent, we create mythical ones. We focus on selected acts, ignoring others, and often burnish the hero's image to a high sheen.

We gave considerable thought to selecting the right pair of leaders to profile, seeking to explore both the reality of a hero's impact and the power of legend. We considered many, including Joan of Arc and Davy Crockett, before deciding to begin with Zheng He, a fifteenth-century Chinese admiral with little name recognition in the West. Castrated as a boy by Ming dynasty captors he would later serve, and purported to be seven feet tall, and leading a fleet of improbably huge ships, Zheng He seems more apocryphal than real—akin to a Paul Bunyan or Pecos Bill caricature. But nearly six centuries after his death, far from a forgotten sailor, Zheng has a considerable, and growing, stature in modern China, and his story reflects much about the society that reveres him.

To pair with Zheng He, we profiled former slave turned abolitionist and Underground Railroad conductor Harriet Tubman. Dramatically smaller in physical stature than the admiral, with an equally unlikely path to her place in the pantheon of heroes, Harriet Tubman is a figure who grew larger with closer examination. The impression she created through her life of service left an impossibly more significant mark than her circumstances should have allowed, and she was also intriguingly more complex and human than her tale suggests.

Admittedly, few of us can truly appreciate the unthinkable, yet omnipresent fear of reenslavement, but we can immediately admire the unwavering courage of an illiterate middle-aged woman in daunting circumstances.

More than any other genre of leaders, heroes are a function of the judgment and needs of others. So what need do they fill, and how and why do we follow them?

Key Books

- Edward L. Dreyer, *Zheng He: China and the Oceans in the Early Ming Dynasty, 1405–1433* (New York: Pearson Longman, 2006)
- Louise Levathes, *When China Ruled the Seas: The Treasure Fleet of the Dragon Throne, 1405–1433* (New York: Oxford University Press, 1996)
- Kate Clifford Larson, *Bound for the Promised Land: Harriet Tubman, Portrait of an American Hero* (New York: One World, 2003)

ZHENG HE

Take courage, my heart: you have been through worse than this. Be strong, saith my heart; I am a soldier; I have seen worse sights than this.

—HOMER, *THE ODYSSEY*

At close to four hundred feet long, and nearly two hundred wide, the ancient ship was reported to have been larger than a modern football field. The rudder alone was two stories tall—a size that was necessary to steer the huge craft through the rough waters it encountered on expeditions across the Arabian Sea and Pacific Ocean. To harness maritime winds, nine masts stood atop its deck, complete with twelve sails that stretched across more than sixty thousand square feet. In the words of one contemporary, when unfurled these would have looked "like great clouds in the sky."

The Yongle ("Everlasting Joy") Emperor, born as Zhu Di, became the third ruler of the Ming dynasty after deposing his predecessor in a civil war. Though Yongle's stature was unparalleled in Ming society, we found a more heroic figure in his servant— the eunuch admiral Zheng He, commander of the mythologized Treasure Fleet of ancient China.
(PHOTOGRAPH BY UNIVERSAL HISTORY ARCHIVE/UIG VIA GETTY IMAGES)

The boat displaced around ten thousand tons of water, three times that of the HMS *Victory*, Admiral Horatio Nelson's 104-gun flagship in the Battle of Trafalgar—a boat built 347 years later, and considered the apogee of eighteenth-century technology. According to a later commentator, merely one of this vessel's multiple decks could fit "all the ships of Columbus and da Gama combined."

The emperor of China commissioned the construction of the gargantuan boat in 1408, early in the reign of his Ming dynasty, and well before Columbus, da Gama, and Nelson had even been born. It was called a *bao-chuan*, or "Treasure Ship"—one of nearly fifty such leviathans that the emperor had built in the same decade. Together with hundreds of lesser craft, these Treasure Ships formed their emperor's Foreign Expeditionary Armada, which would go on to establish influence in distant nations across oceans and unexplored continents, many years before European civilizations set foot there.

The imperial armada is recorded to have made seven expeditions between 1405 and 1433, each with hundreds of ships and tens of thousands of men.

All seven of these voyages were led by one man: Zheng He (pronounced "Jung Huh"), the famous eunuch admiral of China and loyal slave to the emperor.

According to the few historic accounts that remain, Zheng He's stature matched his massive ships. He was said to have stood seven feet tall, with a waist that was five feet in circumference—an unbelievable size, the product of both legend and the fact that the Chinese measurement of a "foot" has changed over the years. By the time of the expeditionary armada's first voyage, his skin was already "rough like the surface of the orange," while his "eyebrows were like swords and his forehead wide, like a tiger's." His voice was described as similarly exceptional: booming and clear.

Whatever Zheng's exact physical size really was, he has become a cultural giant in modern China. After nearly six hundred years of relative obscurity following his death in the fifteenth century, Zheng has emerged as a symbol for a China once again setting out beyond her borders to restore her role as a global leader. Schoolchildren across China know of Zheng He, but as with most such leaders, looking at only the individual or the myth would be insufficient. We must understand the man, and appreciate the power of the myth.

"The Stories of Antiquity"

Theseus and Romulus—the founders of Athens and Rome, respectively— usually make up the first chapter of modern, compiled editions of Plutarch's *Lives*. Plutarch knew that these men's stories dwelt partially in fable, and admits as much to his readers:

> Let us hope that Fable may, in what shall follow, so submit to the purifying processes of Reason as to take the character of exact history. In any case, however, where it shall be found contumaciously slighting credibility . . . we shall beg that we may meet with candid readers, and such as will receive with indulgence the stories of antiquity.

Yet Plutarch saw their embellished tales as worthy profiles all the same, conveying them just as he did the less mythological men who constituted the remainder of his *Lives*. Plutarch paired the two because they were the men at the center of their civilizations' founding myths.

Because they were both considered to be "sprung from the Gods," as Plutarch puts it, their stories were canvases on which Romans and Greeks could paint the values each held most dear. But Plutarch was a biographer, not a painter. He also portrayed the shortcomings of both Romulus and Theseus, faithful to how each man fell short of the myths surrounding him:

> Both Theseus and Romulus were by nature meant for governors; yet neither lived up to the true character of a king, but fell off, and ran, the one into popularity, the other into tyranny, falling both into the same fault out of different passions.

We cannot paint a perfectly lifelike picture of Zheng He, whose physical size undoubtedly grew along with his legend. But we can put his legend side by side with the recorded facts of his life to understand how people in his own time and beyond have thought about what the ideal leader—and hero—should be.

Unlike Theseus or Romulus, Zheng He was not the ultimate authority of his society or era. He was the castrated child of a defeated people forced into service to the emperor of China. But Zheng's is a worthy story nonetheless, that of, the servant whose legacy has surpassed that of his master.

Enslavement

Zheng's life was precarious from an early age. He was born as Ma He into a Mongolian family around 1371, in the independent province of Yunnan, bordering the growing Ming empire of China. It was a particularly dangerous time in the region, and especially so for someone with Zheng's background. As the son of a Muslim Yunnan army officer, he would likely face slavery or death should the mountainous territory fall to the Ming.

And fall it did. A quarter-million-strong Ming army invaded Yunnan in 1382, killing more than 60,000 local tribesmen along with "countless"

Mongols in the province. Zheng's father was among those who fell fighting the Ming forces.

At the time of their incursion into Yunnan, Ming rule of China was in its infancy. The Ming emperor, the first of the Ming dynasty, had seized power from the Yuan only four years earlier. The Yuan, ethnically Mongolian descendants of Genghis Khan, had ruled China for over a century as a vassal state. At the time of the Yuan's dethroning, the last of their dynasty took sanctuary in the diverse province of Yunnan.

There the remnant Mongolians stayed defiant against the Ming, whose emperor dedicated himself to restoring Confucian ideals in China—long neglected by the foreign Yuan. When the Ming sent an envoy to negotiate with Mongolian forces in Yunnan, he was beheaded. This action forced the Ming's hand, and they invaded.

In the aftermath of the fighting that killed his father and subjected Yunnan to Ming rule, the ten-year-old Zheng was apprehended by a Ming war party searching for an escaped Yunnan official. When questioned by the soldiers, Zheng lied, telling the soldiers he'd seen the man in question jump into a nearby pond. The Ming officer questioning Zheng found the retort both amusing and brave and, in response, took the young boy into custody.

Inter-kingdom invasions were often followed by efforts to extinguish future resistance from the occupied territory, beginning with eliminating those in power, as well as their lineage. Once Ming soldiers had sufficiently crushed local resistance, they were ordered by the emperor to settle in the local area—diluting the ethnic composition of the province and ensuring that its population would be integrated with the rest of China forever. Castration to prevent the emergence of future opposition leadership was common practice. All told, several thousand sons of Yunnan officers were castrated, Zheng He among them.

Yet despite its unfortunate start, and the obvious challenge of being a conquered Mongol in servitude to a Ming prince, the path ahead of Zheng He held some promise. Even with the death of his family members, and the devastation of his homeland, opportunity would open for Zheng as a result of his newfound place in the royal court, and he would seize it.

Loyalty and "Everlasting Joy"

The son of the emperor to whom Zheng He was bound for life was Zhu Di. The invasion of Yunnan—in which Zheng had been captured—was Zhu's first experience in war. Though Zhu was not yet emperor, he surely coveted the mantle of his father.

The position and status of a Chinese emperor is difficult to fully appreciate today. Considered a "Son of Heaven," the emperor's rule over China was popularly believed to be a result of his divine status. He reigned over his people from a position of perceived holiness, where his leadership of the nation was sanctified by the authority of elaborate ceremonies, and his interactions with his subjects were carefully controlled. No other status of the imperial era approached the reverence accorded the emperor. Therefore, to be in the emperor's personal service was a position shown great respect.

Every emperor's court was a collection of advisers, military officers, courtesans, and scholars subject to choreographed rituals. Eunuchs were responsible for critical administrative functions in these chambers of governance, and, despite their castration and lack of freedom, were envied for their influential status. Not surprisingly, court gossips complained that eunuchs were of weak temperament, often corrupt, and liable to interfere in political matters in order to expand their court influence. And there was a strong perception that eunuchs were a faction in need of restraint and control. Zhu Di's father—the first Ming emperor—directed that eunuchs be kept illiterate, and that any caught interfering in politics would be beheaded.

Zheng appears to have overcome the stereotypes quickly. Early in his service to Zhu Di, Zheng was promoted beyond the roles typically held by eunuchs in the imperial bureaucracy. Taller than most of his fellow eunuchs, with a deeper voice and more stoic demeanor, he also distinguished himself by his martial expertise. Not long after Zheng joined Zhu Di's court in Beijing, Mongolian raiders began attacking Ming caravans. Zhu rallied his ponderous forces to respond to the threat, and Zheng earned the trust of the prince by serving in increasingly prominent roles as a chief military aide and battlefield commander, leading columns of Ming soldiers against horse-mounted Mongols in China's cold northern steppes.

Zheng's competence and demonstrated loyalty to the Mings solidified his position. By 1391, when the leader of the Mongols surrendered, Zheng was still only twenty years old, and he had nonetheless ascended to the highest levels of power within Zhu's court.

In the years ahead, Zheng remained aligned with Zhu and, in the inevitable vacuum that emerged with the death of Zhu's father in 1398, helped him expand his power. Conflict arose between Ming princes for the throne, and also between the different power bases in their respective courts. Confucian advisers strongly insisted, per their doctrine, that Zhu be passed over in favor of the emperor's grandson, the son of the emperor's eldest son. The new emperor, Zhu Di's nephew, ascended the throne and immediately began to purge his family of possible threats to his power. Zhu's brothers, with less military power at their disposal, were systematically eliminated under a policy called "reducing the feudatories." In Beijing, north of the national capital in Nanjing, Zhu at first cleverly feigned madness to help escape his nephew's purge, then organized a formal rebellion.

In the ensuing civil war, Zheng distinguished himself in Zhu's service. Early in the war, as imperial forces surrounded the rebels' capital in Beijing, it appeared the insurrection would be short-lived. Yet at the site of one of the city's major reservoirs, named Zhenglunba, Zheng He led a force of rebel troops against imperial soldiers. During the ensuing battle that would prove a rebel victory, Zheng's horse was shot out from under him. In recognition of his heroism and battlefield triumph that lifted the imperial siege, Zhu renamed his eunuch commander. Known since birth as Ma He, he would now be named for the site of his bravery—Zheng, after Zhenglunba.

Now standing as a peer to conventional military commanders, Zheng organized raids on supply trains around crucial enemy cities and used his troops to cut off grain supplies and harass imperial columns. Always careful to avoid areas where the enemy was known to be concentrated, Zheng seized a series of weakly defended towns and eventually joined Zhu's forces outside of Nanjing.

Resentful of the controls that had been placed on them by a distrustful emperor, the eunuchs in Zhu's court informed Zheng of the locations of imperial forces and of weaknesses in the defenses of Nanjing. Armed with this intelligence, Zhu's army marched victoriously into the capital in July 1402. As was tradition, Zhu Di assumed a new name upon ascending the throne that year. From then on, he would become known to history as the Yongle, or "Everlasting Joy," Emperor.

Among the emperor's first orders was to execute his predecessor's advisers and military officers—those who had successfully denied him power and resisted his attempt to reclaim it—but also their families "to the ninth and tenth degree," as well as their teachers and servants. The purge would be ruthless—and absolute.

The former emperor's Confucian advisers were cleaned out as well. One of the seniormost Confucians, when asked to draft an order formalizing the new emperor's reign, angrily refused. Throwing down his writing brush, the Confucian scribe claimed that he would rather die. The emperor gave the man his wish, ordering execution by *lingchi*—"a thousand cuts." Over the course of several days, the scholar's body was meticulously sliced until little blood remained to be drained from it.

In the aftermath of Zhu Di's victory, there were persistent rumors that the nephew he had unseated had somehow faked his death and escaped overseas to a distant land. For a man as paranoid as the emperor, the possibility that his enemy had survived was a threat that could not be ignored. A mission would be organized to eliminate this danger.

The man entrusted to lead it was Zheng He.

ON A FALL EVENING in Nanjing in 1405, Zheng He, now in his mid-thirties, led his senior officers in prayer and sacrifice to Tianfei, the Chinese patron goddess of sailors. Before the presence of their emperor, the men had each been given gold and silk as a sign of respect for the risks they were about to take on his behalf. The next morning, Zheng would lead more than twenty thousand men on the first voyage of the Treasure Fleet.

At the docks, some 250 ships awaited their boarding. Resources from across the empire had been summoned for their construction: cedarwood for their hulls, elm for the rudders, oars of fir and juniper, as well as massive fir masts. In addition to the flagship Treasure Ships, there were also boats dedicated to carrying water and food, and transportation for the foreign ambassadors they anticipated bringing back.

Among the fleet's crew were 302 military officers, 180 medical specialists, as well as bursars, administrators, translators, judges, and a fortune
teller. The remainder of the rank-and-file included blacksmiths, crafts-
men, and soldiers. Zheng exerted command over this coalition via 70 eunuchs who captained the various vessels. Communication between the
ships was maintained through a complex system of flags, gongs, lanterns,
and carrier pigeons. In addition to personnel, the ships carried silks, ornate
robes, silver, and gold—all intended to be gifted to countries visited along
the way.

According to an unofficial history of the era, the emperor even gave a
specific purpose for the voyage. Zheng was "to seek out traces of" the rumored escape of his predecessor. Yet the size of the fleet, the capabilities of
its crew, and its valuable cargo left room for speculation over the true purpose of the fleet. This first voyage was destined for the Indian spice center
of Calicut, with various ports of call along the way.

Zheng had served his emperor faithfully for decades and confirmed his
worth as a commander during the war for the throne—his proven competence and dedication left no room for doubt. But he lacked any naval expertise, and at thirty-five years old, Zheng was considered old by the standards
of the time. It was a difficult decision for the emperor, and as often happens
in choosing whom to appoint as a leader, it came down to a combination of
both rational and seemingly arbitrary factors.

A counselor told the emperor: "Let not Your Imperial Majesty forget
the saying 'the old horse knows the way.'" According to this adviser, Zheng
had the weather-beaten appearance of someone who could endure years at
sea. Moreover, Zheng was eloquent, "with a mouth like the sea," while the
closeness of his eyebrows indicated that his internal energies were focused
on his service to the emperor. The size of his forehead was also a sign of his
strong character and aptitude for military command. The adviser's augu-
ries accentuated the strength of Zheng's real-world credentials, and his
physical attributes were now considered signs of a god-given capacity for
leadership.

Zheng was the first eunuch ever appointed to so high a command, and
with it the emperor gave him the ultimate authority—blank scrolls bearing

A portrayal of Zheng as he is popularly recalled today—with handsome, heroic, and auspicious features. With a tigerlike "wide" forehead, rough skin, and "eyebrows like swords," Zheng's fortuitous appearance confirmed his suitability for leading the Treasure Fleet.
(CHRIS HELLIERT/ALAMY STOCK PHOTO)

the imperial seal. Zheng, the eunuch servant, now had the power to issue orders abroad on behalf of the emperor, his divine master.

AFTER WHAT HAD BEEN a twenty-five-year rise through the imperial court, Zheng had not forgotten his past.

One month ahead of the fleet's first departure from Nanjing, Zheng, now an important man, had taken the opportunity to return to his homeland in Yunnan. At his father's gravesite, Zheng dutifully erected a tablet to commemorate him:

> The title of this gentleman was Hazhi (*hajji*). . . . The gentleman was diligent, clear-headed, and sharp-witted; modest, respectful, strict, and close-mouthed. [He] did not avoid working hard . . . by observing his offspring one surely can see what the father accomplished during his life and taught by his righteous ways. . . . [Ma Hajji] respected the practice of ritual and righteousness; in his station, [he] was con-

tent as an ordinary commoner yet cherished the bestowal of extraordinary favors.

In this tribute to a man he barely knew, Zheng revealed the values that had become important to him over his lifetime in servitude: loyalty, the concept of "righteousness," and an appreciation for "ritual" and "the bestowal of extraordinary favors."

Accounts celebrate a principled nobility in Zheng's service to the emperor—a man who had helped command the forces who killed his father. Despite an abundance of reasons for bitterness and disloyalty to the Ming, Zheng rose above it and was judged worthy of commanding the largest flotilla ever assembled by that point in history.

Diplomacy, Pirates, and Divine Light

The fleet's arrival in Calicut was surely an intimidating sight: hundreds of masts crowding the view from the shoreline nearly all the way to the horizon, with vast ships bearing exotic weapons, goods, and thousands of crew docked at harbor. For the inhabitants of the various lands that Zheng's fleet visited—in places as far as Champa, Java, Quilon, Ceylon, and Calicut on this first voyage—it must have been difficult to interpret what was meant by this massive, and novel, spectacle. Was this fleet a true armada, a diplomatic tour, a trading mission, a search for an escaped emperor, or some obscure combination of all those things?

The conduct of the fleet at each port provided some answers: unlike the European fleets that would arrive later, Zheng's did not seem intent on either establishing a permanent presence in the nations it visited, nor would it enslave locals. While its military might was brought to bear against locals in certain cases, and commercial trade occurred, the fleet's primary interest was usually in finding local envoys to bring back to China. In doing so, the fleet could ensure that these states recognized the suzerainty and power of the Yongle Emperor.

Zheng's fundamental mission thus appeared to be the establishment of a Ming-centric vassal system. In sending later representatives to the emperor's court, complete with tribute gifts, the nations visited by Zheng's Treasure

Fleet would be symbolically submitting themselves to Ming authority. Still considered by those on the ships as the lands of "barbarians," these countries would nevertheless be granted the privilege of trading with the Treasure Fleet on its future voyages. For the fledgling rule of the Yongle Emperor, such a system would consolidate his domestic legitimacy—something that was almost certainly a concern, given the violent way in which he rose to power.

Zheng's own identity may have assisted him as a commander of such an alliance-minded expedition. On the Treasure Fleet's missions, Zheng often demonstrated an abundance of respect for local faiths and customs. A good example of this came during his 1408 return to Ceylon—in which he was met with hostility—when Zheng erected a multilingual tablet offering dedications to Chinese, Hindu, and Muslim deities in their respective languages, as well as gifts of precious metals, silk, and perfumed oil to each god. Zheng's deft leadership helped secure envoys from a half dozen nations on his first voyage alone.

Not all of the fleet's visits were peaceful, however. In 1407, two years after he'd first set out from China, Zheng demonstrated his forces' martial abilities. Sailing past the Indonesian island of Sumatra, he first offered peaceful parley to a marauding pirate called Chen Zuyi. Zheng had noted the presence of ethnic Chinese among the local population when he first visited in 1405—the descendants of migrants who had left China when it was under the rule of pre-Ming dynasties. These local Chinese and their indigenous allies were now at war against Chen's pirate forces, who had been disrupting commerce in the area. Chen at first accepted Zheng's peace offering, but apparently it was a ruse by the pirate: Chen intended to escape or ambush the Treasure Fleet.

But Zheng had gotten wind of the plot. Once Chen's ships got within range, the sailors of the Treasure Fleet used burning tapers and grenades to incinerate the pirates' sails. After capturing Chen and killing five thousand of his men, Zheng sailed onward to Nanjing.

ON THE VOYAGE NORTHWARD from Sumatra to Nanjing, Zheng's returning ships were suddenly struck by a tempest as they traversed the South China

Sea. Now with both captive pirates and envoys in tow, the Treasure Fleet was in danger of sinking in the violent churn that surrounded them. The sailors were certain that they had sailed over a raging dragon, and began to fearfully pray to their patron goddess, Tianfei, the deity they had worshipped upon their initial departure.

Suddenly, a glowing azure light seemed to emanate from the ships' pointed fir masts. The vessels soon resembled floating lanterns, to amazing effect and the stupefaction of the crew: "As soon as this miraculous light appeared, the danger was becalmed. Everyone on the fleet, set at rest, felt assured that there was [now] nothing to fear."

What the fleet had encountered was almost certainly St. Elmo's fire, a meteorological oddity that European mariners regularly experienced in later centuries. To Zheng and his sailors, however, this was nothing short of a divine blessing bestowed on his first expedition.

When Zheng returned home from his first voyage, after only two years as a sea captain, he could legitimately be hailed as a skillful diplomat, a victorious warrior, and a divinely guarded leader. The emperor conferred new status on Zheng and his fleet. After lobbying from Zheng, the emperor granted greater titles to Tianfei and ordered the rebuilding of a temple to her at her reputed birthplace.

Tribute, Final Voyages, and Death

By 1414, the Treasure Fleet had left and returned to China twice more. In the aftermath of three successful expeditions in the previous decade—to new destinations like present-day Somalia and Kenya—a coterie of African and Arabian ambassadors were now in full-time residence in the emperor's court in Nanjing.

Good omens came along with this growing network of international envoys. The most dramatic symbol came that September: the beast that was brought from overseas before the Beijing court that day was a wonder to those present. It was intended as a gift for the emperor from the king of Bengal. Standing upright on horselike hooves, with a long, smooth head crowned by a pair of rounded cartilaginous horns, it towered many feet above the heads of the silk-robed ministers, ambassadors, and astrologers crowded around it. The animal's naturally crisscrossed hide was a

The arrival of a giraffe from abroad to the Ming court—where it was mistaken for a mythical qilin—*was interpreted as a divine blessing of the emperor's rule and by extension Zheng's fleet. This painting and an associated poem were commissioned in response to the event. The appearance of fortuitous omens like this one would not last, however.*
(GIFT OF JOHN T. DORRANCE, 1977)

stark contrast to the gilded ceilings and rich furnishings of the imperial court.

There was only one possible explanation: this was a *qilin* (pronounced "chee-lin"), a divine being that was said to have appeared before the mother of Confucius. The rumored tradition was that *qilin* would appear to humans to indicate the arrival of great sages. The appearance of a *qilin* in the Chinese capital was interpreted as heavenly endorsement of their ruler's reign.

Of course, this spectacle was just a giraffe. But this omen could not have appeared at a more fitting time for the reign of the emperor: along with the success of the Treasure Fleet, the empire was showing signs of domestic prosperity. In Beijing, the construction of the Forbidden City had begun, with one in fifty of China's total population working on the grand project. At a time when so much of the populace was mobilized to support public works, and when the emperor was the most divine figure in a mysterious world that contained creatures like *qilin*, it's no surprise that the big admiral, the emperor's premier servant, might evolve into something of a hero.

Zheng's ships were on a mission to east Africa at the time, and so he was not there when the emperor was supposedly presented with the *qilin*. In 1416, though, Zheng returned with another giraffe. Zheng and his fleet were at the peak of their influence. Just as his Treasure Ships could safely traverse the Horn of Africa, Zheng's efforts were being received by his patron as favorably as they ever would be over the course of his life.

But it would not last. Soon, domestic pressures would force a reconsideration of Zheng's command.

IN THE SPRING OF 1421, storm clouds brewed over the newly finished Forbidden City in Beijing. After heavy showers, great bolts of lightning struck its three main halls, kindling fires in their high rafters. Before the day was done, the compound looked as though "a hundred thousand torches" had been ignited within its walls. Throughout the Forbidden City, offices, apartments, and ceremonial rooms were destroyed in the blaze.

This was not the first such inauspicious moment for the emperor's rule. Not long beforehand, a hunting horse had been given to him by one of the foreign envoys that now populated his court. When the emperor attempted to use it in the field, it bucked him off and injured him—an incident that had caused much diplomatic consternation at the time.

But after the fires at the Forbidden City, criticism of imperial policies began to flow even more freely behind closed doors.

The empire appeared to be in disarray: open rebellion, fueled by imperial demand for timber for the Forbidden City, had broken out in the province of Annam, while the capital's investment in the Treasure Fleet was coming under closer scrutiny by Confucian advisers to the emperor. Famines had taken place in the countryside, and soon even the emperor's senior ministers were either committing suicide or being jailed for defying his demands.

These crises at home forced a suspension of Zheng's voyages—after his return in 1421 from the fleet's sixth voyage, his boats were kept at anchor for nearly a decade. During this time, Zheng completed one diplomatic mission on his own to Palembang, in Sumatra. As China paused its interactions with the outside world in the midst of chaos at home, the Confucians must surely have felt vindicated and relieved.

In 1424, the emperor personally set out with his troops from Beijing to fight raiding Mongolians in the north of his territory. He died at the front—leaving a power vacuum in his wake, and Zheng He without his chief patron. Zheng heard of the Yongle Emperor's death upon his return from the mission in Palembang, at which point he was given the duty of defending Nanjing, still China's capital after the Forbidden City had burned down in Beijing. Zheng would hold this position for seven years.

BY 1431, Zheng was embarking on what would be the seventh of his fleet's voyages, and one he expected would be his last. The Yongle Emperor's successors had pursued isolationist policies in the aftermath of his death, implicitly endorsing a view that the Treasure Fleet's adventures had been nothing but "wasteful expenditures." On what would in fact be his final expedition, Zheng's mission was to inform the tribute states of the many changes to the domestic situation in China since the fleet's last voyage—a trip that would take his men as far as modern-day Saudi Arabia.

In preparation, he had taken the time to raise a tablet in Fujian that recounted the fleet's past adventures at sea, ascribing their success to divine blessings:

> From the third year of Yongle until now we have seven times received commissions as ambassadors to the countries of the Western Ocean . . . in all more than thirty countries large and small. [We have] traversed over a hundred thousand miles of vast ocean [and have] beheld rolling billows in the great oceans and huge waves like mountains rising as high as the sky.

In 1433, as the fleet rounded India on its return to China, Zheng died of natural causes. He was sixty-two years old. Without its leader, the fleet's arrival back home would be its last.

Not long thereafter, the tribute system Zheng had helped establish gradually broke down, in what some have referred to as the beginning of China's "Great Withdrawal." As interest in maintaining this international network declined, smugglers and thieves began openly posing as envoys from foreign lands, and corrupt local officials began seizing whatever tribute was on its way to Nanjing.

In perhaps the most audacious attempt to remove the memory of Zheng's accomplishments, official imperial records of his expeditions were "accidentally" destroyed—an action that has been blamed on revisionist Confucians in the emperor's court.

With that, Zheng and his fleets were forgotten—at least for a time.

A Convenient Revival

One spring, centuries after the last Treasure Ship had rotted at its moorings in Nanjing, a legation of foreign envoys crowded into a brightly lit receiving room in central Beijing. Even a few heads of state joined in. Taken together, the statesmen assembled represented a hundred nations from across not only Asia and the Pacific Rim, but also Europe and the New World. They promptly took their seats, ready to hear an opening address from their host.

Xi Jinping, general secretary of the Chinese Communist Party, the head of the People's Republic of China, soon took the stage. He was presiding over the 2017 "Belt and Road Forum." Xi's speech explained his country's agenda to the forum attendees: the creation of a new intercontinental Silk Road, a major new infrastructure investment intended to bind together the East and the West in a relationship of "Peace and Cooperation . . . Openness and Inclusiveness."

Near the beginning of his talk, Xi sought to humanize the project and place it in a broader historical context. Using Zheng He, Xi was able to explain that China sought peaceful cooperation, a sort of world order that had been possible in the past thanks to Chinese leadership:

> In the early 15th century Zheng He, the famous Chinese navigator in the Ming Dynasty, made seven voyages to the Western Seas, a feat which still is remembered today. These pioneers won their place in

history not as conquerors with warships, guns or swords. Rather, they are remembered as friendly emissaries leading camel caravans and sailing treasure-loaded ships. Generation after generation, Silk Road travelers have built a bridge for peace and East-West cooperation.

FOLLOWING ZHENG'S DEATH, China no longer wished to extend influence overseas. China's maritime capability, once intercontinental, eventually dwindled to the point that its coast became regularly raided by Japanese pirates in the sixteenth century. By the twenty-first century, however, interest in Zheng and his fleet had resurged.

Embedded in Chinese national memory at the time of this popular resurgence were the traumas of the Opium Wars and the failed Boxer Rebellion—Chinese xenophobia and isolationism had led to military humiliation and foreign dominance that would persist for generations. Perhaps the most wounding moment in this period was the British burning of the Imperial Summer Palace in 1840, an act deliberately carried out to undermine domestic "pride as well as . . . feelings." This era would be remembered in Chinese history as the "century of humiliation," and gave some Chinese reason to wish that they had not shied away from international engagement and exploration.

Returning Zheng's legacy to public prominence could help salve wounded Chinese pride. This intent is best represented in the Communist-era writings of Huang Hui-zhen and Xue Jin-du in their work *Eighty Years of Researching Zheng He*:

> From the age of Zheng He until the new period of socialist construction, the achievements of Zheng He during his voyages to the Western ocean have been excellent materials for conducting patriotic education for the Chinese nation.

Eventually, such education was aimed at both foreign and domestic audiences. Chinese authorities could use Zheng He's memory to shape the minds of future generations. In elementary school, Chinese schoolchildren were taught about Zheng He's life. Trillions of Chinese government dollars went to infrastructure projects along Zheng's old routes. These assertive international moves—like the trillion-dollar "Belt and Road Initiative" establishing massive trade infrastructure throughout the Asian continent, and a network of commercial naval bases constructed around the Indo-Pacific—provided a framework like that of the tribute system Zheng had helped put in place six hundred years before.

In 2005, the Chinese Communist Party commemorated the six hundredth anniversary of Zheng He's voyages with nationwide celebrations, and in 2008 the Opening Ceremony of the Beijing Olympic Games offered a dramatization of the journeys of his Treasure Fleet. As China approached superpower status, Zheng's image had been fully rehabilitated by the Chinese Communist Party—even elevated to a height greater than it had reached during his life. By 2012, a Zheng He theme park was opened on the site of the Nanjing dockyards where his *baochuan* had been built. With China literally extending its influence to new shores, the Party wanted to project an image to the outside world, as well as its own citizens, that the nation was returning to its rightful place on the global scene. No man embodied those ambitions more perfectly than the emperor's loyal servant Zheng He.

Since his appointment in 2012, Premier Xi Jinping has begun to cite Zheng He in speeches. When mentioning Zheng's legacy, remarks from Communist Party officials follow a similar pattern: make sure to underline the Treasure Fleet's peacefulness, Zheng's respect for other cultures, and the mutually beneficial nature of the historic ties he had helped create. In this narrative, certain realities of Zheng's life had to be erased—including the complex nature of his relationship to the emperor, as well as the battles his fleets sometimes fought *against* locals in faraway lands.

But even though both the ancient and party-line descriptions of the man defy belief, Zheng He, the "seven-foot-tall" eunuch with a "five-foot waist" who became a hero in service to China's imperial court, must have been a remarkable leader. And despite a period in which Chinese interactions with the wider world were downplayed, Zheng's role is again being celebrated. Almost six centuries after his death, Zheng He, and more important the idea of Zheng He, is being used to instruct the citizens of his country, and the broader world, about how the newly resurgent nation wants to consider itself, and how it wants to be considered.

HARRIET TUBMAN

Much of what you have done would seem improbable to those who do not know you as I know you.
—FREDERICK DOUGLASS

As she boarded the USS *John Adams* that evening, the white officers tipped their caps to the black woman they knew as "Moses." Apart from this polite gesture, she was paid no special attention. The 300 troops had business to take care of, and Harriet Tubman was a part of the team, with duties of her own.

At 9:00 p.m. on Monday, June 1, 1863, three steamers—the *John Adams*, along with the *Harriet A. Weed* and the *Sentinel*—set off from Beaufort, South Carolina, and headed twenty-five miles up the Combahee River. Their objective was to raid a set of plantations about a mile inland from either side of the riverbank. In doing so, Colonel James Montgomery, commander of the 2nd South Carolina Volunteer Regiment, hoped to test his new outfit of black troops, disable rebel lines of communication and burn their supplies, and free slaves who could also then fight for the Union.

When the boats set off upriver, Tubman, as head scout, assumed her place next to Colonel Montgomery. It's an incongruous scene: a five-foot-tall, forty-one-year-old black woman going on a raid to free slaves in the middle of the Civil War. Headed to a battle, the officers and soldiers of the 2nd South Carolina didn't show concern with the symbolism of a middle-aged, formerly enslaved woman wearing a dress amid all the men in blue uniforms. All they cared about was her competence as a scout. Montgomery's men relied on Tubman and her team to guide the regiment safely upriver; and in the weeks leading up to the raid, Tubman and the handful of men under her command had gotten word out among the nearby slave community that Union troops were coming to rescue them.

By the time Montgomery's soldiers set off for their raid, their encampment at Port Royal was at the cutting edge of a slow-moving Union Army

A photograph of Harriet Tubman.
(PHOTOGRAPH BY MPI/GETTY IMAGES)

experiment that was learning how to cope with newly free black Americans. Two years earlier, in November 1861, the Union Navy had bombarded two rebel forts guarding Port Royal Bay, South Carolina. The forts' Confederate defenders and the area's white plantation owners quickly fled, leaving behind some ten thousand slaves. Known as "contrabands," the former slaves who were now behind Union lines in and around Port Royal attracted the attention of Northern abolitionists, who flocked there to help. When Tubman, ever duty-bound, decided that she would go to Port Royal, she recalled making the decision out of a calling to work "among her people." This choice of hers to go south also speaks to the evolution of her motivations: by this point in her career, she had become deeply committed to dismantling the institution of slavery.

John Albion Andrew, the governor of Massachusetts, knew Tubman through abolitionist circles, and personally arranged her travel to South Carolina, with the idea that "she would be a valuable person to operate within the enemies' lines in procuring information and scouts." After all, Tubman had spent the entire decade beginning in 1850 guiding slaves from the confinement of Maryland's Eastern Shore to the relative freedom of the North, having rescued some eighty slaves in all. And while South Carolina was hotter than her home state, the terrain was similar. By the outbreak of the Civil War, Tubman was an expert at inconspicuously navigating through fertile, overgrown lowlands, sluiced with brackish water. She was a black woman, scouting behind enemy lines, in a slaveholding state, in the middle of a war about slavery. It was risky business, and while she was driven by her faith and a steady commitment to a cause, she was also a seasoned professional—the result of how she'd lived the first forty years of her life.

Liberty, or Death

On August 29, 1849, the *Cambridge Democrat*, a newspaper covering Maryland's Eastern Shore, announced a slave auction:

NEGRO FOR SALE

I WILL sell at public sale to the highest
bidder for cash, at the Court house door in the
town of Cambridge, on MONDAY the 10th day
of September next, a negro woman named
KIZZIAH, aged about 25 years. She will
be sold for life, and a good title will be
given. Attendance given by
JOHN MILLS,
Agent for Elizabeth Brodess.

Just over a month later, on October 3, 1849, the same newspaper posted the following:

THREE HUNDRED DOLLARS
REWARD.

RANAWAY from the subscriber on Monday
the 17th ult., three negroes, named as
follows: HARRY, aged about 19 years, has
on one side of his neck a wen, just under

the ear, he is of a dark chestnut color, about
5 feet 8 or 9 inches hight [*sic*]; BEN, aged aged [*sic*]
about 25 years, is very quick to speak when spoken to, he is of chestnut color, about six feet
high; MINTY, aged about 27 years, is of
a chestnut color, fine looking, and about 5
feet high. One hundred dollars reward
will be given for each of the above named negroes, if taken out of the State, and $50 each
if taken in the State. They must be lodged
in Baltimore, Easton or Cambridge Jail, in
Maryland.
ELIZA ANN BRODESS,
Near Bucktown, Dorchester county, Md.
The Delaware Gazette will please copy
the above three weeks, and charge this office.

The details offered in these two advertisements give insight into how Tubman spent the first twenty-seven years of her life. Both were in the *Cambridge Democrat*, a newspaper serving Tubman's home: Dorchester County, Maryland. The first posting is an advertisement to sell Harriet Tubman's niece at auction. The second is a notice seeking to recapture Harriet and two of her brothers after their first escape attempt.

A few decades before she was born, Dorchester County families began farming less tobacco, relying instead on timber and grain exports. The shift to a less labor-intensive economy meant that it was decreasingly in slave owners' interests to own, feed, and clothe slaves. To reduce costs, many slave owners began manumitting, or freeing, some of their slaves when they were no longer of working age, usually around forty-five. In Dorchester County, from 1790 to 1800, the free black population increased from 528 to 2,365, as the enslaved population dropped from 5,337 to 4,566. As a result, by the time Tubman escaped in 1849, Maryland had a large community of free blacks to aid her along the way. Because there was a community of free blacks, and because of the region's close proximity to nonslaveholding states, far more slaves escaped from the Upper South than the Deep South. In addition to being geographically farther from free states, slaves in the Deep South also lived more isolated lives on plantations, and generally had very little interaction with people who lived outside of their owners' property.

Economic forces increased manumissions on Maryland's Eastern Shore through the 1790s and early 1800s, but they also increased the domestic slave trade. Cotton took over the economy of the Deep South just as the foreign slave trade was outlawed in 1808 and new slaveholding states like Florida, Louisiana, and Texas sought an influx of cheap labor. As a result, many slaves born in the early 1800s on Maryland's Eastern Shore, Tubman included, lived with the constant fear of being torn from their families and sold south. "Going South" meant not only permanent separation from family, but also the specter of a hellish world they imagined had to be far more cruel than the lives they already lived.

Harriet Tubman was born Araminta ("Minty" in the above newspaper clipping) Ross in March 1822. She was owned by the Brodess family and her parents were Ben and Rit Ross. The fortunes of the Brodess family shaped Harriet's relations with her own parents. During Tubman's twenty-seven years in bondage, the Brodess family went through financial troubles and legal battles; in turn, neither Tubman nor her family had predictable lives. The basic fact of instability dominated Tubman's early years. She had no idea if she'd be permitted to be with her family from one day to the next.

Tubman was hired out, or rented, to other families throughout the Eastern Shore for most of her childhood, and was often mistreated by those leasing her body. Tubman's first biographer remembered that even in late middle age her "poor neck was covered with scars which sixty years of life have not been able to efface."

In her early teens, she suffered a trauma that would affect her for the rest of her life. One evening, while hired out as a field hand, she went to a local store. Another slave had come to the store without permission, and when his overseer found him there he picked up a two-pound iron weight and launched it at the fugitive slave. Unfortunately, he missed and instead hit Harriet directly in the forehead. She had been wearing a shawl, and later remembered that the weight "broke my skull and cut a piece of that shawl clean off and drove it into my head." According to a journalist who wrote about Tubman in 1863, her head injury made her "subject to a sort of stupor or lethargy at times; coming upon her in the midst of conversation, or whatever she may be doing, and throwing her into a deep slumber, from which she will presently rouse herself, and go on with her conversation or work."

Though Tubman and her family were deeply religious well before her head injury, her skull fracture marks the time when Tubman began having religious visions, which would stay with her for the remaining eighty years of her life and contributed to what she felt was her calling.

Harriet's being hired out did have some upside benefit. In her twenties, she did work that was usually done by men, to include felling timber and driving oxen. The nature of such work separated her physically from her owners' property, and exposed her to a world of free blacks who moved up and down the Chesapeake's waterways. It was during this time that she met her first husband, John Tubman, a free black whom she married in 1844. She subsequently changed her name from Araminta Ross to Harriet Tubman, her first name coming from a favorite aunt. Spending her life as a hired hand on various farms also gave her a certain confidence. She had the wherewithal to move about on her own, and even if she didn't know how to get to the Pennsylvania-Delaware state line, she did have an intuitive sense of topography.

Though Delaware would fight for the Union in the Civil War, it was a slaveholding state until the war ended. Wilmington, its capital, sits barely ten miles from the border of Pennsylvania, a nonslaveholding state. The Brodesses were aware of the routes most slaves took on the way to their liberty, and Wilmington was often the last stop for escaped slaves from the Eastern Shore before crossing into the North. This is why, in closing their notice regarding their fugitive slaves, the Brodess family asked the *Delaware Gazette*—a Wilmington newspaper—to "copy the above."

The route north to liberty was aided by the emergence of a loosely affiliated network: what we have come to know as the Underground Railroad. A patchwork of abolitionists throughout the Upper South and Northern states, the Underground Railroad was, of course, not a railroad at all. By the time Tubman took her liberty, historian Fergus Bordewich described it as a

> diverse, flexible, and interlocking system with thousands of activists reaching from the upper South to Canada. In practice, the underground was a model of democracy in action, operating in most areas with a minimum of central direction and a maximum of grassroots involvement, and with only one strategic goal: to provide aid to any fugitive slaves who asked for it.

The Underground Railroad was an informal entity, a series of local groups committed to helping fugitive slaves, with networks that connected activists in various towns. With the exception of a handful of truly exceptional people like Tubman, the railroad was forged by thousands of occasional acts of brave kindness. Bordewich cites "a knock on the door, a bed offered, a horse saddled—dramatic only in retrospect." Tubman relied on this network of free blacks and whites to achieve her own liberty on her route from Maryland to Pennsylvania.

It was no accident that the auction of her niece, Kessiah, described in the first newspaper clipping above, preceded Harriet's first escape attempt by only a week. Several of Tubman's family members had been sold south throughout Tubman's life in bondage. Harriet recounted visions in which she "saw the horsemen coming, and heard the shrieks of women and children, as they were being torn from each other, and hurried off no one knew whither."

Tubman and her brothers made their first attempt at freedom on September 17, 1849, but for reasons unknown, the three turned back. Tubman had been motivated by something more than the immediate fear of being sold south, recalling, "I had reasoned this out in my mind; there was one of two things I had a *right* to, liberty or death; if I could not have one, I would have the other; for no man should take me alive; I should fight for my liberty as long as my strength lasted, and when the time came for me to go, the Lord would let them take me." Tubman comes across as a hard woman, which seems easier to understand in the context of her "liberty or death" mindset. And as a result, she was willing to endure pain to live up to her ideals. Within weeks of the failed escape attempt with her brothers, Tubman set out again on her own.

After a journey of several days, she crossed into the North. But she was not satisfied. Tubman described the moment she entered Pennsylvania:

> I had crossed the line of which I had so long been dreaming. I was free; but there was no one to welcome me to the land of freedom, I was a stranger in a strange land, and my home after all was down in the old cabin quarter, with the old folks, and my brothers and sisters. But to this solemn resolution I came; I was free and they should be free also; I would make a home for them in the North, and the Lord helping me, I would bring them all there. Oh, how I prayed then, lying all alone on the cold damp ground; "Oh dear Lord," I said, "I ain't got no friend but *you*. Come to my help, Lord, for I'm in trouble."

Her resolve to return south, and then do it again and again and again, set her apart. This *choice*—to return to the land of her bondage over and over and over—is what took her from being one of brave thousands, who took their own liberty, to one of dozens, who once or twice returned south to help others, to one of one—the Harriet Tubman we remember nearly two hundred years after her birth for going back south thirteen times rescuing around eighty slaves, giving advice to dozens nine, and eventually strengthening the resolve of multitudes.

Be Ready to Step Aboard

The post office inspectors in Dorchester County stared at the line intently. It read, "Tell my brothers to be always watching unto prayer, and when the good old ship of Zion comes along, to be ready to step aboard."

The 1854 letter, apparently signed by William Henry Jackson, the adopted son of the free black Jacob Jackson, was unremarkable correspondence. But the name Jackson was enough to catch the observant inspectors' attention. They suspected Jacob Jackson had facilitated recent slave escapes and also knew that William Henry Jackson, who'd left Dorchester County some time ago, had no "brothers." The inspectors were stumped.

So they went directly to the source to figure out the letter's meaning. But to their chagrin, Jacob Jackson threw down the letter, claiming, "I can't make head nor tail of it," and walked out of the room.

But Jackson knew exactly what the line meant. He was familiar with this type of coded communication with Harriet Tubman, who was alerting him under a forged signature that she would be coming to rescue her brothers. Jackson quickly warned Robert, Ben, and Henry—the trio who would soon be led to freedom by their sister.

The three brothers had attempted to flee the Eastern Shore multiple times on their own without success. Their disobedience angered Eliza Brodess, who, when approached about a potential sale of the three brothers to a local friend, sneered that she'd "rather see them sold to Georgia." By December 1854 it was official: Robert, Ben, and Henry were going to be sold down south around Christmas. When Tubman heard of their impending sale, she began her journey to the very location where she was still considered property of the Brodess family, something she had done many times before and would do again many times after.

Though "Slavery," as she once said, was "the next thing to hell," freedom did not mean happiness if it meant her family was still in bondage. "I was a stranger in a strange land; and my home, after all, was down in Maryland; because my father, my mother, my brothers, and sisters, and friends were there. But I was free, and *they* should be free," Tubman would say later in her life. Her sense of duty to her family was matched by her fierce belief that God would always protect and guide her. When asked about her decisions to return south, Tubman always responded, "T'wasnt't me, 'twas de Lord! I always tole him, 'I trust to you. I don't know where to go or what to do, but I expect you to lead me,' an' he always did."

So in December 1854, after writing her secretly coded letter to Jacob Jackson about her impending arrival (or rather, after having dictated the letter to someone who could read and write), Tubman embarked on her journey to the Eastern Shore, most likely by train and boat.

Tactically, Tubman arrived at the perfect time: Christmas Eve. Eliza Brodess was going to allow Tubman's brothers to travel to their parents' house forty miles away for dinner, providing an excuse for their temporary absence. But Tubman's window for a rescue shrank when she heard that

Robert, Ben, and Henry were due to be sold the day after Christmas at a public auction.

She made plans to meet her brothers that night, and together they traveled to their first "safe house"—their parents' cabin. That same evening, Robert's wife went into labor, which caused him to run late to the meeting. Tubman didn't wait.

Harriet, Henry, Ben, and Ben's fiancée, Jane Kane, who had joined the escapees at the last minute, made it to their parents' cabin, where they hid in the fodder house as a frigid December rain poured outside. Robert, the third brother, eventually caught up and joined them in the outbuilding. Somewhere along the way, two other enslaved men joined the group. The small rescue, in the course of one day, had doubled in size.

Tubman was careful about how she let her parents know of her presence: she sent the two new additions to tell her father about the situation. Tubman's father, without alerting his wife, brought food out to the fugitives. He made sure he did not actually see Harriet and her siblings, even wearing a blindfold at one point. Knowing that slave catchers would eventually come and ask if he'd seen his children, he made sure that he could honestly say that he never had.

Tubman was tough on her passengers for the sake of their own safety. Sometimes, the journey north was so difficult that slaves seriously considered returning to bondage, but Tubman ensured that they kept moving. Carrying a pistol both to protect and to threaten her passengers if they wanted to turn back, she made it clear that, as one Underground Railroad operative described it, "times were very critical and therefore no foolishness would be indulged in on the road." Such discipline is what allowed Tubman, and the fugitive slaves under her charge, to sit in a cold barn on a rainy Christmas Eve while her parents' warm home, presumably with a holiday meal, was within sight.

She'd made her way down south and retrieved her brothers. By nighttime on Christmas Day, Tubman was ready for the final phase of her mission: bringing the fugitives across the Pennsylvania border and beyond.

After passage of the Fugitive Slave Act in 1850, which required Northern authorities to return escaped slaves to their owners, reaching the Pennsylvania state line didn't amount to safety. Tubman needed the Underground Railroad to help her and her family get from Dorchester County, Maryland, all

Harriet Tubman, at the far left, with slaves she helped to rescue.
(BETTMANN/CONTRIBUTOR)

the way to safety in St. Catharines, Canada (now in Ontario), where there was a growing community of black refugees, protected by British laws that had outlawed slavery decades earlier.

The route that Tubman took to rescue her brothers, following a direct path, is about 450 miles each way. She made this journey thirteen times in the 1850s. For an entire decade, Tubman ignored the bounty on her head and the bloodhounds following her scent, and dedicated her life to taking small groups of slaves from the South to the North.

At each stop on her route, abolitionists huddled around parlor rooms eagerly listening to the stories of Tubman's rescues. To many of these activists, her bravery was stupefying. But as remarkable as each of her thirteen rescues was, Tubman's life had a regular rhythm in the 1850s. After bringing her newest group of fugitive slaves all the way up to Canada, she swung through New England to raise money and meet with her widening circle of abolitionist friends. During the summer, she would try to find work as a cook or laborer to make enough money to eat.

In the hours she was not working she would travel to the homes of abolitionists to tell the story of her escape from slavery and subsequent rescues of others with the hopes that impassioned and sympathetic listeners could spare a few dollars for her cause. In the fall, she'd head back to the area around Philadelphia to make preparations for the next season's raids.

In the winter, when the nights were longer, Tubman secretly made her way back to the Eastern Shore. After hiding for up to three months, she gathered more charges. In her rundown shoes, Tubman led the escaped slaves from safe house to safe house through Maryland, Delaware, Pennsylvania, New York, and usually all the way to Canada.

Despite cold, sickness, complaining passengers, crying babies, slave catchers, and the seizures caused by her head injury, Tubman guided each of the eighty or so slaves she rescued all the way to freedom in the North. Immediately after settling the family members and friends she loved enough to go back and retrieve, she left them and started over.

But late in the evening of Christmas Day in 1854, Tubman's mind was focused on the task at hand. Under cover of darkness, Tubman, her brothers, and the rest of her charges continued north. When they finally reached Wilmington, they came to a familiar home.

"Trumpet Her Noble Deeds"

A couple days after Christmas in 1854, Thomas Garrett heard a rap at his door, the knock a bit less cautious than usual. He and the rest of the family were accustomed to late-night visitors. To his wife, Rachel, the noise could hardly have been more alarming than a creaky floorboard in the home at 227 Shipley Street.

Thomas rose from his chair as quickly as his sixty-five-year-old body would let him, already considering where to send his guests. He opened the door with his typical warmth, but when he noticed a friend standing in the threshold he smiled a bit more broadly. Most of the thousands of folks passing through his home in Delaware were on a one-way ticket north, and Harriet was an old comrade. As she and her six charges came into the house, Rachel readied the tea.

As they sat down, Thomas noticed that Harriet and one of the men—who turned out to be her brother—had worn the shoes off his feet. The members of the Garrett household listened in rapt attention as Harriet told the story of her latest journey to her eager audience.

Between the early 1800s and 1865, Thomas Garrett, a white Quaker, assisted 2,700 slaves in taking their liberty—he was the most important abolitionist in his state. In his correspondence between 1854 and 1868, out of all the former slaves he'd helped, only Tubman is repeatedly referred to in heroic terms.

In December 1855, writing to two famous women in Scotland who raised and sent money for the US abolitionist cause, Garrett introduced Tubman to the ladies for the first time: "I feel as if I could not close this already *too long* letter, without giving some account of the doings of a noble woman, but a *black* one. . . . She is strong and muscular." After spending two paragraphs regaling the women with the stories of Tubman's high adventures, Garrett closes: "Were a *white person*, man or woman, to peril life & health, & spend everything he or she had earned in such a noble & disinterested cause, the name would be trumpeted over the land; but be sure you *do not trumpet* her noble deeds in the Newspapers." A year later, Garrett thanked the ladies for a donation they sent on Tubman's behalf. As always, this and other letters sent between 1855 and 1857 recall the eventful details of Tubman's "missions of love and daring."

In a summary note shared with Tubman's first biographer in 1868, Garrett opened up about "the remarkable labors of Harriet Tubman, in aiding her colored friends from bondage," and explained to posterity what made her unique in his eyes:

For in truth, I never met with any person, of any color, who had more confidence in the voice of God, as spoken direct to her soul. She has frequently told me that she talked with God, and he talked with her every day of her life, and she has declared to me that she felt no more fear of being arrested by her former master, or any other person, when in his immediate neighborhood, than she did in the state of New York, or Canada, for she said she never ventured only where God sent her, and her faith in the Supreme Power was truly great.

The majority of this letter, like all the others, tells stories of "Harriet's . . . remarkable incidents." She'd left quite an impression on the man, just as she had done with other key abolitionists from Thomas Garrett's home in Wilmington, Delaware, all the way to black refugee communities in Canada.

In 1854, after keeping them safe for a day or two of rest, making the proper arrangements, and outfitting Harriet and her brother with new shoes, Garrett forwarded Tubman to J. Miller McKim and William Still, two leading abolitionists in Philadelphia. Still later recalled that "Harriet Tubman had been their 'Moses.' . . . Harriet was a woman of no pretensions, indeed a more ordinary specimen could hardly be found. . . . Yet, in point of courage, shrewdness and disinterested exertions . . . she was without her equal. . . . Her like it [sic] is probable was never known before or since."

From Philadelphia the railroad went on to New York. There, Sydney Gay, in his "Record of Fugitives," an account of all the slaves he helped move through the city in 1855 and 1856, devoted six pages to the woman he referred to as "Captain Tubman." While other entries got hardly more than a paragraph, Gay related nearly all of Tubman's rescues through 1856. Oliver Johnson, another New York–based Underground Railroad conductor, remembers "that heroic woman, Harriet Tubman. . . . She always told her tale with a modesty which showed how unconscious she was of having done anything more than her duty. No one who listened to her could doubt her perfect truthfulness and integrity."

New England was the next "stop" on the railroad. In a letter to his mother in 1859, Thomas Wentworth Higginson, a Worcester minister who went on to command the 1st South Carolina Volunteers in the Civil War, wrote: "Her tales of adventure are beyond anything in fiction and her ingenuity and generalship are extraordinary . . . the slaves call her Moses. She . . . will probably be burned alive whenever she is caught, which she probably will be, first or last, as she is going [to Maryland] again."

The end of the "tracks" was typically St. Catherines, Canada. William Wells Brown, a prominent black abolitionist and former slave, remembered, "While in Canada, in 1860, we met several whom this woman had brought from the land of bondage. And they all believed that she had supernatural power. Of one man we inquired, 'Were you not afraid of being caught?' 'O, no,' said he, 'Moses has got the charm.' 'What do you mean?' we asked. He replied, 'The whites can't catch Moses, cause you see she's born with the charm. The Lord has given Moses the power.'"

———

IN ADDITION TO BEING fascinated by what she'd done, leaders in the abolitionist movement leveraged Tubman's story to raise money. And by rescuing as many slaves as she did, she was proof that the money was going to
good use. But in the final accounting, her leadership was about something
more than the numbers. By one estimate, between one thousand and five
thousand slaves escaped annually from 1830 to 1860. In the 1850s, then,
Tubman freed between 0.14 percent and 0.80 percent of escaped slaves, and
a higher percentage of all slaves who escaped from Maryland during that
time (a very rough estimate is around 3 percent).

The depth of her fame suggests that she did something larger than these
modest numbers. Tubman's particular actions took on symbolic significance. In the tone of the letters about Tubman, her actions—and the stories
they inspired—deepened others' resolve, and inspired abolitionists to take
more dramatic action than they otherwise might have. That happened, in
Tubman's case, through the serendipitous confluence of a remarkable time
with a remarkable woman.

It was never Tubman's intention to be called a leader, or a hero. While
the abolitionist movement had leaders across the country, its most prominent figures were in the Northeast, where Tubman spent most of her time.
She was one type of leader the movement needed, at the precise moment it
needed a leader like her, and she was building relationships with other
movement leaders out of sheer necessity.

And while Tubman was politically savvy, her day-to-day aims were
practical. Even when speaking publicly, she was usually trying to raise
money for her next rescue attempt. Except to the dozens of slaves she freed
and led north from bondage, Tubman never chose to become a leader. She
engaged with the abolitionist movement and the movement in turn held her
up as a leader—she needed funding and they needed a symbol. It was a role
that was never explicitly defined, but is easily perceived in the correspondence of Tubman's contemporaries.

Though the Underground Railroad was a loosely affiliated network, its
leadership corresponded regularly. Tubman was the only person who physically accompanied slaves on a route from Maryland to Canada several times

A depiction of Harriet Tubman leading slaves to Canada.
(NATIONAL GEOGRAPHIC CREATIVE/ALAMY STOCK PHOTO)

over the course of the 1850s, and so she had to forge strong relationships with abolitionist leaders up and down the East Coast. Tubman had a personal relationship with each of these key leaders, and in turn they corresponded with one another about her. She unknowingly became a node in their network.

She also used these relationships to gain safe passage down to South Carolina to serve in the Civil War.

Nurse, Scout, and Spy

When Tubman arrived in South Carolina in 1862, she spent most of her days as a field nurse. Because she wasn't paid for her work mending the wounds of Union soldiers, in the evenings she ran a small business. Every night, she baked pies and gingerbread, brewed two casks of root beer, and then hired someone to sell her products in the Union camp. On other days, according to an official report about her service in the Army, she "rendered much, and very valuable service acting as a spy within the enemies' lines and obtaining the services of the most-valued Scouts and Pilots in the Government employ in that department." She recruited a small squad of about seven local black men who knew the terrain. Her team went behind Confederate lines, gathered intelligence for Union commanders, acted as guides for the Union Army in South Carolina, and presumably opened lines of communication with the still-enslaved community of blacks behind Confederate lines inland from Union positions.

Her work as a spy likely accelerated when, in August 1862, Edwin M. Stanton, the US secretary of war, authorized the creation of five regiments of black troops. A couple months later, Colonel Thomas Wentworth Higginson, the white abolitionist minister from Massachusetts, arrived in Port Royal to take command of the 1st South Carolina Volunteers, the first regiment of former slaves in the Union Army. When he arrived at the Union camp, Tubman would have been one of the few blacks Higginson already knew. She had spoken at his Worcester congregation a few years earlier, and in a letter to his mother after her talk, Higginson had called Tubman "the greatest heroine of the age."

Colonel Montgomery, who as commander of the 2nd South Carolina Volunteers led the Combahee River raid, was himself an old abolitionist who'd fought with John Brown in Kansas in the mid-1850s. Montgomery had known about Tubman for several years by the time he arrived in South Carolina.

Given her proven track record of operating undetected in the South, and her preexisting connections with two of the highest-ranking Union commanders in South Carolina, it was natural that Tubman would be considered a "valuable woman" to the US Army, as a government report on her military service puts it. While it would have defied outsiders' expectations, the men in Port Royal assumed that Tubman would take a leadership role.

Harriet Tubman's specific job during the Combahee River raid (the outset of which was described at the beginning of the profile) was to serve as Colonel Montgomery's head scout. In this role, she—or perhaps a member of her team who had grown up in the area and would have been natively familiar with the waters of the Combahee—guided the *John Adams*, *Harriet A. Weed*, and *Sentinel* upriver on the evening of June 1, 1863. On the way, the *Sentinel* ran aground, but after boarding the remaining two boats, all 300 Union troops reached their objectives by 2:30 a.m. on June 2.

Throughout the morning, Colonel Montgomery's soldiers won several skirmishes with Confederates, disabled a pontoon bridge the rebel troops were using to usher supplies between positions, and destroyed approximately a million dollars' worth of enemy property.

Hundreds of slaves emerged from inland plantations. Their numbers threatened to overwhelm the Union transports, so, according to Tubman's later recollections, "Montgomery shouted from the upper deck, 'Moses, you'll have to give em a song.'" To calm the crowd of newly free slaves clamoring to hop aboard, she sang a tune that was popular in abolitionist circles at the time: "'Of all the whole creation in the East or in the West / The glorious Yankee nation is the greatest and the best / Come along! Come along! Don't be alarmed / Uncle Sam is rich enough to give you all a farm.'"

In the end, thanks to the collective effort of the 2nd South Carolina's troops, officers, and scouts, the raid rescued 727 slaves and was a success. While Tubman hadn't commanded, she did play an important role. According to a telegram sent by Colonel Montgomery in July 1863, Tubman was a "most remarkable woman, and a valuable scout."

As the boats came back to Beaufort, a reporter from Wisconsin recorded the scene. His account notes that, a day after returning from the raid, both Colonel Montgomery and Tubman addressed the newly free blacks in a Beaufort church, and that "for sound sense and native eloquence, her address would do honor to any man, and it created quite a sensation."

Predictably, the same article romanticized Tubman's role in a few places, allowing its reader to believe that Tubman herself might have been the one in complete command. According to the Wisconsin correspondent, Tubman was "the black woman who led the raid, and under whose inspiration it was originated and conducted." This language, skewed beyond the author's original intent, has contributed to a misunderstanding about Tubman's particular role in the Civil War, including a myth that she actually attained the rank of general.

While it may be predictable that a reporter overstated Tubman's role in the Combahee River raid, it is more interesting to consider why and how Tubman became the sort of person about whom a reporter would want to exaggerate. To the men of the 2nd South Carolina—who understood her as a competent scout and a leader among the black community in Port Royal and Beaufort—it was natural that Tubman would be sitting with the regimental commander during the raid, and she'd have been expected to speak to the freed slaves the next day. To a reporter who needed a good story, it was also natural that such a scene would have been too good for him to pass up.

After the War

On Sunday, October 22, 1865, Harriet Tubman came to the pulpit at the Bridge Street African Methodist Episcopal (AME) Church in Brooklyn, New York, her hand wrapped in a bandage. A conductor on the train she'd taken from Philadelphia a few days earlier didn't think a black woman should be riding on a soldier's half fare. When the conductor called her a "nigger," Tubman took exception. The bandage was the outcome of the resulting scuffle.

Behind her were forty-three years of a hard life: twenty-seven years in bondage, a decade of trips back to the South to rescue slaves, and the last few years as a nurse, scout, and spy in the Union Army. In front of her stood a full congregation, about half white and half black, so packed that even the gallery above the ground-floor pews was full.

The Reverend Dr. William Howard Day introduced Tubman to the congregation by reading several letters of recommendation, including three from some of the most famous men in the country: William Seward, the secretary of state; Edwin Stanton, the secretary of war; and General David Hunter, who most recently was head of the military commission that tried the conspirators who had assassinated President Abraham Lincoln the previous April. Dr. Day concluded by asking the congregation to assist Tubman by donating some money. For the rest of her life, she fought to scrape together a living.

Though Tubman was a memorable storyteller, a reporter at the Bridge Street AME Church on this Sunday evening recorded that "there was nothing particularly impressive in her remarks." As she gave the crowd the story of her last fifteen years, she spoke in a "plantation dialect and [was] at times not intelligible to the white portion of her audience." She did manage to elicit "shouts of laughter from the congregation," though it's unclear how many people found her accent funny, and how many simply enjoyed the way she recalled her past. Unlike Frederick Douglass, whose main work was speaking, Tubman was not a speaker first and foremost. More important than the stories she told were the stories told about her.

More than a traditional leader, Tubman was a symbol. She personified quiet courage and steadfast commitment. Douglass offered some insight into what made her the sort of person whose particular actions take on broader significance. Distinguishing Tubman from himself, Douglass wrote a letter to her that was included in an early account of her life:

> Most that I have done and suffered in the service of our cause has been in public, and I have received encouragement at every step of the way. I have wrought in the day—you in the night. I have had the applause of the crowd and the satisfaction that comes of being approved by the multitude, while the most that you have done has been witnessed by a few trembling, scarred, and foot-sore bondsmen and women, whom you have led out of the house of bondage, and whose heartfelt *"God bless you"* has been your only reward. The midnight sky and the silent stars have been the witnesses of your devotion to freedom and of your heroism. Excepting John Brown—of sacred memory—I know of no one who has willingly encountered more perils and hardships to serve our enslaved people than you have. Much of what you have done would seem improbable to those who do not know you as I know you.

Leaders like Frederick Douglass shaped the abolitionist movement's ideological contours. Harriet Tubman simply made slaves free, and she did it better and more often than anyone else. She changed the facts on the ground. She never intended to lead, and that turns out not to matter—she became a hero, and a leader, all the same.

A HUMAN NEED FOR HEROES

Heroic leadership is not simply a quality or entity possessed by someone; it is a type of relationship between leader and led.
—JAMES MACGREGOR BURNS

When Hollywood screenwriter George Lucas was ten years old, he asked his mother, "If there is only one god, why are there so many religions?" Earlier in the twentieth century, the Swiss psychiatrist Carl Jung asked a related question after observing that similar legends emerge independently across different cultures. His answer was the existence of an "archetype" within human psychology, such that "myths are first and foremost psychic phenomena that reveal the nature of the soul."

The person who connected Lucas's question with Jung's answer was Joseph Campbell, who in 1949 wrote *The Hero with a Thousand Faces*, an exploration of consistent story lines across the world's various myths. Campbell, who was influenced by Jung, wrote that "the symbols of mythology are not manufactured. . . . They are spontaneous productions of the psyche."

What Campbell saw across the various myths of history was a similar pattern, which has been termed the "Hero's Journey," built around what Campbell called the "Monomyth." George Lucas credited Campbell's description of this narrative form as critical to the development of his *Star Wars* epic. By now, much of Hollywood has studied what Lucas learned from Campbell. Films that retell an epic story, such as *Ben-Hur*, or that follow the Hero's Journey, such as *The Lion King*, are often among the most profitable.

Zheng's and Tubman's paths actually followed what Campbell described as the "nuclear unit" of the Hero's Journey, a "formula represented in the rites of passage: *separation—initiation—return*." As Campbell goes on to explain, "A hero ventures forth from the world of common day into a region of supernatural wonder: fabulous forces are there encountered, and a decisive victory is won: the hero comes back from this mysterious adventure with the power to bestow boons on his fellow man." The parallels between this formula and the epic lives of Tubman and Zheng are obvious. If we accept Campbell's analysis, the stories of Zheng's and Tubman's lives feel ready-made to be retold.

Both rose from relative anonymity before being embraced by elites who recounted these leaders as visceral, extreme, and straightforward symbols of group values. Each literally embarked on epic journeys, one by sea, the other by Underground Railroad. The parts of their lives that are most often recounted—Zheng's voyages and Tubman's slave rescues—involve each hero setting forth into the unknown, emerging victorious, and then returning, or as Campbell says: *"separation—initiation—return."*

And upon their returns—Tubman to Maryland's Eastern Shore and Zheng to mainland China—they each "bestowed boons" upon their fellow man. To their contemporaries, both Zheng and Tubman were symbols of unknowable worlds beyond unreachable frontiers. Tubman, for instance, represented freedom to the slaves she rescued, and could viscerally explain slavery to the abolitionists she motivated.

There are also notable differences in their stories. We know little about Zheng's leadership, for his records were lost to history. By contrast, the record of Tubman's exploits is more complete. And while it matters less whether the details of Zheng's story are true, Tubman's heroism is important precisely because we know it to be true—abolitionists could make her a hero because of her consistent accomplishments, but they needed to make her a hero because of how she could serve their cause.

And they were cast very differently for their stories. Zheng fit the mold and looked the part: big, strong, and with a countenance that was taken as a sign of good character. Tubman, by contrast, broke a mold. She had every reason to be the victim in her story, but that's not how she conducted herself. Rather, she rose up and repeatedly defied expectations that a small black woman wasn't capable of what she did.

Most of all, the stories of Tubman and Zheng suggest that heroes fulfill a need. The status of hero is always conferred by followers, and not the hero herself. This explains why humans create such symbols of heroism as the Nobel Prize or the Medal of Honor. The real achievements of the awardee are often not so distinct from those who are passed over, but the recognition is necessary all the same.

Our tendency for hero worship seems related to what it is that makes leadership so necessary. Both capture an essential part of what it means to be human—our ability to conceive of a different future, even an imaginary one. And in doing so, we create a gap between now and then, a gap that propels us ever forward. The hero is a reminder that something else is possible—particularly in difficult times.

One of the first superhero comic books, *Superman*, was published in 1938 in the wake of the Great Depression. Superhero worship surged again in the wake of 9/11 and following the great recession of 2008. Perhaps, when challenged, we look for others to do what we cannot. For instance, the common theme in the notes written about Tubman by her contemporaries is astonishment bordering on disbelief. Even when sticking to just the facts, there's a touch of something mystical in both heroes' stories.

If hero worship thrives in crisis, then its roots are in courage, which Tubman and Zheng both exuded. Zheng spent his adult life in martial service to the emperor, filled with scenes of physical courage. Tubman attributed her incomprehensible courage to her faith and the pull of family. This does nothing to diminish her accomplishments; rather, it reveals the very human wiring beneath even the most celebrated of heroes.

Finally, no leader, or hero, exists independent of the context beyond their control. Leadership is not magic, and it is an alluring illusion that there are individual heroes. Rather, the apparent magic stems from the alignment of the right person at the right time, surrounded by a group of people who both enable their activities and find meaning in what someone like Tubman or Zheng offers.

It is clear that heroes do not exist outside the mind of the follower, but there's more to it than that. We need heroes because of the values they propagate, and their role as symbols of purpose and possibility. Decades after they've stopped living their epics, master storytellers like George Lucas and Plutarch will continue to use heroes to captivate audiences and communicate values.

Seven

THE POWER BROKERS

*Power is like being a lady. If you have to tell
people you are, you aren't.*

—MARGARET THATCHER

The conference room, referred to as "the Tank," is modest by corporate standards and its major decoration, ironically, is a painting of a meeting. But context is everything: this Pentagon room is where the nation's seniormost military leaders convene, and the painting, appropriately, is an original of Generals Grant and Sherman discussing strategy with President Abraham Lincoln.

The eight four-star admirals and generals who sit at the Tank's solid but spartan-simple wooden table constitute the Joint Chiefs of Staff, composed of the heads of the United States Army, Navy, Air Force, Marine Corps, Coast Guard, and National Guard, led by the chairman of the Joint Chiefs, and attended by his vice chairman. This collection of leaders, each of whom has risen to the top of their profession, represents the most powerful assemblage of uniformed military in the world.

For a year from 2008 to 2009, as the director of the Joint Staff, I was always in the room but did not have a seat at the table. My chair was off to the side, several feet back from the "inner ring" of flag officers that dominated the room. I was the junior officer, expected to take notes and comment—if asked a question. Had I been a young, inexperienced soldier, relegation to that role would have seemed normal. But after thirty-two years in uniform, the previous five years leading a Task Force of Special Operations soldiers in combat in Iraq and Afghanistan, it would seem, at first glance, a humbling reversal of fortune.

Appearances, however, are often deceiving. Although wearing only the three stars of a lieutenant general, compared to the four of the other officers, it became clear to me that power lies in perception. And that perception can be as much about potential or future power as position or authority in the present. In the military, in which most positions are held for a set tenure, ascension to the highest rung of the ladder also begins a clock ticking down toward the leader's departure. The term "lame duck" is never used, but the perception of future power can actually give a junior leader more true power than the senior. It was impossible to measure, but curiously, sitting in the wings, I was likely as powerful as I would ever be.

Power is maddeningly difficult to describe. Like the famous quip about pornography, that you "know it when you see it," we often end up defining power simply—as the ability to get something done. But even then, we struggle with its essential nature. It is, at once, concrete and vaporous, long-lasting and ephemeral. Even in combat, I found I had far less direct power than the mythology of military command implies and would discover vastly more ability to influence things outside my formal authority than I'd anticipated. Power, in my experience, derived more from reputation than rank, more from persuasion than direction, and more from example than prescription.

We considered a range of historically iconic lawmakers and executives before settling on an unlikely but interesting pair. Early on, we decided on Margaret Thatcher, famously the "grocer's daughter," whose improbable journey led to her being Great Britain's best-known prime minister since Winston Churchill, and the longest serving of the twentieth century. Emerging as a winner in the rough-and-tumble world of British electoral politics, the "Iron Lady" entered with a chemistry degree but developed a widely noted (and often criticized) skill for wielding power.

To balance our look at power brokers, we went a bit outside the lines and selected a man born into modest circumstances on New York's Lower East Side in 1823 who died penniless in the nearby Ludlow Street jail fifty-five years later. But in the intervening years, William M. Tweed, the Tammany Hall political machine leader popularly known as "Boss," came to dominate and then symbolize the New York City politics of his era. Tweed's ostentatious corruption eventually sent him to jail, but it was in his deft orchestration of power, exercised through patronage and providing retail-political value to his supporters, that the most intriguing picture emerges.

Power brokers inhabit a central niche as leaders. Beyond genius, courage, charisma, or hypnotic eloquence, they remind us that we often select or follow leaders quite simply because they deliver something, and that means leveraging power, hopefully in their followers' interest. Their personalities and techniques vary, some using facilitation and compromise, others a more unyielding approach. At their best they can reflect selfless, honest service, but quite often they embody excess, greed, and manipulation. Power is about influence over a group—it's inextricably linked to leadership, and yet we shade the idea of "power brokering" with a negative connotation and shine a positive light on the idea of "leading."

Rather than judge, we might just ask: What is the role of power in leadership, how are leaders granted power, and how does it get taken away?

Key Books

- Kenneth D. Ackerman, *Boss Tweed: The Corrupt Pol Who Conceived the Soul of Modern New York* (Falls Church, VA: Viral History Press, 2011)
- Margaret Thatcher, *Margaret Thatcher: The Autobiography* (New York: Harper Perennial, 2013), abridged combined edition
- Charles Moore, *Margaret Thatcher: The Authorized Biography: Volume I: From Grantham to the Falklands* (2013) and *Volume II: At Her Zenith: In London, Washington and Moscow* (2016) (New York: Knopf)

WILLIAM MAGEAR "BOSS" TWEED

A politician coming forward takes things as they are.

—BOSS TWEED

Lunch was important for William Magear Tweed. While eating a piece of oyster pie in the carpeted dining area of his Ludlow Street jail cell in 1877, he told a reporter from the *New York Herald*, "I have never smoked a cigar nor chewed a piece of tobacco. I never liked whiskey. Being a man of large body, I am fond of good eating."

Tweed died alone in a cell in that same jail. But only seven years earlier, in the late spring of 1870, he was still safely in his office and at the height of his power, enjoying lunch with the same colleagues he dined with almost every day. Such meals, delivered to his lower Manhattan office at 85 Duane Street, were catered by the city's premier restaurants, and Tweed often punctuated the feasts by offering his guests some brandy and cigars.

Outside, the city was booming. Down the block was the new County Courthouse, farther north near Central Park were paved and widened boulevards, across the East River the Brooklyn Bridge was just beginning construction, and rapid uptown development had converted what was mostly untrammeled land to "one of the most desirable and picturesque localities for residence." Property values were soaring, and the city was growing: in the last two decades, the city's population had nearly doubled. In the same period, its foreign-born population had grown to make up more than 40 percent of the city's residents.

New York City had more buildings, more people, and more money than ever before, and at lunchtime William Tweed's office was the city's most important room with its most powerful people. Huddled around Tweed's three-hundred-pound frame were Richard Connolly, the city's comptroller; Peter B. Sweeny, parks commissioner; and A. Oakey Hall, the mayor of New York City. None of these men were great friends; they were each there because they'd pursued their own paths to power and the moment called for the four to collaborate.

An 1871 Thomas Nast cartoon of Tweed's "lunch club." At the left, Tweed is the large, bearded man wearing a massive diamond pendant, and to the right are Sweeny, Connolly, and then Mayor Hall wearing an exaggerated pair of spectacles. Printed soon after Tweed's fall, the cartoon depicts all of the guilty parties pointing the blame at everyone but themselves.
(PHOTOGRAPH BY UNIVERSAL HISTORY ARCHIVE/UIG VIA GETTY IMAGES)

Formally, Tweed was the city's commissioner of public works, in addition to holding the simultaneous titles of state senator, director of the New York Bridge Company, "the Erie Railroad, the Tenth National Bank, and the New-York Printing Company, proprietor of the Metropolitan Hotel, and president of the Americus Club." By popular reputation and in practice, of the four men in his office, Tweed was the one in charge—the only one among them who, as he said, "when anything desperate was at hand," would "go to the front."

This quartet's mandate was broad and its authority was firm—it represented informal political power, nearly absolute statutory authority to govern New York City, and vast corruption. The many names for the group reflected those various roles. Widely known as the "lunch club," this clique, or one similar in stature, had been meeting in City Hall, in Tweed's office, or in a nearby restaurant for the last decade to discuss the day-to-day of city and state politics.

By law, Tweed, Connolly, Sweeny, and Hall also made up New York City's Board of Apportionment. In the city's new charter, signed in early

1870, this board "would approve all city spending, fix budgets, and even control judgeships." Appointments for each of the positions (mayor excepted) were for terms of six to eight years, meaning that their appointed terms were meant to extend beyond the mayor who appointed them. They had power, and the perception was that they weren't going anywhere.

History remembers these four men not just as the "lunch club" and the city's Board of Apportionment, but also as the "Tweed Ring." Using a scheme of kickbacks on outstanding payments owed to the city, scholars estimate the ring and its predecessors stole between $25.5 and $45 million from the city's taxpayers. In 1877, city investigators put the figure at closer to $60 million—or the modern-day equivalent of $1.2 billion. To put it in perspective, by 1871 New York City had $90 million of debt on its books. Nearly two thirds of that debt—or around $60 million—was added from 1869 to 1871, through the height of Tweed's corruption. The four men in Tweed's office alone nearly bankrupted the city.

One might assume that the lunch club had indirect conversations about broad generalities, while the daily to-do's were handled by minions and hangers-on. Not so. For them, the application of power was specific and detailed. Tweed once remarked, "Our power, socalled, was always precariously held." Despite their titles, their authority, and the attendant trappings, keeping power required constant coordination and tending. In part, that's because even though their money and power served interim aims along the way, the path was never-ending, and under the leadership of Tweed, the ring only ever wanted more and more.

On any given day, perhaps over some roast duck, oysters, and good champagne (Tweed never overindulged in drink, but he would drink a glass of wine over lunch), the group discussed a range of issues from politics and policy to electioneering and graft, always in practical terms. At some stage, they discussed the draft of the new charter of New York City, along with who needed to be paid off in the state assembly and senate to have it pass. They regularly decided on specific appointments to be made across city government. Once, during an election season, they mused over an idea to delay the wire-reported vote counts by "telegraphing the whole Bible over them, if it was necessary." Such a delay would buy time for Tweed's counters; as he later testified, at the height of his power, "The ballots made no result; the counters made the result." Almost every day, the four men signed the inflated claims for payment that made each of them rich, and Tweed sensationally so.

From 1869 through the summer of 1871, the lunch club controlled and stole from New York City, often from Tweed's office. Their leader had various names—William, Bill, Senator, Director, Congressman, and Commissioner—but he's remembered as "Boss." He got the title by rising through the ranks of the Democratic Party machine of the County of New York—better known as Tammany Hall.

Lead Tiger

New York City in 1850 was cramped and loud. But it was not yet remarkable for its height. Rising only 281 feet above lower Manhattan, the spire of Trinity Church was the highest point in the city. A few blocks north sat City Hall, its cupola a bit shorter than Trinity Church. Twenty-four hours a day, a watchman stood in the City Hall bell tower, on the lookout for fires, a serious danger in a town still mostly constructed of wood. When he spotted smoke, he'd ring the bell, setting off a cascade of other bells positioned throughout the city. If it was daytime, he'd raise a banner, and if it was nighttime, a torch, in the direction of the blaze. Then the dozens of volunteer fire associations around Manhattan would spring to action.

If the banner was raised or the torch lit in the direction of Manhattan's Seventh Ward—only about ten blocks east of City Hall—then the "Big Six" fire company would have answered the call. Under the leadership of twenty-seven-year-old Bill Tweed, they'd race on foot with heavy, man-pulled pump engines to the scene of the fire and hook a leather hose to one of the city's new fire hydrants to fight the blaze. Local citizens would gather outside, watching their local heroes in bold red shirts and white fire coats, or the spectacle of two or more volunteer companies brawling for the honor of being first on the scene. Firefighters were local celebrities. As foreman of the Big Six, Bill Tweed was gaining a reputation as a tough and gregarious young man, well known and respected in his ward, and elected by his peers to run the seventy-five-man company. He was just the sort of talent who appealed to his local political organization. Painted on the side of the Big Six's red engine was a snarling red tiger, an image that came to symbolize the institution that brought Tweed to power: Tammany Hall.

Tweed once pointed out that by 1870, "Tammany Hall got all its powers from us [the Tweed Ring]—not we from them." That may have been true by that late juncture in his career, but Boss Tweed's rise to power was dependent upon the institutions of Tammany Hall—indeed, he oriented his rise toward the pinnacle of Tammany leadership. And while popular lore identifies Tweed as the preeminent Tammany man, Tammany Hall reached its peak only after Tweed's downfall.

Tammany Hall was both a building and an institution. The building was initially located in lower Manhattan before moving to various headquarters around Union Square. More important, Tammany Hall was the institution that controlled the Democratic Party of New York County, or Manhattan. While the building was beautiful (in 1868 it hosted the Democratic National Convention), the organization was much grander: at the height of Tammany's power, they had to rent out Madison Square Garden just to accommodate half of their membership.

The institution lasted for nearly two hundred years, and for about a hundred years from the mid-1800s until World War II, it was the dominant force in New York politics and even shaped national politics. Over its long history, Tammany Hall was many things, from a progressive force for new Irish Americans to an enabler of outright corruption.

In 1850, as Tweed was rising to power in Tammany Hall, nearly half of New York's population was foreign-born, and in the wake of the 1845 potato famine, increasing numbers of these immigrants were from rural, Catholic Ireland. This population reshaped New York politics. As Daniel Patrick Moynihan, the long-serving US senator from New York, put it, the Irish "arrived in America thoroughly alive to the possibilities of politics and they brought with them the phenomenally effective technique of political bureaucracy." Instead of having politics controlled by the privileged few, these new Irish had an organized system for mass political participation and influence—a "Political Machine."

Across Manhattan's twenty-two wards, Tammany Hall had a vast hierarchy of ward bosses, block captains, and building captains. In charge of the entire organization were both a grand sachem, a ceremonial role; and a party boss, selected by the Tammany political organization's general committee. It was through this infrastructure that Tammany doled out patronage jobs, listened to local grievances, made sure everyone voted for the right candidates, and nurtured future leaders. Tweed emerged through this bureaucracy to become both grand sachem and party boss by the 1860s.

By modern standards, the conventional tactics of Tammany would be considered criminal. One common practice was securing patronage jobs for Tammany supporters. As one Tammany leader put it, "I stick to my friends high and low, do them a good turn whenever I get a chance, and hunt up all the jobs going for my constituents." In addition to winning elections by turning out a sometimes-oversized vote and securing jobs for loyal constituents, senior Tammany leaders grew rich by "honest graft," famously described by George Washington Plunkitt, a Tammany man in power from the late 1800s through the early 1900s, as "I seen my opportunities and I took 'em." He goes on to explain what he means: "My party's in power in the city, and it's goin' to undertake a lot of public improvements. Well, I'm tipped off, say, that they're going to lay out a new park at a certain place. I see my opportunity and I take it. I go to that place and I buy up all the land I can in the neighborhood."

While Plunkitt never defined graft so explicitly, he did insist that "honest" politicians like him "didn't steal a dollar from the city treasury." Tammany had institutional norms around what leaders were allowed to do for their own gain, and what they weren't. If "honest graft" gave political bosses unfair advantages over the general public, their justification was that it also got many things built quickly, and created more jobs. As Senator Moynihan remembered, these were people who "could throw up the George Washington Bridge in four years and one month." In other words, Tammany leaders claimed to be supporting the public interest through their private gain—and by representing a constituency that was otherwise ignored by the city's political elite, they were playing a vital role.

Tweed's distinction was not the invention of graft, but his mastery of the system and the shamelessness of his corruption. His theft from the city treasury wasn't simply illegal—it was of an unprecedented scale even by Tammany Hall norms. Tweed's sort of graft was not the kind of low-level corruption often rationalized as the cost of getting things done. He stole directly from the city's taxpayers, but was a popular man for all but a few of his fifty-five years.

Tweed's path to power began with his rise through Tammany Hall—the institution that nurtured him and granted him the public's trust. For every Tammany leader, the journey began at the base unit: the ward.

TWEED GREW UP in the seventh ward. Born on the East Side of lower Manhattan in 1823 into a Scottish-American Protestant family, Tweed spent much of his early adulthood in his family's brush and chair-making business, and turned down an opportunity to run for the city's Board of Aldermen as early as 1843, before coming of age with the Big Six volunteer fire company. In 1850, the same year he was elected the Big Six's foreman, the chief engineer of New York City's firefighters wanted to have Tweed expelled from the department for his role in an assault on another volunteer company. Appealing to the Board of Aldermen, and likely paying a bribe, Tweed was able to have his sentence reduced to a three-month suspension. By 1850, most of the people in the seventh ward knew who Tweed was, and Tweed understood local power.

In 1851, Tammany again asked him to run for office, as an assistant alderman in the seventh ward. He lost this election but tried again a year later and took over his first political office in 1852 as alderman—what today we call a city councilman. The next year, he won a seat as a US congressman but hated it and came back home after just one term in the national legislature. His local rise continued—in 1856 he joined the school commission, became a county supervisor in 1858 and a deputy street commissioner in 1861. This was the same year that construction began on the new County Courthouse, the building standing today at 52 Chambers Street and commonly known as the "Tweed courthouse." Far from the speed of the George Washington Bridge that went up in four years and a month from 1927 to 1931, the Tweed courthouse took eleven years to build and ended up costing the city between $4 and $12 million, after initial cost estimates of just $250,000.

It was in his role on the county board of supervisors that Tweed first wielded citywide power with access to the city's coffers. County supervisors oversaw city funds, and Tweed and a handful of colleagues charged vendors a 15

The 1868 Democratic National Convention. Hosted at Tammany Hall, the convention nominated former New York governor Horatio Seymour as president on the Democratic ticket. Though Seymour eventually lost the presidential election to Ulysses S. Grant, Tammany swept that year's local elections. A federal report said that 1868's elections in New York "comprehend every known crime against the elective franchise."

percent tribute to do business. It was also from this perch that he initially promoted to power future members of his lunch club—Peter Sweeny as district attorney, and Richard Connolly as county clerk. In January 1863, he was elected chairman of Tammany Hall's general committee, beginning what would be a nearly nine-year run as Tammany's political "Boss."

Tweed's rise wasn't just based on backroom deals and a measured ascent into political authority, though those were important. He was also a public figure, and widely understood to wield tremendous power. When a crisis hit New York, he was expected to act. In July 1863, riots roiled the streets of Manhattan when President Lincoln called for a conscription of men to fight in the Civil War. The mostly working-class Irish rioters weren't eager to fight and die for the rights of black Americans, and also railed against the $300 payment—a figure far out of reach for them—that wealthier New Yorkers could pay to avoid going to war. The riots left 120 people dead on the streets of New York City. Among many other buildings, rioters burned to the ground the Colored Orphan Asylum, a home for black children without parents.

In the midst of this crisis, Tweed left the peace of his office and the delicacy of his lunches and led on the ground. As Tweed biographer Kenneth Ackerman puts it, "Tweed recognized the urgent need of being seen on the street that day. He had made Tammany his club, and Tammany over the years had linked its fate to those same immigrants who were now tearing up the city. Many were his constituents; no one knew them better than Tweed and company."

When President Lincoln refused to call off the conscription, Tweed worked with the leading Republican on the County Board of Supervisors, Orison Blunt, to satisfy the federal government's need for soldiers and mitigate the locally felt unfairness of the $300 buyout. Tweed and Blunt traveled together to Washington, DC, to solidify a deal with Secretary of War Edwin Stanton. By their plan, the city raised a $2 million fund through a bond sale. These funds were overseen by a six-member committee, including Tweed, which reviewed cases for draft relief and paid the $300 fee in cases where poor New Yorkers had good reason for avoiding the conscription. In such cases, the committee found volunteers to replace each man unable to go to the front. In cases where a draftee went to the Army, they were able to keep the $300 as an enlistment bonus.

The reviews for Tweed's leadership were soaring, even among usually unfriendly newspapers like the *New York Times*. On September 11, 1863, the *Times* published an editorial praising Tweed's "Supervisors' Committee" for "performing their duties with eminent satisfaction to all parties" and concluding that "no money, no trust was ever more honestly administered."

Tweed's performance in this crisis allowed him to solidify control over Tammany Hall. In the years between 1863 and 1868, he increased the size of Tammany Hall's general committee from 21 to 150 members, making the group more unwieldy and less able to make decisions. Power thus increasingly fell into the hands of Tweed and his lunch club. He began extending his power in other ways as well: in 1867, in addition to his posts on the County Board of Supervisors, as deputy street commissioner, and party boss and grand sachem of Tammany Hall, Tweed won a seat in the state senate.

As Tweed accumulated power, he was also becoming increasingly rich.

In addition to making money through graft, Tweed was involved in several businesses. Among these, he was an owner of the New York Printing Company, the official printer for New York County. By 1868, he owned the paper that his city's election ballots were printed on.

Republicans took the White House as Ulysses S. Grant became president in 1869, but elections in New York were a Democratic Tammany sweep—the governor, mayor, and various other officeholders owed their victories to Tweed. In a congressional report on fraud in the 1868 election, the investigating committee found that election fraud in New York was the worst in the country's history, saying, "These frauds were the result of a systematic plan of gigantic proportions. . . . They were aided by an immense, corrupt, and corrupting official patronage and power. . . . These frauds are so varied in character that they comprehend every known crime against the elective franchise." Among the various schemes were the quick naturalization of new Irish immigrants. Weeks before the 1868 election, a single judge naturalized 955 citizens in one day. According to voter rolls from the 1865 census, voter turnout in New York City was 108 percent.

Tweed once told a reporter: "The fact is New York politics were always dishonest—long before my time. There never was a time you couldn't buy the Board of Aldermen. . . . A politician coming forward takes things as they are. This population is too hopelessly split up into races and factions to govern it under universal suffrage, except by the bribery of patronage or purchase." Such pragmatism was at the heart of Tammany's political philosophy, and part of why it survived for so long. Over time, institutions as vast and enduring as Tammany Hall don't just hold up the best of their culture, norms, and values; they also offer a platform for the most craven representations of the same. Once a leader has charge of an institution, he gets to wield its power, whatever his values are. By the end of the 1860s, Tweed had control over New York politics. The question was how he'd use that power.

"An Astonishingly Frank Rascal"

As usual, he was playing host. At 4:30 p.m. on April 4, 1870, Senator Tweed's suite at the Delavan House in Albany was full. A swanky seven-room apartment, this was where Tweed held court while in the state capital. For the past week, "Mr. Tweed's quarters [had] been thrown open, and a walnut sideboard well stocked with refreshments and cigars of first rate quality [was] liberally patronized by an immense throng of politicians." Today, the room was even more full than usual, owing to general interest in the matter at hand. Tweed chaired the New York State Senate's Committee on Municipal Affairs. That afternoon in his apartment, he was presiding over a final committee hearing before the next day's vote on the most important issue of the legislative session: the New York City charter.

Since the 1850s, most of the day-to-day management of New York City was controlled by the state legislature over a hundred miles away in Albany. It had been thirteen years since New York City had power "over its own health, fire prevention, education, public works, charities, buildings, and docks." Achieving "home rule" for New York City had broad popular support, and the timing was politically opportune to push through legislation. The success of Tammany's electioneering meant that in 1870 Tammany men held office as the mayor of New York City and the governor of New York State, and Democrats held the majority in both the state senate and assembly.

Tweed had one priority at the outset of 1870: pass home rule for New York City through the state legislature.* The Boss delegated the content of the charter to his colleague Peter Sweeny, a member of Tweed's lunch club. Beginning in January 1870, Sweeny had taken up residence down the hall from Tweed in the Delavan House, and within weeks had a draft of what history would remember as the Tweed charter.

Charles O'Conor, a prominent New York lawyer, opined:

> The Tweed charter was an almost perfect instrument—that as a document, under which to administer the affairs of a municipality it seemed to be without a flaw. . . . It had failed . . . because its drafters had not conceived that it was possible for a band of thieves to seize the city, and with great intelligence place at each checking point one of the members of their own clique.

That's precisely what Tweed intended.

---

*The New York State Legislature consists of an upper house, the Senate, and a lower house, the Assembly. A part-time body, the legislature meets for a six-month session beginning in January every year.

Though he delegated the drafting of the charter, the Boss took personal responsibility for its passage. A journalist who covered Tweed once wrote that "he had understanding, cunning, and force. . . . He had no moral consciousness and at times was an astonishingly frank rascal." Without compunction, Tweed did what needed doing to secure his aims. In early 1870, to pass his charter, he had to do two things: ensure that a handful of Republicans in the state senate voted for the bill and win an internal power struggle.

Tweed eventually testified that he promised jobs and, according to him, gave out $600,000 in bribes to ensure passage of the charter. There wasn't any subtlety to what Tweed was doing. He wanted to pass a charter, so he raised cash from supporters, hired a lobbyist to pay assembly members, found out which senators were on the fence, ascertained their prices, and bought their vote. Almost eight years after the 1870 charter was passed, the then-imprisoned Tweed gave testimony to the city's Board of Aldermen. His tone highlights his matter-of-factness. Describing a conversation with a political adviser he'd hired for the occasion, Tweed recounted:

He then asked me if I had Mr. Woodin [a Republican senator]. I said "No." He asked me whom I did have. I told him Mr. Winslow I thought would go with me, and Wood and Minier. He said "You had better get Mr. Woodin, because he is a very powerful active man, and a good talker." I asked him if it was safe to talk to him. He said: "Yes." I said I would try to have a talk with him, and I did the next day.

After a series of similarly dull conversations, Tweed paid a handful of Republican senators—Woodin included—$40,000 apiece to ensure their support for the bill.

A week before the charter eventually passed, Tweed had to win an internal power struggle with the "Young Democrats" of Tammany Hall. The 1870 charter centralized authority—and opportunities for graft—with the mayor and three key appointees in a Board of Apportionment, and stripped the city's Board of Aldermen of the power to confirm mayoral appointments. The Young Democrats, led in part by twenty-nine-year-old county sheriff Jimmy O'Brien, felt that they'd been left out.

On March 28, a meeting of the Tammany Hall general committee—of which Tweed was chairman—had been called to discuss the charter and other matters of city business, but Tweed had been tipped off that the Young Democrats intended to use the meeting to vote him out of his chairmanship, and potentially scuttle the charter. Prior to that evening's meeting, O'Brien and his allies met at Irving Hall, and the Young Democrats thought they'd accrued enough votes of the general committee to take Tweed down. But when the upstarts arrived at Tammany headquarters, they found themselves barred entry by hundreds of police officers. Tweed had phoned the commissioner of the municipal police to warn of a potential riot at Tammany Hall that evening, and had the Young Democrats locked out. A headline in the next morning's paper called the affair "the most stupendous political joke of the century," and by the day after that, it was acknowledged "on every side that the Irving Hall Democracy have been completely outflanked by the Tweed faction," which by March 30 was already pushing the charter bill through the state assembly. Later, the *New York Herald* would report that the Young Democrats "exhibited pluck and pertinacity enough to win any cause if only such qualities were needed to insure victory. But the result proves, after all, that it takes a general to lead an army, and unfortunately for them the generalship was on the other side."

By the time Tweed called to order the Committee on Municipal Affairs' public hearing in his decadent apartment on April 4, this "general" had already won his fight. He had the public's support, he had bribed key Republican senators to support the charter, he had already pushed it through the assembly, and he had eliminated the threat of the Young Democrats.

Three days earlier, dozens of New York City elites signed a petition of support for the charter, saying, "We consider that this bill [the charter] should receive the support of all who desire to give to New York City a symmetrical and honest local government." The next day, April 5, 1870, it passed by a vote of 30–2 in the senate.

The *Herald* noted that "the scene in the Senate was, perhaps, the most remarkable that has been witnessed here in some years. The lobbies were crowded and every inch of space that could be made available was occupied . . .

the opinion was very strong in the Senate, as the vote indicates, that it is the best Charter New York ever had."

And Tweed wasn't just getting support from city elites. At a mass meeting of the "Friendship Democratic Association" at Fourteenth Street and Third Avenue the evening of the charter's passage, part of a resolution adopted by the gathering read, "We especially tender our thanks to Mr. William M. Tweed for recent exhibitions of his talent as a wise and discriminating leader." The charter's passage was met with general glee on Manhattan's streets.

Once it was law, the same charter meant that he would no longer be accountable to the very electorate that now lauded him. Mayor A. Oakey Hall swiftly appointed Tweed's lunch club as the city's Board of Apportionment, at which point Tweed's corruption became legion.

In a fight, Tweed had been ruthless; and in a bribe, generous. This style helped Tweed to get things done, but it also contributed to his downfall.

A $300,000 Necklace

On Wednesday evening, May 31, 1871, according to a front-page article published in the *New York Sun*, "Trinity chapel in West Twenty-fifth street was filled to repletion at 7 o'clock . . . with curiosity seekers, anxious to witness the long-anticipated marriage of Mr. Ambrose Maginnis to Miss Mary Amelia Tweed, second daughter of the Hon. William M. Tweed." It was the social event of the season. After the ceremony, the reception was held at the Tweeds' mansion at Forty-third Street and Fifth Avenue, where "the parlor beggared description," and the whole home was adorned in flowers. In attendance was New York's "aristocracy," including "all the more prominent politicians and their wives." The bride and groom received more than $500,000 in gifts. For his daughter's wedding day, "Mr. Tweed himself wore black evening dress, and a magnificent diamond flashed on the bosom." He'd been wearing the same diamond since he received it as a gift from some friends the prior Christmas Eve: a shiny, ten-and-a-half-karat orb held in place with a necklace, sitting in the middle of his chest. It was valued at $15,000, or the current equivalent of $300,000.

Tweed had extravagant wealth, and he flaunted it extravagantly. There was no need to hide it, for people knew who he was, and they either accepted it or didn't comprehend the nature and scale of his corruption. A year earlier, the *New York Times* had begun attacking Tweed's alleged corruption on the basis that "he is the prime mover in the audacious faction which are now trying hard to ruin this City, and are making their own fortunes in the process." The *Times* was accompanied by attacks from *Harper's Weekly*, including anti-Tammany cartoons drawn by the famous Thomas Nast, who had taken to focusing much of his work on Tammany's corruption, often highlighting Tweed and accentuating his girth and big diamond pendant. *Harper's Weekly* editorials referred to a "'universal conviction' that Tammany was corrupt." The vague, moralistic, nonspecific attacks didn't affect Tweed's public standing.

The attacks weren't incorrect, of course. Tweed was quite straightforwardly stealing from the city's taxpayers. Once the 1870 charter became law, new rules were drawn up to allow for outstanding payments to be made for work done on the city's behalf under its old laws. Tweed's lunch club came up with the idea for the 1870 Tax Levy, which called for a Board of Audit to settle all of the city's bills after claims for payment were submitted by contractors.

The Board of Audit comprised Tweed, Mayor Hall, and Comptroller Sweeny. Through an intermediary, the group passed word to a handful of contractors to submit fake bills. After some internal haggling, it was settled that the contractors' take was to be about one third of the false bills, Tweed himself would receive 25 percent, Connolly 20 percent, Sweeny 10 percent, Hall 5 percent, and 5 percent was to be retained for overhead. Initially, Tweed suggested that the reason for this scheme was to repay those who had given money to ensure passage of the 1870 charter—but the amount of money eventually stolen was well over the $600,000 in bribes that Tweed and his associates had paid. The scheme eventually netted them about $3.6 million, stolen from the city's treasury in the span of about a year beginning in June 1870. To finance the city's bloated budget, the city took on debt in the form of municipal bonds, which meant financiers were profiting and taxes didn't need to be raised. It was a precarious arrangement, but for the moment, it was working just fine.

Decline

Once Tweed got caught, the last six years of his life—from 1872 to 1878—were spent out of power, and featured a complicated series of legal battles, an international escape attempt that took him to Florida, Cuba, and Spain, and ultimately a public reckoning before his death in 1878.

While his criminal prosecution took years and ended only with his death, Tweed's descent from power was a rapid culmination of events beginning with a poorly managed crisis in the summer of 1871. It could not have happened without a group of journalists and politicians poised to strike and a house of cards built on corruption, but serendipity had as much to do with Tweed's collapse as any other factor.

As they'd done before, Protestant Irish New Yorkers, called "Orangemen," had planned for an annual march on July 12, 1871, to celebrate the anniversary of the Battle of the Boyne. The planned parade caused a controversy among Irish Catholics. On July 10, the superintendent of police, with Tweed's backing, banned the parade. The next day Governor John T. Hoffman came down from Albany, rescinded the ban, and offered the Orange marchers National Guardsmen as escorts. On the morning of the twelfth, the parade descended into chaos, and the National Guard fired on the crowds. In the end, sixty civilians were killed and more than one hundred wounded. The next morning, the opening of the *New York Tribune*'s front-page article read: "The cowardice of Tammany and the hesitation and incompetency of the officials with which it afflicts us, has brought terrible but natural fruits of shame and of sorrow to the city."

This time the attacks on Tammany stuck. Months before the riots, Tweed's old political rival, Jimmy O'Brien—the leader of the Young Democrats movement—had paid a clerk in the comptroller's office to record suspicious ledger entries. Sensing an opportunity, within a week of the Orange Riots, O'Brien gave a copy of the ledger to the *New York Times*. On July 22, 1871, the *Times* ran a headline at the top of page one: THE SECRET ACCOUNTS. In it were copies of the fake, inflated payments from the Tweed Ring's tax levy scheme. Most of the false payments were tied to the County Courthouse on Chambers Street—the "Tweed courthouse." As one history neatly summarizes, among other outrageous payments, "One member of a

Tweed-affiliated club was paid $23,553.51 for furnishing thirty-six awnings, boosting the per-awning price from the market rate of $12.50 to a Ring rate of $654.26. Construction of the county courthouse allowed for an orgy of such creative accounting, and the building wound up costing four times as much as the Houses of Parliament and twice the price of Alaska."

Over the summer, the crisis stemming from the Orange Riots worsened. Unlike his sharp response to the draft riots back in 1863, when he was on the streets, this time Tweed spent almost the entire summer at his estate in Greenwich, Connecticut. Thomas Nast, who was fast becoming America's best-known political cartoonist, began drawing more and more cartoons in *Harper's Weekly* focused on Tweed and the corruption of Tammany. Assisted greatly by the investigatory work of Samuel Tilden, an old Tweed rival and the Democratic candidate for president in 1876, the *Times* eventually published a record of all of its ledgers in a book titled *How New York Is Governed: Frauds of the Tammany Democrats*, which went on to sell 500,000 copies.

Tweed wasn't brought down by a moral crusade. In July 1871, he was viewed as all-powerful, so when a riot happened, Tweed and the city's leaders were held responsible for mismanagement. In the same week, one of Tweed's political rivals sensed an opportunity and gave the *Times* his stolen ledgers. In the immediate aftermath of the *Times'* reporting and *Harper's Weekly's* cartoons, there were mixed reactions as to whether Tweed and his ring were really at fault, or if the *Times* and Nast were just do-gooders acting on hearsay provided by people with political axes to grind. Tweed didn't come tumbling down for good until the city's creditors grew wary of continuing to finance its debt, and a "Committee of Seventy"—a group of city elites—banded together and began a reform movement that swept Tammany out of office.

By the fall of 1871, Tweed was out of power—arrested and eventually kicked out of Tammany Hall. In elections that November, reformers beat out Tammany candidates in thirty-four of thirty-five races.

A Last Victory

The lone Tammany victor in the November 1871 elections was Tweed. Though he never claimed his seat, he was elected as senator from New York's fourth senatorial district for the third and final time that fall. Three months after the initial evidence of his corruption had been published, Tweed maintained support from the local political class. On October 23, a "Tweed Club" was opened at 105 East Broadway, near where Tweed had grown up. In a scene redolent of the Delavan House, the room was full with "almost all of the city Judges, members of Assembly, [and] Aldermen. . . . 'The Boss' himself sat in the large hall surrounded by many of those who have been attached to his fortunes since he began to illuminate the political horizon." The gathering consisted of "hundreds," and the festivities lasted until "an advanced hour." Two days later, the *Times* published its most damning, and precise, accounts of Tweed's corruption and the Boss was arrested shortly thereafter. The class of people in this room largely abandoned Tweed at this point—his power no longer ensured theirs.

But for those who elected Tweed to office just after his arrest, the story wasn't so straightforward. In October 1871, Tweed turned out no fewer than 1,500 people at a rally for his state senate race, at a corner not far from where he'd once fought fires. As the *New York Herald* described, "the stairway and sidewalks were fairly crowded with an enthusiastic throng, who amused themselves, in anticipation of the formal proceedings, principally by giving deafening cheers for William M. Tweed at every suggestion, however frequently made." To this group, the *Times*, Nast, and all the reformers were just outsiders attacking their man. For them, following Tweed wasn't just a choice, it was also habit—as much a part of their identity as their neighborhood.

MARGARET THATCHER

Freedom works—and it costs less.

—MARGARET THATCHER

Standing before her local Conservative (or "Tory") Party branch in North London, England, in 1976, Margaret Thatcher was again preaching to the converted. But her sermon had changed for a golden opportunity had presented itself. Earlier, Thatcher's indispensable political strategist,

Gordon Reece, had rushed enthusiastically into her Westminster office, interrupting her as she was preparing her remarks.

Reece was usually concise with his advice, but he was now distracting her, telling her about an edition of the Soviet newspaper *The Red Star*, and asking if she owned a sequined red dress. The paper had referred to her as "the Iron Lady of the Western world," and he insisted that her speech should now be changed, but first, that her usual "power suit" also needed an update.

Thatcher took his advice. Following a trip to the dressmaker and some notable edits to her speech, the United Kingdom's first female leader of the opposition delivered some carefully scripted and now-famous lines:

> I stand before you tonight in my Red Star chiffon evening gown, my face softly made up and my hair gently waved . . . the Iron Lady of the Western world! A Cold War warrior! An Amazon philistine! Even a Peking plotter! . . . Yes, I am an Iron Lady, after all it wasn't a bad thing to be an iron duke; yes, if that's how they wish to interpret my defense of values and freedoms to our way of life.

The speech was a classic example of what would become Thatcher's winning rhetorical formula. With her fierce opposition to socialism in Britain and to detente with the Soviets, Thatcher often blended policy with transcendent British ideals. At the time, her assertiveness raised eyebrows, partly because of the discord between her gender, periodic charm, and fiery political dogma. Her strong sense of belief, and self-belief, were rich tools of persuasion.

And here, with the Conservative Party faithful, it seemed to be working. Earlier, at a Conservative Party Conference at which she spoke, one party official who was not a part of her ideological camp had watched from the sidelines and later reflected: "She cheered up the troops more than any party leader since Churchill."

Into the Political Fray

Thatcher's campaign against socialism had begun early, but it took twenty-nine years for her to refine and perfect its implementation, and for the British people to recognize its true potency.

That story begins in 1945, as Thatcher, then Miss Margaret Roberts, a nineteen-year-old Oxford undergraduate, spent her university summer vacation campaigning for a Conservative candidate in her hometown of Grantham, northern England. Leading the Tories was the formidable wartime prime minister Winston Churchill, who had just shepherded Britain through its "darkest hour" to emerge victorious in the Second World War.

At the height of the June–July 1945 campaign, Thatcher traveled around her constituency giving up to half a dozen speeches each night at local town hall events to ensure that Conservatives were delivered to power again, rather than the left-wing Labour Party, which had been out of office since 1931. Years later she recalled her characteristically unswerving message of national strength and pride: "The British Empire, the most important community of peoples that the world had ever known, must never be dismembered."

But while Thatcher was campaigning for her local candidate, and by extension the Conservative Party, it was also about her hero: "The main argument I advanced for voting Conservative was that by doing so we would keep Winston Churchill in charge of our foreign policy."

In the United Kingdom votes are not cast directly for a prime minister. Across the roughly 650 districts in Britain, voters select local Members of Parliament (MPs) to represent their constituency at the House of Commons in London. After votes have been tallied across all of the constituencies, the MP leading the party that has won the most seats in Parliament requests permission from (or "kisses hands with," as the term goes) the monarch to form a government. Once permission has been given (which has never been denied in the modern era), the leader, now formally the prime minister, announces, "Her Majesty the Queen [or King] has asked me to form a government and I have accepted."

In parliamentary systems such as Britain's, transformational prime ministers are a rarer breed than in countries with presidential structures. Walter Bagehot, a British constitutional theorist, wrote in 1867 that Britain had "efficient" and "dignified" parts to its constitution (unlike in the United States, the UK constitution is noncodified, and spread across many documents of different types and times, rather than being formalized in one). The "dignified" parts include institutions like the monarchy and the House of Lords (the "Upper Chamber," like an unelected version of the US Senate), whereas the "efficient" parts include the House of Commons (the elected "Lower Chamber") and the government that is formed from its most senior members.

Her Majesty's Government, which consists of more than one hundred elected MPs appointed by the prime minister, includes at its most senior level the heads of each government department. As a result, the leadership of Britain's government tends to be made up of career politicians, often experts in both subject area and practical knowledge of the national political machine. Most prime ministers emerge from this system, with extensive personal experience, before rising to the top job. Churchill, for example, held eight different government positions, ranging from secretary of state for war (1919–21) to chancellor of the exchequer (1924–29) before becoming prime minister in May 1940.

Leadership in UK politics is therefore formed in a cluttered landscape of institutions, norms, and individuals. The prime minister is a servant and subject of the monarch and, while leader of His or Her Majesty's Government, exercises powers that are ill defined, and to a great extent based on historical conventions rather than formal authorities. The power of the prime minister, as the early twentieth-century prime minister H. H. Asquith put it, "is what the holder chooses and is able to make of it."

Still, in the 1945 general election, in which Thatcher had a very small part, the outcome would be momentous. While the voter's *X* was scrawled by the name of a local candidate, the vote was as much, or more, about choosing a party and its leader—it was Winston Churchill's Conservatives versus Clement Attlee's Labour Party. Britons, having watched the world leaders who had dominated the stage during World War II, likely believed that the direction of postwar Britain would be shaped by the individual who rose to power.

As the election approached, Thatcher recalls a Churchill who, after five years bunkered in the fury of conflict, was ill placed to judge the political sway of the populace. Churchill spoke divisively of Labour's more socialist policies as requiring "some sort of Gestapo" to enforce. At a time when

Britain and its empire—both brought to the teetering edge of economic collapse—were in urgent need of reconciliation and renewal, Thatcher saw Churchill's grumbling tone as counterproductive.

Though still a political novice, her instinctive gauge of public opinion was on the mark. On July 26, 1945, less than three months after Nazi Germany's surrender, Thatcher and her father—a working-middle-class grocer, and a name in local Conservative politics—sat in despair as results of the election came through. She remembered:

> It was bad, and it became worse. . . . Incomprehension deepened. At the time I felt that the British electorate's treatment of the man who more than anyone else secured their liberty was shameful. But was it not Edmund Burke who said: "A perfect democracy is the most shameless thing in the world?"

To Thatcher, the failure of the Conservatives to win the 1945 election was a major reason for the country's swerve toward socialism, and in turn why Britain declined. For her, this path betrayed the values of individualist freedom and state sovereignty, based on a capitalist system, that the country had spent much of the twentieth century defending.

But Churchill's ousting by British voters was within historical precedent, for Great Britain has a history of firing powerful leaders. Prior to her own ascent, Thatcher observed Clement Attlee, Churchill's successor and an architect of the postwar modern social state, have his premiership torn apart by a divisive cabinet. And she would herself experience a painful finish to her time in office: after eleven and a half years as prime minister (1979–90), she was politically assassinated by her own cabinet. In a country where there is no maximum number of terms a prime minister and her government can serve, voters take seriously their role of deciding when it's time for a leader to go. Fellow members of Her Majesty's Government do the same, always cognizant of the safety of their own constituency seats in the case of an impending election, and the possibility of advancing their own careers by ousting their leader.

If the fall can be bruising, the rise is no easier. Gaining political office

in Britain can take decades before a government career becomes a viable
path, much less entry to high office. Thatcher's own aspirations to political
leadership began with two electoral defeats. But as she watched Britain lose
its greatest leader, its empire, and its confidence in the aftermath of the
Second World War, she grew impatient for the opportunity to redirect its
course.

Member of Parliament

Thatcher had two unsuccessful political campaigns seeking a seat in
Parliament, in 1950 and 1951. To have run for office at all showed impressive courage, and an ardent belief in her own ability. At the time, it was
far from typical that an unmarried woman should seek elected office.
Thatcher, still Miss Margaret Roberts, was just twenty-four years of
age when she first ran, and was running just twenty-two years after the
Equal Franchise Act (1928) was passed, which granted all women the right
to vote.

It is not, then, so surprising that the grassroots organizers who worked
with Thatcher in her first campaign referred to her in explicitly gendered
terms: "plump, smart, pretty, loved hats, lovely skin," and a woman who
"always looked right." In the UK, it would not be until 1975 that a woman
could open her own bank account, and not until 1982 that she could buy
her own drink in a pub.

Her breakthrough came nine years later. In 1959, Mrs. Thatcher—now
married to Denis Thatcher, a well-off businessman—finally won a seat in
the House of Commons, in the upwardly mobile constituency of Finchley,
North London, a district she would represent for the following thirty-
three years. She made gains with the middle-class vote and was particularly successful in attracting the significant Jewish minority. She declared
Jews to be "the people of the Old Testament: how can you believe in the
New unless you believe in the Old?" She spoke of her instinctive respect for
tradition, as well as a profound religious faith, both of which would be
lodestars guiding her career ahead.

Thatcher saw her Jewish constituents as the most exemplary of citizens,
being "one of the most scholarly races," and "good citizens . . . not just talking, but doing and giving." They were "natural traders" who managed

*Margaret Thatcher, then Miss Margaret
Roberts, in 1950, an aspiring young
Tory candidate. She married Denis
Thatcher, a successful businessman,
the following year.*
(PHOTOGRAPH BY CENTRAL PRESS/GETTY IMAGES)

"positively to get on by their own efforts." She believed fervently that with
the right guidance the British people might do and be the same.

After her first electoral victory, Thatcher took a junior government post
with limited responsibility over pensions and national insurance, becoming the youngest female government minister, and the first ever with a
young family. Not surprisingly, observers still spent more time focusing on
her gender than on either her leadership ambitions or nascent political
agenda. One newspaper reported: "She was dressed like any other housewife up to town for the day. A cossack hat in coney fur covered most of her
fair hair which is just going grey at the temples. She was wearing a green
wool jersey dress and a fine two-row necklace of pearls gleamed at her
throat."

In 1959, it was still easy to underestimate Margaret Thatcher. Later, one
of her inner circle of advisers would comment on her subsequent, unlikely,
and spectacular rise to power:

There is . . . the sheer romance of it. . . . A woman from the provincial
lower-middle class, without family connections, oratorical skills,

intellectual standing or factional backing of any sort, established herself
as the leader of a great party which had represented hierarchy, social
stratification and male dominance.

While Thatcher's political success was improbable, it placed her on a
trajectory toward a historic moment that called for a leader of strong
conviction—a role she would grasp as though it had been crafted for her.

By 1968, that opportunity was one step closer. Her Conservative Party,
now out of power, was seeking new political direction. Margaret Thatcher,
nine years into her tenure as an MP, and identified as a rising talent brimming with ideas, was given the prestigious opportunity to speak at the
party conference. Still, few would have considered her a serious candidate
for leadership. In fact, one would-be ally wrote as late as 1973: "Thatcher
will probably go a good deal further without reaching the top. She is not
prime ministerial material."

In her conference speech, Thatcher summarized a belief that would
characterize her political philosophy until her death, that conviction was
better than consensus, and drive better than appeasement: "No great
party can survive except on the basis of firm beliefs about what it wants to
do. It is not enough to have reluctant support. We want people's enthusiasm
as well."

Thatcher became especially convinced about the limited role that the
state should have in a person's life. She identified an apparent—but false—
contradiction between seeing ourselves as interdependent people within a
society, but nonetheless being individuals with certain responsibilities. Her
powerful claim was that "the whole of political wisdom consists in getting
these two ideas in the right relationship to each other."

These neat binaries, not unique for a midcentury conservative, came to
dominate her political discourse—consensus and conviction, or the individual and society. They reveal Margaret Thatcher's core beliefs and fore-
shadow the kind of leader she would become.

In time there were many who saw Thatcher's embrace of dogma as
symptomatic of an unrelenting pursuit of power. But for others, her conviction, among other personal qualities, meant that she was uniquely

capable of driving Britain's interests forward. It was not, however, her conviction and political ideology that first brought her into the national spotlight. It was about something far less grandiose: a question of milk.

Mrs. Thatcher the Milk Snatcher

To some degree, Margaret Thatcher owed her career to Edward Heath, who led the Conservative Party for a full decade beginning in 1965. Heath had himself broken the Conservative leadership mold, having attended a selective public high school (known as a "grammar" school in the UK), rather than one of the elite private schools (so-called public schools) like Eton and Harrow that have dominated British political life for centuries.

Thatcher too was an alumna of one of these provincial grammar schools, and when Heath won the 1970 general election he believed that the role of secretary of state for education and science (which she accepted and held in the 1970–74 Conservative government) might suit such a middle-class woman as Mrs. Thatcher—one who, few thought, harbored any pretensions to party leadership.

Despite her sense of political vocation, the new role was not an entirely comfortable fit. Early in her tenure as a cabinet minister she complained to departmental bureaucrats—civil servants in Britain's celebrated apolitical government machine—about the excessive number of Marxist books on sale at the University of London bookshop. Later, in her memoirs, she spoke of the "self-righteously socialist" atmosphere in the Department for Education. She also described the National Union of Teachers as a "closed world" with Communist affinities.

Within a week, she took her abrasive tongue to the page, writing a minute at the bottom of an interim departmental report of a flagship research program, "This is one of the most disappointing and frustrating documents I have read. Not a penny [in funding] after Dec. 1971." She had a disparaging habit of refusing to send out substandard documents given to her for signature, instead ripping the tops off those pages she thought inferior.

This period was Thatcher's first opportunity to exercise executive power. Unsurprisingly, neither her manner nor her overtly political way of speaking with civil servants made her popular within her own department. Her attitude toward career bureaucrats foreshadowed a bruising approach toward the civil service she would often display as prime minister. She would periodically arrive impromptu at government departments as though trying to catch them in the act of opposing her political agenda.

It was partly this simmering unpopularity within her own department that allowed her to be embroiled in the biggest, but most banal, scandal of her pre-premiership career.

"SCHOOL MILK! SCHOOL MILK!" protesters cried, interrupting Thatcher's speeches as she toured Britain's schools. She became known as "Mrs. Thatcher the milk snatcher," a catchy turn of phrase that seemed to genuinely upset her.

The backstory contained little real drama. Since the summer of 1970, Treasury officials had been hounding the new minister to pursue cuts to her departmental budget. Free school milk, given to children in their morning break, was an easy target, and was expected to save tens of millions of pounds.

Thatcher accepted the necessary cuts, but a government attempt to package them covertly as part of wider legislation was bungled. And as the minister with responsibility for the proposed cuts, she shouldered the worst of the public backlash. Milk was a rallying cry, and an easy campaign because it had such a tangible impact on daily life. And it could be packaged into a broader critique of Tory ideals of a slimmed-down welfare system and small state. The popular press ripped into her. "Is Mrs. Thatcher human?" asked the tabloid *Sun*, which later characterized her as "The Most Unpopular Woman in Britain."

Amid the milk imbroglio, Heath considered firing her, which could have prematurely ended Thatcher's frontbench career.* But he demurred, partly in order to keep his only woman in position in the cabinet, and also

---

*In the House of Commons, frontbenchers are ministers in government, while backbenchers are Members of Parliament who are not part of the government.

because he, the media, and the public became distracted by disruptive miners' strikes from January 1972 onward.

The strikes represented a national trauma. Although the memory of these strikes has dimmed with the passage of time, they caused power cuts and a national state of emergency (a worse situation occurred in 1974, when a second round of major strikes forced the government to introduce a three-day working week). In this politically divisive atmosphere, Heath came to Thatcher's public defense in the House of Commons in January 1972. His move was tactical, suggesting that he saw her as a prop to support his waning authority, rather than someone who posed a threat to his leadership.

In the end, his attempt to consolidate support didn't work. Heath lost the next two general elections, both held in 1974, each of which saw Harold Wilson's Labour Party win office (albeit by exceptionally slim margins). Out of government office, Thatcher became ill at ease with Heath's approach to regaining power. He proposed "national unity" to heal a divided country, implying a willingness to participate in a coalition with left-wing parties.

Her disquiet was to be expected. This tenor was far out of line with Thatcher's belief that politics in Britain should be adversarial: Britons must choose. Appeasement, she felt, was not going to resolve the impending crisis of national confidence, and Britain's economic and geopolitical malaise was only worsening. She watched as Uganda's strongman ruler, Idi Amin, unilaterally nationalized all British businesses and expelled people of Indian descent, requiring Britain to take in the refugees from the fallout. Iceland boldly declared that no British fishing ship would be allowed access to waters within two hundred miles of its shores, seeming to mock the memory of Britannia ruling the waves. And at home, Britain's own "red scare" was afoot, with accusations of Communist infiltration in the National Union of Mineworkers. When in office, Heath had even been briefed about the prospect of an armed uprising. One memo that crossed his desk read: "The social revolution need not be destructive—although a growing number of people begin to think that it will have to be."

British decline had become the expectation. A leaked memo by a retiring British ambassador to Paris woefully concluded: "We can no longer play our historic role . . . there would also appear to be a need to stimulate a sense of national purpose." Compromising the national values that Thatcher held dear was not an approach she would entertain. In her eyes, pretensions of unity in the face of obvious discord were one major reason for Britain's postwar decline.

Adrift off the back of two electoral defeats, Thatcher and her fellow Conservatives did to Heath what is expected at the terminus of a British political leader's career: they cut *him* adrift.

Winning the House

In March 1977, one of the old Tory grandees—one born with a silver spoon in his mouth, and who was distant from her socially, culturally, and politically—said to another: "Well, what are we going to do after she gets in if she gets in?"

By this time, Thatcher had been leader of the Conservative Party, and by implication also leader of Her Majesty's Most Loyal Opposition (effectively the "government-in-waiting"), for two years. But despite being party leader, she had limited room to maneuver. After his ouster, Ted Heath refused to speak to Thatcher again, but she nonetheless found herself surrounded by his allies, so-called Heathites, and lacked the power to sack them.

To be in a position to reform her party, and in turn her country, for years Thatcher had to work closely with those who were the old "centrist," conciliatory wing of the Conservative Party. As one Conservative parliamentarian put it, her election was a "peasants' revolt" against Heath and the party grandees. But the real work came in convincing both party and country that she could lead. In Britain, effective public relations traditionally requires gaining an authoritative command of the House of Commons.

A successful performance in the Commons is no easy task, and Thatcher's early time as leader of the opposition was especially difficult. In her tailored dress suits and patent leather pumps, she sat in stark contrast to the sea of gray flannel wool and receding hairlines. And each week, Thatcher was expected to go head-to-head with the country's leader in the House of Commons, in a debate called Prime Minister's Question Time.

At the beginning, Thatcher literally struggled to make her voice heard. An opposition party operative present at Thatcher's first Question Time spoke of her lackluster performance: "She looked very pale and sounded harsh. This was in some ways a trial run before the election, and we came away feeling very confident." This is hardly the Thatcher history remembers, a political leader with a unique ability to win the House over with well-timed wit and rhetorical panache.

In these early wars of words, Labour backbenchers would make "female-type whoops" as she rose to the podium. Her adversary, Prime Minister James Callaghan, sidestepped her barbed remarks to him, addressing the "Right Honourable Lady" (these first two words being standard for how members of the House of Commons address one another) sitting across the aisle: "I still have hopes that one day Question Time will be a serious period, without Members [of Parliament] just thinking up clever phrases in advance and then shouting them across the Dispatch Box. . . . I am sure that one day the Right Honourable Lady will understand these things a little better." It was the height of condescension, but the kind of challenge that Thatcher faced day in and day out.

To emerge as a leader who could command the male-dominated House, she had to adapt. She sought formal oratory training with the famed Shakespearean actor Sir Laurence Olivier, bringing in a coach to help deepen her voice and generally improve her delivery. While there were those who would complain of the artificiality of her speech, this polished sound and appearance became a part of Thatcher's political brand. To British voters Thatcher sounded like a self-made middle-class woman, hailing from outside the ranks of the British elite.

But increasing the strength of her own voice was not enough; others needed to join her vocal barrage to gain the auditory upper hand. Beyond her own private office, Thatcher's first circle of allies was a group of parliamentarians nicknamed the "Gang of Four."

From 1975, Thatcher's Gang, Norman Tebbit, George Gardiner, Nigel Lawson, and Geoffrey Pattie, all Thatcherite firebrands, developed a staunch allegiance to their new leader. While without any formal control over the parliamentary Conservative Party, they did much of Thatcher's groundwork in the House of Commons.

The Gang of Four prepared her for Prime Minister's Questions, comprehensively anticipating queries she should expect and drafting witty

Thatcher's first Conservative government frontbench (elected 1979) in the House of Commons on April 11, 1981. From left to right are Prime Minister Margaret Thatcher, Chancellor of the Exchequer Geoffrey Howe, Education Secretary Keith Joseph, Defence Secretary John Nott, and Employment Secretary Norman Tebbit.
(PHOTOGRAPH BY CENTRAL PRESS/GETTY IMAGES)

one-liners that would resonate with the Commons' notoriously raucous politicians. With the booing and wahooing that have become a feature of the modern British political system, the gang helped to increase the decibel level of heckling whenever Labour Party politicians stood to speak, making for an adversarial atmosphere in which Thatcher's conviction politics would most powerfully come into play. Additionally, they circulated their own questions for Conservative members to pose so that Thatcher could rail against the Labour Government on the issues on which she and they felt strongest.

In time, Thatcher became a formidable opponent to the embattled Callaghan administration, which looked increasingly sclerotic in comparison to the campaign mounted by the Tory leader and her colleagues. As Thatcher's assessment of the country seemed to ring truer with each new crisis, and her forthright, hectoring style gained credibility, Callaghan's condescending put-downs began to ring hollow. Congratulating her in early 1979 for a speech on the industrial crisis, he crowed, "It was the best manner of our debates and the style in which it was delivered was one of which the right [Honourable] Lady can be proud. . . . I wish I could offer quite the same compliment about some of the content."

Winning the Nation

As Thatcher asserted herself in the House of Commons, she was also courting a nation feeling increasingly at odds with itself. Artfully, Thatcher cloaked her radical agenda in broad concepts, rather than prescriptive policies that could be attacked in detail. To gain power, she needed to establish the conditions of the political moment that would come to resonate with millions of voters. In the grandest sense, it was about reframing the political spectrum, and the system on which it was based.

Voters could observe the manifest fact of economic troubles, but were much less likely to appreciate the potential policy solutions. Thatcher was a fan of quoting Rudyard Kipling's lines "Suddenly, all men arise to the noise of fetters breaking, / And everyone smiles at his neighbor and tells him his soul is his own." These lines resonated with Thatcher's belief that Britain's economic problems had their roots in more fundamental moral ones; that socialism's forward creep was undermining the human freedoms that underpinned British democracy. It was through this moral and social lens that she tried to mobilize a beleaguered nation behind her.

To bring definition to this agenda, annual Conservative Party conferences were a focal point in Thatcher's calendar. It was at these events, again preaching to the party faithful, that she laid out in stark but communicable terms both her rejection of the existing political consensus and her political philosophy. In 1975, her first conference as party leader saw her start as she intended to go on:

> Let me give you my vision: a man's right to work as he will, to spend what he earns, to own property, to have the state as servant and not as master—these are the British inheritance. They are the essence of a free country and on that freedom all our other freedoms depend.

While these statements might seem uncontroversial, Thatcher was drawing battle lines against consensus British politics, where an array of industries had been nationalized, a tax regime saw top earners paying 83 percent in income tax, and where trade unions were akin to an additional branch of government. But when Thatcher came to grapple with what she perceived as a slow rot, one searches this or indeed many of her speeches before her 1979 rise to power for tangible policy detail, and it is almost entirely, and intentionally, absent.

Thatcher mixed an ideological palette for the public that involved taking the moral high ground, inculcating a visceral sense of impending crisis, and condemning consensus-style government as impotent.

As a result, she, her colleagues, and no doubt also her opponents knew that she would never succeed in an environment of political coalition.* She could not offer reconciliation under the conditions of combat she had described, and the kind of leadership she had come to represent.

Prospects for a general election grew through 1978–79. Thatcher and her team doubled down, acting like meteorologists forecasting the country's growing storm. She would quote the eighteenth-century founder of modern conservatism, Edmund Burke, to frame the choice between the Conservatives and their opposing parties: "All that is necessary for the triumph of evil . . . is that good men do nothing."

She told an audience in Houston, Texas: "Never have our basic values, the Christian values which rest on Hebrew and Hellenic foundations, been so menaced as they are today."

To Thatcher, a cesspool of social and economic malaise was being drip-fed into the body politic. She continued: "Family life, the innocence of children, public decency, respect for the law, pride in good work, patriotism, democracy—all are under attack."

The motif of Thatcher as the grocer's daughter standing for or against broad philosophical schools, and doing so with conviction, proved simple and effective. Given that she was still only in the opposition, fostering such an environment left little room for, and made it unnecessary to speak of, actual policy.

---

*A coalition government is where two or more political parties agree to form a government together, because no single party gains a majority of seats in the House of Commons. In such a circumstance, constant compromise and consensus building are required.

"Now Is the Winter of Our Discontent"

Thatcher's diagnosis of the country's woes was not in itself enough to bring her to power. Until 1978, her protestations had acted like tea leaves portending an imminent national crisis of conscience. But her whirlwind leadership style gained solid national—as opposed to grassroots conservative—support only when buffeted by a real crisis. As Britain approached the precipice, Thatcher's oppositional style of politics felt increasingly viable and, to many, required. Events, and Thatcher herself, had brought her to a crossroads in history.

The long and wet British season of 1978–79, still popularly known as "the Winter of Discontent," invoked the famous opening lines from Shakespeare's *Richard III*: "Now is the winter of our discontent / Made glorious summer by this son of York." It was this season of reckoning that enabled Thatcher to rise to the occasion and present herself as the path forward for Great Britain.

There was no shortage of absurd, yet ultimately distressing, events on which she could capitalize. Strikes crippled the nation. There were whisperings of a military-organized coup. The head of Prime Minister Callaghan's policy unit painted his own grim portrait of a country under siege in his memoirs:

> . . . mobile pickets were blocking ports and there was a serious shortage of food and medical supplies—ministers considered sending tanks into the [Imperial Chemical Industries] medical headquarters to retrieve drugs and essential equipment. The strike of water workers had deprived many places in the north-west of England of fresh water since the New Year. The sewage workers were threatening to join the water workers. The lorry drivers had turned down a 15 per cent [negotiated pay increase] offer and were demanding over 20 per cent. The railwaymen had called a national strike because they wanted a 10 per cent bonus on top of their 20 per cent wage demand. The nightly television pictures of violence and the brutal face of trade unionism were doing terrible damage to the government and to the trade union movement itself. . . .

Even death appeared to offer little respite, with the National Union of Public Employees declaring that they would not allow the sick into hospitals:

> . . . an official stood before the television cameras and stated that "if people die, so be it." In many places members of the dismal union also refused to allow the dead to be buried.

Thatcher threw the gauntlet down, filled the void of statesmanship, and announced in a nationwide political broadcast that—uncharacteristically— she saw compromise and unity between the political parties as the only way out of the crisis. Unsurprisingly, she could not resist spelling out Labour's reliance on funds and interests from the very unions crippling the nation before she concluded: "We have to learn again to be one nation, or one day we shall be no nation. . . . What we face is a threat to our whole way of life." Finally, after a long journey, she had ascended to the position of high matriarch of British politics.

Callaghan soon faced a motion of no confidence from the House of Commons (passed with 311 votes to 310 in favor). Such was the farcical showdown facing the country that the House of Commons' catering staff was on strike that day, and Mrs. Thatcher's aides had to buy food—and plenty of alcohol—from a local delicatessen to be participants and spectators in the showdown. Fittingly, Britain's newspaper of record, *The Times*, was not reporting these political developments, its printing suspended due to an industrial dispute.

Callaghan lost the motion of no confidence, and soon his job, when Thatcher and her fellow Conservatives were swept into power in the general election of May 1979. Her victory and ascent to the office of prime minister was a decisive pivot point in British political history, and a bookend for a style of politics that had dominated since the Second World War. Prime Minister Callaghan observed: "There are times, perhaps once every thirty years, when there is a change in politics. . . . There is a shift in what the public wants. . . . I suspect there is now such a sea-change—and it is for Mrs. Thatcher."

Thatcher campaigns for the 1979 general election at Ilford Conservative Club,
East London, accompanied by candidate Neil Thorne. Both went on to
win their prospective seats in Parliament.
(PHOTOGRAPH BY GRAHAM WILTSHIRE-GETTY IMAGES)

10 Downing Street

Around 4:00 p.m. on May 4, 1979, the day she became prime minister,
Mrs. Thatcher arrived at 10 Downing Street and toured her new offices,
including the small flat on the top floor that would become her home for
the next eleven and a half years. Between 4:00 p.m. and the start of her first
"proper" day in office, she read, thoroughly reviewed, and responded to a
steady stream of memos that arrived at her desk. There was no reason to
start slowly. She had waited for this moment for years: her ideas could now
become reality.

A former lawyer, and a known stickler for detail, Thatcher that evening
was already offering inline comments in briefing memos about how she
wanted things done. She expressed irritation at the quality of a memo on
energy policy, and suggested that an imminent visit from German chancellor Helmut Kohl was an unnecessary burden on her time. Many more
memoranda passed her desk—on the economy, defense, education, energy,

the situation in Zimbabwe—briefing her for the burdens and responsibilities of her first days in office.

Those who worked with Thatcher would swiftly become used to this distinct style of written command. Thatcher was a leader who found her sense of political direction through the spoken rather than the written word. As part and parcel of this, she rarely wrote her own memos or directives, and would instead underline key points and emblazon "Yes," "No," or "Agreed" next to specific action points. A flourish of "MT," and occasionally longer directives written in hurried script, and they would be placed back in a red box, gold-embossed "Prime Minister," ready for dispatch to the relevant recipients. On May 4, she was starting as she meant to go on.

But a prime minister does not lead by force of memo alone. The formal institution of the cabinet, the most senior part of Her Majesty's Government, contains the ministers who lead major government departments. In these first years as prime minister, despite having led her party into government, Thatcher continued to have a tenuous position at her top table, with each minister leading his or her relatively independent fiefdom. Compared to the White House machine, a British prime minister's office, housed at 10 Downing Street, is a diminutive entity. Moreover, the prime minister's responsibilities and powers are, like the British constitution itself, amorphous. She is *primus inter pares*, or "first among equals," relative to her cabinet. Ministers, meanwhile, lead sprawling bureaucracies, with a much more substantial team who have subject expertise.

Thatcher had a popular reputation for being her own expert. One of her economic advisers described her approach:

Rather than seeking a change in policy through formal channels, she often preferred to "make policy on the trot" or simply ignore the official line. She often spoke of "their policies" in relation to a department's policies that she did not like—when the policy in question was the government's own official policy.

She is also remembered as a leader who had a centralized grip on power. At first glance, the British political system might seem ill suited to the

Thatcher style. But Thatcher was willing to listen to expertise when it came from allies—and if it allowed her to strengthen her hand.

Like many leaders, Thatcher used informal channels to bolster her support. But her way of leveraging these channels had the distinctive imprint of her adversarial leadership style. She hosted an exclusive "breakfast club" that consisted of her closest allies, who came to be known as the "Dries." Thatcher's missionary zeal left little room for doubters, and those who were "soft" on her political agenda became known as the "Wets" for their lackluster commitment to Thatcherite ideals. The name stuck, and two years later, a commentator who had been hoping for a watery demise to Thatcherite policies would observe: "The trouble with the Tory Wets is that they are so bloody wet." Her opponents could not keep up with the sheer energy she threw into her first government.

Her breakfast clubs met on Thursdays because the arguments ahead required the most preparation: meetings with her disunited cabinet. Her guests were welcomed into what was both her home and office. Thatcher and her husband, Denis, lived in the small Downing Street flat occupied by British prime ministers of the modern era. Thatcher seemed to have been born for the space, and loved the idea of living "over the shop," just like she had over her father's grocery store as a youngster in Grantham, northern England.

In these early years, while combative by nature, Thatcher was in a vulnerable political position. The Heathites, or Wets, were the people most likely to challenge her during cabinet meetings, opposing policies or approaches she took—in private she referred to them as "dumb bunnies." Instead of confronting sources of division head-on in cabinet, Thatcher changed the way the government machine functioned.

While at face value collegial, breakfast at No. 10 shared a fundamental similarity with the earlier Gang of Four: it was crafted to help Thatcher personally fortify her belief system and command of policy matters. This personal style helped build momentum for her ideas, but it also caused her government to become increasingly polarized: you were either with her or against her.

These early years were especially tough for Thatcher. Everyone expected her to cave from her radical legislative program, and return to the previous consensus style of governing. But as the economic medicine she and her first chancellor of the exchequer, Geoffrey Howe, saw as the only cure to the ailing British economy began to bite, she doubled down. As Howe put it repeatedly to colleagues: "There Is No Alternative."

Breakfasts at No. 10 were there to shore up Thatcher's support, but in fact their occurrence helped fuel her detractors' critique of her leadership. Inclusion carried with it a certain mystique. Even Geoffrey Howe, Thatcher's "number two," who records himself as an attendee, admits, "there was no certainty even among close colleagues about who was 'in' and who was 'out.'" Thatcher could have used such off-the-record meetings to build coalitions of support as a strand of wider strategy. Instead, she used them to reaffirm her entrenched beliefs and apply them to the institutions of government. She fired herself up with her "insiders" in order to prepare a resolute stand in the cabinet.

In doing so, once in a full cabinet meeting, she avoided substantive discussion, often having determined her position ahead of time. One former adviser writes of how this tendency for close-mindedness developed through her premiership, where "all too common in her later period as Prime Minister . . . officials and ministers . . . put up advice that they anticipated she would want to hear."

It was on economic policy that she was most vociferous, and least willing to engage with colleagues outside of the Thatcherite core. And the gloomier the economic news became in her first term, the less likely she was to look for discussion on whether the policies were right in the first place. One such issue was interest rates, which if raised could cripple business investment, but which, in accordance with Thatcher and Howe's economic policies, could reduce the money supply that they believed was causing runaway price inflation.

"To those waiting with bated breath for that favorite media catchphrase, the U-Turn," she told her most ardent supporters in October 1980, "I have only one thing to say: You turn if you want." Deadpanning the crowd as they clamorously applauded, she concluded: "The lady's not for turning." The Wets, meanwhile, wanted a more measured economic policy, one that would not lead to considerable unemployment, partly through the anticipated collapse in business investment, and possibly subsequent social unrest.

Rather than trying to solidify support from these nervous colleagues, Thatcher simply sidelined them. Howe records in his memoirs that at this stage it was mostly he and Thatcher executing decisions as a power pair. And as the economic news worsened through the winter of 1979–80, instead of trying to build consensus within her own party, she surrounded herself with her closest supporters, who prepared her like a boxer before a fight, to identify how she might present herself as unyielding in the face of significant cabinet unease.

Maintaining this divisive code of Wets and Dries, conciliators and firebrands, was arguably an effective method of leadership in these early years, as the still-new prime minister tried to force through a radical political and economic agenda. Perhaps some exclusion was necessary. Certainly, the scale of the fallout before the economy began to bounce back in 1983 caused significant ill feeling, shook confidence in the political system, and was a cause of large-scale riots. But Thatcher survived.

Hers was a leadership style whose sustainability and effectiveness were often brought into question. One Conservative MP quoted her as saying, "Well, really it's very lonely. It's really Geoffrey [Howe] and me against the rest of them." Her naturally adversarial character shaped the way that she practiced leadership and saw the world. That adversarial behavior was part and parcel of her political philosophy, as she reflected to a journalist:

> I must say the adrenaline flows when they really come out fighting at me and I fight back and I stand there and I know "Now come on, Maggie, you are wholly on your own. No one can help you." And I love it.

But despite her workhorse capacity to direct affairs from 10 Downing Street with fierce determination, Thatcher had rather less in the way of strategy and policy coordination. The institutions she used, like her exclusive and secretive breakfast club, were personal, rather than established vehicles of governing. As one of the chief architects of Thatcherism, Nigel

Lawson, put it, "She never saw herself as the captain of the team, but as the coachman flogging the horses." In the long-term, this style would prove one of her very real vulnerabilities.

For all her unpopularity—holding, in this first term, the lowest approval ratings of any prime minister in the postwar era—Thatcher still won two more general elections, a metric that is hard to ignore. Part of this is cultural: to the British electorate, with a monarch as head of state, the personality of the political leader simply matters less than it does in a presidential system. Partly because they do not directly vote for them, the British do not need to fall in love with their political leaders. Moreover, Thatcher was assisted by a weakened Labour Party, who, partly with her nudging, had exiled themselves to the far left of the political spectrum.

But one ingredient in her success was the gift of an unforeseen crisis, where her perceived attributes of decisiveness and belief in British strength came to the fore, and in fact helped to give validation to her leadership style: war.

At the soldier's level, Britain's Falklands War of April 1982 was a cold, muddy slog. But from a distance, and for a resolute British leader, it looked like the kind of victory not experienced for generations. The landslide election that Thatcher and the Conservative Party won in June 1983 was in part a product of this foreign policy success that occurred in the South Atlantic, off the Argentine coast. These events brought Thatcher into the international limelight. As biographer Charles Moore writes: "It was not mere flattery to say that only she could have done it." He goes on to reiterate how novel Thatcher's position was in British—and indeed world—history: "She was the first female war leader with executive power in the British Isles since Elizabeth I, and the first ever in the democratic age." The event captured the popular imagination, as one Tory MP writes: "The war became a vast sporting event watched nightly by the nation."

It is difficult to think of an event more uniquely capable of showing Thatcher as a determined, patriotic leader capable of getting the job done. It is also typical of an exceptional moment in history that few leaders can anticipate or prepare for, but where the leader's response becomes an

*On the twenty-fifth anniversary of the end of the Falklands War, celebrated on
June 17, 2007, Margaret Thatcher, by then Baroness Thatcher of Kesteven,
meets Falklands veterans on The Mall in London, England.*
(PHOTOGRAPH BY ANWAR HUSSEIN COLLECTION/ROTA/WIRE IMAGE)

indelible part of the legacy they leave. Thatcher's second electoral victory
gave her the mandate to truly change Great Britain.

Victory Is Bittersweet

"Don't worry, Michael," Mrs. Thatcher beamed, "Nigel and I have fixed
the whole thing—it's all done." The forty-one-year-old civil servant Michael Scholar, until 1983 Thatcher's Treasury private secretary, stared at the
reelected prime minister and newly appointed chancellor of the exchequer,
Nigel Lawson. He had arrived "desperate," late for a meeting with the most
powerful woman in the land. But far from being haughty, Thatcher and
Lawson were "wreathed in smiles" at the productivity of their forty-minute
bilateral meeting.

Scholar recalled this time being "a very sweet time for both of them."
Thatcher and Lawson were in the honeymoon period of their working relationship, of one mind in their attitude that, finally, now was the time that
government expenditure should be reduced to allow for substantial tax

cuts. They had just determined their strategy for the coming term of office. All appeared congenial—and Scholar could breathe a sigh of relief that his tardiness had caused no ill feeling for the gathering.

It was in these heady days after her landslide electoral victory of June 9, 1983, that Thatcher began to relish her perceived indispensability to the Conservative Party, and to Great Britain. On that midsummer day, Thatcher looked like a queen at court, on a weekend getaway at her favorite residence and official countryside retreat, Chequers, to discuss economic strategy with her new chancellor. This was a break for Thatcher after a job well done. One of her aides recalls her style of electoral campaigning: "It's a shooting war, and she's a foot soldier. She's not the general back at HQ. She's in the front line." The next year would be the high-water mark of Thatcherite politics. And yet there was little attempt to marry her electoral strength with the coalition building necessary to convince those still unsure of her methods and intentions.

Nonetheless, Thatcher wanted to remain tough but not tyrannical in the public eye. Discussing with the BBC her major cabinet reshuffle in the aftermath of the 1983 landslide, Thatcher used a metaphor appropriately combining the grocer and housewife motifs she had developed as personal insignia in her two previous, successful major elections: "I'm not a good butcher, but have had to learn to carve the joint."

Since the Falklands War, Mrs. Thatcher had become a national and international icon, despite the reservations many had with her policies and leadership style. Such stunts as arriving at the island constituency of the Isle of Wight, headscarf fluttering in the wind, at the helm of a hovercraft, and going on "manic pretend shopping trips" to ask for British (certainly not imported!) bacon saw her become an audacious yet sturdy fixture of the British political landscape.

Thatcher used her 1983 victory to argue that the policies of her previous administration, controversial though they were, had been vindicated by her considerable electoral success. It also very much helped that the economy was now picking up steam after its downturn. She continued to frame her mandate as a battle for the nation's soul, to resecure Britain's place as a great power, and to expel socialism from its shores. Her 1983 victory had been the biggest majority since Clement Attlee's 1945 rise to power in postwar Britain, and like Attlee, both Thatcher and Lawson knew that playing their cards right could transform the socioeconomic norms of the nation. A Conservative MP from outside the Thatcherite camp refers to this time as her "imperial period," with the 1983 campaign seeing "Mrs. Thatcher inexhaustibly feeding off her own zealotry."

Increasingly, Thatcher used informal "kitchen cabinet" meetings like the one with Lawson, and with nonelected private secretaries, to assert her vision for Britain's new direction. Meanwhile in the cabinet, Thatcher became hostile to dissenters, fostering an environment where many felt unable to stand up for themselves, or to support colleagues when Thatcher was humiliating them through a public dressing down.

There is a common perception that Thatcher fell from power over the so-called poll tax, a property tax that was the cause of widespread riots and resistance in 1990. This was the most visible division that occurred during her final administration and was coincidental with her demise later that year. Yet the rot had begun earlier, and in fact involved a division at the beating heart of the Thatcher-Howe-Lawson troika of power.

A triad of issues confronted them, issues that ran to the core of her government: economics, leadership, and Europe. A major point of contention, the European Exchange Rate Mechanism (ERM) was a lethal cocktail of these three things. A highly technical, but ultimately ideologically charged policy, it dealt with the question of whether the British pound sterling should be pegged to other European currencies. Thatcher, who by instinct sought sovereign independence from the Europeans, did not like the idea of supposedly compromising British interests by tracking the pound sterling with the German deutsche mark. She would have been even more skeptical about the ultimate end point of the ERM (which Lawson would himself in fact oppose), the inception of a common European currency, which eventually emerged as the euro.

On the specific issue of the ERM, Thatcher's two closest advisers, Howe and Lawson, stood against her. The division was not a one-off event but had simmered since early in the Thatcher premiership, when Lawson had first expressed his support for joining forces with the Europeans. Thatcher and her top economic team agreed to postpone entry into the ERM "until the time is right," an ambiguous statement of intent that would remain a sticking point. By early 1985, a run on the pound forced the issue of exchange rates to the fore. Battle lines were drawn. In late September of that year, a calamitous meeting convened with the intention of ironing out tensions saw Thatcher cornered, with few supporters against the greater economic clout of Howe and Lawson.

Thatcher's ensuing tactics exposed something of both her pride and her approach as a political tactician. While Lawson had lobbied all ministers attending a showdown meeting scheduled for November 13, Thatcher had neglected to do so. Lawson, the most economically literate minister on Thatcher's top team, could demonstrate forcefully the benefits of joining the ERM, while Thatcher, normally well prepared, rejected the ERM as much on gut instinct as on the economics. And Thatcher had not tapped her most shrewd allies to defend her stance when the moment came. Characteristically, Thatcher did not sink to coalition-building tactics, nor did she have a cohesive plan to accommodate the divergent interests that had developed around her top table—ones that had by now been causing division for years.

When the time came for the meeting on November 13, like sheepish schoolchildren, the gaggle of conspiring pro-ERM cabinet members entered from neighboring 11 Downing Street. What followed was what one attendee called "a bitter, nasty, unpleasant meeting" in which Thatcher refused to shift from her ambiguous deferral of "until the time is right." Another attendee reflected that Thatcher would have resigned as prime minister before she agreed to a change in policy.

And for three years, that was that. Unable, as ever, to gain momentum in opposing their leader, the conspirators shuffled back to 11 Downing Street, considering how on earth they might respond to this unrelenting dissent from the most powerful woman in the world.

Gradually, Chancellor Nigel Lawson and Geoffrey Howe made further inroads in mustering support for the ERM, in doing so undermining Thatcher's credibility. But ultimately, the three senior leaders reached an impasse. No one would budge. Working relationships deteriorated, and one journalist observed that the arrangement showed Lawson and Howe as "painfully subordinate figures . . . victims of the Prime Minister's utterly insatiable desire

Thatcher, ever an icon at the Conservative Party conference, is cheered at the event in Blackpool, England, in 1989. The man on the far left is John Major, who would succeed her as prime minister in November 1990.
(JOHNNY EGGITT/AFP/GETTY IMAGES)

for domination." With his gift for the ironic understatement, in his memoirs, Howe writes that the journalist "was uncomfortably close to the truth."

Despite growing popular disaffection, in 1987 Thatcher won an unprecedented third term. The Tories held a reduced but still substantial parliamentary majority. "No British Government has ever been defeated unless and until the tide of ideas has turned against it," Nigel Lawson boasted to Conservative supporters. Thatcher and her team still largely controlled that tide, but the image of unity she and her team sought to project had worn thin. By this time, on the foreign policy stage, Thatcher was the most successful prime minister since her hero Winston had held office. During her tenure, Britain had solidified itself as Europe's great power and America's closest partner. And Thatcher had an extraordinary impact in brokering an end to the Cold War through highly personal relationships with Ronald Reagan and the Soviet Union's Mikhail Gorbachev. Yet for all her verve at foreign policy, Thatcher's personal insecurities were cleaving divisions at the heart of her government at home.

The Assassination

By the time of her fall, both Mrs. Thatcher's supporters and critics were able to agree that she had achieved a remarkable amount in the previous decade. Today, a bronze statue of her likeness stands alongside three other heavyweight British prime ministers in the House of Commons' Members' Lobby: David Lloyd George, Winston Churchill, and Clement Attlee. In office, Thatcher had realigned the underpinnings of British politics, broken the trade unions, privatized an array of industries, resuscitated Britain's influence as a global player, and been a towering presence on the international political landscape. In her time, she became the most recognizable woman in the world, holding one of the most powerful offices in human history. But Thatcherism was not made possible by the woman at its helm alone.

By late 1990, only one member of Thatcher's original cabinet, Geoffrey Howe, had survived the Iron Lady's periodic reorganizations, purges, and public fallings out. Thatcher had always bristled with irritation at his slower, softer, more diplomatic persona. He had been shuffled to the position of deputy prime minister and leader of the House of Commons in 1989, but the prime minister recognized his indispensability to Thatcherism.

Despite her international celebrity and the intricate tentacles of her power, like almost all leaders, Thatcher lasted only so long as her core team of allies publicly supported her position. But she had for some time been undermining this core, perceiving them as rivals rather than as partners. When she moved Howe to the position of deputy prime minister, despite the title, it was in fact a demotion for Howe from his previous role as foreign secretary (and before that, chancellor of the exchequer). While she never said so to Howe, it was a move made out of spite for the way she felt Lawson and Howe had cornered her on the issue of joining the ERM. Her cabinet moves often reflected an underlying effort to marginalize old allies whom she perceived as challengers to her authority.

Nigel Lawson resigned on October 26, 1989, due to the intertwined issues of the ERM and Thatcher's increased reliance on an inner circle of advisers whom she had housed at 10 Downing Street. Rather than trusting him as the man holding the economics brief, Thatcher tried to centralize

*Margaret Thatcher addresses the Conservative conference in Blackpool in October
1986. From left to right are Nigel Lawson, Geoffrey Howe, William Whitelaw,
and Norman Tebbit. In different ways, these four parliamentarians
formed part of the narrative of Thatcherism.*
(PHOTOGRAPH BY KEYSTONE/GETTY IMAGES)

policy at Number 10. As Lawson argued: "Prime Ministers have an unfettered right to dismiss any Cabinet Minister, however senior. . . . What is
unacceptable conduct in a Prime Minister . . . is to recoil from sacking a
Minister, and systematically undermine him instead."

The loss of Lawson brought the internal ruptures of Thatcher's political
machine into sharp, and public, focus. Her belligerence toward the ERM
had morphed into a more generalized opposition to Europeanism, a division that then simmered in the Tory Party for decades, emerging most
prominently in the 2016 referendum in which the British people voted to
leave the European Union. Howe, although hardly a neutral bystander, be-
moaned "the increasingly nationalist crudity of the Prime Minister's whole
tone" and the increasing "tantrums" she was throwing in the cabinet.

Perhaps more key than her policy positions was her standing in the
polls. Her popularity hit record lows (as Labour's approval headed toward
50 percent, she was personally polling at 20 percent), and the same conviction politics that had enabled her rise now began to appear politically
reckless. Almost to confirm his growing doubts about his role in the

cabinet, Thatcher rebuked Howe for what would be the final time in a cabinet meeting on October 31, 1990, for perceived errors in a planned legislative program. In hindsight, Thatcher writes in her memoirs that she had attacked him that day "probably too sharply"—sharply enough that Howe resigned.

Five days later, Howe delivered a political death blow to his old boss. Playing the role of Brutus, he delivered a retirement address to Parliament from the crowded backbenches of the House of Commons. It was Thatcher's greatest public embarrassment. Two rows in front of him, with her back to Howe, she sat and listened closely to her former colleague, confidant, and the "tapestry-master of Thatcherism."

Howe stood in front of his peers, Conservatives and Labourites alike. He delivered a version of his private resignation, including a few tongue-in-cheek quips at the expense of his old boss. At moments the entire Parliament roared in laughter at Howe's cutting jokes. It was a surreal moment, and an unraveling of the power and propriety that Thatcher had cultivated in the House of Commons for the last thirty-one years. She remained impassive throughout the dissection.

Thatcher seemed incapable of admitting how she had alienated her closest allies, or of reading the writing on the wall. The hollowing out of her core team, coupled with bungled policy efforts such as the poll tax, led to general realization that the party and country had a leader who was unwilling to adapt her leadership style, but willing to attack her closest elected supporters, to sustain her grip on power. That grip had already been weakening, and Howe, whether or not he anticipated the full impact of his defection, abandoned his leader. She was left an isolated figure, wounded but soldiering on with her unique approach to the political game whose rules she had so substantially remade.

On November 2, Michael Heseltine formally challenged Thatcher for the leadership of the party. The rank-and-file MPs of the Tory Party— responsible for selecting their leader—had been fairly isolated from direct interactions with Thatcher for a while. They were afraid of losing their seats by associating with such a polarizing figure at the next election.

After failing to win enough votes in a first ballot, Thatcher, who had lost much of her authority in the Houses of Parliament, withdrew from the leadership race on November 22, and returned to being a backbencher for the remainder of her term in Parliament.

Margaret Thatcher was a leader of unparalleled conviction, and at her helm, Britain became a different country. The two men who, for all intents and purposes, ended her career—Howe and Lawson—recognized her unique power and capacity to pursue her cause. Yet the convictions of one individual need both the unwavering support of the few and the buy-in of the many. As Lawson puts it, "Margaret could not have done it without her core team, who translated her strong will, courage and conviction— wayward and self-contradictory though it could be—into a coherent and consistent course of action."

Even at her fall, Thatcher retained her pride, and by the end she was able to raise a half-knowing smile. During her last speech in the House of Commons on November 22, 1990, she was heckled by Labour MP Dennis Skinner. While Thatcher was answering a question on whether she'd continue crusading against the European Central Bank when out of office, Skinner interjected, "No, she's going to be the [Bank's] Governor!"

Both benches burst out laughing, the floor returning to Thatcher only when the Speaker of the House, who is effectively the moderator, commanded it half a minute later. The ousted prime minister let out a smile. Civility restored, the Iron Lady, her inimitable voice if not her dignity fully intact, retorted: "What a good idea!"

At which point, raucous laughter filled the chamber anew.

THE HALLS OF POWER

To say that a leader is preoccupied with power is like saying that a tennis player is preoccupied with making shots his opponent cannot return.
—JOHN GARDNER

In October 1984, Margaret Thatcher stood motionless at the podium, allowing the prolonged applause of a standing ovation to wash over her. More than heard, such approval is felt from inside out, stimulating confidence.

She knew the feeling well, but halfway through her second term as Britain's prime minister, few crowds had been this welcoming.

The veteran power broker had just addressed a normal gathering of the Conservative Party, but not six hours earlier a bomb had ripped apart one side of the Brighton Hotel, killing five people and shattering the prime minister's private bathroom minutes after she'd left it. The Irish Republican Army claimed responsibility for the attack, and she had been its target.

Her presence at the podium, so soon after the attack, was a clear show of defiance. True to form, the Iron Lady had overruled her security team and arrived at the conference hall through its main doors, seizing an opportunity for the media to capture her as the symbol of a nation newly united against terrorism. It was, all at once, political theater, strong leadership, and a chance to consolidate her power.

The very term "power broker" implies an individual who manages influence, as though it were a tangible commodity, like a barrel of oil or a single-family home. But power is more ephemeral than we generally admit. The primly dressed Iron Lady couldn't have carried a twelve-ounce can of power in her handbag any more than Boss Tweed could keep it at the ready in a vest pocket. In fact, power is found mostly in people's perception of the leader, and at the point when people believe that a leader has lost it, they likely have.

Perception matters greatly, because power rarely resides within just an individual. Power is not an absolute state but an arrangement among stakeholders. It is bestowed upon the leader as much as it is taken by the leader. While we speak about power as something that a leader seizes and dispenses, it is more accurate to say that power exists within the system that envelops a leader, and reflects that system's expectations of its leaders.

This explains why so many power brokers can seem frustrated and feckless despite their apparent positional authority. Quietly, they know that their power is contingent and derived from elsewhere, whether it is another branch of government, a board of directors, shareholders, an electorate, or a fan base.

For all the blatant differences in their leadership, Thatcher and Tweed were both political leaders in democratic systems, and their stories of leadership contain parallel elements. To gain power, each had to have it granted it by electorates and institutions. Thatcher had to persuade the citizens of Finchley to vote for her, but more substantively, she had to use her rhetoric to win a battle of wills for the soul of the Tory Party and the nation. Through her rigid adherence to an ideology she transformed party lines, and gave Britons an opportunity to resurrect a feeling of national pride. Tweed's following flowed in part from basic patronage and in part from social identity—people from Tweed's neighborhood, and much of poor, immigrant New York, voted only for Tammany men.

If you wanted to be the most powerful man in New York in the nineteenth century, you had to lead Tammany Hall. And if you want to rule Britain, you have to get to the top of one of its major parties. Leadership is rife with such institutions that exist in part to promote leaders. A leader's power derives from the system that promotes them, and they get power only so long as they buy in to that system and play by its rules. They can bend the rules, but they do so at their own risk.

The flip side, of course, is that the followers' choices are limited to the options granted them by those very same institutions. When she was elected as head of the Conservative Party, Margaret Thatcher wasn't tremendously popular within it—on the first ballot of her Tory leadership race with Ted Heath, she beat him by 130 votes to 119 before Heath withdrew on the second ballot. Whether by 11 or 100 votes, she would become head of the party all the same.

Once a leader is granted power, maintaining it is just as precarious. A seemingly brave act, Thatcher's decision to walk through the front doors of the conference hall—mere hours after the assassination attempt against her—was an act designed as much to protect her power as to display it. Failing to maintain the persona she'd marketed to the British people could quickly result in the power bestowed upon her being withdrawn.

Once they had power, our power brokers consolidated the groups with which they actually made decisions. Some of this consolidation was temperamental, for neither Thatcher nor Tweed cared for elaborate process and each preferred a personal touch. But some of it was practical, for both also had to get things done. The regular meetings of Tweed's "lunch club," and Thatcher's "breakfast club," as unseemly as they were, were the more operational, less symbolic side of how they managed their power.

The full arc of Thatcher's trajectory was attributable to her very closest confidants, such as Howe and Lawson. Without the subtle influences and actions of such core followers, Thatcher would never have risen in the way she did. And over time, that group would become marginalized and frustrated by Thatcher's style. With their eventual defection, her erstwhile supporters became her assassins. Thatcher had survived the IRA's bombing, but she would not be so lucky when her closest supporters left her.

Tweed's fall from power was a cascade of events that began with a failure of governance in the Orange Riots. Between then and his eventual indictment, every constituency that had enabled him—Tammany, his lunch club, the city's elites—abandoned him. Though it would take longer for him to lose his popular support, the Orange Riots were a turning point—after a decade-long rise to power, and a decade more as the city's most powerful man, it was all gone in a matter of a few months.

We play along with the mythology that power resides in the single person, in part because we have to. Entitites like corporate boards, electorates, and governments exist, in part, to decide who gets to have power, and then to dictate rules for how they can use it. Because power is so tightly tied to specific institutions, a leader who wants power can at least chart their course, even if getting the top job requires lots of luck and skill. The challenge is that, while the leader is leading, the situation is constantly changing and those constituencies and institutions that endowed the leader with power are always on the lookout for who might do a better job. To see the leadership of power brokers, one must look away from the leaders and toward the followers and institutions that enable them.

Eight

THE REFORMERS

*Human progress is neither automatic nor inevitable. . . . Every
step toward the goal of justice requires sacrifice, suffering,
and struggle; the tireless exertions and passionate
concern of dedicated individuals.*

—DR. MARTIN LUTHER KING JR., IN *A STRIDE
TOWARD FREEDOM: THE MONTGOMERY STORY*

I remember the glow in the night sky. Several hours earlier, at 6:01 p.m., a soft-point, metal-jacketed .30–06 bullet fired from a high-velocity rifle perched in the bathroom window of a Memphis rooming house had cracked across 207 feet to strike Dr. Martin Luther King Jr. on the right side of his face—knocking him to the balcony floor of the Lorraine Motel outside Room 306. It was April 4, 1968, and King was murdered while in the city to support striking sanitation workers. As with the assassination of President John F. Kennedy not quite five years before, the killer, allegedly a lone rifleman identified as escaped convict James Earl Ray, became the subject of significant controversy. But that came later, and at about 11:00 that night, rioting erupted in Washington, DC.

Reflected light from the blaze was visible from across the Potomac River where we lived in northern Virginia. Before the violence subsided on April 8, more than a thousand buildings suffered extensive damage or complete destruction, and twelve citizens died. The economic heart of the city, primarily African American communities, was devastated. Washington, DC, was only one of the hundred-plus cities where violence erupted in the wake of the assassination. There are few leaders whose loss could have produced such a reaction.

Though not yet fourteen years old, I was intensely aware of Dr. King. My mother, raised as a liberal in Alabama and Tennessee, was instinctively, and viscerally, opposed to figures like Alabama governor George Wallace, so King was a subject of frequent discussion in our home. I recall the March for Jobs and Freedom on Washington, DC, in August 1963, and Dr. King's evangelical "I Have a Dream" speech on the steps of the Lincoln Memorial. But, as for many Americans, my memories tended to focus on the high points—the marches, protests, arrests, and celluloid-captured glimpses into the painful process of social and political change. I had only a superficial appreciation for the complex interactions working just below the surface of the reported news, and even less for the leaders who were involved.

Martin Luther King Jr. was only twenty-six when he emerged on the national scene leading the Montgomery bus boycott. He was only thirty-nine when he died. In those intervening years, however, he was the best-known leader in an extraordinary reform movement pushing against tremendous resistance in a society that, after 350 years of inequity, had grown accepting of prejudice.

Dr. King's namesake, Martin Luther, the German monk and theologian who instigated the Protestant Reformation, preceded him by more than four hundred years. A devout believer wracked by doubts surrounding the contradiction between the religion he accepted and the way he saw it in operation, Luther is less familiar to us, but had a greater influence on the arc of history. Both men freely chose the church and pushed reforms beyond the confines of religion.

Reformers are a unique type of leader. Seeking to change the status quo, they must often simultaneously serve as a champion of the need for change, the architect for its design, and the on-site engineer for its execution. More than revolutionaries seeking to overthrow a regime, or political power brokers attempting to master and ride the beast of government, reformers work to change people's actions and, ultimately, what they believe.

We chose Martin Luther because his story is fundamental to Western and Christian history. Many of us identify with, and worship in, churches descended from Luther's movement. King was an even easier choice. A key figure in my youth, Martin Luther King Jr. epitomized courageous leadership. As with Robert E. Lee, it felt as though any book I might write about leaders must include him because he was a key figure in framing how I thought about leading.

Both of our reformers were thrust into leadership of massive, complex, continent-wide movements. The Protestant Reformation and the civil rights movement each comprised complex permutations of intersecting ideas, interests, and leaders—so how, and why, did each of these men emerge as *the* leader of their respective movements, with the authority to speak for millions?

Key Books

- Lyndal Roper, *Martin Luther: Renegade and Prophet* (New York: Random House, 2016)
- Taylor Branch, *Parting the Waters: America in the King Years, 1954–1963* (New York: Simon & Schuster, 1988)
- David Garrow, *Bearing the Cross: Martin Luther King, Jr., and the Southern Christian Leadership Conference* (New York: William Morrow, 1986)

MARTIN LUTHER

When I preach here I adapt myself to the circumstances of the common people. I don't look at the doctors and masters, of whom scarcely forty are present, but at the hundred or the thousand young people and children. It's to them that I preach, to them that I devote myself, for they, too, need to understand.

—MARTIN LUTHER, 1537

Flames licked up the sides of the altar. The violet cloth at its base began to twitch and shrivel. Soon the orange color of fire was dancing around the holy centerpiece, a solitary cross in the middle of the altar. It too became ash as the flames enveloped it, then ascended upward into the wooden roofing.

Shards of richly colored, lacquered ceramic strewn across the floor added to the kaleidoscopic fury. These sacred fragments had once been the torsos and flowing garments of religious statues, icons smashed by the assailants before they set the blaze. A few remained standing, but most littered the floor, as fallen warriors left by a ransacking army. The fractured statue of the Virgin Mary lay as the protagonist in this gory feast of flame, for it was she for whom they had come.

Outside, the plunderers stood victorious, their bounty—a chest, coins, goblets, and a candelabra—glinting from the flames now snaking their way through the seams of the chapel, sizzling and popping. In their eyes this had been a divinely ordained mission, the violent but necessary birth of a movement soon to sweep Christendom.

The destruction of the pilgrimage chapel at Mallerbach in March 1524 was the first church burning in a bloody conflagration that soon spread through central Europe and would become known as the German Peasants' War (1524–25). The peasants were frustrated with their economic exploitation by the landed classes; Luther's religious teachings promised to liberate the oppressed. A connection was made between economic and theological frustrations, and that connection sparked a conflict in which more than 100,000 people were killed.

SOME EIGHTY MILES TO THE EAST, Martin Luther, a forty-year-old monk of a provincial German town, was in his home, a cavernous abode that had previously been an Augustinian monastery. He was joined by a host of close supporters, many of whom had come to Wittenberg seeking refuge, unaware of the violent events that had just transpired at Mallerbach. News circulated by letters and gossip along modest roads upon which carts, horses, and people traveled slowly. Because he was considered an enemy of the pope and the Holy Roman Empire, Luther's movements were largely contained within a small geographic area in the Electorate of Saxony (one of the two states in the Saxony region) governed by Elector Frederick the Wise.

But little else about Martin Luther had been contained. Over the previous eight years the monk-turned-reformer had, through his writings and public actions, conveyed an increasingly intoxicating message of opposition to a pope and Catholic Church he considered to be corrupt. Luther's leadership of what became known as the Protestant Reformation severed the bonds that had united Catholic Europe for centuries. Luther wasn't at Mallerbach, but his ideas lit the fire there, and they continue to hold energy nearly five hundred years later.

Still, the daunting leader and high-profile reformer was just a man with human emotions and vulnerabilities. He was characterized by a dark, prophetic temper. This included disturbing, virulent anti-Semitism that was embedded deep within his theology and went well beyond even the norms of the time. Yet Luther could also be a more lighthearted, convivial soul, one able to poke fun at his own religious devotion. Years of dinnertime conversations were recorded by the people who knew him in a collection called *Table Talk*. One entry records: "When Luther's puppy happened to be at the table, looked for a morsel from his master, and watched with open mouth and motionless eyes, he [Martin Luther] said, 'Oh, if I could only pray the way this dog watches the meat!'"

In the country outside, however, Luther's forceful propagation of what were—for their time—highly incendiary ideas created a tumultuous environment. Five years after the famous (but perhaps apocryphal) posting of his Ninety-five Theses to the door of All Saints' Church in Wittenberg, followers inspired by Luther's teachings had begun burning objects and images. Luther, at home, was largely powerless to stop the descent into violence.

Through a modern lens, Luther and the era in which he lived can be difficult to comprehend. It was an age of intense religiosity, in which Christians' waking hours and practical concerns—work, marriage, taxes, personal conduct, and the steady rhythm of religious worship—were largely defined by the Church. Life on earth, most believed, was only a waystation on the path to eternal unity with God in heaven.

Against this backdrop, Luther's actions had enormous repercussions, and his ideas shaped how we live and think today. Martin Luther, it might be said, led to Puritan pilgrims landing at Plymouth in 1620. Luther and his contemporaries' furious debate over religious images, it could be argued, resulted in the Washington Monument being built as an obelisk, rather than an equestrian statue. Indeed, American civic republicanism reflects

Reformation concerns that the idolization of leaders and institutions can lead to despotism.

Ironically, as Martin Luther urged the Church to get rid of its idols, Luther's followers came to idolize him. And ultimately, they heeded the idol more than the man himself. For all his divine-like authority, the German peasants whom Luther inspired—including those who'd burned down the chapel in Mallerbach—didn't necessarily follow his instruction. The German Peasants' War was conducted by hundreds of thousands of peasants who celebrated Luther and his teachings, but ignored the former monk of Wittenberg when he implored them to put down their arms.

Like many leaders, Luther's practical impact came not through battlefield heroics or diplomatic skill, but emanated instead from the use of his pen and his deft way with words. Luther often stayed at home, far from frontline battles, leveraging his spiritual authority and his fame. And to understand Luther's appetite for celebrity and passion for reform, we first need to appreciate his revolutionary spirit. Luther was a contradictory and internally conflicted man, characteristics that began at a young age, when he rejected his father's chosen path for a favored child.

From Miner's Son to Scholar, to Cloister, to Wittenberg

When he was a boy, Martin Luther's eventual journey to religious influence and historical prominence would have been difficult to predict. One of eight children born to a copper miner and his wife in Eisleben and raised in the gritty mining town of Mansfeld, Luther was expected to fulfill his father's dream of having his eldest son attend university, study the law, and return to his hometown. In doing so, he would help the Luther family rise in Mansfeld's social structure.

Beyond being a resident of Mansfeld, Luther was also a Saxon, a German, and a citizen of the Holy Roman Empire, in which Catholicism was the official and predominant faith. The empire was an alliance of states and territories spanning from Tuscany in central Italy to Holstein in northern Germany. The most senior ruler was the Holy Roman Emperor, a seat that from 1519 was filled by Charles V, who was elected by a number of prince electors, including Luther's local ruler, Frederick the Wise.

In 1498, the young teenager and lawyer-to-be Luther moved to Eisen-ach, his mother's hometown, to attend school. Then, in 1501, he entered university at Erfurt, the oldest German institution by charter. When Lu-ther arrived, it was abuzz with debate. At issue were matters of personal morality and state authority. In particular, theologians could not agree if a person reached heaven through faith alone, or through faith *and* good works during their life on earth. This raised fundamental questions about how God's justice worked—whether God took people's good actions into account or if, conversely, He was totally unknowable and "irrational."

Discussion about these issues made Church and state authorities wary. Their authority rested on the belief that they had worked out what a rational God would want of His subjects. Without this, they feared that many people would ignore their instruction, or even revolt against their rule.

Luther later rejected both sides of the debate, in the process tearing through the traditional hierarchy of institutions whose role it was to medi-ate such matters. But for now, he drifted away from the law and toward religion, becoming an arch-adherent to those very institutions. And it was that intimacy with them that became essential to his understanding of their most patent flaws.

THE ROUTE TO AND FROM home had special significance for Luther. On the road to Erfurt, dry scholarly material awaiting, he might have considered whether the calling of the law was really for him. And on the way back to Mansfeld, he had to reconcile this feeling of listlessness with an expectant father's ambition, and his parents having privileged his education over that of his siblings, concerned for their reaction if he let them down.

On one occasion, traveling back to Mansfeld, Luther managed to injure himself with his own sword, severing an artery in his upper leg. As the wound swelled and bled profusely, Luther prayed "O Mary, help!" A doc-tor was summoned and tended to him, but that same evening, the wound burst, at which point Luther again prayed to Mary to save him. Because the wound healed, Luther came to believe that it was God who had intervened to heal him.

Key locations in
Martin Luther's life
1483–1546

◩ Significant
location

NORWAY

SWEDEN

N
W — E
S

50   0   100 Miles

0   50 Kilometers

DENMARK

○ Copenhagen

Baltic Sea

North
Sea

Flensburg ○

○ Hamburg   ○ Szczecin

○ Bremen   Elbe R.

POLAND

Vistula R.

The Hague ○   ○ Amsterdam   ○ Hanover   ○ Berlin   ○ Poznan

○ Dover   ○ Münster

Rhine R.

Weser R.

Mansfeld
(1484–1498)   ◩ Wittenberg
(1511–1546)

◩◩ ○ Leipzig

○ Breslau

Oder R.

○ Antwerp   ○ Bonn

Meuse R.

◩ Eisleben
Luther's birthplace
(1483)

○ Koblenz

◩ ◩ Wartburg Castle
(1521–1522)

○ Würzburg

◩ Erfurt
(1501–1511)

○ Prague

○ Luxembourg

○ Reims

○ Paris

Seine R.

○ Metz

Worms
(1521)

HOLY
ROMAN
EMPIRE

Danube R.

○ Vienna   ○ Bratislava

○ Orléans

FRANCE

○ Strasbourg

○ Munich   ○ Salzburg

HUNGARY

○ Dijon   ○ Basel

○ Innsbruck

Mur R.

Allier R.

A   l   p   s

○ Lyon   ○ Milan

VENICE

┐ Trieste

Rhône R.

○ Turin   Po R.

○ Venice

OTTOMAN
EMPIRE

○ Genoa

Ligurian
Sea

○ Florence   PAPAL
STATES

Adriatic Sea

Marseille ○

Mediterranean
Sea

Rome ◩
(1510)

Tiber R.

NAPLES

Note:
Boundaries
shown
reflect the
time period
of about
1500 CE

Map by Gene Thorp

A second, more famous incident occurred when Luther was returning to Erfurt from Mansfeld. Four miles outside Erfurt, amid a breaking thunderstorm, Luther called on St. Anna to protect him, vowing to enter a monastery if she did so. At the time, storms were commonly thought to be caused by the Devil or witches, and so he was quite literally praying for protection from their evil spirits. Having survived the storm, Luther was good to his word: on July 17, 1505, he joined the Augustinian order in Erfurt. He had escaped a life of the law—but in order to do so, he had had to leave his family and former life behind.

THE AUGUSTINIANS WHO RESIDED in the "Black Monastery" were a strictly observant order, holding to the principles of obedience, poverty, and chastity with militant diligence. Here Luther faced a punishing existence in servitude to God that included subjecting himself to bodily mortification. For instance, the wearing of a cassock made of coarse wool chafed his skin and meant his wounds stayed open and raw. The requirements of religious observance also meant sleep deprivation, waking in the middle of the night to attend a service to say the first prayers of the new dawn, the matins, before going to similar services at six, nine, midday, and on a further three occasions throughout the afternoon and evening.

All of this was punctuated with hours of reading and writing of religious material each day, bringing the monastery into a state of holy reverie. Luther was known as an especially strict adherent of this regimen, a path he chose for no other reasons than a profound sense of faith and an exceptional fear of God's judgment. Ideas of reform were far from his mind, and the future iconoclast spent the first twenty-nine years of his life as an unremarkable and unpublished conformist.

In time, Luther found himself focusing on one of the only connections to the world outside the monastery's walls that was permitted—that with a new university at Wittenberg, some one hundred miles away. Luther's access to Wittenberg came through his confessor, Johann von Staupitz, a powerful theologian who was influential at the regional court of Frederick the Wise of Saxony. Staupitz became Luther's first father figure since he had entered the monastery, and it proved to be a relationship that served Luther well.

Staupitz saw Luther as a serious young monk, but one who was possessed by fear: that he did not love God enough, and that God's final judgment of him was impending. These were no small matters for a man who was devoting his life to achieving closeness with God.

Despite his mentee's mental turmoil, Staupitz saw that Luther was capable of something beyond his panicked regime of prayer and self-denial. Access to Wittenberg University gave Staupitz, and through him Luther, a window to debates over what it meant to be a citizen and a religious believer. Soon that connection would be Luther's means of escape. Over time it would enable him to take up his central role in the early Reformation.

The Ninety-five Theses and a Revolution in Print

Staupitz had to convince Luther to study for his doctorate. The young monk was doom-laden and world-weary from his life of the cloth, and believed he might not even live to finish his studies. But he did, finishing in 1512 with the qualifications and gravitas to become a full-time professor at Wittenberg. For now, Luther remained in his cassock and committed to his Augustinian vows, living just next to the university building in Wittenberg's own newly established Black Monastery.

Fortuitously, one of the university's founding faculty members, who had departed in 1505, had left behind his printing press, and skillful use of this new technology was already building reputations. The humanist scholar Desiderius Erasmus had used it to become one of Europe's first intellectual celebrities. Between 1514 and 1517, Erasmus was the most published man in Europe, as copies of his Greek New Testament, as well as editions of Seneca and St. Jerome, flooded the market, creating Erasmian disciples all throughout Europe. Print soon became a powerful tool for Luther as well, and by 1518 he had overtaken Erasmus to become the biggest-selling author in Europe. In fact, as the historian Mark Edwards has calculated, between 1518 and 1525, publications by Luther in German exceeded those of the seventeen other most prolific authors put together. This was the outset of a publishing career that would see him translate the Bible into German, a contribution that influences the language to this day. Clearly, from 1517 to 1518, something had changed.

The Attachment of Luther's Ninety-five Theses *by Julius Hübner, 1878.*
Centuries after Luther's death, the posting of the Ninety-five Theses has
become an ingrained feature of the Western cultural imagination,
even though it may never have happened.

MUCH INK HAS been spilled over what exactly happened on October 31, 1517, when Luther is popularly believed to have nailed his Ninety-five Theses to the door of All Saints' Church in Wittenberg. The scholarly consensus is that even if Luther did post the theses—a fact we will likely never know for certain—it was far from being the singular and dramatic event that history has remembered it to be.

Regardless of whether they were nailed to a door or not, the theses became famous across the Holy Roman Empire and incensed clerics at the Vatican. Although no Wittenberg edition is extant today (only two placards survive from other printers' work), Luther printed copies of the Ninety-five Theses and circulated them at the university and beyond.

The theses followed the style of academic arguments of the time, which were based on "theses of disputation." Such theses were a series of related claims, where professors and students would mull over the logical connection of an argument as it progressed. The format of the Ninety-five Theses was typical; it was their content and how they were distributed that made them famous.

In a notable error, one surviving placard numbered his theses in groups of twenty-five; in the other, they were presented as "eighty-seven" theses, because the printer had made several mistakes in his numbering. It's evident from these errors, and various other imperfections in the Ninety-five Theses, that Luther never anticipated that this would become the foundational document for a continent-wide Reformation.

Instead, Luther intended his Ninety-five Theses for an academic and clerical audience, and they were a reaction against the way that the Church, and therefore ultimately the pope, had institutionalized Church practices for lay believers. Ten of the theses began "Christians are to be taught . . . ," and by "Christians" Luther meant common folk. A further eight were "the shrewd questionings of the laity," and read as though Luther were paraphrasing the common complaints he had gathered from his congregation in Wittenberg, to whom he was now preaching regularly. His voice, and the theses, reflected the pulse of what many people were already thinking.

Most notably, the Ninety-five Theses contained Luther's angry opposition to one of the Church's most controversial practices: the selling of indulgences. Indulgences had been a feature of the Church since the eleventh century, when they were first issued to people who fought in the Crusades. They were official certificates that gave the possessor formal reprieve from the cost of sinning. Through accumulating indulgences, a faithful Catholic could reduce the total time his or her soul, or those of loved ones, would need to spend in Purgatory.

By the late fifteenth century, the Church's revenue model had shifted to *selling* these indulgences. The Vatican had made an industry of selling them, and the latest project it was trying to fund through their sale was the building of the formidable St. Peter's Basilica in Rome. Icily, one of Luther's theses asks, in the voice of the laity: "Why does not the Pope, whose wealth is today greater than the riches of the richest, build just this one church of St. Peter with his own money, rather than with the money of poor believers?"

Boldly, Luther sent a copy of his theses to Archbishop Albrecht of Brandenburg, one of the prime actors perpetuating the Vatican's trade in indulgences, who was using their sale to help buy himself the prestigious position of Archbishop of Mainz. In the accompanying letter, he pulls no punches, writing, "I do bewail the people's completely false understanding, gleaned from these fellows [selling indulgences], which they spread everywhere among the common folk." In Luther's view, the sale of indulgences was severing people from true faith in God.

Soon copies of the Ninety-five Theses were printed in Nuremberg, Leipzig, and Basel. While the original version of the theses was in Latin, the historical record suggests that they were also translated into German. By March 1518, Luther published a follow-up text, *Sermon on Indulgences and Grace*, written in German and not Latin, with a style easily digestible by lay readers. Between 1518 and 1520, it went through twenty-five printings.

With this frenzy of publication, Luther became a household name, printing ideas that resonated across Germany. One of the first to print the Ninety-five Theses wrote of a club of "Augustinian diners" where "almost the whole talk over the table was about the one Martin: they celebrate him, adore him, defend him, are prepared to endure everything for him; they recite his work . . . they kiss his pamphlets . . . eagerly they read every word of them." Having spent many years in near silence, Luther had managed to get people talking.

Once the Vatican heard about this dissident young scholar, it bit back—but unlike Luther the Wittenberg monk, its administrative mechanisms were cumbersome and reactionary. On August 7, 1518, nearly a year after he first printed his theses, Luther received a summons to Rome to be questioned on suspicion of heresy. The Vatican sent with it their own piece, ominously titled *Dialogue Against Martin Luther's Presumptuous Conclusions on the Power of the Pope*. Although Luther had been trying to critique a system of authority rather than Christendom's divinely ordained leader, the affront had clearly triggered a deeply personal response from Pope Leo X.

In Wittenberg, as it became clear that their teacher was to be condemned by Church authorities, students joined together and gave his iconoclasm an altogether more violent form. Ignited by the dynamism of Luther's ideas, they became young fire starters. Luther was keen to distance himself from provocative acts like burning books written by Catholic authorities, but he was soon caught with something of a smoking gun, as he sent an ally a charred copy, which he claimed to have seized personally from the flames, of a defense of indulgences written by a pro-Vatican writer.

Kindling the Fire: Exsurge Domine

On December 10, 1520, three winters after the first great mythic act of posting the Ninety-five Theses, Luther's trusted deputy, Philip Melanchthon, posted an invitation to the faculty and students of Wittenberg University to "a pious and religious spectacle, for perhaps now is the time when [the] Antichrist must be revealed." He called on "lovers of evangelical truth" to gather at 9:00 a.m.

Symbolically, the event took place not at or near the university, where formal academic debates were usually held. Instead, Luther and his associates chose the Holy Cross Chapel, a building near the stockyards, the site used for the butchering of cattle, and where the clothes of plague victims, and hospital rags that had touched them, were burned. It was a place of blood and ash, and holding the ceremony there was a provocative statement about the nature of the promised spectacle, one that would involve props people had started believing were infected by devilish forces.

After dawn, a pyre was erected, and a crowd gathered around Luther and his Augustinian accomplices to partake in the mock sacrament. Luther had put together a list of objects that he and his accomplices would proceed to throw into the flames—a record he would soon send, without delay or apparent shame, to Frederick the Wise's court. Frederick had so far given protection to the university at Wittenberg, but this provocation by Luther would make Frederick's job of protecting these unruly theologians that much harder.

Since publishing the Ninety-five Theses, Luther had spent much of his time elaborating on his ideas for reforming the Church. In 1520 alone, he had published twenty-eight works. One of his most far-reaching conclusions was that God's grace comes from faith alone, and not from a man or woman's works, and so no human could ever properly fulfill God's command. This idea—formally called "justification by faith"—was at the heart of Luther's life work and went against the Catholic Church's teaching that

A woodcut by Hans Holbein the Younger, depicting Luther as a German Hercules, circa 1519. Luther has slain Aristotle and Aquinas, among others. In time he would go far beyond enervating the scholarly world.

sinful human beings could be "justified," or made righteous in God's sight, through both God's grace *and* human effort. For Luther, salvation was a free gift, and it was only through simple faith in Christ that God would give grace to a sinner. In sum, Luther's writings claimed that the Catholic Church had lost the gospel and fallen into spiritual bondage.

As the smoke rose into the bracing, late autumn air, Luther now melodramatically revealed a copy of a papal bull—or edict—and proclaimed in Latin, "Because you saddened the holiness of the Lord, so may the eternal fire destroy you." The bull's title, *Exsurge Domine*, meant "Arise, O Lord," and it carried the highest authority of papal law, condemning Luther's writings on forty-one counts. It threatened Luther and his protectors with excommunication in sixty days if he did not recant his teaching.

As he cast the bull into the flames, the inked pages crumpled under the heat. With that, the man who had taken to calling himself Eleutherius

(Greek for "the freed one") was now Martin Luther, a renegade prophet who had just committed the ultimate sacrilege against God's high priest. In Wittenberg, students continued the festivities that Luther had started, kindling new fires and staging a mock-diabolical play that defamed the Church. Across much of the empire, the papal bull had been received with ridicule and civic opposition. Added to that, the Catholic Church was simply not able to match the print popularity of Luther's work. Their struggle with this new technology is reaffirmed by the raw numbers: between 1518 and 1530, Luther's works published in German outnumbered those of his Catholic opponents five to one.

Church and imperial authorities soon decided that it was time they met this man face-to-face, in the hope that he might be dazzled, or intimidated, into submission by the grandeur of the continent's true leaders.

Luther's Grand Tour

On April 2, 1521, Luther set out from Wittenberg knowing that he might never return. For over a year, he had been communicating with George Spalatin, Frederick the Wise's adviser, expressing his profound belief that Christendom was in its Last Days, writing: "I am in terrible anguish because I have almost no more doubts that the Pope is truly the Antichrist popular opinion is universally expecting." The sense of this being his last days, and the Last Days, had in his mind converged into a steady stream of prophetic fatalism. Suppressing any self-doubts, Luther now had tunnel-vision urgency, and could advance as a holy warrior, blind to fear.

A triumphalist serenity possessed Luther as he left Wittenberg. Having lived a life of long and solitary walks, he now traveled in an open carriage, which had been provided for him by Wittenberg's goldsmith. As his students, colleagues, and supporters bade him farewell, he was the city's falsely condemned hero. So as not to upset the delicate balance of domestic imperial politics, especially independent-minded princes like Frederick, Luther had been granted safe passage by Charles V, the Holy Roman Emperor himself, and at the head of Luther's carriage, in which he traveled with several of his closest supporters, rode a herald sporting the imperial eagle. Despite carrying the highest condemnation from the pope, and now branded as a heretic, Luther progressed across Germany magnificently.

His destination was the city of Worms, where an imperial diet, or parliament, was in progress, with the emperor and the most senior princes of the land in attendance. Frederick and George Spalatin were already there, trying frantically to reach a compromise on the infamous "Luther matter." Luther, however, was not minded to reach any sort of compromise: he had by now burned all bridges.

As he traveled across Germany, Luther was welcomed as a prophet on his way to repossess the Church from the dark forces controlling it. He happily milked his status as the most published, most famous, and most wanted man in Germany. Crowds gathered on the roadsides in city after city. In Erfurt, sixty horsemen and the town's rector rode out to meet Luther, now the most renowned alumnus of that town's university.

Mid-journey, Luther received a dispatch from Spalatin telling him that condemnation was the most likely outcome, and that he should not enter Worms. But Luther portrayed his journey as being like Jesus's approach into Jerusalem, replying defiantly: "We shall enter Worms in spite of the gates of hell and the powers of darkness."

Luther finally reached Worms, where, due to the sheer delay of his self-promoting tour, he risked missing the deadline of his safe passage. Despite his tardiness, and the fact that the city was brimming with papal allies, the city trumpets sounded as Luther's carriage approached the town's outskirts.

Now escorted by one hundred horsemen, Luther could hear but not view the crowds of more than two thousand people lining the streets, who had come out to see if the man matched the image. His profile had been circulated by Wittenberg and other cities' presses in famous woodcuts, some of which depicted Luther as a saint. As Luther stepped out of his carriage, a monk reached down to touch his hem three times, completing the striking biblical parallels to the triumphal entry.

At Worms, Luther twice met the emperor, princes, and most important nobles of the empire. The first occasion was on April 17, when Luther entered a room that was decked in furs and finery. Charles V himself sat on a great throne, surrounded by his flowing robes, with a gathering of bejeweled advisers crouched around him on lower steps. One delegate described the diminutive monk who now entered:

> a man was let in who they said was Martin Luther, about forty years old and thereabouts, coarsely built and with a coarse face with not especially good eyes, his countenance restive, which he carelessly changed. He wore a cassock of the Augustinian order with its leather belt, his tonsure [the bald circle in the center of a monk's head] large and freshly shorn, his hair badly clipped.

Luther was shuffled up to a bench, on which sat a great pile of his books, where gruffly, a papal secretary asked if the books were his and whether he would recant their contents. He responded that it would "be rash and at the same time dangerous for me to put forth anything without proper consideration."

It was a clever move by Luther: the imperial court and papal representatives had effectively tried to silence him from giving a case. The following day, April 18, Luther returned. Showing fearless nerve, Luther now proceeded to say why he could not recant his books, explaining that doing so might "add . . . strength to this [papal] tyranny. . . . I should have opened not only windows but doors to such great godlessness." He concluded:

> I have been subdued through the scriptures I have brought forth, and my conscience is held captive to the Word of God, as a result of which I cannot and will not recant anything, because to act against conscience is burdensome, injurious, and dangerous. God help me! Amen.

It was here that Luther is believed to have said, profoundly defiant of the imperial majesty before him, "Here I stand," which would become the most famous three words of the Reformation. It is possible that this famous statement was never uttered. But even if Luther used these words, they did not mean what we might understand them to say today.

"Here I stand" was an expression of his belief in the simple truths of Scripture. Luther believed that he had experienced God's Word, that he was an unredeemable sinner, and that only God's mercy, rather than the laws and institutions of the time, could judge and save him. To the modern ear, "Here I stand" suggests stalwart individual conviction and a powerful and free conscience. But Luther's theology denied that people were free: to him, all of God's people were bound by Scripture. Luther stood in his sinful body, waiting to be judged not by those bejeweled and bedecked in front of him, or by a God he felt he knew, but by a God he saw as inscrutable, and one who exercised a fearsome Old Testament power.

Luther's stand became a profound moment in Western history, but not for the reasons one might think. His was a belief that rejected the idea of human self-improvement and the justice of worldly institutions. "Here I stand" was Luther accepting his total inadequacy before the absolute power of God. It was the fear of damnation that so resonated with people, not the expression of liberal freedom and human conviction that the sentence implies. Having read Luther's theology, people were possessed as much by the virality of fear as by a message of hope.

Coming to the end of this fierce stand of faith, Luther now left the imperial diet. Spalatin recalled Luther saying to him that "if he had a thousand heads, he would rather they were all chopped off than he should recant."

Incensed, that evening Charles V took pen to paper and concluded that Luther and his accomplices should not only be excommunicated but also "eradicated." Luther, however, using his favor at the Saxon court and carrying with him his warrant of safe passage, left Worms unharmed. The formal Edict of Worms that condemned him as a "stubborn schismatic and public heretic" would not be issued until the diet ended, more than a month later.

To Frederick, it was clear that Luther was not going to survive if left to his own devices in Wittenberg. So Frederick engineered his kidnapping outside Eisenach, where the monk was visiting relatives before completing his journey back to Wittenberg. Brought to Frederick's high-walled Wartburg Castle, Luther was forced to hide his identity by dressing as a knight, a curious change for a man who had spent his entire adult life in a cassock.

A Return to Wittenberg

After Worms, Luther's profile was famous across the Holy Roman Empire. Woodcuts of Luther had been copied endlessly over the course of the Reformation, and morphed from a more humble depiction to framing Luther in dazzling light and with a dove above his head, making him out to be a saint animated by the Holy Spirit. In another woodcut, he was depicted as a German Hercules bringing divine vengeance to those who had duped followers into misunderstanding the nature of God.

Before leaving for Worms, Luther had said of religious images that "for the improvement of the Christian estate," legitimate force could be used to oust superstitious ceremonies, and he had even called for the razing of some churches. But the issue of iconographic images was both theological and eminently practical: each community had to decide if they were going to bury their images, smash them apart, or leave them in place for those who still believed in their importance to religious practice.

With Luther absent, on January 6, 1522, Wittenberg's Augustinian order met to institute changes in line with what they believed to be reformist teachings (the "reformist" concept became a deeply ambiguous one, used by many different groups who held different beliefs and allegiances). Against hundreds of years of Vatican precedent, it was decided that anyone who wished to leave the Augustinian order could do so.

Tonsures were allowed to grow back; cassocks were cast aside. The exodus of monks had begun, partly encouraged by the increasingly acrimonious atmosphere for people of the cloth, who had rocks thrown at them and their homes attacked. Four days later, those who remained in Wittenberg decided that they must carry through reformist conclusions to their logical end. The monks who chose to remain "made a fire in the cloister square, went into the church, broke the wooden altars, and took them with all the paintings and statues, crucifixes, flags, candles, chandeliers, etc. to the fire, threw them in and burnt them, and cut off the heads of the stone statues of Christ, Mary and other saints, and destroyed all the images in the church."

ÆTHERNA IPSE SVAE MENTIS SIMVLACHRA LVTHERVS
EXPRIMIT·AT VVLTVS CERA LVCAE OCCIDVOS
·M·D·X·X·

A woodcut of Luther, depicted by	A woodcut of Luther depicted in more
Lucas Cranach the Elder, in 1520.	*exaggerated, saintlike form, pastiching*
(INTERFOTO/ALAMY STOCK PHOTO)	*the original from Cranach's workshop, by*
	Hans Baldung, Strasbourg, 1521.

A woodcut of Luther, depicted by Lucas Cranach the Elder, in 1520.
(INTERFOTO/ALAMY STOCK PHOTO)

A woodcut of Luther depicted in more exaggerated, saintlike form, pastiching the original from Cranach's workshop, by Hans Baldung, Strasbourg, 1521.

The descent into violence played into the hands of Luther's ardent critics, including the many propagandists employed in depicting him as a deranged and Devil-possessed monk. Catholic authorities now threatened the iconoclasts with punishment. The disjointed ribbon of news that traveled across the empire intersected with a tawdry machine of propaganda and political intrigue, further confusing Luther's intentions and actions.

The Reformation Luther had begun was under threat of a violent clampdown, and his seclusion in the Wartburg Castle also left him with at best a distorted view of unfolding events. So Luther felt he had no alternative but to return from hiding, face the possibility of arrest or even summary justice, and instill a degree of moderation into a movement that seemed to have lost control without the guiding hand of its most famous leader.

Eduard Schoen's Luther, des Teufels
Dudelsck (Luther as the Devil's
Bagpipes), *1535.*

Luther arrived back in Wittenberg on March 6, 1522, still dressed in knight's attire. At first, those who recognized him might have concluded that Luther too had decided that cassocks and other strictures were no longer relevant to reformed religious faith. But he again donned the Augustinian habit, which became a symbol of his attempt to reestablish order.

For the next eight days, Luther preached in St. Mary's Church, where five and a half years earlier he had helped spark the Reformation. He laid the blame for disorder at the feet of former supporters who had taken extreme views on the Reformation, and attempted to put the brakes on the Reformation in Wittenberg.

The division that emerged between Luther and the extremists was bad for a movement that had from the outset been accused of revolutionary, rather than just reformist, sentiment. The debate about images, and the inability of reformers to consolidate their gains as a cohesive movement, would become Luther's and the broader Reformation's greatest liabilities.

Unity and Disunity

On Holy Saturday night, April 4, 1523, Luther was awaiting the arrival of herring from a neighboring territory.

Luther had been arranging these fish cart deliveries for some time with a businessman, Leonhard Koppe, who transported herring, loaded in barrels, to the Augustinian monastery at which Luther now lived with an increasingly diverse inner circle of supporters.

That Luther's monastery would require such a quantity of herring was not in itself suspicious. The last Augustinian monks were relieved of their vows in 1523, after which Luther was the only monk residing at Wittenberg's Black Monastery. But from then on, he began using the property as a local center for convening leaders of his Reformation. Others came to Wittenberg simply because they were inspired by Luther's message of religious reform and were seeking shelter, company, and food.

But that April night, it was not fish that the herring cart carried. Instead it was religious refugees. Like monks and other clergy, nuns were starting to digest Luther's teachings and were reconsidering their commitment to their vows. They found their way to Luther, through covert means if necessary. Koppe and Luther had reached an arrangement whereby nuns wishing to leave their convents were smuggled out and brought to Wittenberg to start their new lives as secular women.

It was a risky business for Koppe: a conviction for this kind of abduction carried with it the death penalty. Luther's justification was that he simply wanted to offer these nuns a home after their life in the convent. But it was a flagrant challenge to neighboring rulers: these nuns were the patrimony of their convents' territory, and they did the job of praying that their local rulers' souls went to heaven.

The April 4, 1523, herring shipment arrived from the Nimbschen convent, in the territory adjacent to Frederick's. Among others, it carried in it Staupitz's sister, Magdalene, and a woman called Katharina von Bora. Staupitz likely would have been incensed with the tactics of Luther's circle once the former nuns arrived. A Wittenberg student recalled, tongue in cheek: "Several days ago a wagon arrived here with a load of vestal virgins, as they are now called. They would like to marry as much as to stay alive. May

Portraits of Martin Luther and his wife, Katharina von Bora, by Lucas Cranach the Elder, circa 1529. By this point, Luther was fuller-faced and dressed like a middle-class German civilian. The Cranach workshop produced many of these doubles of Luther and his wife.

God provide them with husbands so that in the course of time they won't run into greater need!"

Luther began to marry off these new female immigrants. Perhaps it was Luther's role as matchmaker that inspired changes to his own persona. While he had donned a monk's clothing again on his return from Wartburg Castle, after at least three years of indecision, Wittenberg's leader finally shed himself of his cassock.

And then, a full two years after Katharina von Bora's clandestine arrival, Luther married her on June 13, 1525. It was a rejection of established Church values, breaking both a nun's and a monk's oaths of chastity. Luther said that he married Katharina to spite the Devil and the pope—but in the end it was a loving and fruitful relationship.

The German Peasants' War (1524–25)

After the burning of the church at Mallerbach in March 1524, the smell of the ashes and the glint of the broken icons precipitated a peasant-led war.

The uprising swept across upper Germany into Austria and into the regions of Alsace, Franconia, Thuringia, and Frederick's Saxony. Violence
that had been simmering in pockets of the empire for decades now spread
like ink across blotting paper.

Luther had already shown his inclination for siding with secular authorities rather than the common man when he had returned from Wartburg and
ousted iconoclast leaders. Against a violent backdrop, the Peasants' War now
forced him to further develop his beliefs on the rule of secular laws: to consider how far it was a Christian's responsibility to follow the laws of the
land—or whether, as he had at Worms, each individual should follow his or
her conscience. It was an issue that had animated Christian thinking since
Christ's cleansing of the Temple depicted in the Gospel.

Much to Luther's chagrin, the peasants were inspired by his message of
liberation and scoffing at authority. He was the ultimate symbol of reform,
excavating the truths of the Bible, and in doing so leveling individual believer's access to the Gospel. Across Europe, peasant bands had been uniting after
reading the "Twelve Articles of the Peasants," which had been coauthored by
a peasant who traded in furs and a preacher who espoused Luther's teachings.
Their work now spewed out of Europe's printing presses and found its way
into the hands of a plurality of literate local community leaders. For Luther,
who had previously dominated the unregulated print market, it would have
been a shock that others now wielded the tool to similar effect.

Each article contained a demand, such as the abolition of serfdom, which
was backed up by a biblical source giving authority to the peasants' assertions. As if to underline that Luther had a determined role to play in the
matter, the leaders soon asked Luther to judge their own case in the "Twelve
Articles." Luther could no longer withhold his verdict as the violent wave
spread across Europe.

Luther eventually went to press with two publications, which were intended to make as forthright a split as possible between him and the insurgent peasants who claimed to act in his name. First, in April 1525 he wrote
*Admonition to Peace: A Reply to the Twelve Articles of the Peasants of Swa-
bia*, where he appealed to the peasants: "No matter how right you are,"
Luther said, "it is not for a Christian to appeal to law, or to fight, but rather
to suffer wrong and endure evil; there is no other way."

His spiritual guidance was largely ignored, the war was intensifying, and Luther heard in May that his childhood home of Mansfeld, down the road from Wittenberg, had been swamped by marauding peasants. The insurgent theologian had lost control.

He took pen to paper again, this time titling his work *Against the Robbing and Murdering Hordes of Peasants*. He left no room for readers to doubt his allegiance to secular authorities, and his condemnation of the peasants:

> Let everyone who can smite, slay, and stab, secretly and openly, remembering that nothing can be more poisonous, hurtful, or devilish than a rebel. It is just as when one must kill a mad dog: if you do not strike him, he will strike you, and a whole land with you. . . . Stab, smite, slay, whoever can.

As Luther remained in his Wittenberg monastery home with wife, advisers, tenants, and guests, the prospect of a single, pan-European movement of Reformation against papal authority was crushed. Between 70,000 and 100,000 were massacred in the fallout of the German Peasants' War, and most of the dead were peasants. It seems as though Luther did not regret his clerkish role in quashing the rebellion. He said solemnly at a dinner table some years later: "It was I, Martin Luther, who slew the peasants during the rising, for I commanded them to be slaughtered." This was Luther at his melodramatic best, but there was more than a grain of truth in his gloomy words.

Building from the Ground Up

By the end of the Peasants' War, particularly following Luther's decision to side with secular princes, the Reformation split into a series of many Reformations. This fracturing has traditionally been divided into two movements: the Magisterial Reformation, headed by Luther and John Calvin, both of whom generally believed in the importance of princes and other secular authorities; and a Radical Reformation, the leaders of which Luther had fallen out with along the way, and who rejected secular authority over matters of religion. As always, building new institutions would prove vastly more complicated and protracted than the initial tearing down of the previously indomitable papal walls.

So Luther, now more firmly rooted with a growing young family in Wittenberg, worked with the limited materials he had at his disposal to rebuild new religious institutions. To do so, he went back to first principles, to writing and to education—the two activities that had consumed much of his life's work up to the bloody events of 1524–25.

With frequent bouts of plague coursing through Germany, Luther was also acutely aware that his days were numbered. New leaders of the nascent Lutheran Church were needed to guide the reformed flock. "Lutheranism" had begun as an abusive nickname and was used to dig at its leader's pretensions to popelike religious leadership. But the insult was prescient of what did in the end become a formal denomination of Christianity, largely thanks to the seeds Luther and his followers sowed. In part, the success of Lutheran evangelism came about because Luther's idea of education was so expansive. He left behind a powerful legacy for establishing universal provision of education, including for women, girls, and peasants.

Luther also wanted to secure a new, enduring system of religious faith, and that would require the support of the state to educate the young with Lutheran values. Luther believed that schools were "for raising up people who are skilled to teach in the church *and* govern in the world." Luther had learned the hard way that for his reforms to be carried through, an alliance of diverse kinds of authority was required.

However, because Luther's Reformation relied on alliances with secular institutions, this also meant that the success of his reforms was dependent on the stability of a number of factors largely out of his control. But stability from secular leaders was not forthcoming: out of the ashes of the Peasants' War came a more organized and princely warfare. Each prince would declare himself as for or against reforming the Church—and by extension, for or against Luther. When war came in 1546, Luther had already died, and those protesting against Vatican and imperial control were now called not just Lutherans, but also "Protestants."

Castle Church, Wittenberg, Germany, 1547

In mid-1547, Charles V found himself staring down at Luther's grave. He had arrived in Wittenberg shortly after his forces had captured the city and, tradition has it, headed straight for the castle church in which he knew the simple memorial was housed.

It must have felt like a hollow victory. This dogmatic theologian from a German backwater had been a thorn in his side for some twenty-six years, when the errant monk had first escaped the Diet of Worms in 1521. Now, just over a year after Luther's death, Charles had had to commit considerable resources to defeat the Schmalkaldic League of "Protestant" princes to whom Luther had been a core strategist, polemicist, and adviser.

Given Charles's status as victor, he would have been well within his rights to deliver appropriate posthumous penalties to this maverick dissenter, heretic, and outlaw who had caused him such tribulation. Queen Mary I of England would do so a decade later to the graves of Protestant leaders, having remains disinterred and burned alongside copies of Protestant books. But by this grave in Castle Church, Wittenberg, the emperor held back, perhaps as a mark of solemn respect. Or, more likely, Charles left Luther's grave alone because he knew from the divisive debate over images and icons that destroying sites of holiness could have far more destructive repercussions.

Plumes of smoke ascended from the conquered city that had been the home and headquarters of the Reformation's most famous leader. The trail of destruction that followed in the wake of the Reformation, culminating in the Thirty Years' War (1618–48), cannot be laid at the foot of any one person. But Luther's bravery and strength in tearing down the papacy's most corrupt practices were never matched by an equal determination to finish the job of rebuilding a Lutheran Church, one that coexisted peacefully with the Catholic Church in Rome.

Charles's decision to leave Luther's grave intact was a recognition that not even the emperor's authority was absolute. That was the myth that the imperial courtiers liked to present, but Luther had scuffed much of the imperial luster in his defiant acts, as at the Diet of Worms. Leaving the grave intact was the kind of quietly astute political decision Luther would never have been capable of, but one thing these two erstwhile enemies could agree upon was that their images, as presented to the empire, belied the messier and less determined realities that a life of leadership had brought them.

DR. MARTIN LUTHER KING JR.

... it relied upon the active participation of people who had a daily task of action and dedication. The movement did not rely exclusively on a handful of leaders to carry through such fundamental change.
—BAYARD RUSTIN, IN A LETTER TO DR. KING

At about 9:45 in the evening on Monday, January 30, 1956, Martin Luther King Jr., the pastor of the Dexter Avenue Baptist Church and recently elected president of the Montgomery Improvement Association, stood on his porch and addressed the crowd on his front lawn. Inside the one-story white clapboard house that served as the backdrop for King's impromptu press conference were several policemen, news reporters, and friends, as well as King's shaken wife, Coretta, and their sleeping seven-week-old daughter, Yolanda. Immediately behind King were the four front windows shattered by a bomb—either a hand grenade or a half stick of dynamite—that had been thrown at the home thirty minutes earlier. Among other dignitaries sharing the makeshift dais with King were the mayor, W. A. Gayle, just over King's right shoulder and wearing his Alabama National Guard uniform, and to King's immediate left, Police Commissioner Clyde Sellers.

On this particular evening, Mayor Gayle insisted, "I am going to work with my last breath if necessary to find and convict the guilty parties," and Commissioner Sellers pointed out that "I do not agree with you in your beliefs, but I will do everything within my power to defend you against acts such as this." Just two days before, the same mayor had insisted he was done "pussyfooting around" with Montgomery's bus boycotters, and Commissioner Sellers's police had arrested King for driving 30 miles per

Dr. Martin Luther King Jr.
on his porch the night of
January 30, 1956.

hour in a 25-mph zone. In front of King, tightly packed in the thirty feet between the porch and street, stood three hundred of Montgomery's black citizens, men and women who'd been walking and carpooling to work since the bus boycott had begun the previous December 5.

King stood in the midst of the crime scene—and in the middle of the varied interests personified by his family, the press, his followers, and Montgomery's white leaders—and spoke. In his sharp double-breasted tan overcoat, tailored suit, pressed white shirt, and trim black tie, the hand-some twenty-seven-year-old began by telling the crowd that it should not get "panicky" or "get your weapons," because "I want you to love your enemies." After insisting that nothing get out of hand, he reminded every-one that "I did not start this boycott. I was asked by you to serve as your spokesman . . . if I am stopped this movement will not stop. . . . What we are doing is just. And God is with us." With that, the crowd went home, and Montgomery's blacks sustained their bus boycott for another 325 days.

King hadn't started the bus boycott, others had. But circumstances thrust him into the role of leader. The young pastor was entirely depen-dent upon the movement he was a part of. And yet on this night, that movement was dependent upon him for its direction. The role of leader, or "spokesman," as he put it, required him to communicate multiple mes-sages to stakeholders with opposing viewpoints in an impromptu speech on the same evening his home had been bombed while his infant daughter slept.

The task was considerable. King had to calm a justifiably angry crowd while at the same time encouraging them to continue their bus boycott in the face of extralegal violence. He had to stand stone-faced, but peacefully, between two men who were trying to align the power of the state against him and the movement, while convincing them that he would not be intimidated by further threats of violence. And at some point, he probably had to tend to his frightened family. As the civil rights movement pulled him along as its leader, King would spend the last twelve years of his short life considering crises as fractious as this one and more.

1955–1957: Giving People Something to Belong To

Two months earlier, on the afternoon of December 1, 1955, Rosa Parks was riding the bus home from work and famously refused to give up her seat to a white man when the bus driver ordered her to do so. She was promptly arrested for violating Montgomery's segregation laws.

The black community in Montgomery was well organized and had been planning for some sort of action to protest mistreatment on public transportation. Unlike Ms. Parks, two other women arrested in the previous year for violating segregation laws on Montgomery's buses weren't considered good candidates around whom to launch a concerted effort. But Parks, in addition to her job as a seamstress at a local department store, was a respected citizen and the secretary of the Montgomery chapter of the National Association for the Advancement of Colored People (NAACP).

Once in jail, she called her mother, who in turn called E. D. Nixon, a local black leader who, among other roles, had been president of the local and state NAACP chapters. Nixon went to the police station along with a prominent local white family, the Durrs, to bail out Ms. Parks. Soon after, when asked, she agreed to fight the case.

A community swung into motion. Jo Ann Robinson, a member of the Women's Political Council, gathered up friends and headed to a nearby college to use its mimeograph machine. Overnight, they printed thousands of leaflets calling for a bus boycott the following Monday. Robinson phoned Nixon at 3:00 a.m. to tell him about the idea, and he agreed with the approach. By 5:00 a.m. he was calling other leaders in Montgomery, informing them of the planned boycott and inviting them to a meeting that evening—Friday, December 2—at the Dexter Avenue Baptist Church, where King was pastor. That meeting convened fifty local black leaders, mostly pastors, and approved plans for the Monday boycott. Through the weekend, they spread the word about the boycott using press contacts, leaflets, and their Sunday pulpits.

The Monday boycott was a surprising success. Hardly any blacks rode the bus, and about five hundred of them were in the courthouse when Parks was convicted and Nixon went to post her bond. Instead of taking the $14 fine, Parks's lawyer appealed the verdict to the state's court of appeals. The fight was on.

That afternoon, leaders met at Reverend L. Roy Bennett's Mt. Zion AME Zion Church to plan for the evening's mass meeting. At 3:00 p.m., eighteen of those present withdrew to Bennett's study. Nixon, along with two local ministers, suggested creating a new organization, the "Montgomery Improvement Association," or MIA for short, to oversee the continuance of the boycott and the bubbling enthusiasm of Montgomery's black community. Next Bennett called for nominations to serve as president. Rufus Lewis—a prominent local businessman and a parishioner at Dexter Avenue Baptist Church—unexpectedly nominated King. Lewis's friend seconded King's nomination, and no other candidates were put forth. Bennett asked King if he'd accept the job. To the surprise of some in the room, King accepted, replying, "Well, if you think I can render some service, I will."

At twenty-six years old, King may have been the youngest person in the room. And he hadn't even grown up in Montgomery—he'd only lived there for about fifteen months, since taking over as the pastor at his church. He was the son of a prominent minister from Atlanta and had just six months before received his doctorate from Boston University. Three weeks before the bus boycott broke out, he had declined to run for the presidency of the local NAACP on account of a desire to focus on his church and his new family.

It is unclear why King was chosen for this role. He was a good speaker with solid connections and an impressive pedigree. Perhaps, in a black community with lots of history and rivalries, his newness meant he could lead without baggage. As King biographer Taylor Branch suggested, it could have been a cynical choice whereby "established preachers stepped back for King only because they saw more blame and danger ahead than glory." Or maybe Rufus Lewis just spoke more quickly and forcefully than the other seventeen men in the room when nominating his preferred candidate. Whatever the case, that evening King was elected as president of the Montgomery Improvement Association and accepted the post. Immediately, that meant he was expected to give the primary talk at the evening's mass meeting and to oversee an organization tasked with, as indicated in the MIA's founding minutes, continuing the protest "until conditions are improved."

In the four days between Parks's Thursday arrest and Monday's pivotal decision to sustain the momentum of the boycott, King did far less than dozens of other leaders in Montgomery's black community. But for reasons of circumstance, he was elected the MIA's president, and those circumstances altered the course of his life.

Now his main task was to sustain the energy that had propelled the first four days of the burgeoning movement—an energy that had people accepting phone calls at 3:00 a.m., staying up all night to make photocopies, and forgoing the convenience of the bus—through an unforeseeable future and against a powerful foe.

ON MONDAY, DECEMBER 5, 1955, Holt Street Baptist Church was at capacity hours before the 7:00 p.m. start time. Less than four hours after becoming the MIA's president, King was on the agenda as the evening's keynote speaker. The overfull mass meeting marked the start of a long and challenging campaign that would end segregation of buses in Montgomery over the coming year and create a legal framework for ending segregation outright.

But on that first evening the MIA started with a more modest set of demands. The board resolved that it would end the boycott if blacks received more courteous treatment on the buses; if seating arrangements were changed to a first-come, first-served basis, with blacks loading from the back and whites from the front (an arrangement already in place in other Alabama cities); and if the bus company hired black bus drivers. The path from the exciting but limited beginning to the unexpected and victorious end was not a straight one—King grew as a leader by playing a role in a movement that unfolded as a series of crises and contingencies. The movement was built around King, not by King.

Over 382 days in Montgomery, King learned how to lead a nonviolent movement that utilized the tactics of mass action. King was familiar enough with the idea of nonviolence to invoke it at the very beginning of his leadership: "I want to say that we are not here advocating violence," he told the crowd in his first speech at Holt Street Baptist Church; the "only weapon we have in our hands this evening is the weapon of protest." But nonviolence as an ethos for the movement emerged over a series of confrontations with Montgomery's white power structure. As Bayard Rustin, a longtime organizer who came to Montgomery in February, remembered:

> [King] had not been prepared for [the job] either tactically, strategically, or in his understanding of nonviolence. The glorious thing is that he came to a profoundly deep understanding of nonviolence through the struggle itself, and through reading and discussions which he had in the process of carrying on the protest.

He learned on the fly how a complicated movement was orchestrated and sustained, and developed the beginning of a network that would support, advise, occasionally spar with, and confound him over his twelve years of civil rights leadership. Ralph Abernathy, the chair of the MIA executive committee, for instance, would be at King's side when he was killed more than a decade in the future.

As important as such friends were, during the bus boycott King also discerned the personal sense of purpose that would carry him forward. Prior to his election, King had envisioned a life as a pastor and eventually as an academic. But on Friday night, January 27, 1956, one night after briefly being jailed for his speeding ticket (the first of dozens of trips to jail for King), King received a call from a man who threatened his life. Unable to sleep, he went to the kitchen and poured himself a cup of coffee. It wasn't the first time his life had been threatened, but at that moment, King said he "was ready to give up . . . with my cup of coffee sitting untouched before me I tried to think of a way to move out of the picture without appearing a coward." After a long set of prayers, and an acknowledgment that his life to this point had been relatively easy, he came to see himself as having a divine purpose. He remembered "an inner voice saying to me, 'Martin Luther, stand up for righteousness. Stand up for justice. And lo I will be with you, even until the end of the world.' . . . I heard the voice of Jesus saying still to fight on." King biographer David Garrow calls this "the most important night of his life, the one he would always think back to in future years when the pressures again seemed to be too great."

Such conviction was essential. While King never would have risen to leadership without the civil rights movement, the movement itself needed a leader to play specific roles. In Montgomery, King began to understand what some of those roles would be. First, he would need to be a unifier for the movement—sometimes this meant quietly settling disputes behind closed doors, other times it meant staking out positions that no one would publicly oppose. Second, he had to be thoughtful about the mechanics of actually leading an organization. Over the course of the boycott, the MIA evolved from an ad hoc coordinating body to an enterprise with a budget and a staff, and that required funding and oversight.

Third, he had to act as a spokesperson. This was a task for which he was uniquely gifted and had prepared for his entire life. Among his pastor colleagues, it was common to riff on sermons late at night, like musicians in the back room of a club. Beyond the cultural heritage of pastor-as-performer, King had honed his speaking ability by taking at least nine courses on "the art of pulpit oratory" while pursuing his divinity degree. As the Montgomery movement gained national attention, it was also relevant that this Southern preacher's graduate education came entirely in the North: at Crozer Theological Seminary just outside of Philadelphia and then Boston University. King was the movement's designated spokesperson and had to communicate its undergirding philosophy to a diverse national audience.

Fourth, he was a symbol for the movement. Over the course of the bus boycott, many Montgomery blacks were arrested. None gained as much attention as King. What King did with his body, and where he spent his time and attention, communicated something to the movement in Montgomery as well as to its enemies, and also to the country as a whole.

Finally, he had to maintain relationships with everyone, especially those he was opposing. Even if he vehemently disagreed with their viewpoints, as the president of the MIA, King sat at the negotiating table across from the formal civic leadership of Montgomery.

By the end of 1956—as a unifier, organizational head, spokesperson, symbol, and chief negotiator—King had played a part in the bus boycott that gave the civil rights movement its best-known win. At a local level, he helped to sustain an environment in which Montgomery's blacks prioritized their rights more highly than segregationists did the status quo. Up close, it was as much about 382 days of walking in the cold or taking a 3:00 a.m. phone call as it was about any particular speech. But stories, like movements, are most effective when all of their complication and struggle can be focused into the relatable image of a single figure. Rosa Parks precipitated the struggle, but as the story of Montgomery reached a national audience, King was at the front—or, more properly, in the middle.

AS FAR AWAY AS NEW YORK CITY, the desegregation of buses in Montgomery, Alabama, was front-page news. A *New York Times* article on December 22, 1956, starts with a nod to the movement: "The Negroes of Montgomery, victors in a year-long boycott to end segregation in public transit here, quietly and in determined numbers went back on the city's desegregated buses today. . . ." Although King had never used public transportation in Montgomery prior to the boycott, an image of him riding a desegregated bus was the lone picture accompanying the *Times* article. The story lifted up King as the boycott's most important member: "The Negroes, under Dr. King, held almost 100 per cent to their campaign. . . ."

Committed civil rights activists also saw something worth mentioning in King's leadership. Bayard Rustin, the national organizer who'd helped King in Montgomery, had been involved with the civil rights movement since 1941. He and two other longtime activists, Stanley Levison and Ella Baker, "began to talk . . . about the need for developing a force that would somewhat become a counterbalance, let's call it, to the NAACP." While the NAACP was well organized, it pursued change mostly through litigation. And though the NAACP had been effective, in 1956 it had little interest in using mass action as a primary strategy. Court injunctions had also shuttered NAACP operations in several Southern states. For activists like Rustin, there was an organic desire to build upon the MIA and King's leadership, but also to create an organization that was grounded in nonviolent mass action.

Rustin best summarized the necessity of building upon Montgomery's success in a letter to King on December 23, 1956, just two days after King took his ride on Montgomery's first desegregated bus. In Rustin's thinking, "Montgomery possessed three features which are not found in other movements or efforts." First, it had "given people something to belong to which had the inspiring power of the Minute Men, the Sons of Liberty, and other organized forms which were products of an earlier American era of fundamental change." Second, through its sheer competence, the Montgomery movement had won the respect of whites. Third, it had "relied upon the active participation of people who had a *daily* task of action and dedication. The movement did not rely exclusively on a handful of leaders to carry through such fundamental change."

In the same letter, Rustin recommended convening a region-wide leadership conference. And so on January 7, 1957, King and other leaders called for a "Southern Negro Leaders Conference on Transportation and Nonviolent Integration." The conference convened sixty leaders from twenty-nine different communities at King's father's church in Atlanta. Over the course of the year, and a couple of follow-on conferences, the group grew, elected King as its president, and changed its name to the Southern Christian Leadership Conference (SCLC). Its mandate was to use nonviolent mass action to end racial injustice in the South. In short,

SCLC's aim was to replicate regionally what the MIA had accomplished locally.

1958–1962: "Where Is Your Body?"

King and SCLC were thrust into the midst of a movement that was well under way.

King had a quick and unexpected rise to national prominence, and SCLC was a regional organization that lent its support to local efforts that had already generated momentum on their own. And because SCLC focused on mass action, the group most regularly engaged with communities that were actively in crisis. The combination of King's fame and SCLC's strategy caused the fault lines of the civil rights movement to array themselves on either side of SCLC, and King in particular.

Should the movement pursue litigation or mass action as the best way to force change? Would leadership rely on individuals, or the power of the masses? How should the movement proceed when there were inevitable conflicts between consolidating local gains and pressing for national victories? When situations reached a flashpoint, must the movement pause to negotiate, or press its advantage?

These are the questions that kept civil rights leaders awake at night, and they all defy simple answers. While he was becoming the movement's most famous spokesperson in the wake of Montgomery, King also committed himself to the hard and thankless work of wrestling with, and trying to forge consensus around, each of these impossible questions. For the next twelve years, King found himself in the middle of a struggle to define what, exactly, the civil rights movement should be.

He never settled on a final answer to any of these questions. While King is remembered for leading nonviolent mass movements, he sometimes delayed protests in favor of negotiations. In other situations, he shunned the advice of more conservative advisers, calling for mass action while others wanted negotiation. For King, the struggle to answer these questions was so intensely personal that the dynamics of his leadership from 1958 to 1962 can be explained by examining his decisions about whether or not he should submit himself to imprisonment. To the people in the civil rights movement who looked to King for leadership, his answer to the question "Should

MLK after refusing bail and being led away in Decatur, Georgia, on October 25, 1960.
(BELTMANN/CONTRIBUTOR)

I go to jail?" communicated more powerfully than any speech possibly could. He was never able to satisfy everyone.

ON WEDNESDAY MORNING, October 19, 1960, Martin Luther King Jr. sat at a snack bar on the second-floor bridge of Rich's department store in downtown Atlanta. He told reporters who'd come to track the day's events that, despite the attention being given to him, "I am not the leader. It was student planned and student originated, and student sustained." King was soon arrested for trespassing. That morning, fifty-one other protesters, mostly young college students, were arrested for similar sit-ins at various eateries in Atlanta department stores—a mass action planned by a new student-run civil rights organization.

At his arraignment the same day in Atlanta's municipal court, King told Judge James Webb:

I don't feel that I did anything wrong in going to Rich's and seeking to be served. We went peacefully, nonviolently, and in a deep spirit of love. If we lived under a totalitarian system, communism or under the Gestapo, then it would be wrong to go. One of the glories of living in a democracy is that citizens have the right to protest for what they believe to be right.

In a tactic developed by the sit-in movement's student leadership, King also refused bail, saying that he would "'sit in jail 10 years if necessary,' rather than post his $500 bond." He told reporters that "staying in jail 'is a way to bring the issue under the scrutiny of the conscience of the community.' Jail-not-bail . . . 'grows out of the whole idea of non-violence that you must accept suffering.'" Before he was arrested, King said that students had "requested my participation and I felt I had a moral obligation."

King explained his decision with a straightforward moral clarity that belied how fraught his choice to go to jail had actually been. Earlier that same month, an old friend passed by King as he was headed out of Atlanta Airport. He saw King sitting in the terminal "surrounded by a half-dozen students. King was on the verge of tears, with his head in his hands." The young activists were pressuring King to join the Atlanta sit-ins, and he wasn't sure what to do.

In early February 1960, King had moved his family back to Atlanta, where he took over as assistant pastor at Ebenezer Baptist Church, his father's parish. The move allowed King to focus on SCLC, whose headquarters were there. Though he'd nominally been the pastor at Dexter Avenue Baptist in Montgomery for the past three years, he had in fact preached there fewer than half of the Sundays during that time. As president of SCLC, he had several speaking engagements daily, and after appearing on the cover of *Time* magazine in February 1957, he had been traveling nonstop—it was the starting line of a frenetically paced life that wouldn't slow down until it stopped suddenly, and violently, in 1968.

King's distress over whether or not he should to go to jail in Atlanta was a reflection of how three forces, all with the same nominal goal of racial justice, were pulling on his moral convictions. Student civil rights activists,

Atlanta's black establishment, and the future president of the United States all wanted something different from King.

At the time, Ella Baker was serving as SCLC's interim executive director. A few months after King's move to Atlanta, she convened a conference in Raleigh, North Carolina, to consolidate the gains of hundreds of sit-ins that black college students had led across the country. The result was the founding of the Student Nonviolent Coordinating Committee (SNCC). In October 1960, it was SNCC leaders who wanted King to join a series of Atlanta sit-ins and go to jail with them.

The SNCC sought King because he was a son of Atlanta, and the primary protest would strike at Rich's department store—an Atlanta institution, and one where prominent black Atlantans spent lots of money. By the time they reached out to King, SNCC's sit-ins were foundering. If King believed nonviolent mass action was the key to achieving justice, here was a specific opportunity for him to practice what he preached. And the publicity surrounding his potential arrest would surely give a much-needed jolt of energy to the students' fight for desegregation.

On the other hand, Atlanta's more conservative black leaders, including King's own father, felt that progress was achievable short of protest. They thought mass action was flashy but counterproductive: protests made headlines, but muddied the relationship between Atlanta's upper-class blacks and the white power structure, slowing the process of desegregation.

And with presidential elections less than a month away, King was on the verge of securing his second meeting with John F. Kennedy. The meeting was set to take place in Miami, but would only be possible without the complication of protests. Having a sit-down with a presidential candidate south of the Mason-Dixon line would be a symbolic victory for all black Americans, and in cultivating a relationship with Kennedy, King could help to sway the traditionally segregationist-oriented Democratic Party toward the cause of civil rights. Even if such a sweeping victory was not achievable in a single meeting, it was important that King begin to sit in rooms of power traditionally occupied only by leaders of more conservative civil rights organizations like the NAACP. At some point, presidents needed to understand that nonviolent mass action wasn't just a nuisance, but a credible strategy to bring about change.

Finally, there was a practical concern that argued against an extended stay in prison for King. SCLC was short on cash, and King had a speech scheduled in Cleveland that promised to bring in $7,000 for his growing team. If he was in jail for too long, it could bankrupt the organization.

When he sat and requested service at the second-floor bridge in Rich's department store on October 19, 1960, King's choice to go to jail was a trade-off. The SNCC's student activists were energized by King's heroic act, and the sit-in movement in Atlanta gained some national attention. But King had seemingly lost his audience with Kennedy. Atlanta's black elite were upset with him, and given their relationships with the mayor and other powerful whites, it would be easy for them to begin negotiating above the heads of student activists.

As was often the case in the civil rights movement, however, an overstep by the white authorities changed everyone's calculus. Atlanta's mayor had arranged the release of all the demonstrators, but a judge from De Kalb County ordered King to remain in custody on account of a parole violation for a minor traffic offense. The judge convicted and sentenced King to four months hard labor in a Georgia state penitentiary.

The judge refused King's release on bond pending appeal, an outrageous action given the original charge was a misdemeanor. In response, the Kennedys intervened on King's behalf, and King was released a week later. The show of support inspired King's father, as well as a number of other black Georgians who traditionally voted Republican, to come out in full support of Kennedy. Within a year of King's original protest, Atlanta's lunch counters were desegregated. It's impossible to know if King's stand played a pivotal role, or if it just gave a little boost of energy to a faltering movement. King's decision ended up working out, but it's hard to see how the result stemmed from the morality of his original act.

ON MAY 4, 1961, a group of six whites and seven blacks set off in a pair of buses from Washington, DC, on what was supposed to be a seventeen-day trip through the Deep South to New Orleans. Organized by the Congress of Racial Equality (CORE), the so-called freedom riders would use nonviolence to test *Boynton v. Virginia*, a December 1960 Supreme Court decision that made segregation illegal in interstate bus terminals. The group included Albert Bigelow, a white, fifty-three-year-old Harvard-trained architect, and John Lewis, a short, twenty-one-year-old black man from Tennessee who'd led student sit-ins the previous summer.

At each bus station, one black "tester" would enter the segregated portion of a bus terminal and seek service, while the others waited in a line. Based on the reception of the tester, the rest of the group would join, help, or regroup and determine a course of action. Because it was the site of a famous student sit-in, in Rock Hill, South Carolina, John Lewis volunteered himself as the tester. When two young whites blocked him from entering the segregated waiting room, Lewis gave his rehearsed line: "I have a right to go in here based on grounds of the Supreme Court decision in the *Boynton* case." He was punched in the face, and more young whites joined in. Second in line, Albert Bigelow came forward and stood unmoving in front of Lewis's bloody body, letting himself be beaten.

Things got much worse. One of the group's Greyhound buses was firebombed on the highway between Anniston and Birmingham, Alabama; and at the terminals in each of those cities, several of the freedom riders were beaten by white mobs. As a result of the violence, the group was starting to get national attention, and more riders joined.

Twenty-one activists took buses from Birmingham to Montgomery on Saturday, May 20. Upon their arrival at the bus terminal, thugs from a thousand-person mob attacked the freedom riders. Violence raged for more than two hours, with twenty people injured. One young black bystander was doused with kerosene and set on fire. A white assistant to US attorney general Robert Kennedy was beaten in the back of the head for trying to help a young female freedom rider escape the melee. That night, four hundred US marshals were sent in to keep the peace.

The next day, King flew in to Montgomery. By his presence, King conferred a sense of prestige on the freedom rides, brought increased national attention, and ensured that influential leaders in the federal government would be personally committed to the crisis. Because King went to Montgomery, a wider range of Americans would see the blatant injustice there.

But King's presence also increased tensions on the ground. His first night in Montgomery, King oversaw a mass meeting at Abernathy's church that was nearly overrun by a white mob before a contingent of national guardsmen intervened. Alabama's governor blamed the violence on King: "They caused that rioting by bringing King to Montgomery," whom the governor called a "menace to the city."

The freedom riders and other civil rights leaders waited in Montgomery, deliberating how they'd be able to continue their ride to Mississippi and beyond. Some twenty of them, including King, were staying in the home of Richard Harris, a local pharmacist who lived just across the street from King's former home on South Jackson Street. Over the course of two days in the Harris house, the freedom riders tried to persuade King to join them. "Where is your body?" they asked. Diane Nash, a leader of the group, believed that he could "set an example of leadership that might raise the standard of nonviolent commitment everywhere."

James Bevel, who had helped organize the freedom riders before their departure and planned to join them on the trip from Montgomery into Mississippi, remembers arguing that "King would be best mobilizing and motivating people to join the Ride, in terms of church support and student support. The rest of us could go join in and create the kinds of discipline within the jails." While they weren't in Harris's home that day, other civil rights leaders like Roy Wilkins of the NAACP agreed that the freedom riders were "registering a personal and powerful moral protest against injustice," but thought they'd already achieved their objective of testing the *Boynton* Supreme Court case. Freedom riders had already been arrested, and so there was a test case that could be used in raising the issue through the courts.

The freedom riders forced King to make a choice between his role as the movement's spokesman and its symbol. If the former was more important, he should live to speak another day, continuing to attract attention and resources to the freedom riders' cause. If the latter, he should face the same potentially mortal consequences that faced all the freedom riders in

Mississippi. After all, these were the most ardent followers of King's philosophy of nonviolence. That choice certainly would have satisfied King's morality.

James Farmer, the head of CORE, recalls that King communicated his decision in biblical terms. King said he didn't want to join the freedom riders because he was on probation, and his arrest would mean an extended stay in jail. After some of the riders made the point that they, too, were on probation, King retorted that "I think I should choose the time and place of my Golgotha." Farmer remembers some of the riders "laughing and joking" about King's heavy-handed refusal. Their reaction was understandable: many of the young freedom riders, after all, had been inspired to act by the example of King's leadership. John Lewis remembers that he joined the civil rights movement because he read a comic called "Martin Luther King and the Montgomery Story," whose cover featured a gleaming picture of a sharply dressed King centered on a yellow background towering over Alabama's capital city, the words "How 50,000 Negroes Found a New Way to End Racial Discrimination" in block letters to the right of the leader's stern face.

On May 23, King announced at a press conference that the ride would go on, and that "I'm sure that these students are willing to face death if necessary." The next day he went to the Montgomery bus station, where he said a prayer and saw the freedom riders off to Mississippi without him.

King decided it was best for him to avoid the risk of joining younger activists in jail. The decision nagged at him. Many of the student activists languished for months in Mississippi prisons. In an issue of *Jet* aptly headlined "Who Speaks for the Negro," in response to criticism for not joining his followers, King hedged. "I don't believe in this business of leaders staying outside of jail. But," he went on, "my advisers on the SCLC board urged me not to. . . . [They said] you'll be out of circulation too long. . . . People will say you have absolutely no regard for the law, that you are a publicity seeker with a martyr complex."

On November 1, 1961, the federal Interstate Commerce Commission issued an order to desegregate all buses and terminals across the country, the final result of the initiative of a dozen activists who'd set out from

Washington, DC, six months earlier. King didn't join the activists riding across the South. He had made a different choice from the one he'd made in the Atlanta sit-ins, but the results were the same.

KING SPENT PART OF 1962 in and out of jail in support of the "Albany Movement," an effort with mixed results to end racial injustice in Albany, Georgia. As King would tell an interviewer, "The mistake I made there [in Albany] was to protest against segregation generally rather than against a single and distinct facet of it. Our protest was so vague that we got nothing, and the people were left very depressed and in despair." He could have made the same general criticism of SCLC. The organization had been chasing crises since its inception in 1957 and was in search of a single place to concentrate its attention, resources, and leadership. At the outset of 1963, SCLC was still trying to reanimate the spirit of the Montgomery bus boycott.

1963: Birmingham and Washington

By 1963, SCLC had about fifty people on staff and an annual budget of around $400,000. Much of the budget was financed by King's extensive speechmaking, which was also helpful in catalyzing King's celebrity and spreading the idea of nonviolent mass action. Every year he traveled hundreds of thousands of miles and averaged well over one speech per day. While SCLC responded to crises as in Atlanta, the freedom rides, and Albany, they were also running programs—among them nonviolent training workshops and voter registration projects.

Because of SCLC the idea of change through nonviolence was in the air, but the general public didn't yet have an acute understanding of its power. For the better part of a year, Fred Shuttlesworth, the secretary of SCLC's board, was prodding King to concentrate SCLC's efforts in Birmingham. King tasked SCLC's executive director, Wyatt Walker, with thinking through a plan for SCLC there. In a technique he used dozens of times after 1963 whenever there was a weighty strategic issue to be hashed out, in January 1963 King convened a small task force of key leaders at a retreat center in Dorchester, Georgia, for two days.

Water cannons spraying protesters in Birmingham, Alabama, in May 1963.
(PHOTOGRAPH BY MICHAEL OCHS ARCHIVES/GETTY IMAGES)

At the meeting, Walker briefed a plan called Project C, standing for "Confrontation," to deploy SCLC to Birmingham, Alabama. Walker's plan had four phases:

First, they would launch small-scale sit-ins to draw attention to their desegregation platform, while building strength through nightly mass meetings. Second, they would organize a generalized boycott of the downtown business section, and move to slightly larger demonstrations. Third, they would move to mass marches—both to enforce the boycott and to fill the jails. Finally, if necessary, they would call on outsiders to descend on Birmingham from across the country, as in the Freedom Rides, to cripple the city under the combined pressure of publicity, economic boycott, and the burden of overflowing jails.

The plan reflected the distillation of SCLC's first six years of institutional knowledge. Project C was approved, but events in Birmingham would, of course, unfold much differently than what Walker briefed in Dorchester. More important than the plan was the decision: SCLC and King were committed to Birmingham.

KING ONCE CALLED BIRMINGHAM "the most segregated city in America."

Segregation was deeply ingrained in almost every facet of Birmingham life. Illuminated bold letters above a theater read COLORED BALCONY. Arrows on bathroom signs distinguished the "White" from the "Colored" entrances. A laundromat claimed in all caps, WE WASH FOR WHITE PEOPLE ONLY. At a diner counter advertising 35¢ tuna fish salad sandwiches and 39¢ banana splits, Birmingham's blacks were prohibited from eating. Black citizens were not even allowed to put their hand on the same Bible as whites when taking an oath. "If Birmingham could be cracked," King wrote in an SCLC newsletter, "the direction of the entire nonviolent movement in the South could take a significant turn."

Historically, Birmingham had been governed by a system in which three commissioners shared power. In 1962, the most prominent of the three was Theophilus Eugene "Bull" Connor, the commissioner for public safety, who controlled the police and fire departments and was a ruthless segregationist. In an action emblematic of his character, Connor had let Ku Klux Klan members beat freedom riders passing through Birmingham in 1961. This and other intense scenes of white-on-black violence were hurting the city's reputation, which in turn hurt the city's business class. By late 1962, Birmingham residents took action and voted to change the form of government to a mayor-council system instead. Reform was in the air before SCLC ever hit the ground.

On March 5, 1963, Connor ran for mayor against Albert Boutwell, a conservative moderate who promised to change negative perceptions of Birmingham, and Tom King, a liberal. No candidate received the majority vote, so Connor and Boutwell, the top two vote getters, competed in a runoff election about a month later on April 2. Boutwell won the election by 7,982 votes, largely due to the black vote. But Connor challenged the validity of the new government in Alabama's Supreme Court. Until a final decision could be reached, Boutwell and Connor divided power by occupying the office on alternating days. This was the volatile, and peculiar, context into which SCLC would have to launch its most heavy-hitting campaign yet.

Project C was delayed twice to avoid tipping the electoral scales in Connor's favor. In the confusion after the runoff, there was some consideration of continuing to hold off, but they decided to forge ahead.

Even after the long wait, the first day of the campaign, which centered on lunch counter protests, didn't meet expectations. The *New York Times* reported, "An attack by the city's black community on racial segregation in Birmingham continued today. But it was much less than the 'full-scale assault' that had been promised." The movement reoriented by organizing protests to city hall. While the first march on April 6 was a success—more than forty people went to jail—volunteers dwindled, along with public support.

As the marches lagged, the movement's enemies tried to strike a death blow. Governor George Wallace signed a bill to raise the maximum bail for misdemeanors in Birmingham from $300 to $2,500 in an effort to deplete SCLC's bail funds. Shortly thereafter, the City of Birmingham sought an injunction against the movement, citing "mass street parades . . . 'sit-in' demonstrations," and other tactics, "calculated to provoke breaches of the peace in the City of Birmingham." Around 1:00 a.m. on Thursday, April 11, as he sat in a motel restaurant with Abernathy, Shuttlesworth, Walker, and other leaders, King was handed the injunction by a deputy sheriff. He and other named leaders would go to jail if they continued to participate in demonstrations.

In response, about eleven hours later, King wrote in a news release, "We cannot in all good conscience obey such an injunction." He also committed that they would "continue their demonstrations and activities or movement 'today, tomorrow, Saturday, Monday, and on through.'"

But information King received after his proclamation complicated his decision: SCLC was almost out of money to post bail for volunteers in jail. As King himself recalled, he faced a conflict between raising money so he could fulfill the movement's "moral responsibility for our people in jail," on the one hand, and "[putting] into practice what I had so passionately preached" on the other. King recalled how he made his decision: "Good Friday morning, early, I sat in Room 30 of the Gaston motel discussing this crisis with twenty-four key people. . . . Finally someone spoke up and, as he spoke, I could see that he was giving voice to what was on everyone's mind." King's advisers told him not to go to jail. Then he left the room to think in solitude:

> I walked to another room in the back of the suite, and I stood in the center of the floor. I thought I was standing at the center of all that my life had brought me to be. I thought of the twenty-four people, waiting in the next room. I thought of the three hundred, waiting in prison. I thought of the Birmingham Negro community, waiting. Then my tortured mind leaped beyond the Gaston Motel, past the city jail, past the city and state lines, and I thought of the twenty million black people who dreamed that someday they might be able to cross the Red Sea of injustice and find their way into the promised land of integration and freedom. There was no more room for doubt.
>
> I whispered to myself, "I must go."

He made the wrenching decision to prioritize downtrodden but nominally free millions over the imprisoned hundreds—the national and universal over the local and particular. That afternoon, April 12, King, alongside Abernathy, led a group of fifty people from Zion Hill Church toward city hall. King remembered being "hauled off by two muscular police-men, clutching the backs of our shirts in handfuls."

King was placed in solitary confinement with no outside contact for roughly three days. It wasn't until King saw Clarence Jones, his lawyer, the following Monday that he received an update on how the movement was going. During his visits, Jones smuggled in newspapers for King to read. In one of the papers, King read an editorial written by religious leaders condemning him and his movement, prompting King to reply with the now-famous "Letter from Birmingham Jail." It started, as King recalled, "on the margins of the newspaper in which the statement appeared." Though much of his leadership was about navigating crises, he never forgot the purpose behind all the day-to-day challenges, and he was exceptionally adept at communicating the movement's basic philosophy.

After just over a week in jail, King was bailed out on April 20. It had been seventeen days since the movement started in Birmingham, and Project C was not going according to the plan Wyatt Walker had briefed back in January. Sit-ins had flopped, public opinion was not in the movement's favor, funds and volunteers were fading, and King had been imprisoned with little outside contact for nine days.

King and his advisers decided they needed a highly publicized mass action to relaunch the effort and set May 2 as the date. Their model was a 1961 protest on city hall in Nashville, Tennessee, that involved four thousand black activists. In order to compensate for the lack of volunteers, King made the highly controversial decision to let kids participate in the Birmingham campaign.

The risks were high—parents and outsiders could easily use the decision as grounds to criticize the movement, SCLC leadership could be charged with crimes relating to minors, and above all, kids would inevitably be facing down the harshness of Birmingham's police and the deprivation of Alabama jails.

James Bevel, who was running daily nonviolence workshops, saw that kids were his most consistent and energetic trainees, and they were clamoring to get involved. He argued to King that Birmingham's black youth would make the difference the movement needed.

After King consented in principle, he and his advisers debated the required age for kids to join in the events of May 2. They eventually settled on the age of six—when a child could be part of a church. This wasn't in the plans for Project C, but the situation in Birmingham demanded a tough choice. The protest scheduled for Thursday, May 2—which became known as "D Day"—would be a students-only protest.

In the afternoon, police officers were waiting expectantly when fifty student protesters emerged in two parallel lines from Sixteenth Baptist Church. While they were arresting the group, another set of students appeared from the church. Then a third wave, a fourth, and so on. "Altogether on 'D' Day, May 2," King later wrote, "more than a thousand young people demonstrated and went to jail." They swarmed the streets. "At one time, demonstrations by groups of from ten to fifty boys and girls were going on simultaneously at four different places several blocks apart. . . . Every available police vehicle was pressed into service to haul the young demonstrators to jail or juvenile court." Eventually, the city had to use school buses to haul all the kids to jail.

By the time the demonstrations ended around 4:00 p.m., activists began to fill the pews of Fred Shuttlesworth's church for a sermon. It was the same rhythm that sustained every crisis in which King participated. Demonstrations would occur in the afternoon. Then a nightly meeting at a local church or churches would be held to spread information, synchronize the community, and rally support. After the meeting, King and his advisers would meet late into the night to strategize and debate decisions. After a little bit of sleep, the cycle would start over again. This structure allowed the movement to make quick, effective decisions in a difficult campaign where conditions changed rapidly.

The next afternoon, more than one thousand kids were ready to protest. "The first wave of young demonstrators came out of the 16th Street Church at 1:00 pm heading in several directions," the *New York Times* reported. "When a group of about 60 reached the corner of 17th Street and Fifth Avenue, Police Captain G. V. Evans ordered them to halt and disperse 'or you're going to get wet.'"

As they began to spray water, some of the crowd dispersed, but ten students held firm. The police drew closer, and the students defiantly sat down. The police resorted to a new weapon—monitor guns. By concentrating the water pressure of two hoses into a single, powerful stream, these weapons were capable of "knocking bricks loose from mortar or stripping bark from trees at a distance of one hundred feet." As more students emerged, the police used their dogs. Animals and high-pressure water were now beating back protesters. As King later wrote, "The newspapers of May 4 carried pictures of prostrate women, and policemen bending over them with raised clubs; of children marching up to the bared fangs of police dogs; of the terrible force of pressure hoses sweeping bodies into the streets."

Those images brought national attention to the crisis. And on May 7, there was another massive, surprise protest in Birmingham's business district. That day, leaders in the city's business community, with assistance from two Justice Department aides who had been dispatched by Robert F. Kennedy, reached an initial agreement with Birmingham's black leadership. And on May 10, after King served another short stint in jail for violating his injunction, segregation in Birmingham ended with a four-part agreement.

Over the course of thirty-eight days in Birmingham, Project C changed dramatically. Facts on the ground had necessitated risky decisions, ones that happened to work out but might not have in different circumstances. While Wyatt Walker's plan had changed, the results were what SCLC had always envisioned.

KING AND OTHER LEADERS wanted to consolidate the success of Birmingham and pressure Congress to pass the civil rights legislation that President Kennedy had recently put together.* A. Philip Randolph, the founder of the Brotherhood of Sleeping Car Porters and a longtime civil rights leader, suggested a march on Washington. Wednesday, August 28, 1963, was set for what was called the "March on Washington for Jobs and Freedom."

Rustin was the chief organizer, and he intended to keep things on time. To avoid any trouble, he planned for downtown Washington to be vacant by dusk. A large part of his job was managing the leaders of the national civil rights movement, who made up the day's speakers and performers. Speakers were given seven minutes each, and everyone had a specific role to play. Number 13 on Rustin's agenda was Roy Wilkins, the head of the NAACP, who focused his remarks on the president's legislation.

Mahalia Jackson, the famous gospel singer, followed Wilkins. With her first song, "How I Got Over," she had the crowd in an uproar; through the second, "I've Been Buked and I've Been Scorned," those assembled were in solemn but smiling reflection, bursting into a standing ovation only at the conclusion.

She exited and stood to the side of the stage on the steps of the Lincoln Memorial. After remarks by Rabbi Joachim Prinz came King, number 16

----

*Passed the following July, this would become the Civil Rights Act of 1964.

on the agenda and the day's featured speaker. Jackson watched A. Philip Randolph introduce him as "the moral leader of our nation," and saw King approach the podium, thirty minutes ahead of schedule.

In front of the old friend she knew simply as "Martin," Jackson gazed at 250,000 people crammed into every inch of space between the Lincoln Memorial and the Washington Monument. The assembly for which she'd just sung included some 190,000 black Americans—nearly 1 percent of the entire black population of the United States. Though the temperature was a pleasant 83 degrees and there was low humidity, the crowd was so dense that many in attendance recall the day as sweltering. Some spectators climbed trees to get a better view above the sweating masses, while others took off their socks and put their feet in the wading pool on the national lawn, more content to listen and cool off.

Unbeknownst to Jackson, King had spent part of that afternoon locked in a tiny guard station underneath the Lincoln Memorial with Randolph, John Lewis, and a white clergyman. Rustin had tasked them with resolving a crisis by tamping down some of the rhetoric in Lewis's prepared remarks before he spoke, sixth on the agenda.

As King finally approached the podium, the last speaker of a long day, Jackson listened as the crowd roared in anticipation. The boom of the crescendo was matched by the intensity of the utter silence when King began to speak. Of all the speakers that day, people expected that King would give them something to remember—his leadership on August 28, 1963, is found as much in the sense of expectation as it is in the words he ended up giving to history. Some just wanted from King a few stirring words; for others, King's message might help legitimize and energize the thousands of local fights that many in attendance were carrying on across the country; for others still, King might provide more universal meaning for acts of protest they'd already taken.

When he began, he spoke from some prepared remarks he'd finished up around four o'clock that morning, his preacher's timbre punctuated by brief glances down at his notes. About eleven minutes into what became a sixteen-minute speech, Jackson noticed that the fellow performer now behind the microphone was beginning to riff—perhaps the cue was a look King gave, or an inflection in his tone.

She recalled a set of lines King had given before and urged him to "tell them about the dream, Martin!" It's unclear if King heard what she said, but he proceeded to give his famous lines. For the last five minutes of the speech, he looked directly at the crowd and occasionally up into the sky as he told the world about his dream. Back in the White House, President Kennedy, like many Americans at home, was watching King speak for the first time on television. "He's damn good," remarked the president.

JUST OVER A YEAR LATER, in October 1964, King was in an Atlanta hospital bed, wearing his dark silk pajamas, the same type he'd worn on previous stints in prison. A telephone was perched on his belly, and he was holding its receiver to his left ear. His frenetic life had landed him in the hospital—he was overweight and suffering from a virus caused by what the doctors said was exhaustion. By one estimate, King was working twenty hours a day, traveling 325,000 miles, and making 450 speeches per year.

The phone call informed him that he'd need to make yet another long trip, this time to Oslo. Dr. King, at thirty-five years old, had just become the youngest recipient of the Nobel Peace Prize. The March on Washington and the Nobel Prize altered the public's perception of King, but it's striking how little the recognition changed him. He felt a heightened sense of responsibility on account of his icon status, but he changed his approach very little. Above all, King was responsive to the weight of the civil rights movement's institutional knowledge, which pushed him willingly into crisis after crisis. The simple logic was that action forged change. The Civil Rights Act of 1964, in other words, passed precisely because of Birmingham in 1963.

That fall, in his annual report, King emphasized that the "mainstay of SCLC program is still in the area of non-violent direct action." He went on: "When we are idle, the white majority very quickly forgets the injustices which started our movement and only think of the demands for progress as unreasonable requests from irresponsible people." Little time was spent savoring the gains they had made. King wielded his moral authority, and endured the frenetic pace of his life, to find the next crisis, which in turn might forge the next great advance in justice.

Martin Luther King Jr. on March 25, 1965, speaking to marchers
at the end of the Selma to Montgomery march.
(PHOTOGRAPH BY STEPHEN SOMERSTEIN/GETTY IMAGES)

1965: Turning Around in Selma

A week after President Johnson's 1964 landslide election victory over Barry Goldwater, King convened an SCLC staff retreat at the same Gaston Motel in Birmingham that had been his headquarters during the campaign there in 1963. Since that campaign had ended, tensions remained high in the city. Less than a month after the March on Washington, four young girls were killed there when white terrorists detonated a bomb in the basement of a church.

In the immediate aftermath, Diane Nash sent a report to King on the mood in Birmingham. Among other conclusions, she wrote: "You can tell people not to fight only if you offer them a way by which justice can be served without violence. There is no other honorable alternative. Just to tell people not to fight after children are murdered and leave it at that is wrong and you are expecting and appealing to them to be less than men."

The same day, she and James Bevel sent King a "Proposal for Action in

Montgomery," a two-page memo detailing mass action aimed at removing George Wallace from the governorship of Alabama and registering every black Alabaman of legal age to vote. While the details of that memo changed, its spirit evolved into the "Alabama Project." The purpose of SCLC's November 1964 staff retreat was to determine whether the Alabama Project should be focused specifically on Selma, which at the time was the most staunchly segregationist city in the state. By the end of the retreat, King agreed to have a team deploy to Selma.

After a handful of SCLC staff spent all of November and December 1964 making plans, King kicked off the campaign in Selma at a seven-hundred-person mass meeting there on January 2, 1965. He announced that the focus of the effort would be "to establish in the mind of the nation that a lot of people who want to register are prevented from doing so. We hope this will lead to a revision of the voter registration laws in this state." Beyond the state, SCLC was also hoping that their actions in Selma would eventually lead to a new voting rights bill in Washington, a bill that President Johnson had said was not possible in the current political climate.

King came back to Selma and on Monday, January 18, led a march of four hundred residents to the county courthouse, where they waited all day without being able to register. King then went to Selma's Albert Hotel to attempt to become one of its first black guests. He was attacked by a white man who landed two punches to King's temple before being pulled away and arrested. In the same rhythm that had sustained the campaigns in Montgomery and Birmingham before, after the day's activities, King oversaw a nighttime mass meeting before late-night strategy sessions with key leaders.

Unlike other campaigns, King did not remain in Selma for the duration. He came in when his staff told him he could be helpful. After he'd left Selma in mid-January, several hundred blacks had been arrested, and SCLC's staff decided it would be best for their president to go to jail as well. On Monday, February 1, 1965, King was arrested along with 260 others and refused bail.

Fifty-two days after accepting the Nobel Prize in Oslo, Norway, King spent the night in a central Alabama jail cell. Now, almost nine years since his home had been bombed at the outset of Montgomery's bus boycott,

King was a seasoned veteran of the civil rights struggle. His first night in jail, he gave twelve numbered instructions to an aide. Far from the sweeping rhetoric he'd just delivered in his Nobel Prize address, the staccato orders are more redolent of a general than a preacher: "Do following to keep national attention focused on Selma," wrote King. His list began:

1. Make a call to Governor Collins [of the Community Relations Service] and urge him to make a personal visit to Selma to talk with the city and county authorities concerning speedier registration and more days for registering.
2. Follow through on suggestion of having a congressional delegation come in for personal investigation. They should also make an appearance at a mass meeting if they come.

The list continued with ten more bullets, each highly specific and steeped in the wisdom of experience.

Three days later, on Thursday, February 4, 1965, after communicating with King's aides, President Johnson issued a statement in which he said, "I hope that all Americans will join with me in expressing their concern over the loss of any American's right to vote. . . . I intend to see that that right is secured for all our citizens." The next day, just as King's instructions from jail had indicated, a fifteen-person congressional delegation arrived in Selma, and King left jail to meet them. The following week he headed to Washington to press the president for voting rights legislation.

Over the next month, as King shuttled all over the country, violence in Selma was escalating. Sheriffs and state highway patrolmen had been using billy clubs and cattle prods in the process of making arrests. The evening of February 26, a twenty-seven-year-old black man was killed by a state trooper after a night march in Marion, thirty miles northwest of Selma. In response, leaders on the ground planned a fifty-four-mile march from Selma to Montgomery scheduled to begin on Sunday, March 7.

Governor Wallace warned that state troopers would block the march "by any means necessary." On the advice of SCLC staff on the ground, King did not return to lead the march. After a Friday meeting in Washington, he returned home to Atlanta and preached at his church that Sunday. As the six hundred Selma marchers crossed Edmund Pettus Bridge on Highway 80, state troopers blocked their way. After the march's leaders—SCLC's Hosea Williams and SNCC's John Lewis—refused an order to move, the troopers attacked. The resulting carnage is remembered as "Bloody Sunday."

The following Tuesday, the movement planned to renew their attempted march, and King was called in to head the column. Leading up to the march, a federal judge had tacitly agreed to endorse a march if Tuesday's events could be postponed, but King, in part to satisfy his own conscience and in part to satisfy his followers, insisted upon pressing ahead. The potential for another violent confrontation was high. Then, just before Tuesday's march stepped off, representatives of President Johnson informed King that they had arranged with Alabama authorities to allow King and his followers to walk to the same place they had the previous Sunday, say some prayers, and then turn around.

Without time to deliberate with his team, King agreed to the compromise, but qualified his response on the grounds that "I cannot agree to do anything because I don't know what I can get my people to do." As events unfolded, King led his procession of marchers to within fifty yards of the troopers arrayed on the Pettus Bridge, sang "We Shall Overcome," and then turned around. The marchers followed. In the aftermath, the SNCC leaders were irate at King for striking what they described as a backroom deal with the government; and President Johnson's representatives, in turn, were irate that King had allowed the march to go on at all given their assurances that a delay would provide a federally protected march.

King had conceived neither the tactics used in Selma nor the idea to go there at all. And he was not in the city when the movement there met the most violence—Bloody Sunday. Rather, King was called in to lead in a difficult moment. He made a decision that was ambiguous and angered people on all sides. It ended up working out—marchers walked from Selma to Montgomery under protective orders from the federal government, and Selma ultimately led to passage of the Voting Rights Act of 1965 that August. But his leadership was not in a speech or a plan. In this particular moment, King's leadership could be found not in a speech or a plan but rather in his willingness, after ten years in the movement, to serve as its symbol and the keeper of its deepest pain. He both stood at the head of

King's assassination at the Lorraine Motel in Memphis, Tennessee.
(PHOTOGRAPH BY JOSEPH LOUW/THE LIFE IMAGES COLLECTION/GETTY IMAGES)

the column and was willing to be held accountable for a wrenching decision. Just as in Montgomery nine years before, he was part of the movement, but also had a distinct role. His leadership was characterized by
simultaneous harmony with, and aloofness from, the thing he was charged
with leading.

Struggling Forward

In February 1968, a *Washington Post* staff writer followed King as he
traveled. "Here in Selma, Birmingham, and Montgomery," she wrote,
"where Dr. King's nonviolence stood the test of fire hoses, police dogs, tear
gas, and Southern Sheriffs with bull whips—the Negro leader has been seeking more strength from the past." But King's purpose wasn't sentimental—
he was there to recruit for another march on Washington, this one part of a
"poor people's campaign." King and his team envisioned bringing "wagon
trains of poor to Washington."

In the wake of Selma, SCLC was focusing increasing attention on economic equality. "We must see that the stuggle today is much more difficult," King acknowledged, ". . . it's much easier to integrate a lunch counter than it is to guarantee a livable income and a good solid job." Having always cared about more than just racial justice, King now opted into a long-term, wider struggle, one with no end in sight.

King had only two months to live before being assassinated outside a Memphis motel room. One imagines that, even with foreknowledge of that horrible day in April 1968, he wouldn't have changed too much. Most of us would probably try to spend the time with family, but King's past was rich with memories of how the movement and his family were inextricably intertwined. Twelve years earlier as he'd led the bus boycott in Montgomery, his first daughter, Yolanda, had been only seven weeks old when their home was bombed. His jailing in Georgia, now eight years past, had occurred while Coretta was pregnant with King's youngest son, Dexter. His oldest son, Martin III, would have been entering kindergarten six years prior—just as King had been jailed as part of the Albany Movement. And he'd left for Birmingham five years before, the day after Bernice, his youngest daughter, was born. Selma was now three years behind him, and how many motels, guest rooms, and jail cells had he slept in since then?

But now it neither stopped nor slowed. On that February 1968 day, with the reporter in tow and using a chartered plane, Dr. Martin Luther King Jr. visited all three Alabama cities in a single day.

MINERS, MONKS, AND MINISTERS

You see, fellow-soldiers, that perseverance is more prevailing than violence; and many things which cannot be overcome when they are together, yield themselves up when taken little by little.

—PLUTARCH, "LIFE OF SERTORIUS"

At birth, Martin Luther King Jr. had been named Michael King Jr. But in 1934, when Michael King Sr. went to Europe for a world Baptist conference, they both got a new namesake. The older King, so the story goes, was so moved by what he learned about Martin Luther on the trip that he changed his name, and also his five-year-old son's, to honor the Protestant Reformation leader. According to one of the elder King's grandsons, the name change was "proof positive of . . . the vision he would plant inside his namesake son."

Each of our reformers had fathers with large and firm expectations. As King Jr. said of his upbringing: "I grew up in the church. My father is a preacher, my grandfather was a preacher, my great-grandfather was a preacher, my only brother is a preacher, my daddy's brother is a preacher. So, I didn't have much choice." Martin Luther's father, a copper miner, had envisioned his son as a lawyer, but Luther defied him by becoming a monk. While the two took different routes to their similar professions, these professions—Baptist preacher and Augustinian monk—were critical in establishing each Martin as a leader.

When King emerged, the church was the beating heart of black activism, and preachers were de facto political leaders. The meeting on the night he was unexpectedly elected as the president of the Montgomery Improvement Association was held in a church. Of the eighteen people in the room that night, about half were preachers, and Rufus Lewis, who nominated King, was one of his parishioners.

Luther's path was through the same Catholic Church that he eventually upended. A strict monk, Luther was eventually asked by his mentor to help out at a new university. Becoming a Catholic intellectual put him in a position to comment on the issues of the day, so it wasn't abnormal for him to do something like write out a set of theses. Luther was an overnight sensation, on account of the fact that his approach to faith resonated with thousands of Europeans.

Their emergence as leaders wasn't preordained. MLK became a national leader because he happened to become the MIA president, and the Montgomery bus boycott—a boycott that was instigated by other well-established leaders—became a watershed event in a civil rights movement that had been lurching ahead for decades. Similarly, the ideas that Luther wrote down in his Ninety-five Theses were already in the air in Wittenberg in 1517. His ideas weren't novel—he happened to articulate those ideas in a particular way at a particular moment, and they unexpectedly struck a chord with the Holy Roman Empire's pious masses.

Neither of our leaders intended to spark their movements, but each of them agreed to shoulder a burden at the moment that leadership was made available to them. While each of our reformers left an indelible mark as a leader, we attribute too much to them as individuals if we neglect the systems that asked for them to lead.

For both, the process of reform was more difficult than they could have imagined. Luther spent many years under the specter of a violent execution, and King was murdered for his leadership. But more simply, the path to reform was arduous and irreducible to a single playbook and involved navigating a constantly changing landscape. King's leadership emerged through the framework of an organization and its strategy, as he was formally the president of either the MIA or SCLC for the entirety of his career. In those roles, he was constantly negotiating the fault lines between nonviolent mass action and other approaches to forging change.

By contrast, Luther's proclivity was more as a commentator than an organizer. He didn't respond to the outbreak of the Peasants' War, for instance, by attempting to negotiate with other leaders or broker a resolution, but instead by publishing tracts establishing his position.

As leaders, they both leveraged new technologies—specifically, the printing press and television—as if they had been invented expressly for their use. Luther was by orders of magnitude the best-selling author of his time. For King, the television beamed images of protests and riots, as well as his speeches and press conferences, to living rooms across the country; and he is among the greatest orators in American history.

Beyond reading and hearing their written and spoken words, why were people so moved by Luther and King? In retrospect, it's clear that each leader forged substantial change. But taken day-by-day as events were unfolding, the picture was never so clear. Large portions of each of their constituencies disagreed with these leaders at any given moment—whether the peasants whom Luther ultimately condemned or the thousands of times MLK's role in the civil rights movement was to decide between various interests and organizations that had good-faith disagreements on the best way to make change.

Reform, it seems, is irreducible to a single, climactic event, speech, or court case. Instead, it is an extended process—a journey that twists, turns, starts, and stops, as though it were an animate object that defies control by a single individual. Our reformers were riders on an unruly horse, normally expending as much energy to hang on as to direct where, or how fast, the animal was going. While they achieved substantial results, success was never a sure thing. Not only was there no common formula for reform, they were more often the symbols of a cause than the doers of change.

When followers fix their gaze upon symbolic leaders like Luther and MLK, their view of the reformers and the movements they led becomes distorted. In becoming the focal point of so much attention, the reform leader becomes laden with outsized expectations. We followers come to expect things that are unreasonable, and to see things that are not real.

There is, for example, the legendary story that Martin Luther sparked the Protestant Reformation by nailing his Ninety-five Theses to the front door of the Castle Church in Wittenberg. This best-known "fact" about Luther probably never happened, even though the ideas in Luther's writing remain historically significant. Similarly, the most famous lines in MLK's most famous speech weren't even in his speaking notes for the day. As usual, he intuited what the crowd wanted and gave it to them. It's a good analogy for his years of civil rights leadership. Neither King nor Luther knew exactly what they were getting themselves into when they were handed the mantle of "leader." But they accepted the role and carried on.

A leader often becomes a discrete symbol. It is easier for followers to wrap their expectations around a singular person at the top than it is to think about the myriad complex actions occurring at multiple levels. And while the real agenda and power come from those nearer the bottom, that agenda is often made coherent by the person-symbol at the top. Reform movements need these apex leaders not so much to tell them what to do, but to unify them with a sense of integrity—especially when these movements are so granular, as they always are, beneath the surface.

When the two Michael Kings became Martin Luther Kings, the father responsible for the name changes probably wasn't thinking about the burdens of leadership—perhaps he was excited about the prestige it might have conferred upon his son. When they were thrust into their roles, each of our reformers had one basic choice: Did they want to lead, or would they let someone else take the burden? Saying yes meant both assuming control and giving it up.

Nine

THREE MYTHS

Myths are not deliberately, or necessarily consciously, fictitious.

—JAMES ROBERTSON, AUTHOR OF *AMERICAN MYTH,*
AMERICAN REALITY

In 1922, at roughly the midpoint and well short of the apogee of his political career, Winston Churchill wrote of "a medium at your disposal which offers real power if you only can find out how to use it." Churchill would become Britain's most beloved and studied prime minister, but the "power" of which he wrote came not from leadership, but from painting. And it was a discovery made at the nadir of his power.

As Britain's First Lord of the Admiralty, Churchill had political control of British naval forces in the First World War. In late 1914, he championed a risky naval and later amphibious operation in the Dardanelles, designed to defeat the Turkish Ottomans and unite forces with Britain's ally, Russia. The campaign was "dependent on speed, ferocity, and sheer audacity," as historian Daniel Butler assessed, and "could have been one of the great masterstrokes of strategy . . . had it succeeded."

Early on the operation (known as the Gallipoli campaign) faltered, but Churchill pressed its continuation, and Britain suffered a humiliating defeat, with the loss of 44,150 Allied lives. The ambitious forty-year-old Churchill was blamed, banished to a lesser posting, and left government soon after. "I thought he would die of grief," his wife, Clementine, later reflected.

It was then, in the darkness of his failed "masterstroke," that Churchill first picked up a brush as an escape from his anguish. "Like a sea-beast fished up from the depths, or a diver too suddenly hoisted, my veins threatened to burst from the fall in pressure. . . . And then it was that the Muse of Painting came to my rescue. . . ." Painting became a lifelong friend that kept Churchill company until his death. It was a companionship that ultimately produced more than five hundred pieces.

Churchill chose the paintbrush out of despair, and his tendency toward depressive moods may have been the reason he never put it down. He would speak of his "black dog," a cryptic way of referring to his darker moods, which could be severe enough that he preferred not to stand "near the edge of a platform when an express train is passing through." He explained, "I like to stand back and if possible to get a pillar between me and the train. I don't like to stand by the side of a ship and look down into the water. A second's action would end everything."

Six years after Gallipoli, in his essay "Painting as a Pastime," Churchill explained how his easel and oils had become a source of personal tranquility because the canvas was an outlet for his risk-accepting tendencies. "The first quality that is needed is Audacity," he explained. "There really is no time for the deliberate approach."

CHURCHILL FELT PAINTING'S "POWER" not just as artist but also as subject. In 1954, the British Parliament unveiled a portrait of Churchill painted by Graham Sutherland for his eightieth birthday that Churchill characterized as combining "force with candour."

The words were a veiled criticism. Privately Churchill hated the painting, which he said made him appear "half-witted." He had the portrait banished to his basement, and it was never seen again. In 1978, his widow, Lady Churchill, revealed that at some point before his death, she secretly had it burned in the middle of the night.

With a quick look at the painting, one can see why. In a tight-fitting three-piece morning suit, Churchill is depicted as rotund and uncomfortable, a caricature of a frail and irritable old man. The problem with the painting was not that it was so bad, but that it was so accurate, and it likely

*The portrait of Sir Winston
Churchill by Graham Sutherland,
1954. It was later destroyed at
Lady Churchill's instruction.*
(ZUMA PRESS, INC./ALAMY STOCK PHOTO)

clashed with how Churchill and his wife wanted the world to think of him.
But Sutherland, as a modernist artist, was instinctively committed to "set
down what he saw," as one of his obituarists put it.

In writing this book, we too wanted to set down what we saw. And
Churchill's vain rejection of Sutherland's realism is a fitting metaphor for
the disconnect between how leaders think of themselves, how followers
memorialize them, and the starker realities. This can be hard and discom-
forting as often fact and fiction bleed into one another. Moments in time,
such as paintings, statues, and speeches, too easily become a way of interpreting leaders, despite the fact that such symbols hardly reflect what the
individual person was or could ever be.

In reality, what we most remember Churchill for—his leadership—is as
much a product of a myth we have created and continue to sustain as it is
the undoubtedly extraordinary, yet more complex and disputed, reality of
the man he was.

Still, Winston Spencer Churchill has become a name synonymous with
wartime leadership. In much the same way that Einstein is the paradigm of
genius, people speak of Churchill's leadership in similarly hyperbolic
terms. Even those who knew of his painting skill couldn't help but relate it
to his leadership; art historian Sir Ernst Gombrich once credited Churchill's

painting, and its role in preserving his sanity, with helping to "save Western Civilization."

And yet Churchill's record was hardly consistent and only occasionally deserving of such hyperbole. It was audacity that made him effective as a painter and became the hallmark of his leadership, but how well it served him depended greatly on the particulars of the situation. Churchill's audacity gave him the courage to fight rather than negotiate terms with a seemingly invincible Nazi Germany, but periodically also resulted in some disastrous forays, such as at Gallipoli.

And that famous wartime audacity also made for a far less effective peacetime leader. During his second tenure as prime minister, Churchill bungled vital efforts for bilateral talks with Russia concerning nuclear weapons, and far too much of his administration's energy was taken up deciding who should be anointed as his successor. Attributes that had been essential to his wartime leadership could not be readily transformed to the new realities of postwar Britain. Nonetheless, over time the legacy of his bold successes would eclipse his audacious failures, and his record as a wartime leader relegated his pastime of painting to become a mere footnote in a storied career.

Like our remembrance of Churchill, our thirteen profiles reveal a disconnect between the ideal of leadership we're often led to believe and the reality of how it occurs. Through our exploration of this baker's dozen of famous leaders, we were reminded regularly of how we all, authors included, tend toward the static ideal of a leader, hesitant to grapple with the more complicated reality.

BOOKS THAT PROFILE A collection of leaders—politicians, generals, CEOs, etc.—will at this point typically try to answer the question: What did they have in common?

In our case, all of our leaders could fairly be characterized as effective in their own contexts, although radically different in their styles, dispositions, and personalities. In fact, it was impossible to distill their effectiveness into a formula for success, even within a single genre. What constitutes effective leadership in one setting or with one group of followers may well produce poor results in another. A single trait—or indeed the bundle of traits that make up any person—can help produce radically different outcomes, depending on the winds of history, the particulars of that situation, the resources available to the leader, and so on.

We came to call this tendency, to seek that holy grail of effective leader traits, the "Formulaic Myth," our first of three related myths surrounding leadership. The Formulaic Myth reflects our desire to tame leadership into a static checklist, notwithstanding the reality that leadership is intensely contextual and always dependent upon particular circumstances that change from moment to moment and from place to place. Throughout the pages of this book are case studies and stories of important leader achievements, but each of them makes sense only in their particular context, and they defy our efforts to generalize across their varying circumstances.

Martin Luther's celebrated posting of the Ninety-five Theses, for example, highlights this tendency to neglect the role of context. Putting aside whether or not the nailing of paper onto a church door actually occurred (and it appears unlikely), the theses were not in and of themselves so important. Luther thought they would be ephemera; they were poorly written, and the original copies were thrown in the trash, lost to history. What was important was the timing of the event, and its alignment with the readiness of others to deem Luther as the leader uniquely responsive to the pulse of the moment.

Luther managed to poke his finger at the Church at just the right time, when it had debased itself by commercializing faith through the sale of indulgences. And his ideas found ready-made audiences who were already convinced by his arguments. The Ninety-five Theses were audacious but not revolutionary, the product of a period of fervent piety and intellectual curiosity in Europe. One must look before and after the epochal, and perhaps imaginary, posting of the theses to really understand the context of Luther's leadership.

In effect, Luther's theses were a lit match in a dry forest. Luther knew he was being controversial, and potentially incendiary—but he had no way of knowing that a gale-force wind would come along and carry his little flame across an entire continent. Luther was courageous and intelligent, but those qualities wouldn't have become legendary had they not been accentuated by the particular dynamics of Wittenberg in 1517.

This question of timing is often overlooked. What we call "leadership" is often some combination of the leader's actions, along with serendipity or other contextual factors that make for a positive result. Deciding to "do a Luther" is unlikely to lead to a similarly memorable outcome—most of us would simply be branded a crazed monk.

All in all, our leaders are separated not only by time and place, but also by what kind of leadership style would make them effective in their specific roles and place in time, moment, and framework. And yet too often we revert to vague assessments of "strong" or "moral" leaders, as though those things consist of formulas to be replicated in diverse contexts. Thatcher and King, for instance, though both undeniably strong leaders, offered wholly different kinds of day-to-day leadership in order to be effective. Lee became the "Marble Man" as a young cadet at West Point because he so closely adhered to the leadership formula prescribed to him by the US Army. But at the very moment it mattered most, that checklist proved insufficient.

Another problem with treating leadership like a checklist of successful leaders' traits is that we sometimes miss the complete picture. Chanel was inspirationally glamorous, but that only mattered to the extent that she also spent countless hours in her studio. Tubman was indeed brave, but that bravery would have been short-lived if not for her basic tactical competence.

Furthermore, to the extent that leader traits do contribute to successful leadership, they are often not portrayed accurately. For instance, Lee was held up as a paragon of decision making despite the fact that he abdicated the most strategic and ethical decision of his lifetime. And even if we're more truthful in depicting a leader's traits, the honest depiction of what was effective is often not the same as what we hold up as desirable.

For instance, you might fairly critique both Chanel and Disney as being imperious. And yet without the sort of perfectionist mania that was at the core of their abrasive styles, neither would have been as creative as they were. And it was this very creativity that inspired Walt's animators to work for him, and why Chanel's employees came flocking back to her after her fifteen-year hiatus. Chanel and Disney were founders of companies whose success was built on compelling brands, yet the symbols they promoted— the warm Uncle Walt and haughty socialite Chanel—were at odds with the day-to-day realities of their grating micromanagement. Often what we call "good" and "bad" traits are an irreducible mix that somehow add up to effectiveness.

Robespierre and Zarqawi were psychological outliers at best, and yet their unique personas and dogged pursuit of their worldviews allowed them to be seen by their followers as purists. That purism in turn meant that they became the centerpiece of their respective movements, despite the covert, often nondescript realities of their daily existence. We can see clearly—but still look past—the awkward reality that effective leaders often have traits that most leadership guides would either spurn or not even see fit to discuss.

The real problem with the Formulaic Myth is that we neglect the reality that leadership is dynamic and must be modulated from situation to situation. Consider King, for instance. Taken as a whole, his choices to go to jail or not were logically inconsistent. King couldn't always be "resolute" or "practical," he had to be a bit of both at different moments. He constantly sought to discern what his followership and his mission required of him, and as a result found himself in constant tension with the very movement he led. At each of these moments, no matter which attribute he chose to exhibit, or which role he chose to play, some in the civil rights movement viewed it as the wrong choice.

This first essential flaw in the mythology of leadership is our quest for something that can be boiled down to a prescriptive theory, or an equation with fixed coefficients. This is a sticky tendency both because this is how we see the world and because leaders seem to matter so greatly. Plutarch taught that we should seek to *emulate* effective leaders, which necessarily implies a need to put a finger on the recipe of success.

But the mythology goes deeper than our quest for a formula of leadership. Then, as now, we believe in the special and peculiar difference that leaders make in creating desirable outcomes. And this too is more myth than reality.

COPIES OF PLUTARCH'S *LIVES* adorn few bedside tables today, but in the nineteenth century they were ubiquitous. At its peak, sales of the *Lives* in America were second only to the Bible, and the authoritative edition through this period was edited by Oxford scholar Arthur Hugh Clough, who published his full translation in 1859. Clough was good friends with Scotsman Thomas Carlyle, a linkage that is not surprising once you are familiar with Carlyle's dubious contribution to historiography.

Carlyle's 1841 book, *On Heroes, Hero-Worship and the Heroic in History*, codified the long-standing idea that history's arc is bent by the discrete actions of singular men with particular traits. Indeed, it was Carlyle who coined the term "great man," born out of his now-famous claim that "the history of the world is but the biography of great men."

Carlyle was concerned that strong, character-driven leadership was in decline. *On Heroes*, a survey of history's notables, began as a series of lectures. In the first four he profiled a god (Odin), a prophet (Muhammad), two wordsmiths (Shakespeare and Dante), and a priest (Martin Luther). For his readers, Carlyle sought to make the idea of the heroic persona intoxicating, collapsing the intervening millennia and making leaders of yesteryear feel relevant and exciting. But in doing so he also distorted the role of "great men" in determining the course of history.

The myth of the "great man" theory is, of course, patently patriarchal. Historical records are dominated by such "great men," and it's only recently that this trend has begun to become more balanced. Still, not even all Great Man leaders in history were men, and Cleopatra and Joan of Arc are classic counterexamples, as was Margaret Thatcher within our list. Nonetheless, the gender imbalance in leadership is both disturbing and unhealthy, and has deep roots in the history of leadership.

Recent indicators show how far we still have to go. For example, it is not surprising that there were more men than women among the CEOs of the S&P 1500 in 2015. But it is disconcerting to learn that there were more men named John than there were women. And there is ample data to suggest that gender inequality is counterproductive to firms and to society as a whole. Studies have shown a relationship between gender diversity and organizational preference. As with much of the research on leadership, this is generally a matter of correlation, and not causation, but it seems clear that organizations with more female senior leaders might be at an advantage. A range of plausible explanations has been offered as to why.

Some studies suggest that organizations with more women leaders are higher performing because women have higher emotional intelligence, which improves the general health of interpersonal relationships and the firm as a whole. If this is true, it is rarely recognized as such. In a 2015 McKinsey study, a female business leader offered a simpler explanation for why diverse organizations might be more efficacious: "Women executives have to be at least twice as good as their male counterparts to get to that level."

Gender bias is but one of a handful of factors in which we think of leadership as being embedded in personal attributes, behaviors, and traits. Evidence suggests how flippant and superficial people can be in rationalizing what leaders should ideally look like. Study after study shows that one's leadership opportunities are a function of gender, height, and even face width. Six hundred years after Zheng He was selected as admiral, in part because his facial features prophesied loyalty to his emperor, it's a reminder that not too much has changed.

Still other studies show how, when people respond to the innocuous and neutral request to "draw an effective leader," their sketch typically reflects male features, even when a woman is holding the pencil. These stereotypes seem to be decreasing, and vary among cultures, but they nonetheless remain prevalent.

It seems clear that the problem of gender disparity in leadership positions is at least partly due to our leader-centric ways of thinking. But it is only one of many toxic effects of this deeply entrenched approach to leadership. Great man theory, as the name would suggest, encourages people to become great individuals, rather than encouraging a whole organization to become great together. Great man theory suggests that it's more about the attributes of the single leader than the attributes of the system; more about the "I" than the "we."

The lens of Carlyle's great man theory is not only too focused on the leader, its rose coloring also introduces romantic and myopic distortions. We tend to embellish the leader we want to remember, not the one who was. Rather than a real-time recording, their legacy is more a canvas upon which we can paint over those details we feel would be better left out of the historical record. This biased form of tunnel vision focused on the leader, neglecting all that surrounds her, was our second prevailing myth of leadership, which we termed the "Attribution Myth."

The Attribution Myth misrepresents leadership as little more than a process directed by the leader and, in this view, outcomes are attributable mostly to that leader. We see this myth in action when we adjudicate what success and failure should be laid at leaders' feet, and when leaders' followers demand too much of them. As a result, our typical framing of leadership neglects the many other factors embedded in the leadership ecosystem. We overstate the influence of individual leaders, and neglect that the real agency in leadership is bound up in a system of followers.

Accounts of Thatcher's leadership during her premiership often implied that she led as though her hand was at the tiller of a ship, steering as she pleased. But Thatcher was less a hand on the tiller and more a star on the horizon, suggesting a general course to steer for a ship being buffeted by a stormy sea. She stood for a vision that was always kept blurry enough that it might just as well have been over the horizon.

Moreover, Thatcher's vision was meaningless in the absence of a British parliamentary system, which illustrates the significance of the institutional framework that envelops the leader. Leadership is never about the capacity and impact of a single person. And to be judged fairly, leadership styles must be viewed not just at a specific time but also in a particular framework. The context of an enabling institution is often necessary to substantiate leadership.

Both Martin Luther and Martin Luther King Jr., for instance, were selected by and encapsulated within institutions that enabled their rise and their effectiveness. Luther joined the Catholic clergy as a pious believer whose devotion to his church pushed him to reform what he saw as decrepit. His failed attempt to reform from within allowed him to reposition himself as a leader independent of the Catholic Church. Martin Luther King Jr. emerged as a leader in a civil rights movement that was already well under way. Lee rose through the ranks of the US Army, Tweed maneuvered his way to the top of the Tammany machine, Zarqawi rose on the fringes of a burgeoning movement of violent jihadists, Tubman became a hero of the abolitionist movement, and Robespierre was one of many politicians striving to shape revolutionary France. Even two of the more iconoclastic of our leaders—Einstein and Bernstein—needed their respective fields to give meaning to their frontier-expanding contributions. It seems obvious that a leader is meaningless when considered alone, and yet this is often how we see and talk about leadership.

At its extreme, and with enough time, the Attribution Myth can grow to become a form of hero worship. In the case of Zheng He, the myth has become more useful to modern Chinese national identity than the man himself. Still, we chase the hero behind the patina of dubious history, and are intrigued by his Hercules-like body proportions. In such cases, we intentionally live with the gap between myth and reality not just because a flimsy historical record gives the excuse, but also because we like to do so.

In a different age and context, we caught the myth escaping the man when Colin Powell made his speech at the United Nations referring to Abu Musab al-Zarqawi a full twenty-one times. Without seeking to, the United States helped solidify the threat of Zarqawi's leadership to its own interests in the Middle East, and in turn amplified Zarqawi's ability to project himself as the most serious leader opposing the American-led coalition in Iraq.

The myth of the standout hero is almost always embellished, and is certainly an incomplete picture. Consider our pair of geniuses, who remind us that it is all too easy to overattribute efficacy to the "lone genius." But genius has both individual *and* social components, and its form and effect are shaped by the surrounding contexts.

These first two myths, that we tend to make our view of leadership too formulaic and attribute too much cause and effect to the leader, are not new ideas. Indeed, these myths have framed much of the debate about how leadership works for the last half century. And yet these debates remain unresolved.

Perhaps this is because there is a deeper aspect of the mythology, one we've not yet paid enough attention to.

CHURCHILL'S FIRST NATIONAL RADIO address as prime minister was on the topic of war. "Our heavy bombers," he reported, "are striking nightly at the patterns of German mechanized power, and have already inflicted serious damage upon the oil refineries, on which the Nazi effort to dominate the world directly depends." Churchill was characteristically audacious despite the fact that few outside observers believed Britain could or would stay the course of war.

In this 1940 speech, and in the subsequent and more memorable recordings of Churchill's voice crackling through British radio sets (such as "their finest hour" and "we shall fight them on the beaches"), Churchill's aim was to inspire a downtrodden people. Historians who heard these speeches in real time with their own ears might even struggle to distinguish the legend from memory. One wrote seventy-two years later: "What he did, almost more in my recollection of my nineteen-year-old state of mind, was to produce a euphoria of irrational belief in ultimate victory."

Churchill's unique delivery held a lingering hint of a childhood speech impediment. Since 1897, he had been seeing doctors to get a diagnosis, and at one point even asked a doctor to do surgery on his tongue, which Churchill self-diagnosed as being "tied." Accordingly, he toiled to resolve his lisp by repeating phrases like "The Spanish ships I cannot see for they are not in sight." He was so attentive to his enunciation that when writing his speeches he deliberately avoided such sibilant s sounds. The work had paid off, and he came to move Britain through the power of his spoken words.

Fascinated by the power of oratory, Plutarch paired Greek orator Demosthenes and the more straitlaced Roman statesman Cicero. Like Churchill, Demosthenes had a speech impediment that, according to Plutarch, produced an "inarticulate and stammering pronunciation." Demosthenes subjected himself to a strict personal regimen to improve his oral delivery. Rather than tongue-twisters, Demosthenes took to talking with pebbles in his mouth and reciting speeches while running up hills. His work also paid off, and he joined Cicero in swaying important audiences with his words.

Today, when leadership is discussed, we usually purport to be discussing what leaders do, rather than what they say, as if this were a more clear-eyed approach. This brings us to the third myth, the "Results Myth," capturing the falsehood that the objective results of the leader's activity are more important than her words or style or appearance. The truth is that when we look closely, we see leadership as much in what our leaders symbolize as in what they accomplish.

For each of our heroes, their particular actions took on broader significance because the results they achieved resonated with group values. Tubman's leadership, for example, was rooted in her impressive track record of success, but she became more broadly influential when other abolitionists recalled her story, mystified as they were that she accomplished what she did. In recalling that the actual number of slaves she freed was a small percentage of the total who escaped in the 1850s, we're reminded that her leadership was less in the tangible results she achieved, and more in the expectations she defied and the symbolism she upheld.

Our zealots were similarly effective as leaders because of what they stood for, not just because of what they did. Robespierre is remembered as a populist, and yet it was in the moments when he stood alone, in opposition to the majority of his own Jacobin allies, that he secured his reputation as "The Incorruptible." And Zarqawi, when he was able to, led in person and on the ground. But these behaviors themselves were less important than the values that their actions communicated to their networks of followers, most of whom would never meet the men they were following.

Both Robespierre and Zarqawi rode a wave more than they summoned it. Their adherence to principle, especially when compared with other leaders with whom each was vying for authority, allowed them to bind the energy of their movements—until, of course, their moments passed and the energy they'd once harnessed crushed them. Both of our zealots were more symbols of their movements than they were decision makers within them, and each emerged as a leader because he reflected a particular set of values.

Consider also the moment that Disney convinced his animators to buy into the production of *Snow White*. As he acted out what was to become his most important film, he wasn't just professing his own vision, he also embodied the expectations that his animators had set for themselves when they made the decision to come work for him.

To enable his rise and his corruption, Tweed had to deliver on his promises of jobs, a new city charter, or even bribes; such results mattered. Yet what mattered more was how his constituents saw him—a view based as much in the dynamics of power and the sway of identity as the hard currency of a job. When Tweed's neighborhood constituents voted him back into his state senate seat when every other Tammany man lost their election in the fall of 1871, it was not simply because he was more effective than the others.

With Chanel, we encountered a leader whose entire brand was based on the self-reinforcing pull of her persona. While her craftsmanship was important, the success of her company had less to do with the smell of a perfume or the decadence of a fabric than with women's desire to be more like Coco. In these instances, leadership was only in a deferred sense about driving results.

Martin Luther King Jr. is rightly remembered for his rhetoric; "I Have a Dream" is perhaps the most memorable speech given in twentieth-century America. Yet we learn as much about leadership from the silence that swept over the crowd—before he spoke—as we do from the indelible mark his words left during and after the speech. He could give that sort of rousing speech not so much because it was inside of him, but equally because it was what was expected of him as a symbol of the civil rights movement.

Or consider Bernstein's symphony, wherein the orchestra "makes" the music, while the conductor "makes" none. Nonetheless, the conductor is still thought of as the leader of the pack, and he is the person whose form and shape audiences are most interested in. As the music becomes more complex, the orchestra becomes increasingly dependent on the conductor as a coordinator, but also more dependent on the cues of one another for nuance and feeling. Increased complexity still means that the music is made from diverse elements to produce the whole. Nonetheless, it remains simpler and more satisfying to see the power to make sound and silence as contained within a single person.

In reality, the complexity at work means that not only are both the "genius" conductor and his collaborators beneficiaries of one another, where the leader and followers are wrapped together in a tangled relationship, but that the conductor holds special meaning for both the audience and his orchestra. That was why, in Bernstein's last ever performance with the Boston Symphony Orchestra, the orchestra could continue playing without him, but it was still set on having him back on the podium so as to continue interpreting the music through him. The iconic conductor was a conduit for the players' and audience's sense of completeness, solidifying the feeling that "something is right in the world . . . something we can trust, that will never let us down."

The prevalence of these three myths is hardly revelatory, and academic theorists have been suggesting elements of them for decades. But somehow their existence is ignored, discussion of them is confined to the kinds of literature that do not make for light reading. Volume after volume, and study after study, have tried to steer us away from individual leader traits and toward relationships among networks of followers. And yet there remains a wide gap between how we think of leadership and how it actually works. Why is this?

It was in hindsight, after we finished writing most of this book, that we found an unexpected answer to this essential question. And the clue was found, of all places, in our approach to the book itself.

IT IS DIFFICULT to step back from Plutarch's masterpiece and see his "top ten" list of qualities one should emulate, for he left no such capstone for how to be an effective leader. His goal was not to offer a programmatic lens for leaders to take away, and Plutarch generally had the good sense to refrain from distilling his observations into generalizations. Instead, Plutarch hoped that his readers would explore how they might emulate his leaders and the dimensions of their virtue. Accordingly, Plutarch's essential question was "What was his character?"

This is where we deviated sharply from Plutarch's method. Our interest was not in the character of leaders, but in leadership itself. Our original research question was different: simply, "How did he or she lead?" We reminded ourselves of this essential question often, asking this of each other as we turned page after page of each biography and scanned each archive. To ask "How did they lead?" feels uncontroversial, with the ring of a familiar shorthand. However, over time, we came to see that very question as nonsensical, itself a reflection of the very myths we sought to explore.

Our question was guilty of suggesting that an answer could be found in the leader, divorced from its relevant context. The more sensible questions, which we came to only through repeated exploration of the wrong question, were "Why did they emerge as a leader?" or, more specifically, "What was it about the situation that made this style of leadership effective?"

In effect, we were our own proof of the stickiness of the great man theory, and the challenge of moving to a more practical concept of leadership. Not only did we fall into the trap of asking the wrong questions, but we also tried to survey a 360-degree landscape of leadership through thirteen discrete portraits. Wittingly, but unable to resist, we were violating the obvious: that revisiting Plutarch's biographies gave credence only to the myths we sought to debunk.

The lesson for all of us who fall into such patterns is that reconciling the mythology of leadership must do more than beat the drum of these age-old myths and dig the grave of the Great Man. As such, the critical question becomes not just why is the great man theory so toxic, but also, what makes it so intoxicating?

There are obvious reasons that Great Man thinking is so sticky. As we learn from Shakespeare, our attention for narrative drama is renowned and familiar. As authors, we know all too well that the pages of a good tale turn faster than those of analytical theory. Most students of leadership prefer to get their lessons from the colorful pages of a CEO autobiography than the dry analysis of leadership literature.

The Great Man also reminds us of our faith in individual free will. For good reason, the Enlightenment ideals upon which the Western world is based insist that individuals have intrinsic worth, and are rational and free-thinking beings, with the capacity to shape their own lives. We think the same of our leaders, and hope that they too have these qualities in abundance. This assumption is too readily translated into the belief that it is individual leaders who make things happen.

Beyond a taste for narrative and belief in our own causality, we also have a preference for simplicity. Boiling things down to discrete action by a certain cast of prime actors is more relatable, and makes attributing success and blame easier. Reductionist explanations are somehow more satisfying than the complex, estranging, but usually more accurate accounts.

Reality is complicated and even boring, and that mundane messiness can be unsatisfying. Life is more interesting and pleasing either when it is simplified or, in the other direction, sensational. And we'll sooner accept the simple or sensational explanation over the accurate one.

These sticky ways of thinking mean that it is difficult to make the Great Man of history move aside in favor of more clear-eyed realities. Efforts to recast our thinking falter. So rather than turning away from these tendencies and continuing to battle these myths—which only deepens the mythology—we would do well to find a way to be more accepting of, aligned with, this awkward reality.

Ten

REDEFINING LEADERSHIP

*As soon as the soldiers saw him they saluted him in their
Macedonian dialect, and took up their shields, and striking
them with their pikes, gave a great shout, inviting the enemy
to come on, for now they had a leader.*

—PLUTARCH, "LIFE OF EUMENES"

As France's Revolution raged on, her king and queen executed, Europe watched in horror, concerned that the virus would spread and threaten the monarchies upon which order rested. By 1792, armies massed on France's borders, and many judged the revolutionaries and their cause to be doomed.

Miraculously, they were not. Maximilien Robespierre and his fellow Jacobin ideologues were able to maintain French sovereignty and continue their experiment to forge a new society. For many, it is a lesson in the power of zealous commitment to a cause—and the influence of individual leaders.

But there was more to the story, for defending France was not solely an ideological exercise. That feat also required effective French cannon and musket fire, which depended on the availability and quality of gunpowder. Eighteenth-century gunpowder required saltpeter, which France had previously sourced from India. But in 1763, France had lost its Indian colony to the British, who now possessed this explosive advantage over their historic rivals. That left France needing to devise its own domestic saltpeter production program.

The French were in luck. In 1777, a chemist-turned-inventor, Antoine-Laurent de Lavoisier, wrote a book on how to establish such a program, and, after the kingdom became a republic, his leadership of a nationalized system of saltpeter mining enabled the young republic to fight back. Lavoisier perfected gunpowder production, refining the optimal proportions, process, and equipment, and ultimately increased output fivefold. His innovations—and the scientific culture they engendered—helped France survive its Revolution.

Yet three months before Robespierre's beheading, Lavoisier also fell victim to the guillotine's blade. The revolutionaries were generally suspicious of scientists, many of whom were thought to be aligned with the royalist elites (in a fit of anti-intellectualism, they even had the Royal Academy of Sciences closed). The presiding judge at Lavoisier's execution condemned France's heroic chemist, summarily stating: "*La Republique n'a pas besoin de savants*"—most simply translated, "The Republic has no need for geniuses." Joseph-Louis Lagrange, Lavoisier's friend and a famous mathematician, wrote sadly: "It took them only an instant to cut off that head, but France may not produce another like it in a century."

While the zealotry of Robespierre and his compatriots is often credited with fueling the Revolution's momentum, tearing apart the ancien régime and propelling France into the modern era, gunpowder was essential to defending her territorial integrity while the Revolution unfolded. This leaves one to wonder whether it was scientists like Lavoisier, rather than politicians like Robespierre, who enabled the Republic to remain intact.

It is tempting to simplify complex dilemmas by invoking such a binary, in this case debating whether it was the science of gunpowder or the art of leadership that saved the Republic. Such dynamics reflect our preference for thinking about the world in either-or dichotomies: science versus art, elitism versus populism, and so on. These false choices abound, and they better reflect our way of making sense of our complex world than they do the reality of how that world operates.

Such approaches are generally inconclusive, and can be frustratingly cyclical, or circular. For example, even if we were to pick a side and credit, for instance, the leadership of the Revolution that saved the day, we'd still be left with a puzzle. After all, the deaths of Lavoisier and Robespierre were gory reminders that while the French Revolution was led by such elite intellectuals, it also killed off intellectual leaders whom it saw as threatening.

It seems clear here that the false choice is unresolvable—followers struggle to beat back strong leaders just as leaders struggle to operate without followers. For instance, and despite all the bloodletting by French revolutionaries, their budding new republic morphed into a dictatorship led by Napoleon Bonaparte, who, having stamped out much of the ancien régime's First and Second Estates, introduced an era that emphasized elitism to an even greater extent than what had existed under Louis XVI.

Napoleon's emergence was partially an answer to the crisis of legitimacy created by the king's beheading, and the inevitable question that followed: What comes next for France? Those left kingless had a newfound opportunity to release the shackles of all that we find toxic with the great man theory. Yet cutting off the king's head is relatively easy compared to dispersing power from the high walls of the castles into the surrounding streets and houses. So what happens when followers are left with their heads to determine what kind of system they want to live in?

We can look for that answer by turning the clocks back even further, to an earlier beheading on the other side of the English Channel.

KING CHARLES I'S FORCES were defeated in the English Civil War in 1645 and again in 1649, when he was condemned and executed for high treason. The philosopher John Locke (1632–1704) lived through the eleven years after Charles I was beheaded, during which England was without a monarch. This period, called the Interregnum (literally, "between kings"), grappled with how authority is made and in whom it resides. Although Thomas Hobbes was the first political theorist to analyze the war, it was John Locke who addressed the question of what came next for England.

Locke's magnum opus, *Two Treatises of Government*, concluded that obedience to leaders at all costs was absurd, dangerous, and ultimately a moral failure by followers. After all, if the English Republic was still able to run itself without a king, then, Locke believed, the real source of authority must be in the followers who continued to function in spite of losing their king.

Locke came to see that it was the followers who must decide if the authority of their ruler is legitimate, and that this legitimacy was rooted in the ruler providing practical things that they needed, like security for their property. As such, Locke effectively repositioned the leader—specifically, the king—as the servant who stewards resources for the followers, his subjects. Locke's *Treatises* shaped the following 350 years of Western political leadership by making a powerful assertion that we do not follow leaders because we have no choice; rather, we empower them because they provide things that we collectively require.

While Locke's writings were a significant shift of emphasis toward follower agency, they stopped short of displacing "trait-based" ways of thinking about leadership. Since the days of Plutarch, such theories carried the assumption that effective leaders could be studied to discover which of their traits led to success. In turn, the theory went, understanding these traits was useful in understanding who should become a leader.

But by the nineteenth century, the inadequacies of these trait-based approaches to leadership were becoming apparent. Even contemporary critics of Carlyle's *On Heroes* objected that such works encouraged the "beating pulse and reddened cheek" of the would-be leader, as one reviewer put it. Carlyle's detractors saw him as encouraging people to emulate "painted idols," rather than real people. This early critique held promise for liberating an outdated concept of leadership and including a more sophisticated understanding of the power of followers, but it was slow in coming.

The first real competitor to trait-based leadership was introduced in the mid-twentieth century by behavioral theorists, for whom leadership involved an education; they insisted that leaders were made, not born. On that assumption, leadership was less intrinsic to a person's character and was more about learned behavior, and therefore more accessible.

Not surprisingly, it was about then, when the Great Man seemed to be losing some of his luster, that would-be leaders stopped reading Plutarch.

This transition also coincided with the post–World War II boom in industrialization, which created strong demand for management of factory workers. In this new reality, leaders could now be fashioned from whole cloth. Also not surprising, this period saw the rise of a for-profit "leadership industry" to train and develop leaders. In turn, the view that leadership could be taught only helped spur the idea that it was a learnable set of skills. And while thinking about leadership as a set of learned behaviors was democratizing in its implications, it ultimately did little to divert attention away from the individual leaders themselves.

The shift toward "followership" didn't occur until the 1970s, when leadership theory took another major step with the arrival of "servant leadership." Fittingly, those who preach and practice servant leadership see power in the system, not in themselves, and they condemn the commanding pull of the strong man as exploitative. Instead, for servant leaders, it's the bottom of the pyramid that matters most. Events and outcomes are made possible by a particular group of people, and it is the leader's job to supply them with whatever they need and to cultivate the environment most conducive to collective success.

More recently, leadership theorists have begun to speak of a "post-leadership" age—one in which systems, rather than individuals, enable us to organize efficiently. In her book *The End of Leadership*, for example, Barbara Kellerman writes of the "arc of history" as being "recent incarnations of the devolution of power and influence and the diminishment of authority."

A much-cited example of decentralized change was the 2011 Arab Spring, where the protesting self-immolation of a sole street vendor and the promise of social media were said to propel bottom-up revolution. In Egypt, the thirty-year incumbent dictator, Hosni Mubarak, was dethroned, only to be replaced by the Muslim Brotherhood's Mohamed Morsi, who was then swept aside after fourteen months in a military coup led by Abdel Fattah el-Sisi. Not unlike the aftermath of revolutionary France, it was a disappointing cycle for the little man seeking power to drive change.

To be sure, there are moments when grassroots activism appears to validate that people can have an impact without a single, unifying leader. Yet there are just as many examples of people emerging as leaders for no other reason *but that they appear strong*. And if this is supposedly the age of the follower, why do management bookshelves still groan with the weight of how-to books on leadership? Why do we still put our faith in strong men who promise us patently more than they can deliver?

In 2014, British politician Boris Johnson published *The Churchill Factor: How One Man Made History*, commemorating the fiftieth anniversary of Churchill's death. Johnson offers Churchill up as the "crowbar of destiny" who placed himself in the wheels of the "Nazi train" rolling across Europe.

For all its merits, Johnson's book still espouses the great man theory in our supposed post-leadership age. Johnson is unabashed in his adoration of Churchill, but he is not alone, and the implicit suggestion contained in so many biographies of Churchill is that his leadership made all the difference to the outcome of the war.

So somehow the Great Man remains alive and well. Despite all the theorizing and progress in enabling followers, we're still wont to think of leadership as an attribute of the individual rather than the system. If we are to move past the mythology of leadership, we need to address why it is that despite much digging, the Great Man theory has yet to lie down in its grave.

CHURCHILL WAS AWARDED the Nobel Prize a decade after he led the Allies to victory over Nazi Germany, but he did not attend his 1953 award ceremony. Instead, Lady Churchill stood and curtsied to the Swedish king, who ceremoniously handed her the small stack of items that constitutes a Nobel Prize, topped by the medal itself, cast as a solid-silver mold of Churchill's 1937 book, *Great Contemporaries*, reflecting the fact that Churchill's Nobel Prize was for literature, of all things. Enscribed across that silver book was the award's citation of his "mastery of historical and biographic description as well as for brilliant oratory in defending exalted human values."

It was both ironic and telling that one of the twentieth century's most lionized leaders received the Nobel Prize in Literature, and his "brilliant" oration. It was ironic because of Churchill's speech impediment as a child. And it was telling because it underlines how often leadership is rooted in communication and narrative.

Churchill mastered communication not just through oration but also in writing, and even writing on oration. In one of his earliest essays, "The Scaffolding of Rhetoric," Churchill wrote that "the climax of oratory is reached by a rapid succession of waves of sound and vivid pictures." Here, as in the French Revolution, we again find art and science, but now they are colliding rather than being presented as a false choice. For Churchill, rhetoric had a tangible and accessible science to it, but it also held a less tangible, inaccessible human dimension. Indeed, Churchill makes clear that it is insufficient to understand oration either in scientific or solely human terms:

> So detailed and disconnected an examination of the structure favours the impression that rhetoric is to be regarded as an artificial science. . . . Experience shows that this conclusion would be incorrect. . . . The subtle art of combining the various elements that separately mean nothing and collectively mean so much in an harmonious proportion is known to a very few.

Bernstein had a similar tendency to speak of the intermingling of art and science in music, and it was clear that he thought about the scientific dimension of music's appeal, and saw music as a vehicle for communicating human ideals. As a composer, Bernstein believed that it was his job to master this juxtaposition between the hidden science and the more palpable craftsmanship.

An example of this science-in-music is found in syncopation, or the use of off-rhythm beats, which research suggests is part of that intangible thing that makes certain styles of music particularly compelling. "So with one syncopation and another, it turns into a pretty hectic boxing match with sudden lefts and rights hitting you where and when you least expect them," Bernstein explained in one of his TV appearances, "and that, plus the insistent repetition of the beat, explains why you want to get up and dance when you hear this kind of music."

Being in the presence of an effective leader often feels akin to the pull of beautiful music or a rousing speech. We are inspired by the charismatic leader even when we can't put a finger on why. We can't quite claim that the answer is "science," for it is a blunt tool that still provides few meaningful answers to the existential questions of leadership. Nor is it acceptable to chock it up to the magical ether of charisma.

Trying to solve this puzzle feels like a doomed journey. It's akin to asking for the single reason that the French Republic did not fall in the face of foreign aggression. As with Bernstein's syncopation, or Churchill's rhetoric, perhaps the more powerful answer is to be found in avoiding the false choice and accepting the juxtaposition of two seemingly opposing things.

Such an approach might be useful for reconciling the mythology of leadership. Any number of leadership theories has sought to debunk and dethrone the Great Man, only to find that hordes of followers still kneel before him. Could it be, as with art and science, that choosing between the Great Man and any of his alternatives is a false choice? If so, more rigorous answers in leadership should look toward a third way of understanding its contours.

Fortunately, there are precedents for such an approach. In particular, a subfield of economics recently bridged the gap between its own classic theories and the psychology of how humans actually behave.

ON DECEMBER 8, 2017, Richard Thaler stood at a lectern in Stockholm and accepted the Sveriges Riksbak Prize, popularly known as the Nobel Prize in Economic Sciences. He began lightheartedly: "I've been interested in gravitational waves for a long time . . . ," to audience laughter. More earnestly, he then told them the story of one of his earliest and simplest experiments, involving a dinner party of economists he hosted while in graduate school.

As the party began, he served drinks and a bowl of cashews. But after a while, he removed the nuts so as not to spoil his guests' appetites. To his surprise, the guests thanked him for doing so and were notably happier. This effect is contrary to theory, particularly for a group of economists, for conventional economic theory taught that people prefer to have *more* options, not fewer. But in this case, the opposite was true, in large part because removing the cashews resolved the challenge of self-control.

In the 1990s, neoclassical economics faced many such puzzles, with gaps between how the theory suggested "economic actors" behaved and how real humans actually behaved in practice. For a long while, economics had been rooted in the concept of the "rational actor," who was supposed to behave in predictable ways. For instance, as the theory goes, people respond to a rise in the cost of a good by buying less of it. Yet there is ample evidence that the economic choices of humans often defy this simple and logical principle.

The solution to this disconnect was to bridge and blend the fields of behavioral science and classical economic theory, a marriage that would become known as behavioral economics, and which disrupted the "rational actor" assumptions. This new discipline was immediately valuable for its explanations of why and how people demonstrate seemingly irrational behavior when it comes to decisions as simple as saving for retirement or spending on material goods. The foundational theorists of this field, such as Thaler, Daniel Kahneman, and Amos Tversky, have, since their cashew-rationing days, mapped out systemic cognitive biases that affect decision making, producing a social systems map of how outcomes often don't accord with what conventional economic theory would suggest.

This merging of economics and psychology is both a monumental achievement and an ongoing reformation, whereby the rules of economics are being rewritten to account for how human actors actually behave, instead of holding them to some theoretical and aspirational model. Thaler writes that the problem with classical economic theory was its highly idealized nature, and that the reality is that "we don't play chess like a grandmaster, invest like Warren Buffett, or cook like an Iron Chef. . . . It's more likely that we cook like Warren Buffett (who loves to eat at Dairy Queen)."

One might say the same for theories and myths of leadership. Not only are we incapable of leading like the legend of Churchill; it's not clear that even Churchill was capable of leading like the legend of Churchill. And there are similar disconnects between our theory and our experiences. Take, for example, the simple fact that leadership theory promotes the virtue of humility, and yet narcissists are overrepresented in senior leadership positions.

To understand leadership more fully, we need to accommodate for how it actually occurs. The field of leadership needs a reformation akin to what transpired with economics. More than anything, this would involve leadership theory that better accounts for real human behavior. As with behavioral economics, we need to come to terms with how myths continue to dominate how we think about leaders and leadership.

WHEN SHE ENTERED 10 Downing Street as prime minister for the first time in 1979, Margaret Thatcher read a prayer from St. Francis of Assisi: "Where there is discord, may we bring harmony. Where there is error, may we bring truth. Where there is doubt, may we bring faith. And where there is despair, may we bring hope." Thatcher professed a moral code based on such binaries: "every one of us has a choice between good and evil from which nothing can absolve us."

Thatcher was, of course, a unique leader for a particular moment in British history. Nonetheless, she was dealing with perennial tensions in leadership, such as the desire for simplicity in a complex world, the need for reassurance amid chaos, and our often conflicting desires for both autonomy and strong leadership.

We encounter such contradictions in what we want from leaders because human nature is itself similarly conflicted. Sometimes we are concerned about the collective, but we can be equally and irreconcilably self-regarding. Sometimes we ask for what is fair and reasonable; other times we are driven by more emotional forces. These human dualities are what makes leadership so complex and often so confounding.

And of all the binaries, that which most readily captures human attention is the reality of the present versus the possibility of the future. Thatcher was speaking to this when she recited St. Francis's prayer, highlighting that leadership is less concerned with *past or present* results, and more about *future or expected* results. It is pulled less by what is and more by what could be, either in positive terms of hope or in negative terms of fear. Humans are uniquely adept at obsessing over their future state, and leaders often exploit this tendency to exert the influence they seek.

This was perhaps the only common denominator among our profiles. Many of our leaders were made powerful not so much by what they did, or even by what they said, but by what their followers perceived they had to gain either individually or collectively by buying into what their leader was asking. They stood for the hopes and fears of a future state of being, and their role as leaders was in crafting a visceral sense of the possible.

For example, our zealots served principally as north stars of clarity in chaotic moments. In Zarqawi's case, beneath all the violence and religiosity, the caliphate represented an alternative future for political Islam. For Robespierre, many citizens of the new republic believed that he embodied Rousseau-inspired *vertu*. The ideal itself was unattainable, so the best many could do was to associate with the man thought to be its closest living representative. So too with geniuses like Einstein, who was the most relatable face in the world of physics and stretched the bounds of the knowable to create new possibility.

Our profiles are a reminder that those who emerge as successful leaders are not necessarily those with the best values, or the most comprehensive record of results, but those who cohere with sources of human motivation. This explains why followers might turn their attention to the hollow but optimistic leader, or be pulled by the leader who talks a big game but who holds a weak record. Just as we look to heroes as a symbol of what could be, we look to leaders more generally because we hold out hope for an alternative future, or because we fear a coming threat, and the leader becomes the repository of that hope or the guardian against that fear. This is compelling, and even necessary, since hope and fear are both essential to pulling human society forward.

For all our evolution and progress as a species, mythmaking remains a part of what keeps us going, and we are still easily captured by the symbols that help craft our identity. Myths give us individual and collective meaning. So perhaps we've been frustrated by the mythology of leadership because we've yet to see leadership for what it is: a reflection of what makes us human in the first place.

If so, we would do well to start from square one and revisit our basic definition of leadership.

IN CHAPTER 1, we outlined how leadership is often construed as a process-driven, action-oriented practice, frequently described as the process of influencing a *group* toward some defined *outcome*.

In other words, leadership is typically thought of as something that is executed by the leader, and its effectiveness measured by whether the leader mobilizes the group to achieve the desired result.

But our three myths suggest that this definition is at best incomplete, and possibly just plain wrong. This typical definition quite directly perpetuates the Attribution and Results Myths, giving the leader considerable causal influence and measuring the leader by what he or she achieves in concrete terms. It also offers little to address the deeper complexities of leadership, or even to speak to our typical notions of leadership and the expectations of followers.

For example, consider Robert E. Lee, who became an archetypal model of leadership to many, despite failing in both the morality of his judgment and the outcome of the Civil War. By any objective measure, he was not successful on the basis of his morals or outcomes. Lee would nonetheless become a legendary folk hero by virtue of his style and persona (and a good measure of academically spurious history). If we were serious about the usual results-based definition, Lee wouldn't have stood for more than a century as a paradigm of leadership.

Defining leadership as a process to achieve results makes sense only if you're the leader who is trying to achieve something. For the rest of us, we need something that speaks to why we follow in what are often unusual or surprising ways, decoupled from mere organizational outcomes. Without this, leadership is left with not just a disconnect between theory and reality, but also between what leaders perceive and what their followers experience.

For starters, an improved definition of leadership should at least address our three myths about leadership and account for their corresponding realities:

1. Leadership is contextual and dynamic, and therefore needs to be constantly modulated, not boiled down to a formula.
2. Leadership is more an emergent property of a complex system with rich feedback, and less a one-directional process enacted by a leader.
3. The leader is vitally important to leadership, but not for the reasons we usually ascribe. It is often more about the symbolism, meaning, and future potential leaders hold for their system, and less about the results they produce.

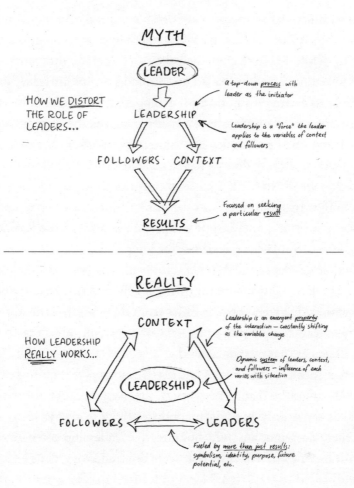

MYTH

HOW WE DISTORT
THE ROLE OF
LEADERS...

LEADER

*a top-down process with
leader as the initiator*

LEADERSHIP

*Leadership is a "force" the leader
applies to the variables of context
and followers*

FOLLOWERS · CONTEXT

RESULTS

*Focused on seeking
a particular result*

REALITY

HOW LEADERSHIP
REALLY WORKS...

CONTEXT

*Leadership is an emergent property
of the interaction — constantly shifting
as the variables change*

*Dynamic system of leaders, context,
and followers — influence of each
varies with situation*

LEADERSHIP

FOLLOWERS ⟷ LEADERS

*Fueled by more than just results:
symbolism, identity, purpose, future
potential, etc.*

If we were to circumscribe these three realities with a more accurate definition, we might say that *leadership is a complex system of relationships between leaders and followers, in a particular context, that provides meaning to its members.* Sometimes that meaning may take the form of driving and achieving results. Other times it will take the form of achieving some sense of understanding, or hope, or identity. But we miss part of what makes leadership powerful if we confine it to just one aspect or the other.*

---

*Psychoanalyst and anthropologist Michael Maccoby expresses similar frustrations that discussing leadership around processes or as a person motivating followers toward end goals will always fall short. Instead, he proposes, "There is only one irrefutable definition of a leader, and that is someone people follow. . . . Leadership always implies a relationship between leader and led, and the relationship exists within a context." Michael Maccoby, *The Leaders We Need: And What Makes Us Follow* (Boston: Harvard Business School Press, 2007), xvi–xvii.

This reframed definition provides fresh perspective on our three myths.

First, it speaks to the Results Myth, and begins to explain why we're so willing to define leadership as the pursuit of specific outcomes, and still look up to leaders who have failed us. Human systems are oddly capable of selecting or tolerating immoral and incompetent leaders because they provide a different kind of meaning elsewhere, such as social identity or ideological affiliation. Leadership, like humanity, is often ends-focused *and* path-dependent. Rarely do we stop to consider why we follow our leaders, and whether we do so for the sense of purpose they provide or the results they can offer. In some situations we think we need a symbol, and in others, a doer. In reality, and despite the preponderance of the Results Myth, neither alone can suffice, at least not for long.

Second, it speaks to the Attribution Myth, and portrays leadership as a network of relationships, while allowing for the fact that leaders still matter greatly within this web. Also, it shifts from the one-directional process of causality to leadership being a property of a system, subject to the vast array of influences that push it around.

Third, it speaks to the Formulaic Myth, and explains quite directly that leadership cannot be made prescriptive, precisely because effective leadership makes sense only in a given context, which is always changing. Not only is there no "right answer," but effective leadership often emerges as a juxtaposition of two behaviors that seem contradictory, thus necessarily it can't be distilled to the "right" kind of leadership. For instance, this helps resolve the puzzle whereby humble and vulnerable leaders can be just as effective as leaders who present as strong and confident, because we're more open to the idea that both sides of this apparent paradox are true.

Finally, this view of leadership also speaks to what makes leadership both so universally necessary and also so confounding. Leaders are necessary because we tend to understand the world through individuals who organize into various structures as a way of fulfilling collective needs. This is particularly important in our current digitial age, for there will still be a unique niche for human learning and organic intelligence, and it is in this enduring sphere that leadership will remain prized.

In sum, this view of leadership expands rather than diminishes leadership; it is something that helps us to make sense of the world, sustains our common identities, and holds hope for a brighter tomorrow. Like leadership itself, our need for such symbols—meaning, identity, hope—is part and parcel of our human nature, which few ever saw as being so simple. Coming to terms with our own complex selves allows us to recognize that leadership too is necessarily difficult and yet endlessly inspiring.

CHANGING HOW WE DEFINE and think about leadership should help to address some of our frustrations with the mythology of leadership and the frequent disconnects between how we talk about it and how we experience it. This new definition also has practical implications for leaders, followers, and those of us who are students of leadership.

As an enabler of a system, leaders should shift their mindset to think of themselves as a node in a network, rather than the top apex of a triangle. As a node, they shift from mere decision maker to a more powerful cultivator, and serve as both a bottom-up servant to enable action and a top-down symbol to motivate and provide for meaning. In this way, leaders need to be retrained and should come to think of themselves as fulfilling both functions.

Moreover, because this network is complex, behaviors must not only be modulated, but they will often straddle both sides of an apparent contradiction. The crux for the leader is in reading the situation and in knowing how and when to modulate based on the particulars of the dynamic.

This aspect of leadership, along with the science of influencing human behavior, explains why leaders do well to pay attention to those things often seen as peripheral to leadership, such as the use of storytelling or even their appearance. If we were to bring more behavioral science to leadership, the legacies and legends of our heroes serve as a useful reminder of why narratives that offer both understanding and mystery can be a powerful and compelling form of influence.

All of this means that leadership is far more difficult than we realize, and that leaders must become more clear-eyed to the burden they've inherited. Leadership is not glamorous or straightforward. It is painful and perplexing, even at its best. Therefore, it is also not for everyone.

The lesson for the follower is not simply to debunk the mythology, but also to understand the lionization and romanticization of our leaders. To this end, the follower should accept the leader's fallibility, and grow more aware of their limitations and our inflated expectations, even as leaders hold immense value as the symbols and custodians of meaning. In this way, followers are better served in pushing information, feedback, and recommendations up to leaders, rather than waiting for decisions and guidance to flow down. In simple terms, followers should operate via a push system rather than a pull system.

One logical extension of this concept is the requirement for followers to practice reverse accountability, or the process of followers' holding leaders accountable. This view of leadership suggests that a leader's operating parameters are often defined by followers, and that the real efficacy in a leadership system lies with the followers. Thus followers should be more willing to shape and confine their leaders' styles.

There are also considerable implications for those in the business of studying leadership and training leaders. Very few of the thirteen people we profiled were trained in any formal way as a leader. Well before the arrival of the modern leadership industry, leaders still found paths to lead in a great variety of contexts. Many simply fell into the role, or were pulled into it. For most, no one could have told them how to prepare for those roles.

But just as this view doesn't imply that leaders are unimportant, it also can't be taken to mean that leaders shouldn't be trained. Rather, it suggests that the training of leaders is still necessary and important, but *how* leaders are trained and developed should be revisited. In particular, leaders shouldn't be given a checklist of attributes. Rather, they should be equipped with an understanding of leadership as a system, see themselves as the enablers of that system, and learn how to adjust their approach based on the needs of that system.

Finally, and most important, there is opportunity for broader reform if we start seeing leadership through this new definitional lens. Namely, it becomes possible to resurrect the expectation that it is the function of leadership to improve the overall progress of humanity. Too often, results-based leadership has been focused on the bottom line, trying to manage a perceived trade-off between achieving the mission and taking care of people. Through this new conceptual lens, we dispense with such either-or thinking. Rather, the two become positively correlated, and we can more easily see how societal prosperity is linked to workforce fulfillment, and how unit effectiveness is linked to morale. Redefining leadership as the enablement of a human system allows for the relinkage of prosperity and productivity in a more positive way.

Most of all, reframing our definition of leadership should bring with it less frustration and puzzling over the various disconnects between theory and reality. We are not soon going to drop our outsized aspirations about leadership, nor should we diminish our expectations of society and what its leaders owe us. But we should begin to see them as part of us, and ourselves as part of the solution.

In the once-French city of New Orleans, a sixty-eight-foot-high lookout tower watches over the city, and from its construction in 1884 through 2017 its now-bare roof had been adorned with a statue of Robert E. Lee. Befitting such a narrow pedestal, this had been one of the few statues of Lee not on horseback. Instead, his likeness had been standing erect, arms crossed authoritatively, with knee-high riding boots visible beneath his uniform. The stark white tower is one of many such marble and concrete remnants that mark the controversy and revision of Lee's legacy.

On the other side of the Atlantic, in the capital of France, dozens of statues of French leaders stand sentry over the famed glass pyramid of Paris's Louvre Museum. Napoleon is there (the courtyard is named for him), as is Rousseau. But you won't find a monument to Maximilien Robespierre there, or anywhere else in Paris for that matter. As with Lee, Robespierre's legacy is deeply controversial, and the only landmark in the French capital that bears his name is a subway station.

And while Robespierre is notably absent from Napoleon's courtyard, a statue of Antoine-Laurent de Lavoisier proudly stands guard over the Louvre. Its sculptor, Jacques-Léonard Maillet, was himself relatively famous, having received the prestigious Prix de Rome scholarship in 1847. Maillet's depiction of a pensive Lavoisier is fitting, arms crossed with a feathered quill in his right hand and a rolled parchment in his left.

Maillet was also a scholar of the Greek style of sculpture that was prevalent in Plutarch's day, and Plutarch was himself intrigued by the relationship between sculptor and sculpture. In his profile of Pericles, Plutarch considered why it is that we look up to some men and women such that we sculpt them in stone (in his day) and put them atop pedestals.

In particular, Plutarch noted that observers of art tend to admire the subject more than the artist. And true enough, Lavoisier is better known to history than Maillet, and Sutherland is best known for Churchill's hatred of the artist's work.

The real lesson is that what we think we see—in artwork or in a leader—is often more consequential than the reality. For instance, Lee's legacy as a leader is increasingly wrapped up in how he is depicted as a symbol and less in his performance as a former military general. This is again proof that what we mean by leadership can be intensely contextual and shift over time. But it is even greater evidence that leadership is inseparable from how human systems derive meaning.

This is part of what makes leaders ubiquitous across human civilization, manifesting in some form in every culture. They are the beating pulse of change. They start companies, invent things; and they lead nations, courtrooms, and countries; they make others happy and fulfilled, frustrated and desolate, hopeful or inspired.

That's why Plutarch remains so intriguing. While he often seems too distant to be relatable, with a meandering style many centuries removed from the pressing issues of our modern world, the timelessness of his stories speaks across the millennia, giving us a sense of the perennial truths and frustrations of human experience that seem to elude resolution.

Plutarch is a reminder not just of our obsession with leadership, but the fact that it is hardly diminishing. Even those who are not leaders clamor to claim the mantle of leadership. Seventeen-year-old college applicants are keen to ensure that their applications are replete with demonstrated competency in "leadership" positions.

It's easy to see why. Increasingly, leaders are getting paid more, recognized more, and commemorated more. Many aspire to positions of leadership given the association we now hold between leadership, power, and affluence. It is hard to know whether this trend reflects more our sense that leaders really do matter and are therefore so deserving, or if leaders are simply getting better at enriching themselves. Whatever the case, our obsession with leadership seems to be constant, if not growing.

We say this fully aware of the logic about living in a postleadership age. But it is our sense that leaders will become only more important to human society as those societies become more complex. So the mythology of leadership will be a growing source of frustration if we don't come to some more clear-eyed sense about why this is so and why they still matter to us.

One can't help but wonder who Plutarch would have written about today, and how he might have handled the modern leader. Likely, his prose would be a colorful reminder of why he himself became one of history's great men, but also an honest confession that he too was just a man.

Plutarch might have selected Robert E. Lee or Maximilien Robespierre, despite the fact that many would reject both as role models. Times have changed, battles have ended, and most of us act on stages that are hardly so full of intrigue. Still, the many men, and far too few women, who stand atop their pedestals today reflect the ways in which we derive meaning, usually as a symbol of the values and virtues that we collectively espouse or spurn as a society. Some are good, fewer are bad, and most are a mixed bag.

And in our tug-of-war over whether such leaders should be remembered as heroes, mortals, or villains, we'll remain conflicted. Rather than wrestle with the false choice presented, we'd do better to opt for the third way, accepting that leaders matter both more and less than we usually realize. Plutarch's legacy is a reminder that even if we knock the leaders of old from their pedestal, the pedestal we've erected is left standing all the same.

EPILOGUE

Science must begin with myths,
and with the criticism of myths.

—KARL POPPER

The children's book of Greek mythology that my mother read to me is now almost ninety years old, and its binding is held together with aging tape. The stories it tells, the ones that captivated me, are much older. But I still enjoy them. They convey with reassuring simplicity the idea that virtue, heroism, and honor will be rewarded. Part of me wishes, and maybe still believes, that they are true.

Plutarch's towering *Lives* is far older than my orange book, and almost as old as the mythology I enjoyed. It has enthralled generations. And beyond the entertainment and inspiration that his profiles provide, Plutarch conveys the comforting message that leaders are the critical fulcrum upon which history is levered. Get the leader right and all else falls into place.

It is useful to see Plutarch's perspective as the natural result of his complex identity and experiences. Born a Greek citizen just outside of Delphi, Plutarch was a product of Greece's city-state culture in which leaders were personally known and accountable to their local communities. Plutarch would have experienced leaders commanding on a limited stage under careful scrutiny by those communities. But with time and firsthand experience of the world's new superpower, Rome, Plutarch's viewpoint on leadership evolved. He adopted the citizenship and expansionist perspective of the mighty, networked Roman Empire. The scale and complexity of the stage upon which he saw leaders act increased dramatically.

Unlike in Athens, Sparta, Corinth, and Greece's other great city-states, in Rome individual leaders could not dominate this complex environment in person, or by offering the same leadership style in each new context they faced. As the idea and frontiers of Rome expanded, Roman leaders were forced to adapt, looking to the potential offered by the interconnected nature and sheer mass of their new ecosystem.

Most important, Roman leaders had to realize that how they were perceived by diverse Roman citizens—a group of people bound together without a shared religion, race, language, or culture—changed with the very contours of the land the Roman legions passed through. The crafting of the stories told about Rome's great leaders became as important as the oratory in the Senate, or the warriors who held the frontiers against invading barbarians. Plutarch straddled these two worlds, seeing commonalities between the two, but also being willing to look change directly in the eye. Plutarch's world had changed, and with it what was required of its leaders.

Like Plutarch, my perspective changed with age, rank, and responsibility, and also collided with a world gone modern. The roads, ships, and laws that connected the far-flung Roman world were multiplied by technology and millennia of growing interaction. The speed, public nature, and apparent fickleness of society-on-bandwidth changed the tempo and feel of leadership. In the years of one soldier's service, the transition had been stunning—and often stunned those living the experience.

Although facing an undeniably wider, more complex environment in which I must operate, I felt I was—or at least should be—prepared. By most measures I was a competent leader. I'd been educated at West Point, trained at Fort Benning, seasoned with countless challenges, and mentored by a succession of impressive leaders. Proficient at my craft, I was experienced at almost every level of our large Army. Usually I could sense risk or opportunity, then act decisively enough to engender confidence. Facing soldiers, and even their spouses, I had learned to both instruct and inspire. Where I would go, young warriors would follow—or willingly lead me.

Still, leading remained difficult, and it has never gotten easier. It helped somewhat to read history, to emulate successful role models, and to listen to the counsel of others. But the wisdom they provided and the solutions they offered never completely fit. Not once.

Like protean shape-shifters, the challenges I undertook and the people I followed or led changed constantly, creating a series of unique, never-to-be-repeated combinations that demanded unique solutions. Prepackaged solutions never worked.

Particularly as the environments I encountered increased in speed and complexity, the problems intertwined, and the personalities seemed to inflate, simultaneously being the leader I'd been raised to be—with a checklist of admirable traits and behaviors—and being truly effective were often in tension. As a young officer I'd been taught that in combat, "if it's stupid, but it works, it isn't stupid." And over time I faced situations where the leadership version applied, asking: "If it's bad leadership, but it works, is it actually bad?" I saw countless leaders who accepted the premise that the outcome is the best, and only, real measure of the leader's effectiveness.

It's easy to see why they might think so. The extraordinary discipline required for the 850-man crew of a nineteenth-century naval warship, like Admiral Nelson's HMS *Victory*, to function effectively typically included periodic, brutal floggings of poorly performing crew members. Even today, CEOs quickly learn that stockholders are ultimately most interested in profits. While following a checklist or formulaic approach to leadership was never a comfortable fit, neither was an attitude where "the ends justified the means."

My decisions and conduct were viewed from multiple vantage points, each offering a different perspective. For the same leadership approach I was often damned, praised, or ignored—with the disquieting reality that each assessment might be, from the observer's unique viewpoint, absolutely correct. Even my personal judgment of my leadership was often maddeningly contradictory. I could be both proud and embarrassed by the same action, or unsatisfied and uneasy with cases that appeared unequivocally successful.

Success as a leader also looks different through the prism of time. Actions taken may be positive in the near term, but injurious over a longer time horizon. Some situations will demand a here-and-now focus, but having the courage to take a longer view is invaluable.

Eventually, years of seeking to master the techniques of effective leadership brought me to the realization that leadership is a constantly moving target. The solution that works perfectly one day can be miserably disappointing the next. It feels impossible and unfair that the right answer to a problem changes, but it does. It feels absurd that being a good leader is a journey, not a destination, but it is.

Years ago, after many attempts with the analogies that seek to explain Albert Einstein's special theory of relativity, I realized I simply couldn't understand it—and that I never would. It was a bit irritating, but acceptable because I'm not a physicist. But I am supposed to be a leader, and finding similar frustrations with efforts to lead is deeply unsettling.

In the end, I came to an accommodation. I will never master leadership, and yet I will never cease the effort to do so. Faced with uncertainty and change, I will seek to adapt where I can, and endure where I can't. Success, I've found, doesn't always mean you got it right, and failure doesn't mean you got it wrong.

In 1941, twenty-three-year-old Ted Williams dramatically ended the season by going 6 for 8 in a doubleheader to finish with a historic .406 batting average. Amazing, but I remind myself that his historic average still implied that he failed almost 60 percent of the times he strode to bat.

It is impossible to master the countless variables of leadership to guarantee a perfect result. Ultimately, the best you can do is to increase the probability of success. Failure rides alongside, but success demands accepting the risk. I found that being confident of my commitment, but humble about my ability to control the outcome, is the best I can do.

We choose to lead or decide not to. We often won't control whether we succeed or fail, or whether we're celebrated or excoriated for what we do. But we can control what we genuinely *try* to do, and perhaps that is how we should hope to be judged.

Acknowledgments

This book would not have been possible had we not had the good fortune of finding a team of three capable research assistants early in the process. This book is theirs every bit as much as it is ours.

Harry Begg is an Oxford and University College London graduate. In 2017, while a fellow at Harvard, we were very fortunate that his adviser Meghan O'Sullivan introduced us to him. This book quickly sweeps across thirteen complex lives. Without Harry's intellectual rigor, we might have only scratched the surface, for he always forced us to dig deeper.

Charles Goodyear is a Yale graduate and the coauthor of another book, *One Mission*. His steady hand and experience gave us the confidence to complete such an ambitious book as quickly as we did. Choosing which leaders to profile was one of our hardest tasks, and Charlie had a knack for recommending interesting people.

Dixe Schillaci was a senior at Yale as she helped us write this book, having graduated just as we went into copyediting. Nearly every week she shuttled from New Haven to Alexandria, and it takes a special person to make that sort of commitment. Dixe held our whole team accountable for communicating our ideas as stories. If we've produced a readable book, Dixe deserves much credit. We're thankful to Jim Levinsohn of Yale's Jackson Institute for telling us about the amazing young woman who knew how to write so well.

Our next debt of gratitude is to the writers—mostly biographers—whose work we already mention in each of our chapters. We did original research wherever possible, but their scholarship always set us off in the right direction.

Several experts granted us interviews and reviewed chapters. We're grateful to Gary Gallagher for his wisdom about the Civil War and Robert E. Lee, and to Richard Carwardine for introducing us to him. Diane Kormos-Buchwald leads the Einstein Papers Project, and we're thankful that she spoke with us, and also for her team's important work. Ruth Leon graciously introduced a tone-deaf team to the world of classical music and helped us to understand Leonard Bernstein. Peter McPhee and James Simpson helped us to understand two periods—the French Revolution and Reformation Europe—that were difficult for novices to parse, and each spent considerable time reviewing our chapters on Robespierre and Luther, respectively. Flynn Cratty was an indispensable reviewer of the Luther profile as well, and Eric Frazier at the Library of Congress guided us through their trove on the French Revolution. Conversations with Joby Warrick were absolutely essential in framing our understanding of Abu Musab al-Zarqawi. Valerie Hansen's help made our chapter on Zheng He more precise than it was in its original form. Kate Clifford Larson was unusually kind and solicitous of her time, and her commitment to telling Harriet Tubman's story made our book better. Ken Ackerman was a great lunch companion, and his expertise on Boss Tweed helped us to understand him as a leader. Nile Gardiner, Ted Bromund, Sir Tim Lankester, and Lord Charles Powell helped us to distill Margaret Thatcher's half century in British politics, occasionally from firsthand experience. Alexander Schwennicke lent us his expertise on all things Plutarch. David Garrow guided us as we explored MLK's twelve years of civil rights leadership.

Colin Allen, Matilda Aspinall, Toby Huelin, Sara Boutall, Carol J. Oja, Marie-Joseé Kravis, Alixe Buckerfield de la Roche, and Shane Reiner-Roth each reviewed chapters where they had special expertise. Emile Simpson, Arati Prabhakar, Teddy Collins, Michael Maccoby, Jeffrey Pfeffer, Jan Rutherford, Charles O'Reilly, Tom Ricks, Niall Ferguson, John Gaddis, Gregg Hurwitz, Barbara Eggers, Penny Ismay, and Walter Isaacson reviewed various portions of the manuscript, and their feedback was always helpful. Presidents Barack Obama and George W. Bush granted us interviews—and their wisdom and generosity are deeply appreciated. Wherever the book falls short anywhere, it is the authors' fault. And wherever there's a kernel of insight, it's likely we had a lot of help to get it on the page.

Sam Ayres, a talented Army Sergeant, helped us to make the chapter on Zarqawi more readable. In addition to helping with that same chapter, Phil Kaplan gave us the original idea to model a book on Plutarch. Greg Behrman and the NationSwell Council hosted the dinner where we began to discuss the book. Jason Forrester, Elana Duffy, and Craig Wilson of NYU's Veteran Future Lab, helped us to secure office space in Brooklyn. Carolina McPhail and Ross King translated some documents from French. Gene Thorp, Katherine Long, and Lina Than helped with maps and graphics. Eric Robinson suggested that we write about Harriet Tubman.

We had the pleasure of working with an excellent editorial staff. Adrian Zackheim is a master at giving candid advice on big ideas and helping authors be more confident about the book they're writing. Bria Sandford had to comb through countless versions of the manuscript and her thoroughness never dissipated. We're thankful to Helen Healey and everyone else who polished our book into something more worthwhile, as well as Margot Stamas and her team.

Lastly, we owe a debt of gratitude to our families. Two of us are particularly thankful to the caregivers who watched over things while we indulgently read and wrote. Most important, each of us thanks our wives—Annie, Megan, and Kara—for putting up with the early-morning phone calls, weekend disappearances, and the many other disruptions to family life.

Notes

Chapter 1: The Mythology

1 **"The die is cast":** Plutarch, *Plutarch's Lives*, ed. Arthur Hugh Clough, Modern Library Paperback Edition, vol. 2 (Toronto: Random House, 1992), 221.

1 **shin-deep stream:** Fernando Lillo Redonet, "How Julius Caesar Started a Big War by Crossing a Small Stream," *National Geographic History*, April 2017, www.nationalgeographic.com/archaeol ogy-and-history/magazine/2017/03–04/julius-caesar-crossing-rubicon-rome/.

2 **"dictator for life":** Plutarch, *Plutarch's Lives*, 2:235.

2 **conspire against him:** Plutarch, *Plutarch's Lives*, 2:235.

2 **"Et tu, Brute?":** William Shakespeare, *Julius Caesar*, ed. David Daniell, The Arden Shakespeare, Third Series (London: Thomson Learning, 2000), act 3, scene i, line 77.

3 **"when I'm gone":** Christopher Jackson and Lin-Manuel Miranda, "One Last Time," *Hamilton* (Original Broadway Cast Recording), accessed June 11, 2018, https://genius.com/Lin-manuel -miranda-one-last-time-lyrics.

3 **Miranda said later:** The Rockefeller Foundation, Lin-Manuel Miranda: "The Tough Lesson of Leadership," *Insight Dialogues*, accessed June 10, 2018, www.youtube.com/watch?v=ku9z 0tAkF3c.

3 **"ordered a halt":** Plutarch, *Plutarch's Lives*, 2:221.

4 **likely dramatic license:** Shakespeare, *Julius Caesar*, act 3, scene i, line 77. David Daniell, a literary scholar, notes that a similar phrase appears in Greek in the writings of Suetonius, and that *Et tu, Brute* is first recorded in the year 1595.

4 **"Some say that":** Plutarch, *Plutarch's Lives*, 2:242.

5 **"I want to go up against the existing painting":** Corey Kilgannon, "Crossing the Delaware, More Accurately," *The New York Times City Room* (blog), December 23, 2011, https://cityroom .blogs.nytimes.com/2011/12/23/a-famous-painting-meets-its-more-factual-match.

6 **"visitors noted his haggard":** Ron Chernow, *Alexander Hamilton* (New York: Penguin Books, 2005), 505.

7 **a day of argument:** Bernard M. Bass and Ruth Bass, *The Bass Handbook of Leadership: Theory, Research, and Managerial Applications*, 4th ed. (New York: Free Press, 2008), 15.

7 **221 definitions of leadership:** Joseph C. Rost, *Leadership for the Twenty-First Century* (New York: Praeger, 1991), 44.

8 **they generally list exogenous factors:** David Reimer, "For the Board, Leadership Is a Risk Factor," *Medium* (blog), September 13, 2016, https://medium.com/@david.reimer/for-the-board -leadership-is-a-risk-factor-why-that-matters-now-more-than-ever-d005d32bfcdf.

9 **dispatched Captain Alexander Hamilton:** Alexander Hamilton, "To Major General Horatio Gates," November 5, 1777, U.S. National Archives, https://founders.archives.gov/documents /Hamilton/01–01–02–0335.

9 **desperate state of the Army:** Alexander Hamilton, "To George Washington," January 29, 1778, U.S. National Archives, http://founders.archives.gov/documents/Hamilton/01–01–02–0353.

10 **turned his attention:** Alexander Hamilton, "Alexander Hamilton Papers: Miscellany, –1820; Military Papers; By Period; American Revolution, 1775 to 1783; New York Artillery Company Pay

Book, Includes Notes by Hamilton on a Variety of Subjects, 1776, Aug.–1777," 1776, Library of Congress, https://www.loc.gov/item/mss246120811/, Image 146.

10 **"close to a thousand times":** Thomas H. Russell, *Life and Work of Theodore Roosevelt* (L. H. Walter, 1919), 260, www.theodore-roosevelt.com/images/research/scholars/trlifeandwork russell.pdf.

10 **Machiavelli's Florentine court:** Erica Benner, *Be Like the Fox: Machiavelli's Lifelong Quest for Freedom* (New York: W. W. Norton, 2017), 34, 165–66.

10 **John Adams's letters:** G. J. Barker-Benfield, *Abigail and John Adams: The Americanization of Sensibility* (Chicago: University of Chicago Press, 2010), 230; John Adams, "John Adams to John Quincy Adams," October 4, 1790, http://founders.archives.gov/documents/Adams/04–09–02– 0067; Thomas Jefferson, "To John Quincy Adams," November 1, 1817, U.S. National Archives, http://founders.archives.gov/documents/Jefferson/03–12–02–0120.

10 **Montaigne, Montesquieu, Rousseau, and Emerson:** "Plutarch & the Issue of Character," *New Criterion*, December 2000, https://www.newcriterion.com/issues/2000/12/plutarch-the-issue-of-character.

11 **"What sort of man":** D. A. Russell, *Plutarch* (New York: Charles Scribner's Sons, 1973), 103.

11 **"Virtue, by the bare":** Plutarch, *Plutarch's Lives*, ed. Arthur Hugh Clough, trans. John Dryden, Modern Library Paperback Edition, vol. 1 (Toronto: Random House, 1992), 202.

12 **subject of debate:** Russell, *Plutarch*, 113. According to Russell, "How the pairs were chosen, and how the plan developed, must remain largely uncertain." Russell makes a convincing argument that Plutarch wrote about Greeks and Romans because he wanted Greek cultural ideals to influence Roman political power, writing as he did at the height of the Roman Empire. Russell writes that "humanity, to Plutarch's way of thinking, was something that Greek education could contribute to a world governed by the potentially destructive force of Roman armies" (98).

13 **"wildness of extremes":** Plutarch, *Plutarch's Lives*, 1:291.

13 **"own prudence and conduct":** Plutarch, *Plutarch's Lives*, 1:326. In the words of D. A. Russell, "The all-important thing is the proper use of education and environment, not of course to conceal evil but to strengthen the good tendencies and eradicate the pernicious" (87).

14 **"it was for the sake":** Plutarch, *Plutarch's Lives*, 1:325.

Chapter 2: The Marble Man: Robert E. Lee

17 **"In all of us":** J. F. C. Fuller, *Grant and Lee: A Study in Personality and Generalship* (London: Eyre & Spottiswood, 1932), 57.

18 **"the sublimest word":** There is contention over whether Lee ever actually said this, but it has proven to be a quote that many enjoy attributing to him. Elizabeth Brown Pryor, "Thou Knowest Not the Time of Thy Visitation—A Newly Discovered Letter Reveals Robert E. Lee's Lonely Struggle with Disunion," *Virginia Magazine of History and Biography* 119, no. 3 (2011): 277–96.

18 **"Lee was one of":** "Symposium to Honor Lee, Villain or 'the Noblest Ever'?," *The Washington Times*, April 25, 2007, www.washingtontimes.com/news/2007/apr/25/20070425–121951–5499r/.

18 **"one of the greatest captains":** Gary W. Gallagher, ed., *Lee the Soldier* (Lincoln: University of Nebraska Press, 1996), 181.

18 **"All over the United States":** Franklin Delano Roosevelt, "Extemporaneous Remarks of the Unveiling of the Robert E. Lee Memorial Statue," June 12, 1936, US National Archives, n.d., https://catalog.archives.gov/id/197566.

20 **"With my whole command":** S. C. Gwynne, *Rebel Yell: The Violence, Passion, and Redemption of Stonewall Jackson* (New York: Scribner, 2015), 530.

21 **The two generals met at night:** Gallagher, *Lee the Soldier*, 365.

21 **ambitiously named Chancellorsville:** Gwynne, *Rebel Yell*, 523.

21 **the temperature in nearby Washington, DC:** Robert K. Krick, *Civil War Weather in Virginia* (Tuscaloosa: University of Alabama Press, 2007), 98.

21 **But as darkness fell:** Michael Korda, *Clouds of Glory: The Life and Legend of Robert E. Lee* (New York: Harper Perennial, 2015), 514.

22 **additional scouting soon found:** Korda, *Clouds of Glory*, 513.

22 **in response to Union movement:** Gwynne, *Rebel Yell*, 522.

22 **Now, at the night-shrouded:** Korda, *Clouds of Glory*, 513.

22 **discussed the risky option:** Gwynne, *Rebel Yell*, 530.

22 **In violation of conventional:** Gary W. Gallagher and Joan Waugh, *The American War: A History of the Civil War Era* (State College, PA: Spielvogel Books, 2015), 113.

23 **"By a prompt and rapid":** "The Last Victory," *Daily Dispatch*, May 7, 1863, Library of Congress, https://chroniclingamerica.loc.gov/lccn/sn84024738/1863-05-07/ed-1/seq-1.pdf.

23 **against foreign invaders:** Gary W. Gallagher, *Becoming Confederates: Paths to a New National Loyalty,* Mercer University Lamar Memorial Lectures, no. 54 (Athens: University of Georgia Press, 2013), 17.

23 **In the evening, after victory:** Gwynne, *Rebel Yell,* 550–51.

23 **Lee noted the magnitude:** Gallagher, *Lee the Soldier,* 57.

24 **"Were ever men more":** Douglas S. Freeman, *Lee's Lieutenants: A Study in Command,* ed. Stephen W. Sears (New York: Simon & Schuster, 2001), 24.

25 **his own father's:** Korda, *Clouds of Glory,* 13-14.

25 **Lee set a rarely:** Elizabeth Brown Pryor, *Reading the Man: A Portrait of Robert E. Lee Through His Private Letters* (New York: Viking, 2007), 63.

25 **At some point:** Korda, *Clouds of Glory,* 34.

26 **the 6,332-strong United States Army:** "Selected Manpower Statistics," U.S. Department of Defense, 1997, www.dtic.mil/dtic/tr/fulltext/u2/a347153.pdf, 54–64.

26 **as a Lieutenant of Engineers:** Brown Pryor, *Reading the Man,* 72.

26 **Lee's marriage in 1831:** Gallagher, *Lee the Soldier,* 98.

27 **Ulysses S. Grant:** Grant's name was actually Hiram Ulysses Grant, but after an administrative error early in his Army career, he used the name Ulysses S.

27 **"we bullied [Mexico]":** Korda, *Clouds of Glory,* 154.

28 **Ahead of the Battle of Cerro Gordo:** Brown Pryor, *Reading the Man,* 164.

28 **After relaying his discovery back to General Scott:** Korda, *Clouds of Glory,* 135.

28 **"charge them to hell":** Korda, *Clouds of Glory,* 137.

28 **Praise came:** Brown Pryor, *Reading the Man,* 164.

29 **Even the formidable, if somewhat pompous:** Brown Pryor, *Reading the Man,* 160.

29 **frequently mentioned Lee in his dispatches:** Gallagher, *Lee the Soldier,* 99.

29 **"the very best soldier":** "Winfield Scott to John B. Floyd," May 8, 1857.

29 **But he remained in uniform:** Brown Pryor, *Reading the Man,* 212, and Korda, *Clouds of Glory,* 186-87.

29 **The slave-worked estates were poorly run:** Brown Pryor, *Reading the Man,* 252–53.

29 **as in 1859, when Lieutenant Colonel Robert E. Lee:** Brown Pryor, *Reading the Man,* 279–283.

30 **His father's old commander:** Sarah Booth Conroy, "The Founding Father and His Slaves," The Papers of George Washington, at the University of Virginia, 1998, http://gwpapers.virginia.edu /history/articles/the-founding-father-and-his-slaves.

30 **"In view of the vast increase":** "R. E. Lee to James Seddon," January 10, 1863, Lee Family Digital Archive. https://leefamilyar chive.org/press-room/9-family-papers/1180-robert-e-lee-to-james-a-seddon-1863-january-10.

32 **The final straw for most:** James M. McPherson, *Battle Cry of Freedom: The Civil War Era* (New York: Oxford University Press, 1988), 235.

32 **2nd United States Cavalry Regiment:** Korda, *Clouds of Glory,* 220.

33 **Washington's legacy seems to have:** Korda, *Clouds of Glory,* 220.

33 **On January 9:** McPherson, *Battle Cry of Freedom,* 266.

33 **cadets of South Carolina's military college:** "152nd Anniversary of the *Star of the West,*" The Citadel, January 2013, www.citadel.edu/root/star-ofthe-west-152.

33 **On February 1:** McPherson, *Battle Cry of Freedom,* 235.

33 **But Lee was spared the task:** Brown Pryor, *Reading the Man,* 258.

33 **Ironically, en route:** Korda, *Clouds of Glory,* 222–23.

34 **Reaching Arlington on March 1:** Brown Pryor, *Reading the Man,* 286.

34 **Virginia, however, had not yet decided:** Virginius Dabney, *Virginia, the New Dominion,* Virginia ed (Charlottesville: University Press of Virginia, 1983), 294-96."

34 **Opinion in Virginia:** Korda, *Clouds of Glory,* 227.

34 **Virginia's departure from:** McPherson, *Battle Cry of Freedom,* 280.

34 **Lee refused "the offer":** Korda, *Clouds of Glory,* 227–28.

35 **"there is no sacrifice":** Robert E. Lee, "Robert E. Lee to Markie Williams," January 22, 1861, as quoted in Douglas Southall Freeman, *Lee's Lieutenants* (New York: Simon & Schuster, 1997), 106.

36 **one of Washington's swords:** Brown Pryor, *Reading the Man,* 295.

36 **"General Lee is, almost":** *The Fremantle Diary, the Journal of Lieutenant Colonel James Arthur Lyon Fremantle, Coldstream Guards,* ed. Walter Lord (Boston: Little, Brown and Company, 1954 [first published in London in 1863]).

36 **But he did not ascend to his most famous:** Gallagher, *Lee the Soldier,* 40.

37 **"King of Spades":** Bob Duncan, "Robert E. Lee, the King of Spades," *The Columbia Daily Herald* (Columbia, TN: February 16, 2014), http://www.columbiadailyherald.com/opinion/columns /robert-e-lee-king-spades.

37 **in late June 1862:** Gwynne, *Rebel Yell*, 384–86.

38 **One of his former:** Ernest B. Furgurson, *Chancellorsville 1863: The Souls of the Brave* (New York: Vintage Books, 1993), 139.

38 **"Oh, I am heartily":** Quoted in General Horace Porter, "Campaigning with Grant," *The Century Magazine* (December 1896).

38 **flanks at the time:** McPherson, *Battle Cry of Freedom*, 281.

40 **In an age of mass armies:** During the Civil War, 94,000 Confederate soldiers were killed on the battlefield or died of wounds, while 164,000 died of sickness or disease. The Ohio State University n.d., "Statistics on the Civil War and Medicine," https://ehistory.osu.edu/exhibitions/cwsurgeon /cwsurgeon/statistics.

40 **"this lack of appreciation":** Fuller, *Grant and Lee*, 125.

41 **After Gettysburg Lee:** Fuller, *Grant and Lee*, 112.

42 **infantryman in the Army:** Joseph T. Glatthaar, *Soldiering in the Army of Northern Virginia: A Statistical Portrait of the Troops Who Served Under Robert E. Lee* (Chapel Hill: University of North Carolina Press, 2011), 48–50.

42 **In April 1865:** Gallagher and Waugh, *The American War*, 195.

43 **"What General Lee's feelings":** Fuller, *Grant and Lee*, 62.

43 **Although Lee was not present:** Brown Pryor, *Reading the Man*, 424.

44 **"We fell under":** David W. Blight, *Beyond the Battlefield: Race, Memory and the American Civil War* (Amherst: University of Massachusetts Press, 2002), 93.

45 **"He was a foe without":** Benjamin Harvey Hill. February 18, 1874. Quoted by Benjamin Harrey Hill Jr. in *Senator Benjamin H. Hill of Georgia: His Life, Speeches and Writings* (1893), 406.

Chapter 3: The Founders

49 **He had led production:** Bob Thomas, *Walt Disney: An American Original* (Glendale, CA: Disney Editions, 1976), 139.

49 **In doing so, Walt:** Nitin Nohria, Anthony J. Mayo, and Bridget Gurtler, "Walt Disney and the 1941 Animators' Strike," Harvard Business School (case study), May 8, 2014, 5.

49 **They were among:** Didier Ghez, ed., *Walt's People*, vol. 9 (Bloomington, IN: Xlibris Corporation, 2010), 29, 141, 215.

50 **One of the reviewers:** Aaron H. Goldberg, *The Disney Story: Chronicling the Man, the Mouse, and the Parks* (Philadelphia: Quaker Scribe, 2016), 10.

50 **Walt heard himself:** Harry Arends (director), *Disney's Snow White and the Seven Dwarfs: Still The Fairest of Them All* (Burbank, CA: Walt Disney Studios, 2001), https://www.imdb.com/title/tt0344378/.

51 **"I'm not 'Walt Disney'":** *American Experience*, "Walt Disney's Public vs. Private Persona," October 9, 2015, https://www.youtube.com/watch?v=WE57FaPBFpY.

51 **would personally voice:** Neal Gabler, *Walt Disney: The Triumph of the American Imagination* (New York: Random House, 2006), 155.

51 **until the mid-1940s:** Gabler, *Walt Disney*, 426.

51 **During its production:** Gabler, *Walt Disney*, 123.

51 **American audiences were awestruck:** Thomas, *Walt Disney: An American Original*, 96.

52 **This first runaway:** Goldberg, *The Disney Story*, 1–3.

52 **across the country:** Gabler, *Walt Disney*, 134.

52 **"How do you *do* that":** Gabler, *Walt Disney*, 133.

52 **One of Disney Studio's:** Gabler, *Walt Disney*, 225.

52 **In the days immediately after:** Gabler, *Walt Disney*, 134.

52 **in July 1930:** Goldberg, *The Disney Story*, 3–4.

52 **by industry standards:** Gabler, *Walt Disney*, 86. Walt was a perfectly fine animator, but not of the level where he would be considered in the higher tiers of talent by this point in his career.

52 **One evening in 1934:** Gabler, *Walt Disney*, 218.

53 **Remarking on the atmosphere:** Arends, *Disney's Snow White and the Seven Dwarfs*.

53 **two million drawings:** Anne E. Duggan, Donald Haase, and Helen Callow, eds., *Folktales and Fairy Tales: Traditions and Texts from Around the World*, 2nd ed. (Santa Barbara, CA: Greenwood, 2016), 271.

53 **On a multiday excursion:** Ghez, *Walt's People*, 1:93.

53 **similar to "a messianic figure":** Gabler, *Walt Disney*, 212.

54 **He asked about his:** Tom Sito, *Drawing the Line: The Untold Story of the Animation Unions from Bosko to Bart Simpson* (Lexington: University Press of Kentucky, 2006), 108.

54 **Disney acted as their:** Gabler, *Walt Disney*, 210–11.

54 **As he recalled during a later:** Arends, *Disney's Snow White and the Seven Dwarfs*.

54 Later in life: Nohria, Mayo, and Gurtler, "Walt Disney and the 1941 Animators' Strike," 13.
54 While competing studios: Sito, *Drawing the Line*, 108.
54 making them feel as though: Gabler, *Walt Disney*, 211.
54 Ken Anderson . . . later explained: Ghez, *Walt's People*, 1:105.
55 Many of those who: Arends, *Disney's Snow White and the Seven Dwarfs*.
55 Workers were allowed: Ghez, *Walt's People* 1:109.
55 Walt once pridefully described: Gabler, *Walt Disney*, 241.
55 "The first duty": Thomas, *Walt Disney: An American Original*, 125.
56 very few of Disney's: Gabler, *Walt Disney*, 353–54.
56 One such instance: Ghez, *Walt's People*, 1:104.
56 this examination room: Thomas, *Walt Disney: An American Original*, 111.
56 Their boss was exacting: Ghez, *Walt's People*, 1:93.
56 Walt would not be remembered: Ghez, *Walt's People*, 1:111.
57 of far greater importance: Gabler, *Walt Disney*, 231–32.
57 What had previously passed: Leonard Maltin, *Of Mice and Magic: A History of American Animated Cartoons*, rev. ed. (New York: New American Library, 1987), 54.
57 Walt exacted meticulous: Arends, *Disney's Snow White and the Seven Dwarfs*.
57 One key change: Maltin, *Of Mice and Magic*, 53.
57 original German folktale: Gabler, *Walt Disney*, 217.
58 Among the many unused names considered: Arends, *Disney's Snow White and the Seven Dwarfs*.
58 when one animator: Maltin, *Of Mice and Magic*, 53.
58 Walt decided that this motion: Arends, *Disney's Snow White and the Seven Dwarfs*.
58 Similarly, Walt decided that: Leonard Maltin, *Of Mice and Magic: A History of American Animated Cartoons*, Rev. ed (New York: New American Library, 1987), 71.
58 In the words of: Ghez, *Walt's People*, 1:80.
58 These decisions infuriated: Arends, *Disney's Snow White and the Seven Dwarfs*.
58 Even with the studio's manpower: Maltin, *Of Mice and Magic*, 54.
58 Per Disney artist Ward Kimball: Arends, *Disney's Snow White and the Seven Dwarfs*.
58 In particular, he conceived: Maltin, *Of Mice and Magic*, 51.
59 Bank of America—his primary lender: Gabler, *Walt Disney*, 265.
59 As he would later remark: "Walt Disney on The Making of Snow White," CBC, December 16, 2009, www.youtube.com/watch?v=N7ZkWfD0ELE.
59 Roy would creep: Gabler, *Walt Disney*, 416–17.
60 The *New Republic* declared: Gabler, *Walt Disney*, 273.
60 Of greater satisfaction to Walt: Maltin, *Of Mice and Magic*, 57.
60 The film held sales records: Nohria, Mayo, and Gurtler, "Walt Disney and the 1941 Animators' Strike," 5.
60 Walt was presented: The Oscars, "Honorary Award," www.oscars.org/governors/honorary.
60 The movie brought in more than $8 million: Maltin, *Of Mice and Magic*, 57.
61 *Snow White* had been: Goldberg, *The Disney Story*, 1.
61 with a staggering target output: Nohria, Mayo, and Gurtler, "Walt Disney and the 1941 Animators' Strike," 5.
61 construction began on: Goldberg, *The Disney Story*, 1.
61 a custom humidity-control system: Garity and Ledeen, "The New Walt Disney Studio," 10–15.
61 Carpets and drapes were banned: W. E. Garity and J. L. Ledeen, "The New Walt Disney Studio," *Journal of the Society of Motion Picture Engineers* (January, 1941), 14.
61 The temperature was: Gabler, *Walt Disney*, 323.
61 A gym, massage parlor: Garity and Ledeen, "The New Walt Disney Studio," 13–15.
61 although some artists initially: Sito, *Drawing the Line*, 112.
61 convertible into a hospital: Gabler, *Walt Disney*, 322.
61 Aspects of Walt's managerial: Ghez, *Walt's People*, 1:130.
61 during the construction in Burbank: Gabler, *Walt Disney*, 288.
61 lacked the "ramshackle homeliness": Maltin, *Of Mice and Magic*, 64.
61 Predictably, Walt struggled: Ghez, *Walt's People*, 1:81–83, and Thomas, *Walt Disney: An American Original*, 165.
62 his public reputation: Gabler, *Walt Disney*, 351.
62 Oddly enough, it was now: Gabler, *Walt Disney*, 351.
62 the doorman would pass along the message that Walt: Nohria, Mayo, and Gurtler, "Walt Disney and the 1941 Animators' Strike," 7.
62 his Old Men: Thomas, *Walt Disney: An American Original*, 7.

62   **enough to afford multiple cars:** Sito, *Drawing the Line*, 115–17.

62   **Some of the so-called:** Sito, *Drawing the Line*, 108.

62   **for every "gag":** Ghez, *Walt's People*, 1:126.

63   **Sometimes he'd hand out bonuses:** Ghez, *Walt's People*, 1:106.

63   **In 1940, Walt and Roy:** Goldberg, *The Disney Story*, 16–17.

63   **up to Walt's judgment:** Nohria, Mayo, and Gurtler, "Walt Disney and the 1941 Animators' Strike," 7.

63   **hesitant to give:** Gabler, *Walt Disney*, 354.

63   **This was obvious to:** Ghez, *Walt's People*, 1:116.

64   **Walt's office diary:** Gabler, *Walt Disney*, 364.

64   **"I didn't think he'd go against me!":** Sito, *Drawing the Line*, 129.

64   **"We can get along without him":** Gabler, *Walt Disney*, 365.

64   **All told, up to seven hundred:** Gabler, *Walt Disney*, 365.

64   **He was initially enraged:** Maltin, *Of Mice and Magic*, 64.

64   **"I have had":** Gabler, *Walt Disney*, 359.

65   **He rationalized his aloofness:** Thomas, *Walt Disney: An American Original*, 167–68.

65   **Though he acknowledged:** Gabler, *Walt Disney*, 359–60.

65   **"My first recommendation to":** Nohria, Mayo, and Gurtler, "Walt Disney and the 1941 Animators' Strike," 9.

66   **As he realized he was:** Sito, *Drawing the Line*, 119.

66   **Overall, his audacious attempt:** Gabler, *Walt Disney*, 360.

66   **telling sign of this new norm:** Nohria, Mayo, and Gurtler, "Walt Disney and the 1941 Animators' Strike," 11.

66   **He later wrote to a:** Nohria, Mayo, and Gurtler, "Walt Disney and the 1941 Animators' Strike," 10.

66   **Six years later, Walt would testify:** Nohria, Mayo, and Gurtler, "Walt Disney and the 1941 Animators' Strike," 12.

66   **While Walt mourned:** Ghez, *Walt's People*, 1:131.

67   **the Academy Award–winning:** Maltin, *Of Mice and Magic*, 70.

67   **He named it:** Goldberg, *The Disney Story*, 35.

67   **one of those poached:** Gabler, *Walt Disney*, 493–94.

67   **Some at the old studio:** Gabler, *Walt Disney*, 502.

67   **He toured forty sites:** Gabler, *Walt Disney*, 501.

67   **He ordered WED's designers to:** Gabler, *Walt Disney*, 533.

67-68   **He personally helped to spray-paint:** Gabler, *Walt Disney*, 531.

67   **and ate hot dogs:** Gabler, *Walt Disney*, 525.

68   **When one laborer:** Gabler, *Walt Disney*, 527.

68   **He soon made a habit:** Thomas, *Walt Disney: An American Original*, 273.

68   **WED's employees, his select:** Gabler, *Walt Disney*, 534.

69   **Televised by ABC:** Goldberg, *The Disney Story*, 47.

69   **"To all who come to this happy place":** Nohria, Mayo, and Gurtler, "Walt Disney and the 1941 Animators' Strike," 13.

70   **They were successful:** Tilar J. Mazzeo, *The Secret of Chanel No. 5*, cond. ed. (New York: Reader's Digest, 2013), 499.

71   **she desired "a woman's perfume with a woman's scent":** Pierre Galante, *Mademoiselle Chanel*, trans. by Eileen Geist and Jessie Wood (Chicago: Henry Regnery Company, 1973), 74.

71   **Catherine de Medici:** Mazzeo, *The Secret of Chanel No. 5*, 476–78.

71   **The Grand Duke was living on an allowance:** According to Rhonda Garelick, "'Dmitri was the *eminence grise* of Rue Cambon,' wrote Claude Delay, referring to the Duke's habit of hanging around Chanel's studio, looking royal. Chanel enhanced the effect by hiring Dmitri's friend Count Koutouzov, former governor of Crimea, as her *chef de réception*—the first person clients would meet. . . . Chanel's boutique soon took on the air of a miniature Alexander Palace." Rhonda K. Garelick, *Mademoiselle: Coco Chanel and the Pulse of History* (New York: Random House, 2015), 124.

71   **When Chanel started to think about making perfumes:** Mazzeo, *The Secret of Chanel No. 5*, 487–90.

71   **known as aldehydes:** Garelick, *Mademoiselle*, 127.

71   **It was Beaux's task to translate:** Galante, *Mademoiselle Chanel*, 74.

71   **"An artificial perfume":** Galante, *Mademoiselle Chanel*, 67–68.

72   **Chanel had this sort of magnetism:** Paul Morand, *The Allure of Chanel*, trans. Euan Cameron (London: Pushkin Press, 2017), 21.

72   **chose vial number five:** Mazzeo, *The Secret of Chanel No. 5*, 491.

72 **for the Russian royal family:** Mazzeo, *The Secret of Chanel No. 5*, 487–90.

72 **The perfume sold so well:** Mazzeo, *The Secret of Chanel No. 5*, 503, 508.

72 **The Wertheimers put up:** Mazzeo, *The Secret of Chanel No. 5*, 509–10.

72 **She was not always:** Phyllis Berman and Zina Sawaya, "The Billionaires Behind Chanel," *Forbes*, April 3, 1989.

73 **Her head is tilted:** "*Inside Chanel*, Chapter 1, No.5, accessed July 31, 2018, http://inside.chanel.com/en/no5/campaigns.

74 **In them, she recalled parts of her childhood:** Morand, *The Allure of Chanel*, 17–18.

74 **Later in the same book:** Morand, *The Allure of Chanel*, 24.

74 **Later in life:** Garelick, *Mademoiselle*, 203.

74 **The woman history knows as Coco:** Garelick, *Mademoiselle*, 4.

74 **She was impoverished:** Garelick, *Mademoiselle*, 8.

74 **Gabrielle's mother did indeed die young:** Garelick, *Mademoiselle*, 12.

74 **while Gabrielle never saw her father again:** Garelick, *Mademoiselle*, 14–17.

75 **In between sets:** Garelick, *Mademoiselle*, 32–36.

75 **It was common for French:** Garelick, *Mademoiselle*, 36–38.

75 **Coco found herself:** "Although on the eve of their decline, the great courtesans were still the recognized queens of fashionable Paris," Galante, *Mademoiselle Chanel*, 20.

75 **Chanel lived at Balsan's estate:** Garelick, *Mademoiselle*, 47–49.

75 **She claimed that:** Morand, *The Allure of Chanel*, 43.

75 **During her time at Royallieu:** Morand, *The Allure of Chanel*, 34.

76 **Capel, who was covering her expenses:** Morand, *The Allure of Chanel*, 40.

76 **At 21 Rue Cambon:** Garelick, *Mademoiselle*, 53–64.

76 **In 1913, with Capel's encouragement:** Garelick, *Mademoiselle*, 53–64, 68–70.

76 **town of Deauville:** Garelick, *Mademoiselle*, 89.

77 **"Nothing. I didn't even know dressmakers existed":** Morand, *The Allure of Chanel*, 42–43.

77 **Chanel asked him to produce:** Lisa Chaney, *Coco Chanel: An Intimate Life* (New York: Viking, 2011), 107.

77 **By May 1916 in Paris:** "1916: Crazy for Chanel Sportswear," *International Herald Tribune*, reprinted March 7, 2016, https://iht-retrospective.blogs.nytimes.com/2016/03/07/1916-crazy-for-chanel-sportswear/.

77 **She wasn't the first person:** Garelick, *Mademoiselle*, 84–85.

78 **"And Chanel made dresses":** "Coco Chanel Was the Original Jersey Girl," *Vogue Australia*, April 9, 2010, www.vogue.com.au/fashion/news/coco-chanel-was-the-original-jersey-girl/news-story/805ae884ab158711852cf19ee817ceed?.

78 **"Women were full of gussets":** Janet Flanner, "31, Rue Cambon," *The New Yorker*, March 14, 1931, www.newyorker.com/magazine/1931/03/14/31-rue-cambon-2.

78 **"they [women] were bound":** Morand, *The Allure of Chanel*, 51–52.

78 **As a 1931 *New Yorker* article:** Flanner, "31, Rue Cambon."

78 **"I liberated the body":** Morand, *The Allure of Chanel*, 45–6.

78 **As one of her former Biarritz:** Marie-Louise Deray, quoted in Garelick, *Mademoiselle*, 92.

79 **She'd done well enough:** Garelick, *Mademoiselle*, 92–93.

79 **But she was successful:** Garelick, *Mademoiselle*, 91.

79 **"I didn't go out":** Morand, *The Allure of Chanel*, 146.

79 **Glossy floors were covered with furs:** "Cécile Sorel dans Son Appartement du Quai Voltaire," *BNF*, n.d., http://gallica.bnf.fr/ark:/12148/btv1b90252856.r=cecile+sorel.langFR.

79 **"moth-eaten leopard skins":** Taken from Misia Sert's memoir of Coco Chanel, reprinted in Arthur Gold and Robert Fizdale, *Misia: The Life of Misia Sert* (New York: Morrow Quill Paperbacks, 1981), 197.

80 **Dubbed "the Queen of Paris":** Garelick, *Mademoiselle*, 154–55.

80 **At Sorel's dinner:** Gold and Fizdale, *Misia*, 197.

80 **Silently sitting across the table:** See: Joseph Barry, "Portrait of Chanel No. 1," *The New York Times*, August 23, 1964, www.nytimes.com/1964/08/23/portrait-of-chanel-no-1.html?_r=1.

80 **Following dinner, Misia:** Taken from Misia Sert's memoir of Coco Chanel, reprinted in Gold and Fizdale, *Misia*, 197.

80 **As the evening was ending:** Gold and Fizdale, *Misia*, 197.

81 **refusing to pursue lawsuits:** Garelick, *Mademoiselle*, 390–91.

81 **As Misia wrote in the 1940s:** Gold and Fizdale, *Misia*, 199.

81 **According to Garelick:** Garelick, *Mademoiselle*, 155.

81 **She enchanted each of these men:** Barry, "Portrait of Chanel No. 1."

82　**It's no surprise:** Mukti Khaire and Kerry Herman, "Coco Chanel: Creating Fashion for the Modern Woman," Harvard Business School (case study), April 16, 2016, 9.

82　**He wrote his wife:** Letter from Winston to Clementine Churchill, quoted in Garelick, *Mademoiselle,* 187–88.

83　**her fashion empire:** Khaire and Herman, "Coco Chanel: Creating Fashion for the Modern Woman," 9.

83　**Page one of the *New York Times:*** "Chanel Offers Her Shop to Workers to Run, Rather Than Make Contract She Can't Keep," *The New York Times,* June 19, 1936.

84　**tried to use Aryanization laws:** Garelick, *Mademoiselle,* 331–333.

84　**Predictably, the scheme failed:** For a deep discussion of Chanel's involvement in "Modellhut," see Garelick, *Mademoiselle* 340–43.

85　**except perfume:** Garelick, *Mademoiselle,* 305.

85　**"Never was I":** Garelick, *Mademoiselle,* 359.

85　**Skeptically, the matriarch of fashion:** Ashley Senft, "History of Dior," February 2, 2011, http://www.fashionintime.org/history-of-dior/.

85　**upstart Christian Dior:** Garelick, *Mademoiselle,* 370.

85　**"It's quite a revolution":** Elsa de Berker, "The Journey of Dior's New Look from 1947 to Today," *CR,* December 2, 2015, www.crfashionbook.com/fashion/a10224424/the-journey-diors -new-look/.

85　**"He doesn't dress women":** Garelick, *Mademoiselle,* 370–72.

86　**Even she "leapt at the chance":** Garelick, *Mademoiselle,* 372–73.

86　**In a pre–World War II article:** Flanner, "31, Rue Cambon."

86　**Later on, in between yacht rides:** "Inside Chanel: The Vocabulary of Fashion," Chanel n.d., http://inside.chanel.com/en/the-vocabulary-of-fashion.

86　**"I imposed black":** Morand, *The Allure of Chanel,* 47.

87　**As one Chanel model remembers:** Ann Montgomery, *Another Me: A Memoir* (Bloomington, IN: iUniverse, 2008), 138.

87　**There was a hierarchy:** Montgomery, *Another Me,* 143.

87　**"In other establishments":** Morand, *The Allure of Chanel,* 73.

87　**After passing through:** Garelick, *Mademoiselle,* 393.

87　**Princess Odile de Croy:** Garelick, *Mademoiselle,* 393.

88　**"This dress will not . . .":** Morand, *The Allure of Chanel,* 147.

88　**In another instance she threw:** Barry, "Portrait of Chanel No. 1."

88　**shredding their designs:** Garelick, *Mademoiselle,* 395.

88　**Ann Montgomery, a model for Chanel:** Montgomery, *Another Me,* 145.

89　**generous as a boss:** Garelick, *Mademoiselle,* 395.

89　**"I am not the least frivolous":** Morand, *The Allure of Chanel,* 171.

89　**"She was exhausting":** Garelick, *Mademoiselle,* 397.

89　**"make their appearance with all":** Edmonde Charles-Roux, *Chanel and Her World: Friends, Fashion, and Fame,* English translation (New York: Vendome Press, 2005), 360–61.

89　**One review . . . across the Atlantic:** Garelick, *Mademoiselle,* 376, 379.

90　**"I want to go on":** Garelick, *Mademoiselle,* 380.

90　**"Nothing was written":** Morand, *The Allure of Chanel,* 13.

90　**"I would make":** Morand, *The Allure of Chanel,* 175.

91　**"complete, full, undisturbed":** Thomas, *Walt Disney: An American Original,* 217–18.

91　**asked his lawyer:** Gabler, *Walt Disney,* 476.

91　**the most exacting details:** Thomas, *Walt Disney: An American Original,* 214–17.

92　**twenty-pound ornamental hats:** Jessa Crispin, "Hot Coco: The Chanel Bio Is Suddenly En Vogue," *Need to Know on PBS* (blog), September 14, 2010, www.pbs.org/wnet/need-to-know /opinion/hot-coco/3548/.

92　**"I was in the right place":** Morand, *The Allure of Chanel,* 43.

Chapter 4: The Geniuses

98　**rejected for publication:** Kameshwar C. Wali, ed., *Satyendra Nath Bose: His Life and Times (with Commentary)* (Singapore: World Scientific, 2009), xix–xx.

98　**most famous scientist:** In 1921, Bertrand Russell, the famous British philosopher, was touring in Japan. Asked by his hosts who the three most famous men in the world were, and therefore whom they should invite next, Russell said Einstein and Lenin, without naming a third. From Albrecht Fölsing, *Albert Einstein: A Biography* (New York: Viking, 1997), 524, 48.

98   **If you think:** Satyendra Nath Bose, "Satyendra Nath Bose to Albert Einstein," June 4, 1924, *The Collected Papers of Albert Einstein, Volume 14: The Berlin Years: Writings & Correspondence, April 1923–May 1925*, http://einsteinpapers.press.princeton.edu/vol14-doc/501.

98   **except for prints:** An article by Elias Tobenkin in the March 26, 1921, edition of the *New York Evening Post*, quoted in Fölsing, *Albert Einstein*, 428.

98   **the most prolific:** "Einstein Online: An Interview with Diana Kormos-Buchwald," The California Institute of Technology, accessed September 13, 2017, www.caltech.edu/news/einstein-online-interview-diana-kormos-buchwald-44998.

99   **"I have translated":** Albert Einstein, "Albert Einstein to Satyendra Nath Bose," July 2, 1924, *The Collected Papers of Albert Einstein, Volume 14*.

99   **"I cannot exactly":** Satyendra Nath Bose, "Satyendra Nath Bose to Albert Einstein," January 27, 1925, *The Collected Papers of Albert Einstein, Volume 14*.

101   **They move toward the bowling ball:** Walter Isaacson, *Einstein: His Life and Universe* (New York: Simon & Schuster, 2007), 4.

101   **While Einstein is indisputably credited:** John S. Rigden, *Einstein 1905: The Standard of Greatness* (Cambridge, MA: Harvard University Press, 2005), 7.

101   **quantum theory had its roots:** Albert Einstein, "On a Heuristic Point of View Concerning the Production and Transformation of Light," *Annalen Der Physik* 17 (1905): 132–48, http://einsteinpapers.press.princeton.edu/vol2-trans/100. The revolutionary sentence: "In accordance with the assumption to be considered here, the energy of a light ray spreading out from a point source is not continuously distributed over an increasing space but consists of a finite number of energy quanta which are localized at points in space, which move without dividing, and which can only be produced and absorbed as complete units."

101   **Einstein's then-radical idea:** Rigden, *Einstein 1905*, 21.

101   **while his fame is based on:** Frederic Golden, "Albert Einstein," *Time*, December 31, 1999, http://content.time.com/time/magazine/article/0,9171,993017,00.html.

101   **The day after his theory of general relativity:** "Lights All Askew in the Heavens, Men of Science More or Less Agog over Results of Eclipse Observations. Einstein Theory Triumphs. Stars Not Where They Seemed or Were Calculated to Be, but Nobody Need Worry. A Book for 12 Wise Men. No More in All the World Could Comprehend It, Said Einstein When His Daring Publishers Accepted It," *The New York Times*, November 10, 1919, http://query.nytimes.com/mem/archive-free/pdf?res=9b0de3df1e38ee32a25753c1a9679d946896d6cf.

102   **He was awed:** Albert Einstein, *Autobiographical Notes*, trans. Paul Arthur Schilpp (La Salle, IL: Open Court, 1999), 9.

102   **As he put it:** Einstein, *Autobiographical Notes*, 9.

102   **This lucidity and certainty:** Einstein, *Autobiographical Notes*, 9.

102   **In his own words, he had a tendency:** Einstein, *Autobiographical Notes*, 15.

103   **As his sister, Maja, remembered:** Maja Einstein, quoted in Fölsing, *Albert Einstein*, 33.

103   **sent his uncle:** Fölsing, *Albert Einstein*, 35.

103   **He famously pondered:** Einstein, *Autobiographical Notes*, 49.

103   **The two immediately began:** Fölsing, *Albert Einstein*, 53.

104   **the classes he'd skipped:** Einstein suspected the "underhandedness" of one of his professors in preventing him from getting an academic job. Albert Einstein, "Albert Einstein to Marcel Grossmann," April 14, 1901, trans. Anna Beck, *The Collected Papers of Albert Einstein, Volume 1: The Early Years, 1879–1902* (English Translation Supplement), http://einsteinpapers.press.prince ton.edu/vol1-trans/187.

104   **Albert never met his daughter:** There is no record of Lieserl after the age of two, but one theory is that she was given up for adoption to one of Mileva's friends who lived in Belgrade. See Fölsing, *Albert Einstein*, 113–14.

104   **He closes the note by saying:** Hermann Einstein, "Hermann Einstein to Wilhelm Ostwald," April 13, 1901, trans. Anna Beck, *The Collected Papers of Albert Einstein, Volume 1*.

105   **He then spends a paragraph:** Albert Einstein, "Albert Einstein to Marcel Grossmann," April 14, 1901.

105   **Einstein met Marić:** Albert Einstein, "Albert Einstein to Mileva Maric," April 15, 1901, trans. Anna Beck, *The Collected Papers of Albert Einstein, Volume 1*.

106   **He continued to submit articles to:** Fölsing, *Albert Einstein*, 118.

106   **He visited their evening meetings often:** Fölsing, *Albert Einstein*, 113.

106   **The name was an inside joke:** As an example of the good-naturedness of the group, Einstein's "Dedication" into the Academy closed with the line "Infallible high priest of the downtrodden." Anna Beck, "Dedication, Einstein as Member of the Olympia Academy," 1903, *The Collected*

Papers of Albert Einstein, Volume 5: The Swiss Years: Correspondence, 1902–1914, http://einstein papers.press.princeton.edu/vol5-trans/27.

106 **The three met regularly:** Fölsing, *Albert Einstein,* 99.

107 **"The paper deals with radiation":** Albert Einstein, "Albert Einstein to Conrad Habicht," May 18, 1905, trans. Anna Beck, *The Collected Papers of Albert Einstein, Volume 5.*

108 **Planck's support brought needed attention:** Albert Einstein, "Max Planck as Scientist," *Natur-wissenschaften* 1 (1913): 274.

109 **Einstein later credited:** This is a translation of a lecture Einstein gave in Kyoto, Japan, on December 24, 1922. Albert Einstein, "How I Created the Theory of Relativity," trans. Yoshimasa A. Ono, *Physics Today,* August 1982, 46.

109 **In May 1905:** Einstein, "How I Created the Theory of Relativity," 46.

110 **Einstein himself once conceded that:** According to Alexander Moszkowski, whose 1921 book was based on a series of conversations with Einstein. Quoted in Isaacson, *Einstein: His Life and Universe,* 127.

110 **At the end of the note:** Albert Einstein, "Albert Einstein to Conrad Habicht," September 30, 1905, *The Collected Papers of Albert Einstein, Volume 5.*

110 **Einstein scholar John Rigden:** Rigden, *Einstein 1905,* 2.

111 **This thought, whose culmination:** "I could not solve this problem completely at that time. It took me eight more years until I finally obtained the complete solution." Einstein, "How I Created the Theory of Relativity," 46–47.

111 **Einstein cautioned Stark:** Albert Einstein, "Albert Einstein to Johannes Stark," September 25, 1907, *The Collected Papers of Albert Einstein, Volume 5.* Emphasis is Einstein's own.

111 **Over the next four years:** Fölsing, *Albert Einstein,* 328.

111 **"I am no less grateful to you":** Albert Einstein, "Albert Einstein to the Prussian Academy of Sciences," December 7, 1913, *The Collected Papers of Albert Einstein, Volume 5.*

112 **On inducting Einstein:** Max Planck quoted in Fölsing, *Albert Einstein,* 339.

112 **A sort of roundtable of the German intellectual elite:** Fölsing, *Albert Einstein,* 336.

112 **A few weeks after settling in Berlin:** Albert Einstein, "Albert Einstein to Adolf Hurwitz and Family," May 4, 1914, *The Collected Papers of Albert EInstein, Volume 8: The Berlin Years: Correspondence, 1914–1918* (English Translation Supplement), http://einsteinpapers.press.princeton .edu/vol8-trans/41. Fölsing says that the "uncles" referred to were "presumably his fellow academicians." Alternatively, the Einstein Papers Project, in a footnote in the archived letter, say that Einstein is referring to Jacob Kock and Rudolf Einstein, two of Einstein's actual uncles who were living in Berlin at the time.

112 **In his inaugural lecture:** Fölsing, *Albert Einstein,* 336.

112 **For the rest of the lecture:** Albert Einstein, "Inaugural Lecture," July 2, 1914, *The Collected Papers of Albert Einstein, Volume 6: The Berlin Years: Writings, 1914–1917* (English Translation Supplement), http://einsteinpapers.press.princeton.edu/vol6-trans/28.

113 **As Planck continued in his response:** Quoted in Fölsing, *Albert Einstein,* 339–40.

114 **The thought experiment:** Einstein, "How I Created the Theory of Relativity," 47.

114 **as Einstein remembers of this day in 1907:** Einstein, "How I Created the Theory of Relativity," 47.

115 **Einstein described the path to general relativity:** Albert Einstein, "Albert Einstein to Hendrik A. Lorentz," January 17, 1916, *The Collected Papers of Albert Einstein, Volume 8.*

115 **In the paper, Einstein predicted:** Albert Einstein, "On the Influence of Gravitation on the Propagation of Light," *Annalen Der Physik* 35 (1911), in *The Collected Papers of Albert Einstein, Volume 3: The Swiss Years: Writings 1909–1911* (English Translation Supplement), http://einsteinpapers.press .princeton.edu/vol3-trans/393 898–908.

115 **A couple experiments:** Fölsing, *Albert Einstein,* 356–58.

115 **"describing physical laws without reference to geometry":** Einstein, "How I Created the Theory of Relativity," 47.

116 **To learn this complex math:** Fölsing, *Albert Einstein,* 314.

116 **"After two years of struggle":** Einstein, "How I Created the Theory of Relativity," 47.

116 **"In thanking you again":** Albert Einstein, "Albert Einstein to Hendrik A. Lorentz," January 17, 1916, *The Collected Papers of Albert EInstein, Volume 8.*

117 **Ben-Gurion pleaded:** A recollection of Yitzhak Navon, Ben-Gurion's assistant and the future president of Israel. Quoted in Fölsing, *Albert Einstein,* 734.

117 **Thankfully for Ben-Gurion:** Albert Einstein to Abba Eban, November 18, 1952. Quoted in Fölsing, *Albert Einstein,* 733.

117 **In a letter to a friend:** Albert Einstein to Josef Scharl, November 24, 1952. Quoted in Fölsing, *Albert Einstein*, 734.

117 **On November 7, the *Times* of London:** "Revolution in Science; New Theory of the Universe: Newtonian Ideas Overthrown," *The Times*, November 7, 1919.

117 **Three days later:** "Lights All Askew in the Heavens, Men of Science More or Less Agog over Results of Eclipse Observations."

118 **public political disagreement:** At the outbreak of World War I, most of Einstein's German colleagues published a famous letter known to history as "The Manifesto of the Ninety-three." The document was a whitewashing of Germany's role in World War I. It begins: "As representatives of German Science and Art, we hereby protest to the civilized world against the lies and calumnies with which our enemies are endeavoring to stain the honor of Germany in her hard struggle for existence—in a struggle that has been forced on her." It only gets more nationalistic and antagonistic from there. See: Professors of Germany, "To the Civilized World," *The North American Review* 210, no. 765 (August 1919): 284–87, https://www.jstor.org/stable/25122278?seq=1#page_scan_tab_ contents. "The Ninety-Three Today," *The New York Times*, March 2, 1921, https://timesmachine .nytimes.com/timesmachine/1921/03/02/107009542.html?action=click&contentCollection= Archives&module=LedeAsset&region=ArchiveBody&pgtype=article&pageNumber=7. Einstein not only refused to sign, but with his colleague and friend Georg Nicolai, signed a "Manifesto to the Europeans" that called for cultural and scientific cooperation among Europeans on all sides of the war and specifically called out "scientists and artists" who "have thus far only uttered things which suggest that their desire for maintaining relations has vanished . . . Such a mood cannot be excused by any national passion; it is unworthy of what the entire world has now come to understand by the name of culture." Einstein was always outspoken, and his convictions were always more important to him than whatever job he happened to have at the moment. "Manifesto to the Europeans," October 1914, in *Einstein on Politics: His Private Thoughts and Public Stands on Nationalism, Zionism, War, Peace, and the Bomb*, ed. David E. Rowe and Robert Schulmann (Princeton, NJ: Princeton University Press, 2007), 64–67.

118 **wrote about it to his old friend:** Albert Einstein, "Albert Einstein to Michele Besso," December 12, 1919, *The Collected Papers of Albert Einstein, Volume 9, The Berlin Years: Correspondence, January 1919–April 1920*, http://einsteinpapers.press.princeton.edu/vol9-trans/200.

118 **He wrote to Maurice Solovine:** Albert Einstein, "Albert Einstein to Maurice Solovine," March 8, 1921, trans. Ann M. Hentschel, *The Collected Papers of Albert Einstein, Volume 12: The Berlin Years: Correspondence, 1921*, http://einsteinpapers.press.princeton.edu/vol12-trans/92.

118 **Fritz Haber, a chemist and German Jew:** Fritz Haber, "Fritz Haber to Albert Einstein," March 9, 1921, trans. Ann M. Hentschel, *The Collected Papers of Albert Einstein, Volume 12*.

118 **Einstein was exceedingly courteous:** Albert Einstein, "Albert Einstein to Fritz Haber," March 9, 1921, trans. Ann M. Hentschel, *The Collected Papers of Albert Einstein, Volume 12*.

119 **Even seventy years after his vacation:** Corey Kilgannon, "No Sailor, for Sure, but He Had Relativity Down Cold," *The New York Times*, July 21, 2007, www.nytimes.com/2007/07/21/nyregion /21einstein.html.

119 **The two struck up a friendship:** Kilgannon, "No Sailor, for Sure, but He Had Relativity Down Cold."

119 **The note warned:** Albert Einstein to Franklin Delano Roosevelt, August 2, 1939, in Einstein, *Einstein on Politics*, 359–61.

120 **Einstein was not involved:** "By late 1944, however, he learned through Otto Stern that work on atomic weapons was advancing at a rapid pace." Rowe and Schulmann, *Einstein on Politics*, 363.

121 **by the end of his life:** Max Born and Albert Einstein, *The Born-Einstein Letters 1916–1955: Friendship, Politics and Physics in Uncertain Times*, trans. Irene Born (New York: Macmillan, 2005), 179.

121 **The same Max Born:** Quoted in Abraham Pais, *Subtle Is the Lord: The Science and the Life of Albert Einstein* (Oxford: Oxford University Press, 1982), 442.

122 **he mocked his own irrelevance:** Albert Einstein to Niels Bohr, April 4, 1949, quoted in Fölsing, *Albert Einstein*, 553.

122 **comfortably described his "attitude towards the simple life":** Born and Einstein, *The Born-Einstein Letters 1916–1955*, 178–79.

122 **"Now he has":** Quoted in Fölsing, *Albert Einstein*, 741.

123 **"an educational mission":** Harold C. Schonberg, "New Job for the Protean Mr. Bernstein," *The New York Times*, December 22, 1957, 120, https://timesmachine.nytimes.com/timesmachine /1957/12/22/issue.html.

123 **comparatively pedestrian headline:** "Young Aide Leads Philharmonic, Steps in When Bruno Walter Is Ill," *The New York Times*, November 15, 1943, https://timesmachine.nytimes.com/times machine/1943/11/15/issue.html.

124 **Lenny's flamboyant conducting style:** Olin Downes, "Bernstein Shows Mastery of the Score," *The New York Times*, November 15, 1943, https://timesmachine.nytimes.com/timesmachine/1943 /11/15/88579746.html?pageNumber=40.

124 **ringing endorsement of the performance:** "A Story Old and Ever New," *The New York Times*, November 16, 1943, https://timesmachine.nytimes.com/timesmachine/1943/11/16/85134894.html ?pageNumber=22.

124 **As New York's *Daily News* put it:** Quoted in Humphrey Burton, *Leonard Bernstein* (London: Faber and Faber, 1995), 117.

125 **the New Deal instigated a Federal Music Project:** Alex Ross, *The Rest Is Noise: Listening to the Twentieth Century* (London: Harper Perennial, 2009), 303.

125 **he was well aware he might be called on to fill:** Leonard Bernstein and Nigel Simeone, *The Leonard Bernstein Letters* (New Haven, CT: Yale University Press, 2013), 33.

125 **Bernstein's less favorable reviewers:** Quoted in Burton, *Leonard Bernstein*, 117.

125 **Bernstein can be heard stomping his foot:** Humphrey Burton, *Ode to Freedom—Beethoven: Symphony No. 9 Official Concert of the Fall of the Berlin Wall 1989*, DVD, 2009.

126 **a role performed in rotation:** John H. Mueller, *The American Symphony Orchestra: A Social History of Musical Taste* (Bloomington: Indiana University Press, 1951), 310.

126 **the conductor's diminutive role:** Quoted in Mueller, *The American Symphony Orchestra*, 316.

126 **an outrageous power grab by the conductor:** Mueller, *The American Symphony Orchestra*, 311.

127 **to level class signifiers in Soviet Russia:** James Chater, "A Renaissance of Conductorless Orchestras Reveals the Limits of Traditional Leadership," *New Statesman*, July 25, 2016, https://www .newstatesman.com/culture/music-theatre/2016/07/renaissance-conductorless-orchestras-reveals -limits-traditional.

127 **the true conductor was one who had:** Burton, *Leonard Bernstein*, 252.

127 **memorialized in his *New York Times* obituary:** Donal Henahan, "Leonard Bernstein, 72, Music's Monarch, Dies," *The New York Times*, October 15, 1990, sec. B, https://timesmachine.nytimes .com/timesmachine/1990/10/15/issue.html.

128 **creating a feeling shared but also owned:** Burton, *Leonard Bernstein*, 253.

128 **"boyishly bewildered by his success":** Burton, *Leonard Bernstein*, 139.

128 **sent him a "personality analysis":** Bernstein and Simeone, *The Leonard Bernstein Letters*, 186.

129 **first scores produced by an acknowledged American symphonist:** Burton, *Leonard Bernstein*, 135–36, 192–93.

129 **what a desegregated world might look like:** Carol J. Oja, *Bernstein Meets Broadway: Collaborative Art in a Time of War* (New York: Oxford University Press, 2014), 155. We are also grateful to Professor Oja for her personal time and helpful insights into this aspect of Bernstein's work.

130 **One dancer told of the excitement of having Lenny:** Burton, *Leonard Bernstein*, 133–34.

130 **Bernstein reports of Koussevitzky's reaction:** Burton, *Leonard Bernstein*, 136.

130 **the conundrum facing Bernstein at the time:** Virgil Thomson, *Herald Tribune*, 1946, quoted in Burton, *Leonard Bernstein*, 146.

131 **"I like to do everything just once . . .":** Burton, *Leonard Bernstein*, 139.

131 **The dark ambiguities of leading some of these orchestras:** Leonard Bernstein to "Twig" Romney, Scheveningen, Netherlands, June 20, 1948, in Bernstein and Simeone, *The Leonard Bernstein Letters*, 243.

132 **the squalid environs of remaining Jews:** Burton, *Leonard Bernstein*, 175.

132 **"[I] cried my heart out":** Burton, *Leonard Bernstein*, 176.

132 **"stamped and shouted" in appreciation in Budapest:** Leonard Bernstein to Helen Coates, Budapest, Hungary, May 20, 1948, in Bernstein and Simeone, *The Leonard Bernstein Letters*, 240.

132 **the same rapturous public congratulation:** Quoted in Burton, *Leonard Bernstein*, 177.

133 **soaked up the sound of the performances he conducted:** Burton, *Leonard Bernstein*, 162.

133 **a rare self-awareness:** Burton, *Leonard Bernstein*,185.

134 **a more regal Felicia posed:** Agnes Ash, "Philarmonic Expected to Open on a High Fashion Note," *The New York Times*, October 1, 1958, https://timesmachine.nytimes.com/timesmachine/1958/10 /01/81888263.html?pageNumber=41.

134 **he unnervingly concluded:** Burton, *Leonard Bernstein*, 213.

134 **New York socialite Elsa Maxwell:** Burton, *Leonard Bernstein*, 298.
134 **getting young, wealthy New Yorkers to go:** Agnes Ash, "Elegant Styles Are Due at Carnegie Hall Event."
134 **as late as 1955 told journalists that:** Burton, *Leonard Bernstein*, 250.
134 **Respite from the grind of national and international travel:** Burton, *Leonard Bernstein*, 284.
134 **the Bernsteins had a curious definition:** Burton, *Leonard Bernstein*, 285.
135 **the Philharmonic recorded:** Burton, *Leonard Bernstein*, 282.
135 **He used custom batons:** Margalit Fox, "Richard Horowitz, Timpanist and Craftsman of Conductors' Batons, Dies at 91," *The New York Times*, November 11, 2015, sec. Music, www.nytimes.com /2015/11/12/arts/music/richard-horowitz-renowned-timpanist-and-craftsman-of-conductors -batons-dies-at-91.html.
135 **a Byzantine monk frantically:** Burton, *Leonard Bernstein*, 283.
135 **lack of discipline:** Burton, *Leonard Bernstein*, 292.
136 **"demonstrably he was their master":** Burton, *Leonard Bernstein*, 293.
136 **"something is right in the world":** Allen Shawn, *Leonard Bernstein: An American Musician* (New Haven, CT, and London: Yale University Press, 2016), 130.
137 **The three main cultural influences:** Leonard Bernstein, "The Absorption of Race Elements into American Music" (Harvard University, 1939), 4, Harvard Univeristy Isham Memorial Library.
137 **"the mighty American river":** "The Absorption of Race Elements," 73.
137 **"My world changes from one of abstractions":** Leonard Bernstein to Shirley Bernstein, April 18, 1950, in Bernstein and Simeone, *The Leonard Bernstein Letters*, 270.
138 **"a work I've been writing":** Burton, *Leonard Bernstein*, 408.
139 **"slams the door of the Kennedy Center":** Maurice Peress, *Dvořák to Duke Ellington: A Conductor Explores America's Music and Its African American Roots* (Oxford and New York: Oxford University Press, 2004), 143.
139 **President Nixon and his chief of staff:** Leonard Bernstein, "H. R. Haldeman Briefs President Nixon on Leonard Bernstein's *MASS*," accessed March 3, 2018, www.youtube.com /watch?v=iH6ckg4BK7k.
139 **the suspicion Bernstein's creation was held in:** See Burton, *Leonard Bernstein*, 406, 413.
140 **live in ambiguities:** Peress, *Dvořák to Duke Ellington*, 143.
140 **penultimate and last scenes of the work:** Peress, *Dvořák to Duke Ellington*, 146–50.
140 **angrily directing their frustrations at their leader:** Peress, *Dvořák to Duke Ellington*, 148.
141 **Peace! Peace!:** Peress, *Dvořák to Duke Ellington*, 148.
141 **in the days before the first performance:** Peress, *Dvořák to Duke Ellington*, 148.
141 **final, frantic rehearsals:** Peress, *Dvořák to Duke Ellington*, 148.
142 **silver and gold mezuzah:** John Canarina, *The New York Philharmonic: From Bernstein to Maazel* (New York: Amadeus Press, 2010), 67.
142 **helped him keep his attention:** Burton, *Leonard Bernstein*, 437–39.
142 **he had caused Felicia's death:** Burton, *Leonard Bernstein*, 446–47.
142 **a speaker pronounced to a huge crowd:** Burton, *Leonard Bernstein*, 452.
142 **"the most horrible night of my life":** Burton, *Leonard Bernstein*, 452.
143 **"there isn't much time":** Quoted in Burton, *Leonard Bernstein*, 452–53.
143 **According to Ruth Leon:** Personal interview with Ruth Leon.
143 **a tension that he never fully reconciled:** Quoted in Shawn, *Leonard Bernstein*, 266.
143 **"Lenny died a disappointed man":** Personal interview with Ruth Leon.
143 **"I want to devote most of the remaining energy":** Quoted in Burton, *Leonard Bernstein*, 499.
144 **the subtleties of this kind of teaching:** Quoted in Shawn, *Leonard Bernstein*, 133.
144 **No video recording of this performance:** Alessandra Lombardini-Parks, *Leonard Bernstein Final Concert*, accessed March 3, 2018, www.youtube.com/watch?v=6Kyr0MknQec&list=RD6Kyr0MknQec&t=2.
146 **"like everyone else only more so":** "Leonard Bernstein Remembered by His Friends," *The New York Times*, October 21, 1990, sec. Arts, www.nytimes.com/1990/10/21/arts/leonard-bernstein -remembered-by-his-friends.html.
146 **"Why is it":** Daniel Schwartz, "The Einstein Theory of Living," *The New York Times*, March 12, 1944, https://timesmachine.nytimes.com/timesmachine/1944/03/12/96574583.pdf.
146 **"by his friends":** "Leonard Bernstein Remembered by His Friends."
147 **"smoked, dried, canned":** Albert Einstein, "Albert Einstein to Conrad Habicht," May 18, 1905, trans. Anna Beck, *The Collected Papers of Albert Einstein, Volume 5*.
147 **"an introspective person":** Shawn, *Leonard Bernstein*, 89.
147 **"I have to be both":** Shawn, *Leonard Bernstein*, 135.

148 *slightly* **above-average:** Bernard M. Bass and Ruth Bass, *The Bass Handbook of Leadership: Theory, Research, and Managerial Applications*, 4th ed. (New York: Free Press, 2008), 83–84.

Chapter 5: The Zealots

154 **the three waistcoats:** Hector Fleischmann, *Robespierre and the Women He Loved* (London: Long, 1913), 80. Robespierre had "a black cloth coat, a satin waistcoat in fairly good condition, a waistcoat of raz de Saint-Maur rather the worse for wear. . . ."

154 **His face twitched:** Peter McPhee, *Robespierre: A Revolutionary Life* (New Haven, CT: Yale University Press, 2012), 48–49. "He also had an uncontrollable facial twitch, affecting his eyes and at times his mouth."

154 **milling about the room:** McPhee, *Robespierre*, 71. "In the Assembly, deputies unused to parliamentary procedure thought nothing of talking among themselves or moving about the chamber. Robespierre, whose voice was not sonorous and whose accent was sometimes mocked, was interrupted to the point of having to stand down from the podium on at least one occasion."

155 **"Let the bishops":** Quoted in McPhee, *Robespierre*, 65.

155 **spokesman of the left:** McPhee, *Robespierre*, 65; J. M. Thompson, *Robespierre and the French Revolution: A Study of the Ideals and the Realities of the Revolution as Revealed in the Life of Its Most Controversial Spokesman* (New York: Collier Books, 1962), 19.

155 **writings of Jean-Jacques Rousseau:** Ruth Scurr, *Fatal Purity: Robespierre and the French Revolution* (New York: Metropolitan Books, 2006), 25. According to Scurr, "We do not know when Robespierre first read Rousseau. Very probably it was during his time at Louis-le-Grand. What is indisputable is that when he did he took him into his mind as a companion for life." Plutarch's life of Lycurgus, the Spartan lawmaker, was also quite important to Robespierre. Plutarch made up an important part of the schooling for most of the highly educated class in Robespierre's lifetime.

156 **"make him stand out":** Étienne Reybaz, a speechwriter for the famous revolutionary Mirabeau, quoted in McPhee, *Robespierre*, 65.

156 **public procession to Paris:** Thompson, *Robespierre and the French Revolution*, 19–20. "It was not by accident that he was one of those chosen out of 600 to accompany the King to Paris on July 17. . . . His speeches in the Assembly show him increasingly an enemy of the throne and a champion of abstract rights—liberty of possession, liberty of conscience, liberty of opinion—such as were embodied in the first clauses of the Rights of Man."

156 **he made 38 speeches:** McPhee, *Robespierre*, 76, 97.

157 **"natural and imprescriptible rights":** "Declaration of the Rights of Man," August 26, 1789, Yale Law School–Avalon Project: Documents in Law, History and Diplomacy, http://avalon.law.yale.edu/18th_century/rightsof.asp.

157 **up for debate:** McPhee, *Robespierre*, 70. According to McPhee: "While the Declaration proclaimed the universality of rights and the civic equality of all citizens, it was ambiguous on whether all would have political as well as legal equality, and was silent on how the means to exercise one's talents could be secured by those without the education or property to do so."

157 **"All men are capable":** Robespierre, September 11, 1789, quoted in McPhee, *Robespierre*, 72.

157 **getting together at cafés:** Michael L. Kennedy, "The Foundation of the Jacobin Clubs and the Development of the Jacobin Club Network, 1789–1791," *The Journal of Modern History* 51, no. 4 (December 1979): 706.

158 **attempted to flee:** McPhee, *Robespierre*, 89–92.

159 **"share my fear":** Quoted in Scurr, *Fatal Purity*, 165.

159 **required no costume:** Simon Schama, *Citizens: A Chronicle of the French Revolution* (New York: Vintage Books, 1989), 603–4. According to Schama, a year later, when many revolutionaries began wearing the *bonnet rouge* (a red beret) as a sign of their revolutionary fervor, Robespierre refused to wear one.

159 **defend Robespierre's life:** Scurr, *Fatal Purity*, 165–66.

159 **join another society:** McPhee, *Robespierre*, 93.

160 **to around eight hundred:** McPhee, *Robespierre*, 97.

160 **"rare stormy destiny":** A. Jourdan, "Robespierre and Revolutionary Heroism," in *Robespierre and Revolutionary Heroism*, Colin Haydon and William Doyle, eds. (New York: Cambridge University Press, 1999), 68.

160 **become the symbol:** Jourdan, "Robespierre and Revolutionary Heroism," 96. In Jourdan's words: "the personification of unequivocal commitment to the principles of 1789, [and] a refusal to compromise with the persons and practices of the *ancien régime*."

160   **"Long live the Incorruptible!":** McPhee, *Robespierre*, 95–96.
162   **even renamed itself:** Schama, *Citizens*, 604.
162   **Some saw their presence:** Schama, *Citizens*, 604–9.
162   **"I would rather see":** Quoted in McPhee, *Robespierre*, 123–24.
162   **ardently against the presence:** Schama, *Citizens*, 605. "Ironically, Robespierre also opposed the camp of the *fédérés*, seeing in it an attempt by the government to use provincial guards to cow their more politically radical Paris co-citizens."
163   **"of the people myself":** McPhee, *Robespierre*, 118. From a speech by Robespierre in the Jacobin Club on April 27, 1792. The last phrase is among Robespierre's most famous utterances. In French: *"je suis peuple moi-même!"*
163   **"I do not trust":** Schama, *Citizens*, 601.
163   **"the most sacred duty":** Schama, *Citizens*, 612.
163   **a written warning:** "The Brunswick Manifesto," in James Harvey Robinson, ed., *Readings in European History*, volume II (Boston: Ginn, 1906), 443–45, https://archive.org/details/readings ineuro pe02robi_0.
164   **"French Brutuses are now":** Maxmilien Robespierre to Antoine Buissart, quoted in McPhee, *Robespierre*, 125.
164   **The Commune had:** Schama, *Citizens*, 613.
164   **all 600 had been massacred:** Schama, *Citizens*, 614–15.
165   **"In 1789 the people":** Scurr, *Fatal Purity*, 216.
165   **Robespierre's own hand:** McPhee, *Robespierre*, 119.
166   **hundreds of Jacobin Clubs:** Through 1792, some 1,533 Jacobin Clubs were known to have existed throughout France. In August, there is evidence that at least 340 of these clubs were actively in operation. See Kennedy, "The Best and the Worst of Times: The Jacobin Club Network from October 1791 to June 2, 1793," Journal of Modern History, vol. 56, issue 4, December 1984, 635–66.
167   **At its summit:** Thompson, *Robespierre and the French Revolution*, 70.
168   **forty thousand Frenchmen:** "Marie Antoinette and the French Revolution," PBS, September 13, 2006, http://www.pbs.org/marieantoinette/timeline/reign.html.
169   **"What is our aim":** *Papiers Inédits Trouves Chez Robespierre, Saint-Just, Payan, Etc. Supprimes Ou Omis Par Courtois; Precedes du Rapport de Ce Depute a La Convention Nationale*, vol. 2 (Paris: Baudouin Frères, 1828).
170   **"Whereas other members":** McPhee, *Robespierre*, 159.
170   **"Virtue and Terror":** Quoted in Scurr, *Fatal Purity*, 303–4.
171   **salons and dinners:** Marisa Linton, "Fatal Friendships: The Politics of Jacobin Friendship," *French Historical Studies* 31, no. 1 (Winter 2008): 62–65.
171   **aura of incorruptibility:** Marisa Linton, "Robespierre and Revolutionary Authenticity," *Annales Historiques de La Révolution Française*, no. 371 (2013): 153–71.
171   **"the most revealing document":** Thompson, *Robespierre and the French Revolution*, 113.
172   **the opening ceremonies:** Schama, *Citizens*, 831–34.
173   **"Being of Beings!":** Schama, *Citizens*, 834–36; Thompson, *Robespierre and the French Revolution*, 117–18; Scurr, *Fatal Purity*, 478.
173   **Convention received 1,235 letters:** McPhee, *Robespierre*, 198–99.
173   **the exact qualities:** Frank Tallett, "Robespierre and Religion," in *Robespierre* (New York: Cambridge University Press, 1999), 101. The author is quoting Gérarde Walter's *Robespierre*, Volume II Gillimard, Paris, 1946.
173   **"This revolution of ours":** An account of Robespierre given by the Marquis de Condorcet in the November 9, 1792, printing of the *Chronique de Paris*. Quoted in McPhee, *Robespierre*, 138, and Scurr, *Fatal Purity*, 237.
174   **the guillotine itself:** Scurr, *Fatal Purity*, 327.
174   **By these laws:** Schama, *Citizens*, 837.
175   **more than nine hundred people:** McPhee, *Robespierre*, 210; Scurr, *Fatal Purity*, 339; Thompson, *Robespierre and the French Revolution*, 109.
175   **June 18 and July 26:** For accounts of how Robespierre spent his time in seclusion, and different theories as to why he secluded himself in the first place, see: McPhee, *Robespierre*, 207–8; Scurr, *Fatal Purity*, 339; and Thompson, *Robespierre and the French Revolution*, 127.
175   **made up stories:** Linton, "Robespierre and Revolutionary Authenticity," 169–70. According to Linton, "The Thermidoreans perfectly appreciated the need to crush the image of Robespierre as a man of genuine virtue . . . [they] fabricated a series of imaginative stories designed to show that the private lives of the Robespierrists had been characterized by vice rather than virtue."
175   **stopped sleeping in:** Scurr, *Fatal Purity*, 347.

175   **"My speech is":** Scurr, *Fatal Purity*, 349.
176   **"Down with the tyrant!":** Scurr, *Fatal Purity*, 350–52.
176   **For his execution:** Scurr, *Fatal Purity*, 356–58.
178   **In an interview:** "Beheaded Man's Father: Revenge Breeds Revenge," CNN, June 8, 2006, www
      .cnn.com/2006/WORLD/meast/06/08/berg.interview/.
178   **meant to guard:** Joby Warrick, *Black Flags: The Rise of ISIS* (New York: Anchor Books, 2016), 17.
179   **Zarqawi sat patiently:** Warrick, *Black Flags*, 27.
179   **Born in 1966:** Jean Charles Brisard and Damian Martinez, *Zarqawi: The New Face of Al-Qaeda*
      (New York; Other Press), 2005.
179   **Fretting over her son's:** Warrick, *Black Flags*, 51–52.
179   **Only a few weeks earlier:** Bill Keller, "Last Soviet Soldiers Leave Afghanistan," *The New York
      Times*, February 16, 1989, https://partners.nytimes.com/library/world/africa/021689afghan-laden
      .html.
179   **Fighting continued between:** McChrystal, *My Share of the Task*, 281.
180   **According to a peer at the time:** Warrick, *Black Flags*, 52.
180   **In these skirmishes:** Warrick, *Black Flags*, 52–53.
180   **They settled on a name:** Warrick, *Black Flags*, 55.
180   **Bay'at al-Imam's early attempts:** Warrick, *Black Flags*, 19.
180   **After a shooting attack:** Brisard and Martinez, *Zarqawi*, 39.
180   **The group's plotting, however:** Warrick, *Black Flags*, 55.
181   **The Jordanian government eventually:** Warrick, *Black Flags*, 16.
181   **would have been intimidated:** Warrick, *Black Flags*, 51.
181   **hard-line understanding:** Wright, *The Looming Tower*, 72–73.
181   **Zarqawi took to wearing:** Weaver, "The Short, Violent Life of Abu Musab Al-Zarqawi,"
      The Atlantic.
181   **helped doctors administer:** Warrick, *Black Flags*, 25.
181   **He enforced Maqdisi's doctrine within:** Weaver, "The Short, Violent Life of Abu Musab Al-
      Zarqawi."
182   **Whereas the genteel Maqdisi:** Weaver, "The Short, Violent Life of Abu Musab Al-Zarqawi."
183   **In 1999, the death of:** Weaver, "The Short, Violent Life of Abu Musab Al-Zarqawi."
183   **Ayman al-Zawahiri:** Wright, *The Looming Tower*, 60–62, 246–47.
184   **"Iraq today harbors:** Colin Powell, "Remarks to the United Nations Security Council," February
      5, 2003, U.S. Department of State Archive, https://2001–2009.state.gov/secretary/former/powell
      /remarks/2003/17300.htm.
184   **Freed through happenstance:** Weaver, "The Short, Violent Life of Abu Musab Al-Zarqawi."
184   **most notably the 1998 bombings:** "Ex-Bin Laden Aide Sentenced to Life in Embassy Bombings,"
      BBC, May 18, 2015, www.bbc.com/news/world-us-canada-32757609.
184   **in Kenya and Tanzania:** National Commission on Terrorist Attacks upon the United States, ed.,
      *The 9/11 Commission Report: Final Report of the National Commission on Terrorist Attacks upon
      the United States* (New York: Norton, 2004), 115.
184   **While al-Qaeda's:** Weaver, "The Short, Violent Life of Abu Musab Al-Zarqawi."
185   **Apparently, after meeting:** Warrick, *Black Flags*, 67.
186   **Zarqawi accepted:** Weiss and Hassan *Isis: Inside the Army of Terror*, 14.
186   **Zarqawi's camp:** Weisfuse, "The Last Hope for the Al Qai'da Old Guard?"
186   **The group was often called:** Kilcullen, *Blood Year*, 21.
186   **All it needed:** Weiss and Hassan, *Isis*, 13.
186   **Since simplicity was:** Gerges, *ISIS: A History*, 59.
186   **A few of the early camp recruits:** Warrick, *Black Flags*, 68.
186   **from explosives expert Nidal Mohammed al-Arabi:** Authors' interview with Joby Warrick.
186   **Zarqawi took a second:** Warrick, *Black Flags*, 68.
186   **When Saif al-Adel visited:** Saif Al-adel, *Biography of Abu Musab Al-Zarqawi*, n.d., 7.
186   **According to a former associate:** Weiss and Hassan, *Isis*, 14.
187   **He reportedly took to:** Weaver, "The Short, Violent Life of Abu Musab Al-Zarqawi."
187   **By the time of America's:** Weaver, "The Short, Violent Life of Abu Musab Al-Zarqawi."
187   **Yet each of the five:** Weaver, "The Short, Violent Life of Abu Musab Al-Zarqawi."
187   **They had been dispersed:** Warrick, *Black Flags*, 69.
188   **Many of his Ba'athist:** Gerges, *ISIS: A History*, 109–110.
188   **As their unarmored vehicles:** Jeffrey Gettleman, "Enraged Mob in Falluja Kills 4 American Con-
      tractors," *The New York Times*, March 31, 2004, www.nytimes.com/2004/03/31/international

/worldspecial/enraged-mob-in-falluja-kills-4-american.html, and McChrystal, *My Share of the Task*, 125–26.

189 **News of heavy fighting:** McChrystal, *My Share of the Task*, 128–31.

190 **Locals swelled jihadi ranks:** McChrystal, *My Share of the Task*, 136.

190 **In the presence of these foreign agents:** McChrystal, *My Share of the Task*, 145.

190 **In visits to small cells of insurgents:** Authors' interview with Joby Warrick, April 2018.

190 **In an era when:** Authors' interview with Joby Warrick.

190 **On May 13:** Bing West, *No True Glory: A Frontline Account of the Battle for Fallujah* (New York: Bantam Books, 2005), 159.

191 **It was in a Fallujah:** West, *No True Glory*, 274.

191–92 **and it was his networks that were:** Louise Richardson, *What Terrorists Want: Understanding the Enemy, Containing the Threat* (New York: Random House, 2006), 118.

192 **From devastating attacks on:** John Burns and Jeffrey Gettleman, "Blasts at Shiite Ceremonies in Iraq Kill More than 140," *The New York Times*, March 2, 2004, www.nytimes.com/2004/03/02 /international/middleeast/blasts-at-shiite-ceremonies-in-iraq-kill-more-than.html?_r=0.

192 **to truck bombings in Basra:** "Scores Killed in Iraqi Bombings," BBC, April 21, 2004, http://news .bbc.co.uk/2/hi/middle_east/3644733.stm.

192 **wanted no association:** Kilcullen, *Blood Year*, 33–35.

192 **In one letter:** "Zawahiri's Letter to Zarqawi—English Translation.," July 2005, https://ctc.usma .edu/harmony-program/zawahiris-letter-to-zarqawi-original-language-2.

192 **His normalization of suicide bombing:** Warrick, *Black Flags*, 171.

192 **As Marine forces initiated:** Weaver, "The Short, Violent Life of Abu Musab Al-Zarqawi."

193 **In an audio recording:** Warrick, *Black Flags*, 174.

193 **Coalition forces would:** Warrick, *Black Flags*, 151.

193 **at least twenty-two bodies:** Louise Roug, "Baghdad Morgue Reports Record Figures for May," *The Los Angeles Times*, June 4, 2006, http://articles.latimes.com/2006/jun/04/world/fg-iraq4.

193 **In the nearby city of Baqubah:** Louise Roug, "Baghdad Morgue Reports Record Figures for May."

193 **Baghdad's morgue alone:** "Killings in Baghdad, 2005–2007," *Iraq Body Count,* accessed March 11, 2018, www.iraqbodycount.org/database/.

193 **By 2005, AQI:** McChrystal, *My Share of the Task*, 140.

193 **Within each cell:** McChrystal, *My Share of the Task*, 171.

194 **From intercepted maps:** McChrystal, *My Share of the Task*, 188, 204.

194 **"the insurmountable obstacle":** "Zarqawi Letter: February 2004 Coalition Provisional Authority English Translation of Terrorist Musab Al-Zarqawi Letter Obtained by United States Government in Iraq," U.S. Department of State, February 2004, https://2001–2009.state.gov/p/nea/rls/31694 .htm.

195 **These bombings were often:** Mark Oliver, "At Least 143 Killed in Iraq Explosions," *The Guardian*, March 2, 2004, www.theguardian.com/world/2004/mar/02/iraq.markoliver.

195 **On August 31, 2005:** Robert F. Worth, "950 Die in Stampede on Baghdad Bridge," *The New York Times*, September 1, 2006, www.nytimes.com/2005/09/01/world/middleeast/950-die-in-stampede -on-baghdad-bridge.html.

195 **The final breaking point:** Kilcullen, *Blood Year*, 29.

195 **when men dressed as:** Warrick, *Black Flags*, 202–3.

195 **Within hours, Shi'ite militias:** McChrystal, *My Share of the Task*, 204.

197 **The first statue of Robespierre:** Gabriel Schoenfeld, "Uses of the Past: Bolshevism and the French Revolutionary Tradition," in *The French Revolution of 1789 and Its Impact*, eds. Gail M. Schwab and John R. Jeanneney (Westport, CT: Greenwood Press, 1995), 286.

199 **Lenin recognized the power:** Schoenfeld, "Uses of the Past," 286.

Chapter 6: The Heroes

203 **At close to four:** Edward L. Dreyer, *Zheng He: China and the Oceans in the Early Ming Dynasty, 1405–1433* (New York: Pearson Longman, 2006), 116.

203 **The rudder alone:** Frank Viviano, "China's Great Armada, Admiral Zheng He," *National Geographic*, July 2005.

203 **In the words of one contemporary:** Translation of Zhou Qufei, provided in Dreyer, *Zheng He*, 109.

204 **The boat displaced:** Dreyer, *Zheng He*, 113.

204 **According to a later commentator:** Viviano, "China's Great Armada, Admiral Zheng He."
204 **Together with hundreds of lesser craft:** Dreyer, *Zheng He*, 99.
205 **By the time of the:** Levathes, *When China Ruled the Seas*, 87.
205 **His voice was described:** Louise Levathes, *When China Ruled the Seas: The Treasure Fleet of the Dragon Throne, 1405–1433* (New York: Oxford University Press, 1996), 64.
205 **"Let us hope":** Plutarch, *Plutarch's Lives*, ed. Arthur Hugh Clough, trans. John Dryden, vol. 1 (Toronto: Random House, 1992), 1.
206 **"Both Theseus and Romulus":** Plutarch, *Plutarch's Lives*, vol. 1, 50.
206 **A quarter-million-strong Ming army:** John W. Dardess, *Ming China, 1368–1644: A Concise History of a Resilient Empire* (Lanham, MD: Rowman & Littlefield, 2012), 6.
206 **along with "countless":** Levathes, *When China Ruled the Seas*, 57.
207 **The Yuan, ethnically Mongolian:** Timothy Brook, *The Troubled Empire: China in the Yuan and Ming Dynasties* (Cambridge, MA: Belknap Press of Harvard University Press, 2010), 83–84.
207 **At the time of the Yuan's:** Levathes, *When China Ruled the Seas*, 57.
207 **the last of their dynasty took:** Dreyer, *Zheng He*, 12.
207 **whose emperor dedicated:** Brook, *The Troubled Empire*, 86.
207 **This action forced:** Levathes, *When China Ruled the Seas*, 57.
207 **In the aftermath of the fighting:** Levathes, *When China Ruled the Seas*, 58.
207 **When questioned by the soldiers, Zheng lied:** Dardess, *Ming China, 1368–1644*, 5.
208 **overcome the stereotypes:** Levathes, *When China Ruled the Seas*, 64.
208 **Zhu Di's father:** Levathes, *When China Ruled the Seas*, 63.
209 **By 1391, when:** Levathes, *When China Ruled the Seas*, 66.
209 **Confucian advisers strongly:** Dreyer, *Zheng He*, 20.
209 **Zhu's brothers, with:** Dardess, *Ming China, 1368–1644*, 34.
209 **were systematically eliminated:** Levathes, *When China Ruled the Seas*, 67.
209 **Yet at the site:** Dreyer, *Zheng He*, 22–23.
209 **Zheng organized raids:** Levathes, *When China Ruled the Seas*, 70–71.
209 **Armed with this intelligence:** Levathes, *When China Ruled the Seas*, 70–71.
210 **Among the emperor's:** Levathes, *When China Ruled the Seas*, 72.
210 **The emperor gave the man his wish:** Brook, *The Troubled Empire*, 92.
210 **At the docks:** Dreyer, *Zheng He*, 123.
210 **cedarwood for their hulls:** Levathes, *When China Ruled the Seas*, 78.
210 **transportation for the foreign ambassadors:** Dreyer, *Zheng He*, 120.
210 **In addition to the flagship Treasure Ships:** Viviano, "China's Great Armada, Admiral Zheng He."
211 **Among the fleet's crew:** Dreyer, *Zheng He*, 128.
211 **Communication between the ships:** Levathes, *When China Ruled the Seas*, 83.
211 **Zheng was "to seek out traces of":** Levathes, *When China Ruled the Seas*, 73.
211 **A counselor told the emperor:** Levathes, *When China Ruled the Seas*, 65, 87.
212 **One month ahead:** Viviano, "China's Great Armada, Admiral Zheng He."
212 **"The title of this gentleman was:** Levathes, *When China Ruled the Seas*, 63.
213 **Accounts celebrate a principled nobility:** Levathes, *When China Ruled the Seas*, 62.
213 **For the inhabitants of the various:** Viviano, "China's Great Armada, Admiral Zheng He."
213 **While its military might:** Daniel J. Boorstin, *The Discoverers* (New York: Vintage Books, 1985), 192.
214 **Still considered by those:** Dreyer, *Zheng He*, 59.
214 **during his 1408 return to Ceylon:** Boorstin, *The Discoverers*, 194.
214 **as well as gifts of precious metals:** Levathes, *When China Ruled the Seas*, 113.
214 **Zheng's deft leadership:** Dreyer, *Zheng He*, 59.
214 **Chen at first accepted:** Dreyer, *Zheng He*, 55.
214 **the Treasure Fleet:** Dreyer, *Zheng He*, 53.
214 **After capturing Chen and:** Levathes, *When China Ruled the Seas*, 102.
214 **suddenly struck by a tempest:** Levathes, *When China Ruled the Seas*, 103.
215 **What the fleet had encountered:** Levathes, *When China Ruled the Seas*, 103.
215 **After lobbying from Zheng:** Levathes, *When China Ruled the Seas*, 103.
215 **By 1414, the Treasure Fleet had:** Dreyer, *Zheng He*, 76.
215 **Good omens came:** Boorstin, *The Discoverers*, 197.
216 **The appearance of a *qilin*:** Levathes, *When China Ruled the Seas*, 140–41.
217 **In the spring of 1421:** Levathes, *When China Ruled the Seas*, 157.
217 **inauspicious moment for:** Levathes, *When China Ruled the Seas*, 156.

217 **But after the fires at:** Levathes, *When China Ruled the Seas*, 159.
217 **open rebellion, fueled:** Dreyer, *Zheng He*.
217 **Famines had taken place:** Levathes, *When China Ruled the Seas*, 159–60.
217 **These crises at home:** Levathes, *When China Ruled the Seas*, 160–65.
218 **The Yongle Emperor's successors:** Dreyer, *Zheng He*, 151.
218 **Zheng's mission was:** Dreyer, *Zheng He*, 144.
218 **a trip that would:** Viviano, "China's Great Armada, Admiral Zheng He."
218 **"From the third year of Yongle":** Translation of Zheng He's 1431 inscription at Changle, provided in Dreyer, *Zheng He*.
218 **In 1433, as the fleet:** Levathes, *When China Ruled the Seas*, 172.
219 **Not long thereafter, the tribute system:** Boorstin, *The Discoverers*, 198.
219 **As interest in maintaining:** Levathes, *When China Ruled the Seas*, 174.
219 **In perhaps the most audacious:** Dreyer, *Zheng He*, 171.
219 **"In the early 15th century":** "Full Text of President Xi's Speech at Opening of Belt and Road Forum," *XinHua News*, May 14, 2017, www.xinhuanet.com/english/2017–05/14/c_136282982.htm.
219 **led to military:** Dreyer, *Zheng He*, 180–82.
220 **Perhaps the most:** Matt Schiavenza, "How Humiliation Drove Modern Chinese History," *The Atlantic* (online), October 23, 2013, www.theatlantic.com/china/archive/2013/10/how-humiliation-drove-modern-chinese-history/280878/.
220 **"From the age of Zheng He":** Geoff Wade, "The Zheng He Voyages: A Reassessment," *Journal of the Malaysian Branch of the Royal Asiatic Society* 78, no. 1 (2005), 37.
221 **These assertive international moves:** Ankit Panda, "Sri Lanka Formally Hands Over Hambantota Port to Chinese Firms on 99-Year Lease," *The Diplomat* (December 11, 2017), https://thediplomat.com/2017/12/sri-lanka-formally-hands-over-hambantota-port-tochinese-firms-on-99-year-lease/.
221 **the trillion-dollar:** Paul Musgrave, Daniel Nexon, "Zheng He's Voyages and the Symbolism Behind Xi Jinping's Belt and Road Initiative," *The Diplomat* (December 22, 2017), https://thediplomat.com/2017/12/zheng-hes-voyages-and-the-symbolism-behind-xi-jinpings-belt-and-road-initiative/.
221 **In 2005, the Chinese:** Ishaan Tharoor, "Searching for Zheng: China's Ming-Era Voyager," *Time*, March 8, 2010, http://content.time.com/time/world/article/0,8599,1969939,00.html.
222 **tipped their caps:** William Wells Brown, M.D., *The Rising Son, or, The Antecedents and Advancement of the Colored Race* (Boston: A. G. Brown & Co., 1882), 539. According to Brown, a Boston abolitionist who'd known Tubman since the mid-1850s, "The Union officers . . . never failed to tip their caps when meeting her . . ."
223 **attention of Northern abolitionists:** James McPherson, *Battle Cry of Freedom: The Civil War Era* (New York: Oxford University Press, 1988), 371. According to McPherson, after the Confederates around Port Royal fled, the contrabands "soon became part of an abolitionist experiment in freedmen's education and cotton planting with free labor."
223 **"among her people":** Sarah Bradford, *Scenes in the Life of Harriet Tubman* (Heraklion Press, n.d.), 66.
223 **evolution of her motivations:** This line of thinking comes from Kate Clifford Larson, *Bound for the Promised Land: Harriet Tubman, Portrait of an American Hero* (New York: One World, 2003), xvii. "Her total commitment to destroying the slave system eventually led her to South Carolina during the Civil War . . ."
223 **arranged her travel:** Franklin B. Sanborn, "Harriet Tubman," *Commonwealth*, July 17, 1863.
223 **"a valuable person":** Charles Wood, "A History Concerning the Pension Claim of Harriet Tubman," June 1, 1888, 1, Accompanying Papers of the 55th Congress, National Archives, Washington, DC, https://catalog.archives.gov/id/306575.
224 **"I WILL sell":** Larson, *Bound for the Promised Land*, 77.
224 **"RANAWAY from the":** Larson, *Bound for the Promised Land*, 79.
225 **In Dorchester County:** Larson, *Bound for the Promised Land*, 13.
225 **As a result:** Larson, *Bound for the Promised Land*, 15.
226 **"poor neck was":** Sarah H. Bradford, *Harriet Tubman: The Moses of Her People* (1886), 12. The book was released in 1886, when Tubman was in her mid-forties. It's telling that Bradford refers to Tubman being in her sixties.
226 **two-pound iron weight:** Larson, *Bound for the Promised Land*, 42.
226 **"broke my skull":** From Emma P. Telford, "Harriet: The Modern Moses of Heroism and Visions," Cayuga County Museum, Auburn, NY, c. 1905, quoted in Larson, *Bound for the Promised Land*, 43.

227 **"a sort of stupor":** Sanborn, "Harriet Tubman."

227 **Tubman and her family:** For a fuller discussion of Tubman's head injury, including what modern medical science might say about it, see Larson, *Bound for the Promised Land*, 42–45.

227 **her first name:** Larson, *Bound for the Promised Land*, 62.

228 **"diverse, flexible, and":** Fergus M. Bordewich, *Bound for Canaan: The Epic Story of the Underground Railroad, America's First Civil Rights Movement* (New York: Amistad, 2006), 5.

228 **series of local groups:** Eric Foner, *Gateway to Freedom: The Hidden History of the Underground Railroad* (New York: W. W. Norton & Company, 2015), 15. Foner writes that the Underground Railroad should not be understood as a "single entity," but as an umbrella term for local groups that employed numerous methods to assist fugitives."

228 **"knock on the door":** Bordewich, *Bound for Canaan*, xvi.

228 **"saw the horsemen":** Bradford, *Harriet Tubman: The Moses of Her People*, 15.

228 **"I had reasoned":** Bradford, *Harriet Tubman: The Moses of Her People*, 17.

229 **"I had crossed":** Bradford, *Harriet Tubman: The Moses of Her People*, 18.

229 **"Tell my brothers":** Bradford, *Scenes in the Life of Harriet Tubman*, 57. As seen in Larson, *Bound for the Promised Land*, 110. Bradford describes the letter as being filled with "indifferent matters."

229 **The 1854 letter:** Bradford, *Scenes in the Life of Harriet Tubman*, 56. As seen in Larson, *Bound for the Promised Land, 110.*

229 **Jackson had facilitated:** Larson, *Bound for the Promised Land*, 110–11.

230 **"I can't make":** Bradford, *Scenes in the Life of Harriet Tubman*, 58, and Larson, *Bound for the Promised Land*, 58.

230 **"rather see them":** John W. Blassingame, *Slave Testimony: Two Centuries of Letters, Speeches, Interviews, and Autobiographies* (Baton Rouge: Louisiana State University Press, 1977), 415.

230 **"the next thing":** Larson, *Bound for the Promised Land,* 54. Larson cited "The Refugee" by Benjamin Drew.

230 **"I was a stranger":** Bradford, *Scenes in the Life of Harriet Tubman*, 20.

230 **"I always tole him":** Bradford, *Scenes in the Life of Harriet Tubman*, 35.

230 **in December 1854:** Larson, *Bound for the Promised Land*, 111.

230 **their temporary absence:** Larson, *Bound for the Promised Land*, 111.

230 **window for a rescue:** Larson, *Bound for the Promised Land*, 111.

231 **Tubman didn't wait:** Larson, *Bound for the Promised Land*, 111–12.

231 **joined the escapees:** Larson, *Bound for the Promised Land*, 112.

231 **He made sure:** Larson, *Bound for the Promised Land*, 111–13.

231 **"no foolishness would":** William Still, *The Underground Railroad: Authentic Narratives and First-Hand Accounts*, ed. Ian Frederick Finseth (Mineola, NY: Dover Publications, Inc., 2007), 157.

232 **She made this journey:** Tubman's rescue patterns were deducted from Larson, *Bound for the Promised Land.*

233 **Thomas Garrett heard:** James A. McGowan, *Station Master on the Underground Railroad: The Life and Letters of Thomas Garrett*, rev. ed. (Jefferson, NC: McFarland & Company, Inc., 2005), 117.

234 **"I feel as if":** Thomas Garrett to Eliza Wigham, December 16, 1855, in McGowan, *Station Master*, 167–68.

234 **donation they sent:** Thomas Garrett to Eliza Wigham, October 24, 1856, in McGowan, *Station Master*, 171.

234 **"missions of love":** Thomas Garrett to Eliza Wigham, December 27, 1856, in McGowan, *Station Master*, 176.

234 **"the remarkable labors":** Thomas Garrett to Sarah Bradford, June 6, 1868, in McGowan, *Station Master*, 191.

235 **Garrett forwarded Tubman:** Thomas Garrett to J. Miller McKim, December 29, 1854, in McGowan, *Station Master*, 138.

235 **"Harriet Tubman had":** Still, *The Underground Railroad*, 157.

235 **devoted six pages to the woman:** Entry for May 14, 1856, in Sydney Howard Gay, "Record of Fugitives," 1856, 1855, 8–13, Columbia University Libraries Online Exhibitions, https://exhibitions.cul.columbia.edu/exhibits/show/fugitives/item/8845.

235 **"that heroic woman":** Oliver Johnson to Sarah Bradford, March 6, 1886, in Bradford, *Harriet Tubman: The Moses of Her People*, 5.

235 **"Her tales of":** Thomas Wentworth Higginson to his mother, June 17, 1859, in Mary Thatcher Higginson, ed., *Letters and Journals of Thomas Wentworth Higginson, 1846–1906* (Boston: Houghton Mifflin, 1906), 81.

235 **"While in Canada":** Brown, *The Rising Son*, 538.
236 **By one estimate:** Foner, *Gateway to Freedom*, 4.
236 **between 0.14 percent and 0.8:** This is derived by, on the low end, dividing 70 slaves who Tubman directly helped escape by 50,000 total; and on the high end, by dividing 80 slaves who Tubman directly helped escape by 10,000 total over the decade she made her 13 trips back to the Eastern Shore. The number of total slaves escaped from the South uses Foner's estimate above.
236 **around 3 percent:** See Barbara Jeanne Fields, *Slavery and Freedom on the Middle Ground: Maryland During the Nineteenth Century* (New Haven, CT: Yale University Press, 1987), 16–17. In 1850, 279 slaves escaped from Maryland. We arrived at 3 percent by dividing both 70 and 80 by 2,790. We rounded up because we know that the number of escaped slaves decreased over the course of the 1850s.
237 **she baked pies:** Bradford, *Harriet Tubman: The Moses of Her People*, 51.
237 **"rendered much, and":** Wood, "A History Concerning the Pension Claim of Harriet Tubman," 1.
238 **"the greatest heroine":** Thomas Wentworth Higginson to his mother, June 17, 1859, in Higginson, ed., *Letters and Journals of Thomas Wentworth Higginson, 1846–1906*, 81.
238 **Montgomery had known:** Wood, "A History Concerning the Pension Claim of Harriet Tubman," 2.
238 **a "valuable woman":** Wood, "A History Concerning the Pension Claim of Harriet Tubman," 2.
238 ***Sentinel* ran aground:** "A Foray in South Carolina," *Daily National Intelligencer*, June 11, 1863.
238 **Throughout the morning:** Frank Moore, ed., "A National Account from Port Royal, SC" (D. Van Nostrand, June 6, 1863), *The Rebellion Record: A Diary of American Events, with Documents, Narratives, Illustrative Incidents, Poetry, etc., Seventh Volume.*
239 **Tubman's later recollections:** Bradford, *Harriet Tubman: The Moses of Her People*, 53.
239 **"most remarkable woman":** Wood, "A History Concerning the Pension Claim of Harriet Tubman," 2.
239 **reporter from Wisconsin:** Correspondent of the State Journal, "Colonel Montgomery's Raid—The Rescued Black Chattels—A 'Black She Moses'—Her Wonderful Daring and Sagacity—The Black Regiments—Col. Higginson's Mistakes—Arrival of the 54th Massachusetts, &c., &c.," *Wisconsin State Journal*, June 20, 1863, vol. XI, 137 edition.
239 **contributed to a misunderstanding:** For an excellent analysis of the evolution of the "Tubman-as-General" myth, see Milton C. Sernett, *Harriet Tubman: Myth, Memory, and History* (Durham, NC: Duke University Press, 2007), 87–92.
240 **A conductor on the train:** Bradford, *Scenes in the Life of Harriet Tubman*, 46–47, and "Mrs. Harriet Tubman, the Colored Nurse and Scout—The Bridge Street African M.E. Church Last Evening," *The Brooklyn Daily Eagle,* October 23, 1865, https://bklyn.newspapers.com/clip/1065316/the_brook lyn_daily_eagle/.
240 **"there was nothing":** "Mrs. Harriet Tubman, the Colored Nurse and Scout—the Bridge Street African M.E. Church Last Evening."
241 **Douglass wrote a letter:** Letter from Frederick Douglass, August 29, 1868, in Bradford, *Harriet Tubman: The Moses of Her People*, 70.
241 **made slaves free:** Thomas Wentworth Higginson, *Cheerful Yesterdays* (Boston: Houghton Mifflin Company, 1898), 328, https://archive.org/details/cheerfulyesterd00higggoog. Higginson recalled, "My own teachers were the slave women who came shyly before the audience . . . women who had been stripped and whipped and handled with insolent hands and sold to the highest bidder . . . or women who, having once escaped, had, like Harriet Tubman, gone back again and again into the land of bondage to bring away their kindred and friends. . . . What were the tricks of oratory in the face of men and women like these?"
241 **"if there is":** Moyers & Company, "George Lucas Tells Bill Moyers About the Mentors in His Career," Accessed July 6, 2018, www.youtube.com/watch?v=dNs7c41JbTI.
242 **"myths are first":** Carl Jung, *The Archetypes and the Collective Unconscious* (Princeton, NJ: Princeton University Press, 1981), 6.
242 **"the symbols of mythology":** Joseph Campbell, *The Hero with a Thousand Faces*, Commemorative Edition (Princeton, NJ: Princeton University Press, 2004), 3.
242 **George Lucas credited:** John Higgs, "The Hero's Journey: The Idea You Never Knew Had Shaped 'Star Wars,'" *Salon*, November 7, 2015, www.salon.com/2015/11/07/the_heros_journey_the_idea_you_never_knew_had_shaped_star_wars/.
242 **the "nuclear unit":** Campbell, *The Hero with a Thousand Faces*, 28.
243 **Superhero worship surged again:** "The Comic Book Industry Is on Fire, and It's About More Than Just the Movies," *Business Insider Australia*, August 27, 2014, www.businessinsider.com.au/the-comic-book-industry-is-on-fire-2014-8.

Chapter 7: The Power Brokers

248 **"I have never smoked":** "Tweed Talks," *New York Herald*, October 26, 1877.

248 **Such meals, delivered:** "Confession," *New York Herald*, October 10, 1877.

248 **"one of the most":** Edwin G. Burrows and Mike Wallace, *Gotham: A History of New York City to 1898* (New York: Oxford University Press, 1999), 931.

248 **the city's population:** "Total and Foreign-Born Population, New York City, 1790–2000," n.d., NYC.gov, www1.nyc.gov/assets/planning/download/pdf/data-maps/nyc-population/historical -population/1790–2000_nyc_total_foreign_birth.pdf.

249 **New York Bridge Company:** David McCullough, *The Great Bridge: The Epic Story of the Building of the Brooklyn Bridge* (New York: Touchstone, 1972), 263.

249 **"the Erie Railroad":** Kenneth D. Ackerman, *Boss Tweed: The Corrupt Pol Who Conceived the Soul of Modern New York* (Falls Church, VA: Viral History Press, 2011), 2.

249 **"when anything desperate":** "Tweed Talks."

249 **city's new charter:** Ackerman, *Boss Tweed*, 71–72.

250 **$25.5 and $45 million:** Ackerman, *Boss Tweed*, 340.

250 **around $60 million:** Burrows and Wallace, *Gotham*, 931.

250 **"Our power, socalled":** "Tweed Talks."

250 **"telegraphing the whole Bible":** New York City Board of Aldermen, "Tweed Ring: Report of the Special Committee of the Board of Aldermen Appointed to Investigate the 'Ring' Frauds, Together with the Testimony Elicited During the Investigation" (New York: New York City Board of Aldermen, January 4, 1878), https://ia600300.us.archive.org/22/items/reportspecialco00fraugoog /reportspecialco00fraugoog.pdf., 226.

250 **"The ballots made":** New York City Board of Aldermen, "Tweed Ring," 134.

251 **Twenty-four hours:** Greg Young and Tom Meyers, Fire Department of New York, *The Bowery Boys: New York City History*, n.d., http://boweryboys.libsyn.com/-161-fire-department-of-the -city-of-new-york-fdny.

252 **snarling red tiger:** Burrows and Wallace, *Gotham*, 823.

252 **"Tammany Hall got":** New York City Board of Aldermen, "Tweed Ring," 367.

252 **Tammany Hall was:** Terry Golway, *Machine Made: Tammany Hall and the Creation of Modern American Politics* (New York and London: Liveright, 2014), xiii.

252 **Madison Square Garden:** Daniel P. Moynihan, "When the Irish Ran New York," *The Reporter*, June 8, 1961.

252 **nearly two hundred years:** Golway, *Machine Made*.

252 **nearly half of:** The actual number is 45.7 percent. See page no? "Nativity of the Population for the 25 Largest Urban Places and for Selected Counties: 1850," US Census Bureau, n.d., www.census .gov/popu lation/www/documentation/twps0029/tab21.html.

252 **"arrived in America":** Moynihan, "When the Irish Ran New York."

252 **a vast hierarchy:** Moynihan, "When the Irish Ran New York."

252 **a grand sachem:** Golway, *Machine Made*, 6.

253 **"I stick to":** William L. Riordon, *Plunkitt of Tammany Hall: A Series of Very Plain Talks on Very Practical Politics* (New York: Penguin Books, 2015), 46.

253 **"My party's in":** Riordon, *Plunkitt of Tammany Hall*, 3.

253 **"didn't steal a dollar":** Riordon, *Plunkitt of Tammany Hall*, 5.

253 **"could throw up":** Moynihan, "When the Irish Ran New York."

254 **Tweed spent much:** Ackerman, *Boss Tweed*, 18.

254 **expelled from the department:** Burrows and Wallace, *Gotham*, 823.

254 **Appealing to the Board:** Golway, *Machine Made*, 61.

254 **His local rise:** Ackerman, *Boss Tweed*, 18–19.

254 **the "Tweed courthouse":** Ackerman, *Boss Tweed*, 361.

255 **promoted to power:** Burrows and Wallace, *Gotham*, 837.

255 **In January 1863:** Ackerman, *Boss Tweed*, 19.

256 **Colored Orphan Asylum:** Burrows and Wallace, *Gotham*, 890.

256 **"Tweed recognized the urgent need":** Ackerman, *Boss Tweed*, 20.

256 **In cases where:** Ackerman, *Boss Tweed*, 25.

256 **"Tweed's "Supervisors' Committee":** "The Supervisors' Loan," *The New York Times*, September 11, 1863, https://timesmachine.nytimes.com/timesmachine/1863/09/11/78706299.html.

256 **from 21 to 150:** Ackerman, *Boss Tweed*, 49–50.

257 **New York Printing Company:** Ackerman, *Boss Tweed*, 67.

257 **"These frauds were":** "Report of the Select Committee on Alleged New York Election Frauds, Made to the House of Representatives, Fortieth Congress, Third Session" (Washington, DC, February 23, 1869), 4, https://play.google.com/books/reader?id=w58FAAAAQAAJ&printsec=front cover&output=reader&hl=en&pg=GBS.PA5.

257 **naturalized 955 citizens:** "Report of the Select Committee on Alleged New York Election Frauds, Made to the House of Representatives, Fortieth Congress, Third Session," 9.

257 **According to voter rolls:** "Report of the Select Committee on Alleged New York Election Frauds, Made to the House of Representatives, Fortieth Congress, Third Session," 60.

257 **"The fact is":** "Tweed Talks."

257 **on April 4, 1870:** "The State Capital.—The Charter Before the Senate Committee on Municipal Affairs.—Greeley Thinks It Can Be Improved and Sammy Tilden Advises Caution.—The Committee Report It to the Senate Without Amendment.—It Is Made the Special Order for To-Day and Will Undoubtedly Pass.," *The New York Herald*, April 5, 1870, sec. Page 3, Image 3 on Library of Congress website, https://chroniclingamerica.loc.gov/lccn/sn83030313/1870-04-05/ed-1/seq-3.pdf.

257 **seven-room apartment:** Ackerman, *Boss Tweed*, 65.

257 **"Mr. Tweed's quarters":** "Mr. Sweeny's Legislature—Mr. Tweed's Charter to Be Pushed Through To-Day," *The Sun*, March 30, 1870.

258 **more full than usual:** "The State Capital.—The Charter Before the Senate Committee on Municipal Affairs." According to the article, "a multitude of people thronged the rooms . . ."

258 **"over its own":** Burrows and Wallace, *Gotham*, 927.

258 **Tammany men held office:** Ackerman, *Boss Tweed*, 69.

258 **"almost perfect instrument":** William C. Hudson, "'Boss' Tweed and Governor Hoffman," in *Random Recollections of an Old Political Reporter* (New York: Cupples & Leon Company, 1911), 31, https://archive.org/stream/randomrecollecti010640mbp#page/n39/mode/2up.

259 **"he had understanding":** Hudson, "'Boss' Tweed and Governor Hoffman," 33–35.

259 **"He then asked":** New York City Board of Aldermen, "Tweed Ring," 138.

259 **$40,000 apiece to ensure:** New York City Board of Aldermen, "Tweed Ring," 85–87.

259 **The Young Democrats:** Ackerman, *Boss Tweed*, 72.

260 **found themselves barred:** Ackerman, *Boss Tweed*, 74–75.

260 **"the most stupendous":** "Locking Out the Indians—the Most Stupendous Political Joke of the Century," *The Sun*, March 29, 1870.

260 **"on every side":** "Mr. Sweeny's Legislature—Mr. Tweed's Charter to Be Pushed Through To-Day," *The Sun*, March 30, 1870.

260 **"it takes a general":** "The State Capital.—The New York City Charter in the Senate.—It Passes Without Amendment by a Vote of 30 to 2.—Final Rout and Discomfiture of the Young Democracy.—Signing of the Bill by Governor Hoffman.—Passage of the Bill Regulating Elections in the Metropolis," *New York Herald*, April 6, 1870, https://chroniclingamerica.loc.gov/lccn/sn83030313/1870-04-06/ed-1/seq-3.pdf.

260 **"honest local government":** John D. Townsend, "How Citizens Aided the Ring in 1870," in *New York in Bondage* (New York, 1901), 33, https://play.google.com/books/reader?id=Oy8b2XSG_CwC&printsec=frontcover&output=reader&hl=en&pg=GBS.PA32.

261 **"the best Charter":** "The State Capital.—The New York City Charter in the Senate."

261 **"We especially tender":** "Rejoicing in the City," *New York Herald*, April 6, 1870.

261 **met with general glee:** Ackerman, *Boss Tweed*, 80.

261 **$500,000 in gifts:** "A Resplendent Wedding—the Marriage of Mr. William M. Tweed's Daughter—West Twenty-Fifth Street Refulgent with the City's Aristocracy—Half a Million's Worth of Wedding Presents—a Lovely Bride and Princely Fortune," *New York Sun*, June 1, 1871.

261 **valued at $15,000:** Ackerman, *Boss Tweed*, 117.

262 **"ruin this City":** "Why Attack Mr. Tweed?," *New York Times*, September 29, 1870, https://timesmachine.nytimes.com/timesmachine/1870/09/29/83474241.pdf.

262 **a "'universal conviction'":** *Harper's Weekly*, March 13, 1871, quoted in Ackerman, *Boss Tweed*, 136.

262 **it was settled:** New York City Board of Aldermen, "Tweed Ring," 174–78.

263 **As they'd done before:** Burrows and Wallace, *Gotham*, 1003–8.

263 **"The cowardice of Tammany":** "The Riot of 1871—Results of Municipal Cowardice and Tardy State Action," *New York Tribune*, July 13, 1871, https://chroniclingamerica.loc.gov/lccn/sn83030214/1871-07-13/ed-1/seq-1.pdf.

263 **paid a clerk:** Ackerman, *Boss Tweed*, 160–62.

263 **Times ran a headline:** "The Secret Accounts," *New York Times*, July 22, 1871.

263 **"One member of"**: Burrows and Wallace, *Gotham*, 1009.
264 **best-known political cartoonist**: Ackerman, *Boss Tweed*, 181.
264 **sell 500,000 copies**: Ackerman, *Boss Tweed*, 171.
264 **were held responsible**: Golway, *Machine Made*, 94–95.
264 **Tweed was out of power**: Ackerman, *Boss Tweed*, 253–56.
265 **the room was full**: "The William M. Tweed Club," *New Hork Herald*, October 24, 1871.
265 **the *Times* published**: "Our Dishonest Politicians," *New York Times*, October 25, 1871, 1.
265 **"the stairway and sidewalks"**: "Fourth Senatorial District—an Enthusiastic Meeting of Mr. Tweed's Friends," *New York Herald*, October 20, 1871.
265 **"Freedom works—and it costs less"**: Margaret Thatcher, "Article for *Sunday Express* ('It's Your Freedom They Hate')," Margaret Thatcher Foundation, November 23, 1975, www.margaretthatcher.org/document/102808.
266 **"the Iron Lady of the Western world"**: Margaret Thatcher, "Speech to Finchley Conservatives," January 31, 1976, Margaret Thatcher Foundation, www.margaretthatcher.org/document/102947.
266 **"more than any party leader since Churchill"**: Charles Moore, *Margaret Thatcher: The Authorized Biography*, vol. 1 (New York: Alfred A. Knopf, 2013), 326.
267 **"keep Winston Churchill in charge of our foreign policy"**: Margaret Thatcher, *Margaret Thatcher: The Autobiography* (New York: Harper Perennial, 2013), 37.
267 **Britain had "efficient" and "dignified" parts**: Walter Bagehot, *The English Constitution*, Project Gutenberg, accessed May 21, 2018, www.gutenberg.org/files/4351/4351-h/4351-h.htm.
268 **"what the holder chooses"**: Adam Sisman, "Observer Review: The Prime Minister by Peter Hennessy," *The Guardian*, October 14, 2000, sec. Books, www.theguardian.com/books/2000/oct/15/politics.
268 **Churchill spoke divisively**: Thatcher, *Autobiography*, 37.
269 **"It was bad, and"**: Thatcher, *Autobiography*, 38.
270 **explicitly gendered terms**: Quoted in Moore, *Margaret Thatcher*, 1:85.
270 **Jewish constituents**: Quoted in Moore, *Margaret Thatcher*, 1:137.
271 **first ever with a young family**: Moore, *Margaret Thatcher*, 1:158–59.
271 **"dressed like any other housewife"**: Quoted in Moore, *Margaret Thatcher*, 1:159.
272 **"established herself as the leader"**: Richard Vinen, *Thatcher's Britain: The Politics and Social Upheaval of the Thatcher Era* (London and New York: Pocket Books, 2010), 12.
272 **"not prime ministerial material"**: Quoted in Vinen, *Thatcher's Britain*, 42.
272 **conviction was**: John Campbell, *The Iron Lady: Margaret Thatcher, from Grocer's Daughter to Prime Minister* (New York: Penguin Books, 2011), 49.
272 **"the whole of political wisdom"**: Quoted in Moore, *Margaret Thatcher*, 1:350.
273 **a "closed world"**: Moore, *Margaret Thatcher*, 1:217.
273 **writing a minute at the bottom**: Quoted in Moore, *Margaret Thatcher*, 1:219.
273 **ripping the tops off those pages**: Moore, *Margaret Thatcher*, 1:166.
274 **periodically arrive impromptu**: Moore, *Margaret Thatcher*, 1:423–24.
274 **Free school milk**: Moore, *Margaret Thatcher*, 1:220.
274 **accepted the necessary cuts**: Moore, *Margaret Thatcher*, 1:221.
274 **The popular press**: Moore, *Margaret Thatcher*, 1:222–23.
274 **But he demurred**: Moore, *Margaret Thatcher*, 1:223.
275 **"The social revolution need not be destructive"**: Quoted in Vinen, *Thatcher's Britain*, 39.
275 **a retiring British ambassador to Paris**: Quoted in Vinen, *Thatcher's Britain*, 75.
276 **"what are we going to do"**: Quoted in Vinen, *Thatcher's Britain*, 75.
276 **against Heath and the party grandees**: Julian Critchley, *A Bag of Boiled Sweets: An Autobiography* (London and Boston: Faber and Faber, 1995), 146.
277 **her lackluster performance**: Bernard Donoughue, *Downing Street Diary: With James Callaghan in No. 10* (London: Pimlico, 2009), 305.
277 **"I am sure that one day"**: Quoted in Moore, *Margaret Thatcher*, 1:335.
277 **self-made middle-class woman**: Moore, *Margaret Thatcher*, 1:31.
277 **From 1975, Thatcher's Gang**: Moore, *Margaret Thatcher*, 1:329.
279 **"the right [Honourable] Lady can be proud"**: Margaret Thatcher and James Callaghan, "House of Commons Speech [Industrial Situation]," Margaret Thatcher Foundation, January 16, 1979, www.margaretthatcher.org/document/103924.
279 **quoting Rudyard Kipling's lines**: Margaret Thatcher and Robin Harris, *The Collected Speeches of Margaret Thatcher* (New York: HarperCollins, 1997), 57.
279 **her rejection of the existing political consensus**: Ben Jackson and Robert Saunders, ed., *Making Thatcher's Britain* (Cambridge: Cambridge University Press, 2012), 29.

279 **"Let me give you my vision"**: Margaret Thatcher, "Speech to Conservative Party Conference," Margaret Thatcher Foundation, October 10, 1975, www.margaretthatcher.org/document /102777.

280 **"the triumph of evil"**: Quoted in Jackson and Saunders, *Making Thatcher's Britain*, 32.

280 **"all are under attack"**: Quoted in Jackson and Saunders, *Making Thatcher's Britain*, 83.

281 **"the Winter of Discontent"**: William Shakespeare, *Richard III*, ed. James R. Siemon, The Arden Shakespeare, Third Series (London: Arden Shakespeare, 2009), act 1, scene 1, lines 1–2.

281 **a military-organized coup:** Dennis Barker, "Obituary: Sir Walter Walker," *The Guardian*, August 14, 2001, www.theguardian.com/news/2001/aug/14/guardianobituaries1.

282 **"if people die, so be it"**: John Hoskyns, *Just in Time: Inside the Thatcher Revolution* (London: Aurum, 2000), 80–81.

282 **"We have to learn again"**: Margaret Thatcher, "Conservative Party Political Broadcast (Winter of Discontent)," Margaret Thatcher Foundation, January 17, 1979, www.marga retthatcher.org/docu ment/103926.

282 **311 votes to 310:** Moore, *Margaret Thatcher*, 1:401.

282 **Britain's newspaper of record:** "1979: Times Returns After Year-Long Dispute," BBC, November 13, 1979, http://news.bbc.co.uk/onthisday/hi/dates/stories/november/13/newsid_2539000/2539795 .stm#sa-link_location=story-body&intlink_from_url=http%3A%2F%2Fwww.bbc.com %2Fnews%2Fentertainment-arts-22120480&intlink_ts=1526916709360-sa.

282 **"there is a change in politics"**: Quoted in Geoffrey Howe, *Conflict of Loyalty* (London: Pan Books, 1995), 117.

283 **in briefing memos:** Various archival documents obtained from the Margaret Thatcher Foundation, dated May 4, 1979, such as "Germany: Cartledge minute to MT ('Chancellor Schmidt's Visit: 10/11 May') [arrangements and draft programme] [declassified 2009]," "Incoming brief: Cabinet Secretary's incoming brief for new PM ('Energy Issues') [declassified 2009]." and "Incoming brief: Cabinet Secretary incoming brief for MT ('Rhodesia') [declassified 2009]," accessed on July 6, 2018 at https://www.margaretthatcher.org/search?dt=5&w=&searchtype=and&t=0&starty=1979& startm=5&startd=4&endy=&endm=&endd=&onedayy=&onedaym=&onedayd=.

284 **"make policy on the trot"**: Tim Lankester, *The Politics and Economics of Britain's Foreign Aid: The Pergau Dam Affair* (London and New York: Routledge, 2013), 34.

285 **"the Tory Wets"**: Simon Hoggart, "Wet Hopes Revive in Mrs. Thatcher's Watery Britain," *The Observer*, July 26, 1981.

285 **"over the shop"**: Thatcher, *Autobiography*, 258.

285 **as "dumb bunnies"**: Moore, *Margaret Thatcher*, 1:639.

285 **expected her to cave:** Moore, *Margaret Thatcher*, 1:529.

286 **"There Is No Alternative"**: Campbell, *The Iron Lady*, 163.

286 **"who was 'in' and who was 'out'"**: Howe, *Conflict of Loyalty*, 147.

286 **"anticipated she would want to hear"**: Lankester, *The Politics and Economics of Britain's Foreign Aid*, 35.

286 **"The lady's not for turning"**: "Margaret Thatcher, 'The Lady's Not for Turning,' " accessed May 21, 2018, https://www.youtube.com/watch?v=rQ-MOKEFm91.

287 **executing decisions as a power pair:** Howe, *Conflict of Loyalty*, 195.

287 **"it's very lonely"**: Howe, *Conflict of Loyalty*, 195.

287 **"the adrenaline flows"**: Compiled by Laura Pitel, "Margaret Thatcher's Memorable Remarks," *The Times*, April 9, 2013, www.thetimes.co.uk/article/margaret-thatchers-memorable-remarks -9hq7b2mckcj.

288 **"coachman flogging the horses"**: Moore, *Margaret Thatcher*, 2:193.

288 **lowest approval ratings:** Dennis Kavanagh, *Thatcherism and British Politics: The End of Consensus?*, Reprint Edition (New York: Oxford University Press, 2002), 270.

288 **"only she could have done it"**: Moore, *Margaret Thatcher*, 2:752–53.

288 **The event captured:** Critchley, *A Bag of Boiled Sweets*, 180–81.

289 **"wreathed in smiles"**: Moore, *Margaret Thatcher*, 2:66.

289 **"a very sweet time"**: Quoted in Moore, Margaret Thatcher, 2:66.

290 **"It's a shooting war"**: Quoted in Moore, *Margaret Thatcher*, 2:52–53.

290 **"I'm not a good butcher"**: Quoted in Moore, *Margaret Thatcher*, 2:66.

290 **"manic pretend shopping trips"**: Moore, *Margaret Thatcher*, 2:53.

291 **"inexhaustibly feeding off her own zealotry"**: Critchley, *A Bag of Boiled Sweets*, 182, 193.

291 **informal "kitchen cabinet" meetings:** See, e.g., Moore, *Margaret Thatcher*, 2:489.

291 **Thatcher became hostile:** See, e.g., Moore, *Margaret Thatcher*, 2:194, 495–96, 698, 702.

291 **a property tax:** Moore, *Margaret Thatcher*, 2:359–61.

291 **eventually emerged as the euro:** Moore, *Margaret Thatcher*, 2:410.
291 **stood against her:** Moore, *Margaret Thatcher*, 2:413.
291 **joining forces:** Moore, *Margaret Thatcher*, 2:410. The year 1981 is the one that Lawson recalls beginning to favor the idea of Britain's joining the ERM, though it wasn't until he became chancellor in 1983 that he started to think seriously about it. (Personal communication with Sir Tim Lankester.)
291 **"an ambiguous statement of intent":** Moore, *Margaret Thatcher*, 2:421.
292 **a run on the pound:** Moore, *Margaret Thatcher*, 2:411–13.
292 **a calamitous meeting convened:** Moore, *Margaret Thatcher*, 2:417–18.
292 **Thatcher had neglected:** Moore, *Margaret Thatcher*, 2:419.
292 **rejected the ERM:** Moore, *Margaret Thatcher*, 2:420.
292 **Thatcher had not tapped:** Moore, *Margaret Thatcher*, 2:419.
292 **"until the time is right":** Moore, *Margaret Thatcher*, 2:419–20.
292 **Thatcher would have resigned:** Moore, *Margaret Thatcher*, 2:420.
292 **the most powerful woman:** Moore, *Margaret Thatcher*, 2:420.
292 **Working relationships deteriorated:** Moore, *Margaret Thatcher*, 2:421.
293 **"uncomfortably close to the truth":** Howe, *Conflict of Loyalty*, 574.
293 **Nigel Lawson boasted to Conservative:** Nigel Lawson, *Memoirs of a Tory Radical* (New York: Biteback Publishing, 2011), 422.
294 **a move made out of spite:** John Campbell, *The Iron Lady: Margaret Thatcher, from Grocer's Daughter to Prime Minister* (New York: Penguin Books, 2011), 421–22.
295 **unacceptable conduct in a Prime Minister:** Lawson, *Memoirs of a Tory Radical*, 622.
295 **"nationalist crudity of the Prime Minister's":** Howe, *Conflict of Loyalty*, 645–47.
295 **hit record lows:** David Cannadine, *Margaret Thatcher: A Life and Legacy* (Oxford: Oxford University Press, 2017), 103.
296 **sharply enough that Howe:** Thatcher, *Autobiography*, 712.
296 **"tapestry-master of Thatcherism":** Charles Moore, "Geoffrey Howe Was the Tapestry-Master of Thatcherism," *The Telegraph*, October 10, 2015, www.telegraph.co.uk/news/politics/conservative/11924424/Charles-Moore-Geoffrey-Howe-was-the-tapestry-master-of-Thatcherism.html.
296 **Howe stood in front:** Geoffrey Howe, "Full Resignation Speech," https://www.youtube.com/watch?v=kvyAMjGSoKQ. "Resignation Part 2," accessed July 31, 2018, https:/ /www.youtube.com/watch ?v=Y2zOifEPLjY.
296 **Michael Heseltine formally challenged:** Thatcher, *Autobiography*, 718.
296 **failing to win enough:** Cannadine, *Margaret Thatcher*, 109.
297 **"Margaret could not have done it:** Lawson, *Memoirs of a Tory Radical*, 263.
297 **"No, she's going to be the [Bank's] Governor!":** "Margaret Thatcher—November 22, 1990 (Full Speech)," accessed May 21, 2018, www.youtube.com/watch?v=uF_GXMxa-mE&t=1660s.
298 **a bomb had ripped apart:** R. W. Apple, "I.R.A. Says It Set Bomb That Ripped Thatcher's Hotel," *New York Times*, October 13, 1984, www.nytimes.com/1984/10/13/world/ira-says-it-set-bomb-that-ripped-thatcher-s-hotel.html?pagewanted=all.
299 **130 votes to 119:** "1975: Tories Choose First Woman Leader," *BBC: On This Day* (blog), accessed June 9, 2018, http://news.bbc.co.uk/onthisday/hi/dates/stories/february/11/newsid_2539000/2539451.stm.

Chapter 8: The Reformers

303 **"When I preach here":** Martin Luther, *Martin Luther's Table Talks*, ed. Henry F. French, abridged edition (Minneapolis: Fortress Press, 2017), 39.
304 **bloody conflagration that soon:** Diarmaid MacCulloch, *All Things Made New: The Reformation and Its Legacy* (New York: Oxford University Press, 2016), 38.
305 **disturbing, virulent anti-Semitism:** Lyndal Roper, *Martin Luther: Renegade and Prophet* (New York: Random House, 2016), 378–85.
305 **"Luther's puppy happened to be":** Luther, *Martin Luther's Table Talks*, 6–7.
305 **American civic republicanism:** For a brief summary, see Francis J. Bremer, *Puritanism: A Very Short Introduction* (New York: Oxford University Press, 2009), 103–9.
307 **He was totally unknowable:** James Simpson, *Permanent Revolution: Surviving the Long English Reformation* (Cambridge, MA: Harvard University Press, forthcoming), chapter 3. We are grateful to the author for providing a draft of this chapter in its unpublished form.
307 **many people would ignore:** Simpson, *Permanent Revolution*, chapter 3.

309 he joined the Augustinian: Roper, *Martin Luther*, 33–34.
309 the principles of obedience: Brad S. Gregory, *Rebel in the Ranks: Martin Luther, the Reformation, and the Conflicts That Continue to Shape Our World* (San Francisco: HarperOne, 2017), 17–18.
309 strict adherent to this regimen: Roper, *Martin Luther*, 41–42.
309 an unremarkable and unpublished: Roper, *Martin Luther*, 44–45.
309 first father figure since: Andrew Pettegree, *Brand Luther: How an Unheralded Monk Turned His Small Town into a Center of Publishing, Made Himself the Most Famous Man in Europe and Started the Protestant Reformation* (New York: Penguin Books, 2016), 33–34.
310 skillful use of this new: Carlos M. N. Eire, *Reformations: The Early Modern World, 1450–1650* (New Haven, CT: Yale University Press, 2016), 88, 92–93, and see generally Pettegree, *Brand Luther*.
310 seventeen other most prolific authors: Roper, *Martin Luther*, 130.
311 the logical connection: Roper, *Martin Luther*, 80–87.
312 the foundational document: Roper, *Martin Luther*, 82–83.
312 his congregation in Wittenberg: "The 95 Theses," luther2017.de, n.d., https://www.luther2017.de/en/martin-luther/texts-sources/the-95-theses/.
312 the voice of the laity: Quoted in Gregory, *Rebel in the Ranks*, 46.
313 "the people's completely false": Quoted in Gregory, *Rebel in the Ranks*, 43.
313 translated into German: Roper, *Martin Luther*, 83.
313 it went through twenty-five printings: Roper, *Martin Luther*, 108.
313 a club of "Augustinian diners": Quoted in Roper, *Martin Luther*, 85.
314 seized personally from the flames: Roper, *Martin Luther*, 85.
314 "lovers of evangelical truth": Quoted in Pettegree, *Brand Luther*, 141.
314 published twenty-eight works: Pettegree, *Brand Luther*, 120.
315 Luther now melodramatically: Roper, *Martin Luther*, 157–58.
316 the papal bull had been received: Roper, *Martin Luther*, 159–60.
316 Luther's works published in German: Quoted in Roper, *Martin Luther*, 445 at fn 52.
316 Christendom was in its Last Days: Heiko Augustinus Oberman and Donald Weinstein, *The Two Reformations: The Journey from the Last Days to the New World* (New Haven, CT: Yale University Press, 2003), 92.
317 a herald sporting: Roper, *Martin Luther*, 165–66.
317 sixty horsemen and the town's rector: Roper, *Martin Luther*, 166.
317 Jesus's approach into Jerusalem: Quoted in Roper, *Martin Luther*, 167.
317 striking biblical parallels: Roper, *Martin Luther*, 168.
318 the diminutive monk who: Quoted in Roper, *Martin Luther*, 168.
318 "rash and at the same time": Quoted in Roper, *Martin Luther*, 169.
318 he could not recant his books: Quoted in Roper, *Martin Luther*, 171.
318 "I have been subdued through the scriptures": Quoted in Gregory, *Rebel in the Ranks*, 84.
319 Luther's theology denied that: Gregory, *Rebel in the Ranks*, 84.
319 people were possessed as much by the virality: Simpson, *Permanent Revolution*, chapter 3.
319 "if he had a thousand heads": Quoted in Roper, *Martin Luther*, 173.
319 his accomplices should not: Quoted in Roper, *Martin Luther*, 175.
319 The formal Edict of Worms: Quoted in Roper, *Martin Luther*, 183.
320 legitimate force could be used: Oberman and Weinstein, *The Two Reformations*, 91.
320 Against hundreds of years of Vatican: Roper, *Martin Luther*, 214.
321 "destroyed all the images in the church": Quoted in Roper, *Martin Luther*, 214.
322 dressed in knight's attire: Roper, *Martin Luther*, 222.
322 put the brakes on the Reformation: Gregory, *Rebel in the Ranks*, 95–96.
323 arrival of herring: Roper, *Martin Luther*, 264.
323 inspired by Luther's message: Roper, *Martin Luther*, 263.
323 "May God provide them with husbands": Quoted in Franz Posset, *The Front-Runner of the Catholic Reformation: The Life and Works of Johann von Staupitz* (Aldershot, Hants, England; Burlington, VT: Ashgate, 2003), 341.
324 to spite the Devil: Jack Kilcrease, "Katharina von Bora Luther," Lutheran Reformation, December 20, 2016, https://lutheranreformation.org/history/katharina-von-bora-luther/.
325 simmering in pockets: Eire, *Reformations*, 200–201.
325 the violent wave spread across: Pettegree, *Brand Luther*, 238–42.
325 "it is not for a Christian": Quoted in Eire, *Reformations*, 208.

326 **spiritual guidance was largely ignored:** Roper, *Martin Luther*, 250–51.

326 **his childhood home of Mansfeld:** Robert J. Christman, *Doctrinal Controversy and Lay Religiosity in Late Reformation Germany: The Case of Mansfeld*, Studies in Medieval and Reformation Traditions, v. 157 (Leiden; Boston: Brill, 2012), 19–20.

326 **condemnation of the peasants:** Quoted in Eire, *Reformations*, 209.

326 **"I commanded them":** Quoted in Eire, *Reformations*, 210.

326 **Luther had fallen out:** For a comprehensive account, see Eire, *Reformations*, 248–317.

327 **legacy for establishing:** Pettegree, *Brand Luther*, 265–66.

327 **"raising up people who":** Quoted in Pettegree, *Brand Luther*, 263, emphasis added.

327 **more organized and princely warfare:** Pettegree, *Brand Luther*, 283–86, 312–14.

327 **When war came in 1546:** Eire, *Reformations*, 530–31; Pettegree, *Brand Luther*, 254.

328 **headed straight for:** Pettegree, *Brand Luther*, 313, and H. J. Selderhuis, *Martin Luther: Spiritual Biography* (Wheaton, IL: Crossway, 2017), 309.

328 **Queen Mary I of England would:** Erik R. Seeman, *Death in the New World: Cross-Cultural Encounters, 1492–1800* (Philadelphia: University of Pennsylvania Press, 2011), 85.

329 **King's impromptu press conference:** Joe Azbell, "Blast Rocks Residence of Bus Boycott Leader," *Montgomery Advertiser*, January 31, 1956.

331 **Once in jail:** "Minutes of Montgomery Improvement Association Founding Meeting," December 5, 1955, 69, The Martin Luther King, Jr. Papers Project, Stanford University, http://kingencyclopedia.stanford.edu/primarydocuments/Vol3/5-Dec-1955_MIAMinutes.pdf, 5 fn 6.

332 **their Sunday pulpits:** Taylor Branch, *Parting the Waters: America in the King Years, 1954–1963* (New York: Simon & Schuster, 1988), 128–33.

332 **The Monday boycott:** Branch, *Parting the Waters*, 136.

332 **Instead of taking:** "Minutes of Montgomery Improvement Association Founding Meeting," December 5, 1955.

332 **That afternoon, leaders met:** "Minutes of Montgomery Improvement Association Founding Meeting," December 5, 1955.

332 **"Well, if you think":** David J. Garrow, *Bearing the Cross: Martin Luther King, Jr., and the Southern Christian Leadership Conference* (New York: William Morrow, 1986), 22.

332 **Three weeks before:** Martin Luther King, Jr., *Stride Toward Freedom: The Montgomery Story* (Boston: Beacon Press, 1986), 44.

333 **As King biographer:** Branch, *Parting the Waters*, 137.

333 **Immediately, that meant:** "Minutes of Montgomery Improvement Association Founding Meeting," December 5, 1955.

333 **Less than four hours:** Luther A. Huston, "High Court Rules Bus Segregation Unconstitutional," *New York Times*, November 14, 1956. In fact, as a result of the Montgomery bus boycott, the United States Supreme Court eventually made a ruling that "was interpreted as outlawing state or municipal enactments anywhere that require separation of the races on public vehicles." According to the *New York Times*, the boycott placed "a headstone at the grave of *Plessy v. Ferguson*"—the 1896 Supreme Court case that served as the legal justification for Jim Crow segregation, https://timesmachine.nytimes.com/timesmachine/1956/ 11/14/88483373.html.

333 **But on that first evening:** "Montgomery Improvement Association Resolution," December 8, 1955, The Martin Luther King, Jr. Papers Project, Stanford University, http://kingencyclopedia.stanford.edu/primarydocuments/551208_006.pdf.

334 **"I want to say that":** "MIA Mass Meeting at Holt Street Baptist Church," December 5, 1955, The Martin Luther King, Jr. Papers Project, Stanford University, http://kingencyclopedia.stanford.edu/encyclopedia/documentsentry/mia_mass_meeting_at_holt_street_baptist_church/index.html.

334 **"The glorious thing":** Quoted in John D'Emilio, *Lost Prophet: The Life and Times of Bayard Rustin* (Chicago: University of Chicago Press, 2003), 230–31.

335 **"the most important night of his life":** Garrow, *Bearing the Cross*, 57–58.

335 **at least nine courses:** Branch, *Parting the Waters*, 75–76.

336 **The story lifted up:** George Barrett, "Bus Integration in Alabama Calm, Montgomery Quiet on First Day—Slapping of Negro Woman Only Incident," *The New York Times*, December 22, 1956.

337 **He and two other longtime activists:** Interview with Ella Baker, quoted in D'Emilio, *Lost Prophet*, 245.

337 **The movement did not:** Bayard Rustin, "Rustin to King," December 23, 1956, The Martin Luther King, Jr. Papers Project, Stanford University, http://okra.stanford.edu/transcription/document_images/Vol03Scans/491_23-Dec-1956_From%20Bayard%20Rustin.pdf.

337 **And so on January 7:** "Montgomery Improvement Association Press Release, Bus Protestors Call Southern Negro Leaders Conference on Transportation and Nonviolent Integration," January 7, 1957, The Martin Luther King, Jr. Papers Project, Stanford University, http://okra.stanford.edu /transcription/document_images/Vol04Scans/94_7-Jan-1957_Montgomery%20Improvement %20Assoc.pdf.

340 **Before he was arrested:** All details of King's arrest at Rich's department store and arraignment in Atlanta Municipal Court taken from Bruce Galphin and Keeler McCartney, "King, 51 Others Arrested Here in New Sit-In Push," *The Atlanta Constitution*, October 20, 1960.

340 **King was on the verge of tears:** Branch, *Parting the Waters*, 346.

341 **At the time:** Ella Baker and Martin Luther King Jr., "Youth Leadership Meeting, Shaw University, Raleigh, N.C.—April 15–17, 1960," April 1960, www.crmvet.org/docs/6004_sncc_call .pdf.

341 **lots of money:** Galphin and McCartney, "King, 51 Others Arrested Here in New Sit-In Push." The King family actually spent a good amount there the prior year. According to the article, "The minister said during 1959, his family spent $4,500 at the store and added: 'We are welcome at all counters other than the lunch counters.'"

341 **And with presidential:** The two had met privately at the New York apartment of Harry Belafonte in June 1960, and arrangements were being made for another meeting as well. See Branch, *Parting the Waters*, 346–50.

342 **bring in $7,000:** Branch, *Parting the Waters*, 352.

343 **The group included:** Simeon Booker, "Alabama Mob Ambush Bus, Beat Biracial Group and Burn Bus, Attack Riders Forced from Bus by Smoke and Fire," *Jet*, May 25, 1961, 12–15.

343 **Second in line:** Branch, *Parting the Waters*, 415.

343 **As a result:** "Bi-Racial Buses Attacked, Riders Beaten in Alabama," *The New York Times*, May 15, 1961.

343 **A white assistant:** "Freedom Riders Attacked by Whites in Montgomery," *The New York Times*, May 21, 1961.

344 **His first night:** "Montgomery Under Martial Law; Troops Called After New Riot; Marshals and Police Fight Mob," *The New York Times*, May 22, 1961.

344 **"They caused that rioting":** Claude Sitton, "Bi-Racial Riders Decide to Go On," *The New York Times*, May 24, 1961, https://timesmachine.nytimes.com/timesmachine/1961/05/24/101464639 .pdf.

344 **"Where is your body?":** Branch, *Parting the Waters*, 466–67.

344 **"King would be best":** James Bevel, Taylor Branch interview with James Bevel, interview by Taylor Branch, May 16, 1985, Folder 535, Scan 20, Taylor Branch Papers, The Southern Historical Collection at the Louis Round Wilson Special Collections Library, University of North Carolina–Chapel Hill, https://dc.lib.unc.edu/cdm/singleitem/collection/05ddd/id/448920.

344 **Freedom riders had already been:** Alex Poinsett, "Who Speaks for the Negro," *Jet*, July 6, 1961, pp. 18–19.

345 **Farmer remembers some of the riders:** James Farmer, Taylor Branch interview with James Farmer, interview by Taylor Branch, November 18, 1983, Folder 611, Scan 3, Taylor Branch Papers, The Southern Historical Collection at the Louis Round Wilson Special Collections Library, University of North Carolina–Chapel Hill, https://dc.lib.unc.edu/cdm/singleitem/collection/05ddd /id/457330.

345 **John Lewis remembers:** John Lewis, *WBUR Here & Now*: "Rep. John Lewis Looks Back, 50 Years After March on Washington," August 20, 2013, http://hereandnow.legacy.wbur.org/2013 /08/20/john-lewis-march; *Martin Luther King and the Montgomery Story* (Nyack, NY: Fellowship of Reconciliation, 1957), http://kingencyclopedia.stanford.edu/primarydocuments/Comic% 20Book%201957.pdf.

345 **On May 23:** Sitton, "Bi-Racial Riders Decide to Go On."

345 **"But," he went on:** Poinsett, "Who Speaks for the Negro," 18.

346 **As King would tell an interviewer:** Alex Haley, "Playboy Interview: Martin Luther King, Jr.," *Playboy*, January 1965.

346 **By 1963, SCLC:** "SCLC Salaries for Fiscal Year 1963–64," n.d., www.crmvet.org/docs/6410_sclc _staff_salaries.pdf; "SCLC Annual Report, 1962–1963," September 1963, www.crmvet.org/docs /630924_sclc_annualrpt.pdf.

346 **In a technique he used:** Branch, *Parting the Waters*, 688.

347 **"First, they would":** Branch, *Parting the Waters*, 689.

348 **King once called Birmingham:** Martin Luther King Jr., *The Autobiography of Martin Luther King, Jr.*, ed. Clayborne Carson (New York: Warner Books, 1998), 172.

348 **At a diner counter:** Barnett Wright, "1963 in Birmingham, Alabama: A Timeline of Events," *AL.Com* (blog), January 1, 2013, http://blog.al.com/spotnews/2013/01/1963_in_birmingham_ala bama_a_t.html.

348 **prohibited from eating:** S. Jonathan Bass, *Blessed Are the Peacemakers: Martin Luther King Jr., Eight White Religious Leaders, and the Letter from Birmingham Jail* (Baton Rouge and London: Louisiana State University Press, 2002), 90–91.

348 **"If Birmingham could be cracked":** "Southern Christian Leadership Conference Newsletter: Birmingham Issue," July 1963, The King Center, www.thekingcenter.org/archive/document/sclc -newsletter-july-1963.

348 **In an action emblematic:** Branch, *Parting the Waters*, 420.

348 **Boutwell won the election:** "Statistics on Birmingham, Alabama," n.d., The King Center, www .thekingcenter.org/archive/document/statistics-birmingham-alabama; Bass, *Blessed Are the Peacemakers*, 100; "Boutwell, Albert," The Martin Luther King, Jr. Research and Education Institute, n.d., https://kinginstitute.stanford.edu/encyclopedia/boutwell-albert.

349 **"But it was much less":** Foster Hailey, "4 Negroes Jailed in Birmingham as the Integration Drive Slows; Sit-Ins and a Demonstration Plan Fail to Materialize—Dr. King Takes Lead," *The New York Times*, April 5, 1963, https://timesmachine.nytimes.com/timesmachine/1963/04/05/90568484 .html?pageNumber=16.

349 **While the first march:** Branch, *Parting the Waters*, 709–10.

349 **As the marches lagged:** Branch, *Parting the Waters*, 726.

349 **the City of Birmingham sought:** "Injunction Requested by the City of Birmingham against Protests," n.d., The King Center, www.thekingcenter.org/archive/document/injunction-requested -city-birmingham-against-protests#.

349 **Around 1:00 a.m. on Thursday:** "Injunction from the City of Birmingham," n.d., The King Center, www.thekingcenter.org/archive/document/injunction-city-birmingham; Garrow, *Bearing the Cross*, 240; Branch, *Parting the Waters*, 727.

349 **He also committed:** "Injunction from the City of Birmingham," n.d., The King Center, www .thekingcenter.org/archive/document/injunction-city-birmingham.

349 **But information King received:** Garrow, *Bearing the Cross*, 241.

349 **As King himself recalled:** Martin Luther King Jr. and Clayborne Carson, *The Autobiography of Martin Luther King, Jr.* (New York: Intellectual Properties Management in association with Warner Books, 1998), 181.

350 **King's advisers told:** King and Carson, *The Autobiography of Martin Luther King, Jr.*, 181.

350 **"I walked to another room":** King and Carson, *The Autobiography of Martin Luther King, Jr.*, 182.

350 **King remembered being:** King and Carson, *The Autobiography of Martin Luther King, Jr.*, 183.

350 **It wasn't until King saw:** Branch, *Parting the Waters*, 735.

350 **In one of the papers:** Martin Luther King Jr., "Letter from Birmingham City Jail," May 1, 1963, The King Center, www.thekingcenter.org/archive/document/letter-birmingham-city-jail-1.

350 **It started, as King recalled:** King and Carson, *The Autobiography of Martin Luther King, Jr.*, 187.

351 **Their model was a:** Branch, *Parting the Waters*, 752.

351 **The risks were high:** Branch, *Parting the Waters*, 753.

351 **They eventually settled:** Branch, *Parting the Waters*, 755.

351 **"Altogether on 'D' Day":** King and Carson, *The Autobiography of Martin Luther King, Jr.*, 270, and Branch, *Parting the Waters*, 757–61.

352 **Eventually, the city:** Foster Hailey, "500 Are Arrested in Negro Protest at Birmingham," *The New York Times*, May 3, 1963, https://timesmachine.nytimes.com/timesmachine/1963/05/03 /81807492.html?pageNumber=1.

352 **The next afternoon:** Branch, *Parting the Waters*, 758.

352 **Evans ordered them to halt:** Foster Hailey, "Dogs and Hoses Repulse Negroes at Birmingham," *The New York Times*, May 4, 1963, https://timesmachine.nytimes.com/timesmachine/1963/05/04 /81808290.html?pageNumber=1.

352 **Animals and high-pressure:** Branch, *Parting the Waters*, 758–61.

352 **"The newspapers of May 4":** King and Carson, *The Autobiography of Martin Luther King, Jr.*, 208.

353 **And on May 10:** "Southern Christian Leadership Conference Newsletter: Birmingham Issue," July 1963, The King Center, www.thekingcenter.org/archive/document/sclc-newsletter-july-1963.

The agreement called for: "1. The desegregation of lunch counters, rest rooms, fitting rooms, and drinking fountains in planned stages within the next 90 days. 2. The upgrading and hiring of Negroes on a non-discriminatory basis throughout the business and industrial community of Birmingham. . . . 3. The movement has made arrangements for the release of all persons on bond or their personal recognizance. . . . 4. Through the Senior Citizens Committee [city's business leadership], communications between Negro and white will be publicly re-established within two weeks."

353 **Number 13 on Rustin's agenda was:** "Official Program for the March on Washington for Jobs and Freedom," August 28, 1963, www.crmvet.org/docs/mowprog.pdf.

353 **With her first song:** "March on Washington—MAHALIA JACKSON Sings Two Hymns," YouTube—Collectif James Baldwin, 2017, accessed July 31, 2018, www.youtube.com/watch? v=-hQeGDSB6Ss.

353 **After remarks by Rabbi Joachim:** "Official Program for the March on Washington for Jobs and Freedom," August 28, 1963, www.crmvet.org/docs/mowprog.pdf.

354 **The assembly for which:** Campbell Gibson and Kay Jung, "Historical Census Statistics on Population Totals by Race, 1790 to 1990, and by Hispanic Origin, 1970 to 1990, for Large Cities and Other Urban Places in the United States" (Washington, DC: U.S. Census Bureau, February 2005), www.census.gov/population/www/documentation/twps0076/twps0076.pdf; The National Park Service, "March on Washington for Jobs and Freedom," n.d., www.nps.gov/articles/march-on-washington.htm. According to the National Park Service, of 250,000 attendees, 190,000 were black and 60,000 white. Census data records the African American population of the United States as 18.87 million 1960 and 22.58 million in 1970.

354 **Some spectators climbed:** Lewis, *WBUR Here & Now*: "Rep. John Lewis Looks Back, 50 Years After March on Washington."

354 **Unbeknownst to Jackson:** Branch, *Parting the Waters*, 879.

354 **sixth on the agenda:** "Official Program for the March on Washington for Jobs and Freedom," August 28, 1963, www.crmvet.org/docs/mowprog.pdf.

354 **The boom of the crescendo:** E. W. Kenworthy, "200,000 March for Civil Rights in Orderly Washington Rally," *The New York Times*, August 29, 1963.

354 **Some just wanted:** Nathan Connolly, Johns Hopkins University history professor, discusses the significance of the March on Washington, August 26, 2013, https://hub.jhu.edu/2013/08/26/march-on-washington-economic-justice/. According to Connolly, "The march helped to provide local activists with the moral authority to push back against less progressive forces in their respective home states, making 1963 a critical year, and the march itself a critical event in the transformation of local political regimes around the country."

355 **It's unclear if:** Drew Hansen, "Mahalia Jackson, and King's Improvisation," *The New York Times*, August 27, 2013, sec. Opinion, www.nytimes.com/2013/08/28/opinion/mahalia-jackson-and-kings-rhetorical-improvisation.html.

355 **"He's damn good":** Taylor Branch interview with James Farmer, in Branch, *Parting the Waters*, 883.

355 **By one estimate:** Haley, "Playboy Interview: Martin Luther King, Jr."

355 **Dr. King, at thirty-five years old:** "Martin Luther King Wins the Nobel Peace Prize," *The New York Times*, October 15, 1964, https://timesmachine.nytimes.com/timesmachine/1964/10/15/118682825.html?action=click&contentCollection=Archives&module=LedeAsset&region=ArchiveBody&pgtype=article&pageNumber=l.

355 **He went on:** Martin Luther King Jr., "Annual Report of Martin Luther King, Jr. to the Southern Chrisitian Leadership Conference," October 2, 1964. www.crmvet.org/docs/6409_sclc_mlk_rpt.pdf.

356 **Among other conclusions:** Diane Bevel, "Report, September 17–20, 1963," September 1963, www.crmvet.org/docs/6309_nash_report.pdf.

356 **The same day:** Diane Nash Bevel and Jim Bevel, "Proposal for Action in Montgomery," September 20, 1963, www.crmvet.org/docs/6309_nash_actionplan.pdf.

357 **He announced that the focus:** Garrow, *Bearing the Cross*, 372.

357 **He was attacked by a white man:** Garrow, *Bearing the Cross*, 378–79.

357 **a central Alabama jail cell:** Garrow, *Bearing the Cross*, 381–85.

358 **Three days later:** Garrow, *Bearing the Cross*, 387.

358 **The evening of February 26:** Garrow, *Bearing the Cross*, 391.

358 **In response, leaders:** Garrow, *Bearing the Cross*, 394.

359 **The resulting carnage:** Garrow, *Bearing the Cross*, 391–400.

359 **Without time to deliberate:** Garrow, *Bearing the Cross*, 402.

361 **with his team:** Jean M. White, "King Revisits Scenes of Strife, Seeking Aid," *The Washington Post*, February 17, 1968.

361 **In the wake of Selma:** Martin Luther King Jr., "The Other America," April 14, 1967, https://auro raforum.stanford.edu/files/transcripts/Aurora_Forum_Transcript_Martin_Luther_King_The _Other_America_Speech_at_Stanford_04.15.07.pdf.

362 **According to one of the elder King's grandsons:** Martin Luther King Sr., *Daddy King: An Auto-biography* (Boston: Beacon Press, 2017), foreword to the 2017 edition. This question of MLK's name is one of some confusion and debate. But several historians have agreed with the version we tell here, which is also held up by the King family website and the 2017 revised foreword to *Daddy King*, written by one of King Sr.'s grandsons, MLK's nephew. Elsewhere in the same book, King Sr. claims that his father had insisted that his name had always been Martin Luther, the names of two of King Sr.'s uncles. King Sr. says he changed his and his son's name when his father died to honor his father's wishes.

362 **"My father is a preacher":** Luther and Carson, *The Autobiography of Martin Luther King, Jr.*, 1.

362 **held in a church:** "Minutes of Montgomery Improvement Association Founding Meeting," December 5, 1955, The Martin Luther King, Jr. Papers Project, Stanford University, http://kingency clopedia.stanford.edu/primarydocuments/Vol3/5-Dec-1955_MIAMinutes.pdf.

Chapter 9: Three Myths

367 **"a medium at your disposal":** Winston Churchill, *Painting as a Pastime* (New York: Cornerstone Library, 1965), https://gutenberg.ca/ebooks/churchillws-paintingasapastime/churchillws -paintingasapastime-00-h-dir/churchillws-paintingasapastime-00-h.html.

367 **"one of the great masterstrokes of strategy":** Daniel Allen Butler, *Distant Victory: The Battle of Jutland and the Allied Triumph in the First World War* (Westport, CT: Praeger Security International, 2006), 133.

367 **44,150 Allied lives:** Ministry for Culture and Heritage, "Gallipoli Casualties by Country," New Zealand Government, March 1, 2016, https://nzhistory.govt.nz/media/interactive/gallipoli -casualties-country.

367 **"I thought he would die of grief":** Quoted in Roy Jenkins, *Churchill: A Biography* (New York: Plume/Penguin, 2002), 277.

368 **"the Muse of Painting came":** Churchill, *Painting as a Pastime*.

368 **"I like to stand back":** Quoted in William Manchester, *The Last Lion: Winston Spencer Churchill; Visions of Glory, 1874–1932* (New York: Dell, 1989), 24.

368 **"no time for the deliberate approach":** Churchill, *Painting as a Pastime*.

368 **"force with candour":** "The 1954 Sutherland Portrait," The International Churchill Society, accessed June 13, 2018, https://winstonchurchill.org/publications/finest-hour/finest-hour-148/the -1954-sutherland-portrait/.

368 **made him appear "half-witted":** John Ezard, "Forerunner of Lost Churchill Portrait Goes on Show," *The Guardian*, June 30, 1999, www.theguardian.com/politics/1999/jul/01/uk.political news4.

368 **secretly had it burned:** "Churchill's Wife Destroyed Portrait They Both Disliked," *The New York Times*, January 12, 1978, https://timesmachine.nytimes.com/timesmachine/1978/01/12/110762138 .html?pageNumber=4.

369 **"set down what he saw":** John Russell, "Graham Sutherland, Artist; Did Study Churchill Hated," *The New York Times*, February 18, 1980, https://timesmachine.nytimes.com/timesmachine/1980 /02/18/111764065.html?action=click&contentCollection=Archives&module=LedeAsset&region =ArchiveBody&pgtype=article&pageNumber=51.

370 **"save Western Civilization":** Dink NeSmith, "Churchill's Hobby 'May Have Helped to Save Western Civilization,'" *Athens Banner-Herald*, accessed March 27, 2015, www.onlineathens.com /article/20150327/OPINION/303279993.

370 **far less effective peacetime leader:** Jenkins, *Churchill: A Biography*, 868, 882–84, and Geoffrey Best, *Churchill: A Study in Greatness* (Oxford; New York: Oxford University Press, 2003), 310–11.

373 **second only to the Bible:** Rebecca Burgess and Hugh Liebert, "From Cicero to Trump, They're All in Plutarch's 'Lives,'" *Wall Street Journal*, September 1, 2017, www.wsj.com/articles/from-cicero -to-trump-theyre-all-in-plutarchs-lives-1504303373.

374 **Clough was good friends:** Hugh Liebert, *Plutarch's Politics: Between City and Empire* (New York: Cambridge University Press, 2016), 14.

374   **"the biography of great men":** Thomas Carlyle, *On Heroes, Hero-Worship and the Heroic in History*, ed. Henry Duff Traill, vol. 5, *The Works of Thomas Carlyle*, 2010, 29.

374   **more men named John:** Justin Wolfers, "Fewer Women Run Big Companies Than Men Named John," *The New York Times*, March 2, 2015, sec. The Upshot, www.nytimes.com/2015/03/03 /upshot/fewer-women-run-big-companies-than-men-named-john.html.

374   **generally a matter of a correlation:** "Does Gender Diversity on Boards Really Boost Company Performance?," Wharton School at the University of Pennsylvania, *Knowledge@Wharton* (blog), May 18, 2017, http://knowledge.wharton.upenn.edu/article/will-gender-diversity-boards-really-boost -company-performance/, and Robin J. Ely and Deborah L. Rhode, "Women and Leadership: Defining the Challenges," in *Handbook of Leadership Theory and Practice: An HBS Centennial Colloquium*, eds. Nitin Nohria and Rakesh Khurana (Boston: Harvard Business Press, 2010), 389.

375   **health of interpersonal relationships:** Alice H. Eagly, Leire Gartzia, and Linda L. Carli, "Female Advantage: Revisited," in *The Oxford Handbook of Gender in Organizations*, eds. Savita Kumra, Ruth Simpson, and Ronald J. Burke (Oxford: Oxford University Press, 2014), 157–59.

375   **"Women executives have to be":** James Heskett, "Why Does Gender Diversity Improve Financial Performance?," *HBS Working Knowledge*, November 4, 2015, http://hbswk.hbs.edu/item/why -does-lack-of-gender-diversity-hurt-performance.

375   **Study after study:** Daniel E. Re et al., "Looking Like a Leader: Facial Shape Predicts Perceived Height and Leadership Ability," *PLoS ONE* 8, no. 12 (December 4, 2013), https://doi.org/10.1371 /journal.pone.0080957.

375   **"draw an effective leader":** Natalie Proulx, "What Makes Someone a Great Leader?," *The New York Times*, March 22, 2018, sec. The Learning Network, www.nytimes.com/2018/03/22/learning /what-makes-someone-a-great-leader.html.

375   **These stereotypes seem:** Anne M. Koenig et al., "Are Leader Stereotypes Masculine? A Meta-Analysis of Three Research Paradigms," *Psychological Bulletin* 137, no. 4 (July 1, 2011): 616–42, https://doi.org/10.1037/a0023557.

377   **"German mechanized power":** Winston Churchill, "Responses to War and Colonialism, from the Speeches, May 19, 1940," Knomi, accessed May 23, 2018, www.knomi.net/fileServer/textbook /English/britishLit/data/u6_speeches_1940_se.pdf.

378   **"a euphoria of irrational belief":** Jenkins, *Churchill*, 590.

378   **so attentive to his enunciation:** John Mather, "Churchill's Speech Impediment Was Stuttering," The International Churchill Society, August 29, 2008, https://winston churchill.org/resources/ myths/churchills-speech-impediment-was-stuttering/.

378   **"inarticulate and stammering":** Plutarch, *Plutarch's Lives*, ed. Arthur Hugh Clough, Modern Library Paperback Edition, vol. 2 (Toronto: Random House, 1992), 394.

381   **"something is right in the world":** Allen Shawn, *Leonard Bernstein: An American Musician* (New Haven, CT, and London: Yale University Press, 2016), 130.

Chapter 10: Redefining Leadership

386   **scientific culture they engendered:** Steve Jones, *Revolutionary Science: Transformation and Turmoil in the Age of the Guillotine* (New York: Pegasus Books, 2017), 71–79; Seymour H. Mauskopf, "Lavoisier and the Improvement of Gunpowder Production/Lavoisier et l'amélioration de la Production de Poudre," *Revue d'histoire des Sciences* 48, no. 1 (1995): 95–122, https://doi.org/10.3406 /rhs.1995.1223.

386   **"no need for geniuses":** Quoted in Jones, *Revolutionary Science*, 31.

386   **"an instant to cut off":** Stephen Jay Gould, *The Hedgehog, the Fox, and the Magister's Pox: Mending the Gap Between Science and the Humanities* (Cambridge, MA: Belknap Press of Harvard University Press, 2011), 65.

386   **scientists like Lavoisier:** Mauskopf, "Lavoisier and the Improvement of Gunpowder Production," 119.

387   **introduced an era that emphasized:** William Doyle, "Ambiguous Aftermaths," in *Aristocracy and Its Enemies in the Age of Revolution* (Oxford: Oxford University Press, 2009), 311–39.

388   **"beating pulse and reddened cheek":** William Thomson, "From an Unsigned Review in the Christian Remembrancer, August, 1843," in *Thomas Carlyle: The Critical Heritage*, ed. Jules Paul Siegel (London: Routledge, 2013), 171–92.

388   **real competitor to trait-based leadership:** Mary Ann Glynn and Rich DeJordy, "Leadership Through an Organization Behavior Lens: A Look at the Last Half-Century of Research," in

Handbook of Leadership Theory and Practice: An HBS Centennial Colloquium on Advancing Leadership, eds. Nitin Nohria and Rakesh Khurana (Boston: Harvard Business School Press, 2010), 122–23.

389　**the "arc of history":** Barbara Kellerman, *The End of Leadership* (New York: HarperBusiness, 2012), 43.

389　**where the protesting self-immolation:** Jason Brownlee, Tarek Masoud, and Andrew Reynolds, *The Arab Spring: Pathways of Repression and Reform* (Oxford: Oxford University Press, 2015), 10.

390　**"crowbar of destiny":** Boris Johnson, *The Churchill Factor: How One Man Made History* (London: Hodder, 2015), 30.

390　**"brilliant oratory in defending":** Kjell Stromberg, "The 1953 Nobel Prize," The International Churchill Society, accessed June 11, 2018, https://winstonchurchill.org/the-life-of-churchill/senior-statesman/the-1953-nobel-prize/.

391　**"The subtle art":** Winston S. Churchill, "The Scaffolding of Rhetoric," November 1897.

391　**certain styles of music:** Maria A. G. Witek et al., "Syncopation, Body-Movement and Pleasure in Groove Music," *PLoS ONE* 9, no. 4 (April 16, 2014): https://doi.org/10.1371/journal.pone.0094446.

391　**"So with one syncopation":** Leonard Bernstein, "Young People's Concert: The Latin American Spirit," leonardbernstein.com, accessed June 11, 2018, https://leonardbernstein.com/lectures/television-scripts/young-peoples-concerts/latin-american-spirit.

392　**a bowl of cashews:** Richard H. Thaler, "Prize Lecture: From Cashews to Nudges: The Evolution of Behavioral Economics," Nobelprize.org, December 8, 2017, www.nobelprize.org/nobel_prizes/economic-sciences/laureates/2017/thaler-lecture.html.

393　**"cook like Warren Buffett":** Richard H. Thaler, *Misbehaving: The Making of Behavioral Economics* (New York: W. W. Norton & Company, 2015), 47.

393　**narcissists are overrepresented:** Michael Maccoby, *Narcissistic Leaders: Who Succeeds and Who Fails* (Boston: Harvard Business School Press, 2007); Charles A. O'Reilly et al., "Narcissistic CEOs and Executive Compensation," *The Leadership Quarterly* 25, no. 2 (April 2014): 218–31, https://doi.org/10.1016/j.leaqua.2013.08.002.

394　**"Where there is discord, may we bring harmony":** Margaret Thatcher, "Remarks on Becoming Prime Minister (St. Francis's Prayer)," Margaret Thatcher Foundation, May 4, 1979, www.margaretthatcher.org/document/104078.

394　**"nothing can absolve us":** Quoted in Matthew Grimley, "Thatcherism, Morality and Religion," in *Making Thatcher's Britain* (Cambridge: Cambridge University Press, 2012), 84.

401　**Prix de Rome:** "Prix de Rome," L'histoire de Jacques-Leonard Maillet, accessed June 13, 2018, http://jlmaillet.free.fr/frame.php?page=page2.

402　**subject more than the artist:** Plutarch, *Lives*, 1:202.

Index

PENGUIN PARTNERSHIPS

Penguin Partnerships is the Creative Sales and Promotions team at Penguin Random House. We have a long history of working with clients on a wide variety of briefs, specializing in brand promotions, bespoke publishing and retail exclusives, plus corporate, entertainment and media partnerships.

We can respond quickly to briefs and specialize in repurposing books and content for sales promotions, for use as incentives and retail exclusives as well as creating content for new books in collaboration with our partners as part of branded book relationships.

Equally if you'd simply like to buy a bulk quantity of one of our existing books at a special discount, we can help with that too. Our books can make excellent corporate or employee gifts.

Special editions, including personalized covers, excerpts of existing books or books with corporate logos can be created in large quantities for special needs.

We can work within your budget to deliver whatever you want, however you want it.

For more information, please contact
salesenquiries@penguinrandomhouse.co.uk